ABRAHAM IN THE OLD TESTAMENT AND EARLY JUDAISM

Abraham in the Old Testament and Early Judaism

John Eifion Morgan-Wynne

☙PICKWICK *Publications* · Eugene, Oregon

ABRAHAM IN THE OLD TESTAMENT AND EARLY JUDAISM

Copyright © 2020 John Eifion Morgan-Wynne. All rights reserved. Except for brief quotations in critical publications or reviews, no part of this book may be reproduced in any manner without prior written permission from the publisher. Write: Permissions, Wipf and Stock Publishers, 199 W. 8th Ave., Suite 3, Eugene, OR 97401.

Pickwick Publications
An Imprint of Wipf and Stock Publishers
199 W. 8th Ave., Suite 3
Eugene, OR 97401

www.wipfandstock.com

PAPERBACK ISBN: 978-1-5326-9302-1
HARDCOVER ISBN: 978-1-5326-9303-8
EBOOK ISBN: 978-1-5326-9304-5

Cataloguing-in-Publication data:

Names: Morgan-Wynne, J. E., author.

Title: Abraham in the Old Testament and early Judaism / John Eifion Morgan-Wynne.

Description: Eugene, OR: Pickwick Publications, 2020 | Includes bibliographical references and index.

Identifiers: ISBN 978-1-5326-9302-1 (paperback) | ISBN 978-1-5326-9303-8 (hardcover) | ISBN 978-1-5326-9304-5 (ebook)

Subjects: LCSH: Abraham—(Biblical patriarch) | Abraham—(Biblical patriarch)—In rabbinical literature | Abraham—(Biblical patriarch)—Influence | Judaism—History—To 70 A.D.

Classification: BS580.A3 M67 2020 (print) | BS580.A3 (ebook)

Manufactured in the U.S.A.   APRIL 20, 2020

Quotations from the Bible and the Apocrypha are from the text of the Holy Bible, New Revised Version, copyright 1987, by the Division of the Christian Education of the National Council of Churches in the USA, used by permission.

In memory of my parents,
Idris Ffoukes Morgan Wynne (1890–1969)

and

Mary Phyllis (née Thomas) (1902–1955),
in gratitude for all the love and encouragement they gave me

Contents

Preface | ix
Abbreviations | xi

Part I—Abraham in the Old Testament

1 Abraham in the Old Testament | 3
   1.1 Abraham in the Law | 3
   1.2. Abraham in the Former Prophets | 39
   1.3. Abraham in the Latter Prophets | 45
   1.4. Abraham in the Writings | 52

Part II—Abraham in Early Judaism

2 Abraham in Early Jewish Literature | 67
   2.1 Ecclesiasticus | 67
   2.2. The Book of Tobit | 71
   2.3. The Book of Jubilees | 73
   2.4. The Additions to the Book of Daniel and the Book of Esther in the LXX | 86
   2.5 The Dead Sea Scrolls | 89
   2.6. The First Book of Maccabees | 96
   2.7. The Third Book of Macabees | 99
   2.8. The First Book of Enoch (or The Ethiopic Enoch) | 100
   2.9. Fragments of Jewish Writers | 103
   2.10. The Psalms of Solomon | 107
   2.11. The Book of Judith | 108
   12. The Testaments of the Twelve Patriarchs | 110
   2.13. The Wisdom of Solomon | 114
   2.14. The Writings of Philo of Alexandria | 117

2.15. Other Jewish Scholars in Alexandria | 182
2.16. The Fourth Book of Maccabees | 193
2.17. The Biblical Antiquities of Pseudo-Philo | 195
2.18. The Prayer of Manasseh | 203
2.19. The Writings of Josephus | 204
2.20. The Fourth Book of Ezra (or 2 Esdras) | 216
2.21. The Second Book of Baruch (or The Syriac Apocalypse of Baruch) | 220
2.22. The Apocalypse of Abraham | 222
2.23. The Testament of Abraham | 224
2.24. The Pirke Aboth (The Sayings of the Fathers) | 226
2.25. Summary | 227

Bibliography | 235
Index of Ancient Documents | 255
Index of Modern Scholars | 273

Preface

THIS IS NOT A book which I had intended to write—not an enticing way to commence a preface, you might think. My original intention was to write on Abraham in the New Testament and supply an introductory chapter on Abraham in the Old Testament and Early Judaism. Early on it became apparent that this was unrealistic and unfair. The material was just too large to do justice to it, not least due to the explosion of interest and research on the literary sources of Early Judaism. Accordingly, the proposed introductory chapter became two chapters, the second of which on Early Judaism being rather long. In view of the total length of the manuscript, a decision was reached to divide the work into two books.

I hope that I have been fair to Jewish sources in their own right and not just treated them as mere background to the New Testament material. Whether I have been successful is for the reader to decide.

Though the project has taken far longer than I originally intended, in part due to my domestic circumstances, I have found it immensely interesting and rewarding. I hope that I have made adequate acknowledgement of the labours of others into which I have entered.

I wish to thank Dr. Robin Parry, Zechariah Mickel, Zane Derven, and Ian Creeger at Wipf & Stock for their patience and kind help in bringing the project to completion.

I am greatly indebted to my daughter, Leri-Anne, and grandson, Samuel, for their help when I found myself in difficulties with the computer, and I warmly thank them.

The separate publication of this volume enables me to dedicate it to the memory of my late parents for all the love and encouragement they gave me over the years, and for their quiet but firm Christian faith. Gratias Deo. Sadly, they had both passed away before I had published anything.

—J. E. Morgan-Wynne

Abbreviations

AnB	Analecta Biblica
ABSBL	Academia Biblica (SBL)
AB	Anchor Bible
AGAJU	Arbeiten zur Geschichte des antiken Judentums und des Urchristentums
ALGHJ	Arbeiten zur Literatur und Geschichte des Hellenistischen Judentums
AOTC	Apollos Old Testament Commentary
APOT	Apocrypha and Pseudepigrapha of the Old Testament
ATANT	Abhandlungen zur Theologie des Alten und Neuen Testaments
ATD	Das Alte Testament Deutsch
BBB	Bonner Biblische Beiträge
BETL	Bibliotheca Ephemeridum Theologicarum Lovaniensium
BGBH	Beiträge zur Geschichte der biblischen Hermeneutik
BHT	Beiträge zur Historischen Theologie
BJS	Brown Judaic Studies
BO	Biblica et Orientalia

BWANT	Beiträge zur Wissenschaft vom Alten und Neuen Testament
BZAW	Beihefte zur Zeitschrift für die altestamentliche Wissenschaft
BZNW	Beiheft zur Zeitschrift für die neutestamentliche Wissenschaft
CB	Coniectanea Biblica
CBC	Cambridge Bible Commentary
CBQMS	Catholic Biblical Quarterly Monograph Series
CD	The Community Rule of the Qumran Community
CSHJ	Chicago Studies in the History of Judaism
DJD	Discoveries in the Judean Desert
ECB	Die Neue Echter Bibel
EH	Europäische Hochschulschriften
ET	English Translation
EvTh	Evangelische Theologie
FOTL	The Forms of the Old Testament Literature
FRLANT	Forschungen zur Religion und Literatur des Alten und Neuen Testaments
FzB	Forschung zur Bibel
GAP	Guides to the Apocrypha and Pseudepigrapha
HBS	Herders Biblische Studien
HCS	Hellenistic Culture and Society
HDR	Havard Dissertations in Religion
HM	Heythrop Monographs
HTR	Havard Theological Review
HTS	Harvard Theological Studies
HUCA	Hebrew Union College Annual
HUP	Harvard University Press
JBL	Journal of Biblical Literature
JCC	Jewish Culture and Contexts
JSNTSS	Journal for the Study of the New Testament Supplement Series
JSOT	Journal for the Study of the Old Testament
JSOTSS	Journal for the Study of the Old Testament Supplement Series

JSPS	Journal for the Study of the Pseudepigrapha Supplement
JSPSS	Journal for the Study of the Pseudepigrapha Supplement Series
JTS	Journal of Theological Studies
KBANT	Kommentare und Beiträge zum Alten und Neuen Testament
KEKNT	Kritisch-Exegetischer Kommentar über Das Neue Testament.
LCL	Loeb Classical Library
LHB/OTS	Library of Hebrew Bible/Old Testament Studies
LSJ	Lidell and Scott, *Greek-English Lexicon*
LSTS	Library of Second Temple Studies
NCB	New Century Bible
NEB	New English Bible
NEB	Die Neue Echter Bibel
NSBT	New Studies in Biblical Theology
NTOA	Novum Testamentum et Orbis Antiquus
NTS	New Testament Studies
OBO	Orbis Biblicus et Orientalis
OTG	Old Testament Guides
OTL	Old Testament Library
OTP	Old Testament Pseudepigrapha
PA	Philosophia Antiqua
PACS	Philo of Alexandria Commentary Series
RB	Revue Biblique
SANT	Studien zum Alten und Neuen Testament
SAP	Sheffield Academic Press
SBA AT	Stuttgarter Biblische Aufsatzbände Altes Testament
SBL	Society of Biblical Literature
SBL	Studies in Biblical Literature
SBLDS	Society of Biblical Literature Dissertation Series
SBLEJL	Society of Biblical Literature Early Judaism and its Literature
SBLMS	Society for Biblical Literature Monograph Series

SBLSS	Society of Biblical Literature Semeia Series
SBS	Stuttgarter Bibel-Studien
SBT	Studies in Biblical Theology
SBTS	Sources for Biblical and Theological Study
SDSSRL	Studies in the Dead Sea Scrolls and Related Literature
SFSHJ	South Florida Studies in the History of Judaism
SGKA	Studien zur Geschichte und Kulter des Alterums
SJSJ	Supplements to the Journal for the Study of Judaism
SNTSMS	Society for New Testament Studies Monograph Series
SOTBT	Studies in Old Testament Biblical Theology
SPB	Studia Post-Biblica
SPh	Studia Philonica
SPM	Studia Philonica Monographs
STDJ	Studies on the Texts of the Desert of Judah
SUNT	Studien zur Umwelt des Neuen Testaments
SVTP	Studia in Veteris Testamenti Pseudepigrapha
TANZ	Texte und Arbeiten zum neutestamentlichen Zeitalter
TB	Theologische Bucherei
TBC	Torch Bible Commentaries
TDNT	Theological Dictionary of the New Testament
TSAJ	Texte und Studien zum Antiken Judentum
WB	Die Welt der Bibel
WANT	Beiträge zur Wissenschaft vom Alten und Neuen Testament
WB	Die Welt der Bibel
WBC	Word Bible Commentary
WUNT	Wissenschaftliche Untersuchungen zum Neuen Testament
YUP	Yale University Press
ZAW	Zeitschrift für alttestamentliche Wissenschaft

Part I

Abraham in the Old Testament

1

Abraham in the Old Testament

1.1 Abraham in the Law[1]

1.1.1 The Book of Genesis

GENESIS 12:1-4A MARKS THE beginning of the patriarchal history. This passage itself has been prefaced by 11:10-32, which comprises a genealogical table outlining Abraham's ancestors (11:10-27) and a note which recorded how a man called Terah had three sons, Abraham, Nahor, and Haran. The last named died in the land of his birth, Ur of the Chaldees. Without specifying why, the account tells us that Terah left Ur, accompanied by Abraham

---

1. In recent decades, Pentateuchal criticism has been in the melting pot. The idea of Yahwist and Elohist sources has come under sustained criticism. Many scholars have rejected the idea of an E source altogether, while the idea of a J history produced in the Davidic-Solomon era has been abandoned by many in favor of a date for the composition of Genesis in the fourth century BC or even as late as the second century BC, though there are still influential voices adhering to the idea of sources given the nomenclature J, E, and P (the D or Deuteronomist source falls into a different category). Particularly influential in this trend have been the works of Rendtorff, *Das überlieferungsgeschichtliche Problem des Pentateuch* (1977), and Schmid, *Der sogenannte Jahwist* (1976). The third volume of JSOT 1977 was largely devoted to a consideration of the work of Rendtorff and Schmid and various invited responses to or reviews of them. See the articles by Clements, Coats, van Seters, Wagner, Wenham, and Whybray listed in the Bibliography. See also Jenks, *Elohist and North Israelite Traditions*, for a careful and thorough defense of the existence of an Elohist tradition linked with North Israelite prophetic-levitical circles. Haag, *Die Abrahamtradition in Gen 15*, 83–106; Weimar, *Genesis 15*, 361–411, also defend the existence of E.

and his wife, Sarah (who, we are informed, was childless), together with Lot, son of Abraham's deceased brother, Haran.[2] The intention was to journey to Canaan, but they resided in a place called Haran, where Terah died.

We could say that the immediate preface indicated that for the family under consideration there was a situation of uncertainty.[3] The head of the family had died; the eldest son had no heir. We are left to assume that the grandson, Lot, is considered the one who will bear the family name. Thus, key elements of the succeeding story are put before us: Abraham has no heir, and it would seem his responsibility to take Lot under his wing. Yet, in Genesis 12:1–3, God promises that this man who has no heir will become a great nation.

At the same time, the wider, global context, is the story of the building of the Tower of Babel and what was God's response to this act of human pride, *viz.* His judgment which consists of the confusion of human language and the scattering of the human race. It seems as if yet again the human race has thwarted God's beneficent purposes for His creation: first came the disobedience of Adam and Eve; then Cain's murder of his brother Abel; then, there was the increase of human wickedness which resulted in the Flood; and now, the human arrogance and pride in its own achievements. How is God to rectify matters? How is He to get His purposes "back on track"? What Genesis 12:1–3 described was a further response of God to the situation arising out of the human race's frustration of His purposes and His judgment on it.[4]

The section Genesis 12:1–5 consists of three parts. Firstly, God commanded Abraham to leave his country and his father's family and house for a land (not specified)[5] which God would show him (v. 1). Secondly, God

---

2. The narrative does not mention that Nahor accompanied his father. He presumably accompanied or followed Terah as far as Haran, for he figures later in Abraham's story in Genesis 24, on the occasion of securing a wife for Isaac from among Abraham's kinsfolk at Haran, and not from among the Canaanites (Nahor is Rebekah's father according to Gen 24:24, 27).

3. Tretheim, *Abraham*, 31, points out that the Word of God at Genesis 12:1 entered into a point of great uncertainty for the future of this family.

4. See von Rad, *Genesis*, 150; Henton Davies, *Genesis*, 167–68; Westermann, *Genesis 12–36*, 145–46.

5. Ego, *Abraham als Urbild der Toratreu Israels*, 27, maintains that the contrast between the detailed description of what Abraham is called to leave and the unspecified nature of where he is to go illustrates the hardness of the divine command. Flury-Schölch, *Abrahams Segens*, 62, comments that Abraham is called to abandon a social system which it was his duty to support and promote. Actually, strictly speaking, verse 1b is not a promise of land (as Flury-Schölch, *Abrahams Segen*, 64, points out); the promise of the land of Canaan first comes later at verse 7, after Abram has actually reached Canaan and journeyed as far as Shechem.

promised[6] to make of Abraham a great nation; to make his name great; to bless him,[7] to bless those who bless Abraham and curse those who curse him;[8] and to make him a blessing to others—in fact, to all the families of the earth (vv. 2-3). Finally, there is the report of Abraham's obedience to the command (vv. 4-5): Abraham set out immediately in response to God's command.

If there appears to be a narrowing of God's purposes to one man and to the people stemming from him, this is more apparent than real. The universal perspective is not lost sight of, because through Abraham all the families of the earth will be blessed.[9] Abraham and the nation from him will be a conduit for blessing to the world. He receives blessing, but that blessing is (so to speak) to flow through to others. The promises look forward to the future and the nation that comes from Abraham.[10]

The narrative continued with Abraham journeying to the land of Canaan, where the Lord appeared to him and gave him a promise, which picked up and clarified the reference to the land which God would show Abraham mentioned in verse 1. Hereafter, in the promises made by God during the course of the narratives, the Land figures prominently.[11] God promised the land of Canaan to his descendants. Thus, Abraham's descendants are

---

6. See Westermann, *Promise to the Fathers*, for a discussion of the critical issues connected with God's promises to the Patriarchs. Westermann has argued that the original promise was that of a son, which should be distinguished from the promise of the increase of progeny, and that other promises are later developments.

7. Commentators note the link of this stress on God's blessing Abraham and the blessing of humankind by God in the account of creation (Gen 1:28). The importance of blessing is heightened by its coming after the judgment on the Tower of Babel enterprise (Gen 11:9).

8. This implies a measure of divine protection and help, which is noted by several scholars, including Flury-Schölch, *Abrahams Segen*, 90.

9. After an extremely detailed examination, Flury-Schölch, *Abrahams Segen*, 90-121, has convincingly demonstrated that the niphal of *brk* in v.12.3b (and also at Gen 18:18; 26:4) has a passive sense "to be blessed" (through Abraham, and through his descendants), whereas the use of the hithpael of *brk* at Genesis 22:18; 26:4, has a reflexive meaning, with the sense that others will seek for themselves the same kind of blessing that Abraham has experienced.

10. In many of his publications, N. T. Wright has argued the case that Israel was to be the answer to the problem created by Adam's sin, a view widespread in Second Temple Judaism and one which Paul shared (e.g., Wright, *Pauline Perspectives*, 6, 23, 98-99, 107, 116-17, 149, 304, 363, 369, 413, 490-509, 583). The roots of this are there in the Genesis account of the call of Abraham.

11. See Halpern-Amaru, *Rewriting the Bible*, 9, who states that within the triad of promises the Land holds the primary position.

incorporated into the promise of the land.[12] Abraham from his side acknowledged the promised gift by building an altar to Yahweh.

The next episode (12:12–20) reveals a threat to the family under consideration in the form of famine, and also, one might say, to the promise of land, since the famine forced Abraham to leave Canaan and go to Egypt in search of food for his family and his flocks.[13] While in Egypt there was another threat—this time to the marriage and to the sanctity of Sarai and so to the promise of descendants. The threat came from the desires and power of the Pharaoh, who takes Sarah into his harem (12:15). Abraham's ruse to pass Sarai off as his sister has compounded the problem. The situation was only rescued by God's intervention to extricate Sarah by striking Pharaoh with illness until eventually Pharaoh learned the true situation.[14]

God not only preserved the one whom He has chosen and called, but also ensured that he prospered economically, and He brought the couple back to Canaan (12:17; 13:1). Thus, the trustworthiness of God is illustrated.[15]

From the narrator's point of view, the all-important theme was *the protection of the ancestress*, the one who was to be the mother of the heir, the destined recipient of God's promise. God overruled when the enemy of the promise was the bearer of the promise himself.[16]

We are told that Abraham returned to Canaan, but strife broke out between the herdsmen of Lot and his herdsmen. The quarrel was settled amicably by Abraham's giving Lot the choice of where to settle. The two part and settle in different parts: Lot in the Jordan valley and Abraham in the area west of the river Jordan. Following Lot's choice and departure, God spoke to Abram, confirming the two promises of the land and numerous descendants (13:14–18). So by Lot's own decision and by God's decision, Lot has no share in Canaan. In addition, although Abraham rescued Lot when he was taken prisoner and later his intercession for Sodom inevitably included Lot and his family, there is according to the narrative no real

---

12. We can imagine that this promise would supply a ground for hope to those who had been removed from the land by the Babylonians and settled in exile in Babylon or whose situation in Israel was precarious and uncertain.

13. The parallel with the later history of his descendants would not be lost on the hearers/readers of the story.

14. Westermann, *Genesis 12–36*, 167, has pointed out that while God punished Abraham, the punishment consists only in putting him to shame. The story is neither a glorification of Abraham's astuteness nor of the beauty of Sarai.

15. Therein would again lie a message of hope for those in exile or any situation fraught with difficulties and dangers.

16. Von Rad, *Genesis*, 164.

contact between Abraham and Lot. They live separate lives. We are left to conclude that Lot will not be Abraham's heir.[17]

Lot figures in the next episode and so this is a link with the previous material. Chapter 14 is widely regarded as perhaps the latest addition to the Abraham narratives, however this story of Abraham's involvement in the war against Chedorlaomer and his rescue of Lot arose.[18] Abraham is drawn into a conflict between certain Middle Eastern kings by the capture of Lot. He is depicted as a quick-thinking and astute strategist and a bold and competent fighter who gained a victory with his band of 318 retainers, and released Lot. After the victory, Abraham was met by the priest-king of Salem, Melchizedek, to whom he gave a tenth[19] of the captured spoils and from whom he received a blessing (14:18–20).

This episode is unique in relating Abraham to the wider near Eastern political scene. Indeed, the picture of the patriarch has been described by Westermann as having practically nothing to do with the Abraham of the old patriarchal stories.[20]

The story in what is our Genesis 15:1–6, 7–21, used to be assigned to *E or the Elohist stream of tradition*,[21] but that is widely disputed and rejected today, and a whole range of suggestions have been made.[22] However this is decided, the story is not, as it stands, a parallel to Genesis 12:1–3, 4–5, because it does not contain a command for Abraham to leave his family and country. Rather, it seems to presuppose an existing relationship with God[23] and the events narrated in Abraham's life which have preceded the

---

17. See Heard, *Dynamics of Diselection*, 25–61, 172–74, 1822–84, for a discussion of the relations of Abraham and Lot, and the way Lot is excluded from the destiny of Abraham's descendants and from Canaan. Heard amply brings out the many ambiguities in the narratives of Genesis 12–36 and how the narrator leaves the reader to come to his/her own judgments about the various characters and incidents. Kaminsky, *Yet I loved Jacob*, 29–30, says that Genesis 13 makes it clear that Lot will not be Abram's heir.

18. Genesis 14 has been referred to as an erratic boulder among the patriarchal traditions.

19. The aim is "to legitimate the regular payment of the tithe by means of a single event which took place a long time ago" (Westermann, *Genesis 12–36*, 206).

20. Westermann, *Genesis 12–36*, 207. But see Henton Davies, *Genesis*, 174, for the picture of Abraham as one of the commercial princes who were compelled to employ armed retainers for protection.

21. As examples, see von Rad, *Genesis*, 177; Wolff, *Elohistic Fragments*, 67–69.

22. Westermann, *Genesis 12–36*, 214–15, 217, points out that modern scholarship has almost universally abandoned the attempt to assign some or all of 1–6 to E. See Oeming, *Der Glaube Abrahams*, for a list of the numerous opinions.

23. See Henton Davies, *Genesis*, 177.

encounter with God narrated in Genesis 15.²⁴ Through the phrase "After these things," what follows in Genesis 15 is now set in a period after Abraham's military adventure, his meeting with Melchizedek, king of Salem, and his refusal to take a share in the booty captured in the conflict.

We are told that the word of the LORD came to Abram in a vision.²⁵ Yahweh's word initiates a dialogue. A similar emphasis on the word of Yahweh coming to Abraham occurs in verse 4.

First comes the command to Abraham not to be afraid, which presupposes that Abraham was in a situation where a sense of anxiety and fear was present. This command was followed by either God's self-proclamation: "I am your shield and your great reward"—He offered protection and welfare,²⁶ or "I am your shield; your reward will be very great."²⁷ In view of the subsequent dialogue, the latter fits better. God promised Abraham protection (God would be a shield to him) and a reward. Abraham had obeyed the call to leave family and homeland (Gen 12:1–3, 4); he had trusted God in respect of where to dwell (Gen 13); and he had acted courageously and honorably in rescuing Lot and declining a share in the booty for himself (Gen 14).²⁸

In response to what Yahweh had said, Abraham complained that whatever he might receive was valueless without an heir begotten by himself. At the moment his heir was the steward of his household (v. 2). Now we know from Genesis 11:30 that Sarai was childless. It is that problem, in the light of implicit promises of descendants in 12:2 and the explicit reference to them in 12:7 and 13:15–16, which is raised by Abraham in 15:2–3.

But God promised that Abraham would father a son who would be his heir (v. 4), and this promise was confirmed by taking Abraham out to see the myriads of stars in the night sky: "So shall your seed be" (v. 5). The story could end satisfactorily with this promise which is intended to allay Abraham's complaint/doubt. But then comes the phrase, later fastened on by the apostle Paul: "Abraham believed the LORD and He reckoned (this) to him for righteousness" (v. 6). This is a reflection by the story teller:²⁹ it is his comment after the dialogue between God and Abraham, and in it he

---

24. See Westermann, *Genesis 12–36*, 217.

25. For a defense of the use of Yahweh here (and not Elohim) by the Elohist, see Weimar, *Genesis 15*, 395–96n122, 399n135.

26. A possible rendering of the Hebrew, so the LXX; RV; NIV.

27. A possible rendering of the Hebrew, so JB; NIV mg; NRSV; REB.

28. Oeming, *Glaube*, 17.

29. Westermann, *Genesis 12–36*, 222, considers that verse 6 presupposes the understanding of faith shaped by Isaiah.

turns to the reader/hearer.[30] Abraham's trusting acceptance of God's word was counted as the appropriate response (right behavior) for a relationship with God, the donor of the promise.[31]

This translation assumes that Yahweh is the subject of the second half of the verse. This involves a change of subject from that of the first half, where Abraham is the subject. On the other hand, Yahweh is clearly the subject of 15:7, so that there if Yahweh is the subject of 15:6b, there is a continuation of subjects between it and 15:7. But did verses 1–6 and 7–21 originally go together? If not, that is, if verses 1–6 and 7–21 were originally separate units of traditions and brought together, then the question of the subject of 15:6b remains open. Some scholars do argue that Abraham is in fact the subject of both halves of Genesis 15:6.[32] Abraham reckoned God's promise to be based on His righteousness, His faithfulness, to what He had expressed. We shall have to ask whether there is evidence in the way Genesis 15:6 is used later that Abraham was interpreted as the subject of the action of reckoning in verse 6b.[33]

Some comment is necessary on the term "believed." Does the Hebrew express a specific act of believing or an ongoing aspect of Abraham's life? Is Abraham's faith directed simply to the promise uttered by Yahweh recorded in the narrative, or is it directed to Yahweh Himself, although in the end Yahweh cannot be dissociated from His words? These questions involve complicated syntactical and semantic issues.[34] We will content ourselves by

---

30. So von Rad, *Genesis*, 179; Schliesser, *Abraham's Faith in Romans 4*, 94.

31. Von Rad, *Genesis*, 179–80, believed that the formula, used by priests to declare that a sacrifice was acceptable to God (e.g., Lev 7:18; 17:4; Num 18:27; cf. Lev 13:17, 23, 28, 37, 44), was taken up in Genesis 15:6, and that, detached from that background, the declaration has a non-cultic character and is theologically reflective. Westermann, *Genesis 12–36*, 223, while accepting von Rad's view, also accepts that a broader view of the practice is possible.

32. See Gaston, *Paul and the Torah*, 45–63, esp. 48–49 (originally, *Abraham and the Righteousness of God*), who points out that the Jewish scholar, Nachmanides (1194–1270), since the passage referred to God's promise and since God's word is truthful and uttered in righteousness (e.g., Ps 132:11; Isa 45:23), had argued that it was Abraham who had recognized God's righteousness in what He had promised (Gaston mentions that Calvin was acquainted with this line of interpretation, but rejected it). See also Oeming, "Genesis 15:6b," 182–97; *Glaube*, 16–33; Weimar, *Genesis 15*, 410. Flüchter, *Die Anrechnung des Glaubens zur Gerechtigkeit*, 17–25, reviews this issue.

33. To anticipate: Oeming, *Glaube*, 22–31, traces the reception history of Genesis 15:6. Flüchter, *Rechnung*, 267–69, also sees this understanding of Genesis 15:6b to be reflected in Nehemiah 9:8; Philo, *Abr.* 273; Heb 11:11–12, 19.

34. See Schliesser, *Abraham*, 130–40, for a very full discussion.

accepting the view which sees Abraham's act of believing as not just punctiliar, but durative, as expressive of "fixing oneself on Yahweh."[35]

The second unit 15:7–21 opens with a self-proclamation of God: "I am the Lord who brought you out of Ur of the Chaldees, to give you this land" (v. 7). Weimar has pointed to the cross reference with the opening of the Decalogue (Exod 20:2; Deut 5:6; and especially Lev 25:38), and agrees with the suggestion that the leading out of Egypt is relativized in favor of the leading out of Abraham from Ur of the Chaldees.[36] The issue is the land promised previously in the narrative as it stands (12:7; 13:14–17). First, Abraham was promised the land (v. 7). Just as in 15:1–5, Abraham lamented his lack of an heir, so here he asked for some assurance of the promise of such a possession. God then acted, and acted *unilaterally*. He alone acted in a ritual and gave a solemn promise. Abraham was given assurance by means of a ritual confirming an oath (vv. 9–21). The oath asserted that while Abraham himself would die and his descendants would be afflicted in a strange land for four hundred years, they would, however, emerge and settle in the fourth generation in the land from the Nile to the Euphrates (vv. 13–16, 18–21). The story-teller's comment that God gave Abraham a solemn assurance (vv. 18–19) rounds the story off. The story could not end earlier in a satisfactory manner, for we would be left wondering for what purpose was the mention of heifer, ram, dove, and pigeon, and Abraham's effort to keep at bay the carrion birds (vv. 9–11). In some unspecified way, the giving of an assurance or oath is linked with the ritual slaughter of these animals and birds. As with the unit of verses 1–6, so with this second unit the story-teller has rounded off the account with his comment to the addressees. The promise of land to Abraham's descendants confirmed the promise made at verse 7[37] within the context of a solemn obligation.[38]

The actual ritual seems unique in the OT. Something analogous is mentioned in Jeremiah 34:18–20, though there the reference is to a ritual

---

35. Von Rad, *Genesis*, 180; Oeming, "Genesis 15:6b," 190, 195; Schliesser, *Abraham*, 137–39; Dobbeler, *Glaube als Teilhabe*, 119. The Targum Pseudo-Jonathan on Genesis 15:6 paraphrases "believed" as "he had faith," i.e., assuming a permanent quality about Abraham's faith (Schliesser, *Abraham*, 134).

36. Weimar, *Genesis 15*, 409 (he quotes Jacob, *Genesis*, 395: "When now a similar sentence is applied to Abraham, the leading out of Israel from Egypt appears only as a repetition and that of Abraham as the model").

37. Westermann, *Genesis 12–36*, 228. Indeed, it answers the question posed by Abraham's original complaint at verse 2. Cf. Schliesser, *Abraham*, 93.

38. See Westermann, *Genesis 12–36*, 215, 228–29, for a rejection of interpreting *berith* as covenant, and agreeing with the suggestion of a "binding obligation." The comment of Henton Davies, *Genesis*, 179, that "the assurance of the promise is thus embodied in ritual," would still hold good.

with an obligation which is made before God, not by Him, and not to an agreement with Him. What is undoubtedly special in Genesis 15 is that Yahweh took this rite on Himself.[39] There is nothing about Abraham's obligations; it is a matter of Yahweh's laying Himself under obligation by promising the land to Abraham's descendants after delivering them from a future enslavement (an obvious reference to the period as slaves in Egypt).[40] In this way Abraham was promised a future.[41]

That God revealed His future plan to Abraham can be taken as a sign that Abraham was a prophet (in accordance with the belief that Yahweh did not act without disclosing His intentions to His servants, the prophets, as declared in Amos 3:7).[42] Abraham is of course described as a prophet in Genesis 20:7.

Chapter 16 continues the motif of an heir for Abraham: "Now Sarai, Abraham's wife, had borne him no child." She thought of a way by which she might have a child — via her slave girl, Hagar. The initiative in the attempt to solve the problem of her childlessness came from Sarai, not Abraham, although he fell in with her suggestion. When, however, Hagar conceived a child by Abraham, she began to despise her mistress. In response, Sarai treated her harshly and Hagar ran away. In the wilderness, Hagar was confronted by the angel of the LORD who commanded her to return, while at the same time instructing her to call the son to be born Ishmael and indicating what his destiny would be (vv. 7-12). Hagar returned, and duly gave birth to her son, Ishmael (v. 15).

Has Sarai's proposed solution to the problem worked? If we put ourselves into the situation of the hearer/reader of the story, the answer will have to be a negative. What the angel of the LORD said about Ishmael hardly agrees with the idea that blessing will come upon the nations through Abraham's descendants (12:3). Ishmael is to be a rather wild, defiant man of conflict, ever at odds with others and submitting to no one (16:12).[43]

---

39. Von Rad, *Genesis*, 182; Tretheim, *Abraham*, 37.

40. See the comments of Neef, *Aspekt alttestamentlicher Bundestheologie*, 8-9; cf. Mühling, *Blickt auf Abraham*, 57.

41. So Oeming, "Genesis 15:6b," 194; *Glaube*, 17; cf. Christiansen, *Covenant in Judaism and Paul*, 33.

42. So Mühling, *Blickt*, 58.

43. For a less confrontational view of Ishmael's relations with others, see Syren, *Forsaken Firstborn*, 24, who prefers a geographical sense of "opposite" on the analogy of Genesis 25:18, where the sense would be to the east of Egypt as NEB/REB render it. This sense is found in the RV mg and the NIV mg of Genesis 16:12. See also Heard, *Ambiguities*, 69-71, for a discussion of this translation and a less adversarial and more co-operative understanding of the Hebrew. An Israelite reader/hearer would be more likely to take the description of Ishmael in a negative sense.

The problem remains unresolved. At the same time, Hagar was promised by God that He would multiply her descendants (v. 10).

The continuation of the narrative is a theophany: God appeared to Abram (17:1). Genesis 17 represents *the priestly interpretation* of the covenant with Abraham. The encounter began with God's self-revelation ("I am El Shaddai" = "I am God Almighty"), and was followed by a command ("Walk before Me and be perfect"), and a promise in two parts (that God would make a covenant with Abram and that he would have numerous descendants, though there was at this stage no reference to the problem of childlessness, v. 2). This called forth an act of veneration by Abram (v. 3) and further words from God (vv. 3b–8). God declared that His covenant was with Abram (v. 4a, reiterated at v. 7 in terms of an everlasting covenant); He bestowed a new name (Abraham rather than Abram); and promised that Abraham would be the father of many nations; that kings would be among his descendants (v. 6c) whose God He would be; and that the land of Canaan would be an everlasting possession for them (v. 8). Circumcision was instituted as a sign of this covenant (vv. 9–14). It must be carried out on the eighth day after birth (v. 12).

Then God promised that Sarai, now to be called Sarah, would have a son by Abraham (vv. 15–16), a promise reiterated in the face of Abraham's incredulity (vv. 17–19). This son, Isaac, and not Ishmael, would be the inheritor of the covenant (vv. 19–21).[44] The story concluded with Abraham's carrying out the obligation to circumcise every male in his household (vv. 23–27).

The reference to kings suggests the Davidic monarchy, for David was a descendant of Abraham. This is stated at both Ruth 4:18–22, where the genealogy begins with Perez who was a son of Judah who was the great grandson of Abraham, and ends with David; and also 1 Chronicles 2:1–4.

This P account placed the establishment of the covenant with Israel in the story of Abraham (P does not narrate the covenant at Sinai), and stressed that the covenant with Abraham and his descendants was an eternal one (v. 7a); that God would be the God of Abraham and his descendants

---

44. Although Ishmael received circumcision, the account notes that he was thirteen years old at the time. By contrast, Isaac was circumcised on his eighth day (21:4). The Abrahamic covenant is continued with him, and Ishmael is excluded (17:21).

after him (v. 7b);[45] and that circumcision was a vital sign of this covenant.[46] There is an indication of the acceptance of this covenant by Abraham and his descendants and of their obligation to walk in God's ways (vv. 9-14).[47] Abraham has a universal significance, because from him will come many nations.

As has frequently been pointed out,[48] the demand for circumcision as a sign of the covenant with Yahweh became increasingly important, both for Jews in exile among strange people or elsewhere in the Diaspora, and at times of crisis like the threat of Hellenism (both from those Jews in Jerusalem among the ruling classes who assimilated and from a foreign ruler like Antiochus Epiphanes).

When making the promise that Abraham's wife, Sarah, would have a son (previously it had never been actually said that Abraham's heir would be from Sarah), God linked Sarah firmly with Abraham insofar as God said that He would bless her and indicated that she would become the ancestress of many nations and of many kings (v. 16). The narrative indicates that Abraham laughed at the statement (vv. 15-17). That this is not the laughter of joy but of incredulity is shown by the fact that Abraham asked God to let Ishmael be his heir (v. 18). The remark is revealing. It indicates how fond Abraham was of Ishmael and that he still thought of him as his heir in spite of the promise that Sarah would have a son. Reverence and unbelief coexist![49] While God went on to promise blessing to Ishmael for Abraham's sake, He made it crystal clear that His covenant (an everlasting one) would be with Isaac (vv. 19, 21). Although he received circumcision (not, however,

45. Vogel, *Das Heil des Bundes*, 111, maintains that the Sinai covenant is seen by P as the fulfilment of the covenant with Abraham. He bases this on the declaration that God will be the God of the people of Israel in Exodus 25:8 and 29:45-46, especially the latter. Though it must be said that this is not a very strong cross-reference between Genesis 17 and Exodus 29, in general terms Vogel's contention (112-13) that the covenant at Sinai is seen as the fulfilment of the Abrahamic covenant within also the horizon of the Noahic covenant has much to commend it; the existence of Israel as the people of God is based on the promises made in the covenants of the Primeval period (Noah) and the Patriarchal period (Abraham).

46. Circumcision could be practiced in a foreign land, like Babylon, as, e.g., Blaschke, *Bescheidung*, 83, points out. He also (86, 90) draws attention to the numerous references to the household as a cultic unit (vv. 12-13, 23, 27), which he sees as corresponding to the situation in Babylon, and raises the question whether some Jews in exile had become lax in practicing circumcision.

47. See Neef, *Aspekte*, 20: the covenant will be "maintained in the keeping of (God's) commands."

48. E.g., Mühling, *Blickt*, 39.

49. Syren, *Forsaken*, 36, comments that Abraham appears as the skeptical realist rather than the model obedient believer.

on the eighth day obviously), Ishmael is excluded from membership of God's elect people. He and his descendants will form a separate entity over against Israel.[50] At the same time, as Kaminsky points out, not being the elect does not mean being an enemy of God.[51]

When, in the final editing of what we call the book of Genesis, the different streams of tradition, written and oral, were drawn together, it was the P editor who gave the chapters about Abraham their final form.[52]

It is worth pausing at this point and taking stock. Although clearly Genesis 12–17 would have been read/heard as a continuous narrative by Jews once the book of Genesis had been put together, OT critical scholarship for all its differences (and at times these have been and are not inconsiderable), has revealed that different traditions have been blended into our present Genesis 12–17, and that there were different emphases in the way the story of God's dealings with Abraham were set forth. While land and descendants figure prominently, the story is shaped to express particular concerns. Thus, one could say that Genesis 12 evinces an interest in Israel's relations with the world beyond it: Israel is to be a blessing to all the families of the earth. The account in Genesis 15 (whether we accept the presence of an E source or reject it) reflects on how a childless man reacted to God's promise of descendants. Clearly, the Priestly account of Genesis 17 was interested in the institution of circumcision as the badge of the covenant, and stressed that the covenant was an eternal one. Probably also there is an underlying concern to link Abraham with the Davidic house.

That these different emphases are present—especially if some of these traditions go back into the pre-exilic period and thus pre-date the final composition of Genesis by a considerable period—is both fascinating and instructive, and needs to be borne in mind as our study progresses.[53] It might suggest that different portraits of Abraham might well emerge elsewhere and subsequently among Israel's traditions.

---

50. See Syren, *Forsaken*, 37–40.

51. Kaminsky, *Jacob*, 35, a point which he frequently emphasizes throughout his book. The non-chosen sibling is not necessarily excluded from all divine favor (41).

52. See Cross, *Priestly Work*, 293–325, esp. 301–7, 324–25, for the arguments that P was not a narrative source, and that in Genesis 12–25 only 17:1–17 and 23:1–20 are real compositions of P. The P editor reworked JE and some other traditions with priestly orientated material into what we have in our Genesis 12–25 today.

53. See von Rad, *Theology of Israel's Historical Traditions*, 165–75, for discussion of the History of the Patriarchs in J and E, while for the contribution of P see Blenkinsopp, *Abraham as Paradigm*, 225–41. Note the remark made by Konradt, *Die aus Glauben*, 44, to the effect that *projection on to the figure of Abraham of a writer's own concerns about identity was clearly basically true of the OT narratives about Abraham*.

The problem of a son and heir continues to be the theme of 18:1–15, when Yahweh appeared to Abraham by the oaks of Memre, was entertained by Abraham, and promised that Sarah would have a son (vv. 1–10). Sarah laughed at the idea, but the LORD asked "Is anything too hard for the LORD?" and promised to return when Sarah had had a son (vv. 13–15).

Before the account of Sarah's conception and the birth of Isaac, we are given the story of Abraham and the issue of the wickedness of Sodom, which God intended to destroy. This begins with a soliloquy from Yahweh. He asked Himself whether He was right in hiding from Abraham what He intended to do to Sodom. The question was raised because God recognized that Abraham would become a great nation (as He had promised according to Gen 12:2a) and that through him all the nations of the earth would be blessed (the niphael of *brk* is used with a passive sense,[54] as at 12:3; 28:14). For God had indeed chosen[55] him "that he may charge his children and his household after him to keep the way of the LORD by doing righteousness and justice" (v. 18). Here Abraham is basically portrayed as *a teacher of righteousness and justice*. Abraham was a man who both kept God's commands and taught his descendants to behave in a similar way.[56] As the "for" (*ky*) indicates, there is a link between the idea that the nations would be blessed through Abraham and the idea that he would be a teacher of righteousness and justice for his children and household. The sense appears to be that by teaching in this way Abraham would contribute to his descendants' becoming a great nation whose way of life would be so admired that other nations would be attracted by and blessed through their example.[57]

Through the divine soliloquy, Abraham is portrayed as someone standing in a relationship of intimacy with God. Through their subsequent conversation, Yahweh is portrayed as speaking with him and disclosing His plans to him (cf. 18:33).[58]

Through the story about Sodom, questions are raised about *divine justice*—is it right to destroy the righteous with the wicked? Which is more important—the wickedness of the majority or the righteousness of

---

54. Flury-Schölch, *Abrahams Segen*, 138, takes it as a consecutive perfect.

55. The verb *ydʿ* at Genesis 18:19 is the sole text with the sense of choose in the patriarchal narratives (Westermann, *Genesis 12–36*, 288).

56. The significance of this and its application to Jews in the Diaspora is obvious, but no less also when Jews within Israel itself were facing demands to assimilate to Hellenistic religion and customs.

57. Without wishing to suggest any link or influence, one thinks of the role of the Servant = Israel to be a light to the nations in Isaiah 42:1–7; 49:3–6.

58. Flury-Schölch, *Abrahams Segen*, 145, helpfully refers to Numbers 12:8, and suggests that here Abraham stands on a par with Moses in his relationship to God.

the minority? Can the righteousness of the minority avail on behalf of the majority? The story is the vehicle for raising these theological issues. It is hardly a story about Abraham's intercession for Sodom, though it has often been popularly referred-to as such, while it has also been suggested that had Abraham continued to bring the number down below ten, the story would have had a different twist or ending.[59] As it is, it is Abraham who breaks off, not God! This is the impression created by Abraham's remark in verse 32 that he intended to speak just once more, which he does at verse 32c, asking for Sodom to be spared for ten righteous persons.[60]

Again, we can see that this issue would have practical relevance. It was not a purely abstract, theoretical problem. For example, the question of the justice/righteousness of God was raised by the destruction of Jerusalem,[61] even if the finer spirits in Israel acknowledged the sinfulness of both Israel and Judah (as we can see by the way Habbakuk wrestled with the problem of why God was using the evil Babylonians to chastise His own people when they were far worse sinners than the Israelites).

We note that Abraham's standing before God is revealed by a couple of comments in the story relating to Sodom. The first is when Yahweh asked Himself whether He should hide from Abraham what He intended to do to Sodom, seeing that Abraham would become a great and mighty nation and that all the nations of the earth would be blessed in him (18:17–18). Abraham appears to be a kind of trusted confidante of God. Then, secondly, it is said that God saved Lot from being destroyed with Sodom because of Abraham (19:29). So highly did God regard Abraham that He ensured the rescue of Lot from the catastrophe about to engulf Sodom.

Mention of the popular designation "intercession" can lead us on to the story of Abraham's passing off Sarah as his sister in the Kingdom of Gerar, the wilderness area between Shur and Kadesh (20:1–18 ?E). In this story,[62] Abimelech, the king of Gerar, took Sarah, but he is warned in a dream by God not to touch her (20:2). God instructed Abimelech as follows: "Now, therefore, restore the man's wife; for he is a prophet and he will pray for you, and you will live" (20:7). We note that intercession is expected to be

---

59. Unless the number ten simply indicates the virtually smallest conceivable number, as Mühling, *Blickt*, 61n175, supposes.

60. Heard, *Ambiguities*, 44, says that it is God who breaks off the conversation, but He only does so after Abraham's declaration that he intends to make one further request. Heard is correct, on the other hand, to state that Yahweh seems determined to destroy Sodom.

61. As it was after AD 70, as 4 Ezra and 2 Baruch amply testify.

62. See the commentaries for discussion of the literary-historical relationships between it and Genesis 12:10–20; 26:1–11.

what a prophet does. As Aubrey Johnson said "The prophet was a specialist in prayer; he was peculiarly qualified to act in this way as an intercessor."[63]

Sarah is restored to Abraham together with money, animals, and slaves (vv. 14–16).

In this story there is some attempt by the writer to explain Abraham's subterfuge (see v. 12), though there is no rebuke from God contained in the story. Abimelech actually appears in a very favorable light. Indeed, Anke Mühling considers that there are lessons through the story for Jews living in foreign lands. They can have a *modus vivendi* with foreigners, whose moral integrity they should not underestimate, and they can trust in God's leading and preserving care.[64] She sees similar implications in a sequel to this story, in the account about the covenant which Abraham and Abimelech made together with the resolving of a dispute over a well (21:22–34).[65]

The long awaited child comes at last. But the birth of Isaac is recorded in Genesis 21 somewhat prosaically. Care is taken that the reader is reminded that God had not only promised the couple a child, but had specified when it would happen: verse 2 says that the birth occurred "at the time of which God had spoken to (Abraham)." Isaac was circumcised on the eighth day, according to the divine command recorded in 17:12.

Abraham is shown as being upset when Sarah, having given birth to Isaac, later wanted to get rid of Hagar and Ishmael. It was only as a result of a divine command that Abraham dismissed the boy and his mother from his household (21:12–13). Abraham's provision for the two seems extremely meagre and wholly inadequate except for the shortest of journeys.[66] While God promised blessing for Ishmael (vv. 13, 18, 20a) and intervened to ensure that mother and child were saved from death in the wilderness (vv. 14–19), the narrator stressed that Isaac had priority: Abraham's line was to

---

63. Johnson, *Cultic Prophet in Ancient Israel*, 59.

64. Mühling, *Blickt*, 163. The comments of Westermann, *Genesis 12–36*, 329, are more general—the author is warning his contemporaries against a narrow-minded thought pattern of friend versus foe and an attitude inspired by uneasiness about the wickedness of others. Though Heard, *Ambiguities*, does not discuss this passage, it represents a position different from his own (though on 22 he says that Genesis was produced by somewhat more erenic members of Yehud's immigrant elite group, while his statement on 176 is that they supported the Ezra-Nehemiah line on mixed marriages).

65. Mühling, *Blickt*, 65–66.

66. Heard, *Ambiguities*, 87–88, mentions Calvin's suggestion that it is part of Abraham's resistance to Sarah's and God's demand and that he intended that they should only go a short distance and that he would keep in touch with them to provide for their needs.

be traced through him (v. 12; cf. 17:19). As with Lot earlier, so now Ishmael is excluded from the true line of Abraham's descendants.[67]

We move now to Genesis 22, which records what is a crucially important episode, the demand from God that Abraham offer Isaac as a sacrifice.[68] In other words, the recipient of the promise from God is ordered by this same God to offer up as a sacrifice the one through whom the promise is to be fulfilled in the future. This order is stated as being a means by which God tested Abraham (v. 1; cf. vv. 12, 16). Abraham obeyed and proceeded to travel to Moriah with Isaac. When Isaac asked where was the lamb for a burnt offering (v. 7), Abraham said God *yr'h lô hśh* the lamb for a burnt offering (v. 8). Traditionally, this has been translated in English as "God will *provide* etc.," though the verb *r'h* means to *see*. The LXX translated by οψεται.[69] If the normal sense of the Hebrew is followed, the sense would appear to be "God sees the lamb for a burnt offering for Himself" and to refer to Isaac, without this being revealed openly to Isaac.[70]

At the crucial moment, with the knife raised ready to carry out the awful deed, the angel of the LORD commanded Abraham to desist. "Now I know that you have not withheld your son, your only son, from me" (v. 12). Then Abraham saw (*wyr'*) a ram caught in a thicket and proceeded to offer this as a burnt offering (v. 13). As a result, Abraham called the place *yhwh yr'h*. The narrator adds that to his day it is said, *bhr yhwh yr'h* (v. 14). Once again the same problem of translation confronts us. The usual English translation again uses "provide" in both instances, but if we follow the normal sense of the Hebrew verb, we can translate "Yahweh saw" and "In the mountain of the Yahweh he saw." (The LXX renders Κυριος ειδεν = The Lord saw and εν τω ορει Κυριος ωφθη = In the mountain the Lord appeared,[71] respectively. The translator interpreted the event as a theophany—hence

---

67. See Syren, *Forsaken*, 49. Heard, *Ambiguities*, 176, in his concluding summary, suggests that Abraham's action in dismissing Hagar and Ishmael would be seen by those returned exiles in the post-exilic community in Jerusalem-Judah as a paradigm for taking the action demanded by Ezra and Nehemiah in dismissing foreign wives and their children (see Ezra 10; Neh 13). A similar post-exilic setting is assumed by Syren, *Forsaken*, e.g., 41, 54–65, 143–45. He suggests that in the stories of the forsaken first-born there is a place for the "also peoples" within God's plans, even though Israel is conscious of its own special standing as God's elect people (Syren, *Forsaken*, 143–45).

68. Here is not the place to comment on the skill and artistry of the narrator, nor on what is not said in the course of the story (about the human emotions, while Sarah is not mentioned at all).

69. See verse 13 where it renders *wyr'* with ειδεν "he saw."

70. Possibly, the sense of "to see" may be "see to."

71. The passive of οραω means "to become visible, appear" (See Bauer, *NT Lexicon*, 581).

ὤφθη.) There seems to be a move from God seeing Isaac as the sacrifice in verse 8—and knowing thereby that Abraham was obedient—to Abraham seeing the ram in verse 13, which he was able to offer as a substitute for Isaac. But the name of the place is related to the statement in verse 8.

Whatever may be said about the problems of translating r'h, the total story has various levels of meaning. At one stage, the story may have helped to explain the name of the place, of a sanctuary on the mountain (v. 14): Yahweh had appeared there and "seen" the actions. It has been widely believed also that it was used to show that the God of Israel did not require child sacrifice (cf. Exod 13:13b; 34:20b; Lev 18:21; Deut 18:10, though the practice did continue in Israel as we learn from prophetic condemnation of it).[72] It illustrates the obedience of Abraham, his godly fear (v. 12). Abraham is willing to offer up the only child through whom the future descendants would emerge, the only child on whom the promise depended. It is difficult to understand why Westermann objects to this level of meaning when the text at it now stands seems to mention it so clearly. His own interpretation is that the narrator is not seeking to extol a human being but to praise God who had seen suffering, seen the anguish of those in the depths, and had liberated Abraham from his anguish. This interpretation takes seriously the meaning of the Hebrew r'h in verse 14. Whether this was actually what the narrator intended is probably open to doubt, though it certainly accords with the usual theocentric emphasis of the Bible as a whole. Perhaps it is an interpretation which bears witness to what Westermann himself calls the continued vitality of the story.[73] At the level of the final editor, the story could be holding up Abraham as a model of the faithful Jew, who maintains obedience amid the most testing of circumstances. Like the father of the race, Jews in exile or subsequently must remain obedient and faithful.[74]

In verse 15-18, the angel of the LORD called a second time to Abraham. The obedience of Abraham to God's command is stressed at the beginning and the end of the divine speech ("because you have done this thing" [v. 15]; "because you have obeyed My voice" [v. 18]).[75] It is this which becomes the

---

72. But Westermann, *Genesis 12-36*, 354-55, 357-58, firmly rules this out as in any way a prime motif, though the materials in Exodus 22:29 and 34:20 may have been at hand for the author. See also Levenson, *Death and Resurrection*, 111-24, for a severe critique of this view.

73. Westermann, *Genesis 12-36*, 365. I here use the wording of D. E. Green's translation-adaptation of Westermann's 3 volumes for the popular version, *Genesis*, 163, rather than the wording of *Genesis 12-36*, 365 ("what is [essential] is that the narrative lives on").

74. Mühling, *Blickt*, 73.

75. Ego, *Abraham*, 28, says that the obedience of Abraham forms the narrative framework within which the Yahwist presents his work (in reference to Genesis 12:1-4;

basis of what is in fact a confirmation[76] of the blessing previously promised to Abraham in respect of his descendants. Because Abraham had been willing to offer Isaac back to God, God renewed His promises to bless him and to multiply his descendants. There is an additional promise—to give them victory over their enemies. Abraham's seed will possess the gates[77] of their enemies (v. 17e). What, if any, is the link between the victories of verse 17e and the next phrase "and in your seed all the nations will seek a blessing for themselves"? Here the hithpael of *brk* is used (in contrast to Gen 12:3) and has a reflexive sense.[78] If the hithpael of *brk* is a consecutive perfect, then the sense is that when the nations see the victories of Abraham's descendants, the result will be that they will wish for the same kind of success (blessing) for themselves as Abraham's descendants have ("God make us like Israel").[79] This militant note is rather surprising (despite Gen 14), though something very similar recurs in the farewell blessing upon Rebekah uttered by her family at 24:60.[80]

When Sarah died, Abraham purchased a burial place in Hebron (Gen 23). It is as if symbolically he staked a claim to the land promised to him. In the lengthy story in chapter 24, Abraham commissioned his steward to arrange for Isaac to have a wife from his kinsfolk in Paddan-Aram. The steward was made to swear an oath that he would not arrange a marriage

---

22:1-14). Westermann, *Promises*, 130-31, sees the motif of reward for obedience as a sign of later development, and argues that the promises are absolute and not conditional upon any actions of the patriarchs. Halpern-Amaru, *Rewriting*, 12, argues that Abraham's merit does not elicit the covenant so much as offer the justification for it after the fact.

76. Hansen, *Abraham in Galatians*, 177, 267.

77. The gate as the beginning of a city or a sector of it would be a means of keeping at bay an enemy and so a crucial part to capture. See Nehemiah's concern to see to the repair of the gates of Jerusalem which had been burned and left like that, whenever that had happened (Neh 1:3; 3:1-33). Here, in Genesis 22:17, the use of gates is a case of *pars pro toto*.

78. Flury-Schölch, *Abrahams Segen*, 91-116, 152-53, 166.

79. This is the argument of Flury-Schölch, *Abrahams Segen*, 152-53.

80. It might suggest a pre-exilic setting in the royal ideology of the Davidic dynasty as exemplified by Psalm 72. This is the position of Flury-Schölch, *Abrahams Segen*, 226-33, 239-58.

Levison, *Death*, 174, has argued that through these verses 14-18 the event (the aqedah) has become "a foundational event." While it is undoubtedly the case that Abraham's willingness to sacrifice his son came to exercise a tremendous influence on the way the patriarch was later seen (see chapter 2), this verdict may go too far in view of the crucial importance of God's saving acts in the Exodus and gift of the Covenant at Sinai. Within the canonical Hebrew scriptures it is these which are the foundational event.

for Isaac with a Canaanite woman (vv. 2-9).[81] There was also a stress in Abraham's instructions to his steward that on no account was he to take Isaac back to where Abraham came from. Abraham recalled God's promise of the land of Canaan. Canaan was the destiny of Abraham's descendants (vv. 6-8). Divine guidance in the choice of Rebekah is also stressed (vv. 12, 21, 27, 42-44, 48, 56). After Sarah's death, Abraham married again (a woman called Kenturah) and had more children (Gen 25). His death is briefly recorded at 25:8, and his burial alongside Sarah at Machpelah at 25:9-10. Although the narrator states that Isaac and Ishmael buried their father, he records the list of Ishmael's descendants and where he and they dwelt separately, underlining thereby the separateness and distinctiveness of the Ishmael line (Gen 25:12-18) and the Isaac line (25:19-21).

We now look back over the material which we have surveyed. We may agree wholeheartedly with Westermann's comment that *both* the promises of God to Abraham *and* the relationship with God are the basic determining factors of Abraham's existence.[82] God broke into Abraham's existence, called him, uprooting him from his land and family. God made certain promises to Abraham, which are renewed at further points in the narrative. These promises focus on blessing, spelt out as descendants, land, and a name. That blessing stretches out beyond his immediate descendants to the families of the earth. But how can these promises be realized when Abraham and Sarah are childless? This *Leitmotiv* runs through many of the stories, and only reaches its resolution with the birth of Isaac, but then seems jeopardized by the demand to sacrifice Isaac on Mount Moriah, to be resolved when a ram is substituted for his son and when Abraham arranged for his son to have a wife from his wider family (and not from the Canaanites). Abraham is seen as the father of Israel, under God. Although not a "plaster saint," and although at one stage he attempted to ensure the fulfilment of the promise by having a son from Hagar and seemed to continue to hope that Ishmael might be his heir, he is presented as one who trusted God (15:6) and obeyed when put to one of the most excruciatingly painful tests imaginable (22:12, 18b). Abraham is also portrayed as a teacher of the Law, who instructs his descendants in the ways of Yahweh (18:19), and as a prophet who can act as an intercessor (20:7).

If we may assume that our present Genesis does combine different streams of tradition (using that phrase rather than documents), then the different emphases in Genesis 12, 15, and 17, for example, suggest that

---

81. The issue of endogamy was certainly a post-exilic problem as the books of Ezra, Nehemiah, and Jubilees amply testify.

82. Westermann, *Genesis 12-36*, 404.

reflection on the figure of Abraham had gone on fairly early in the history of Israel. If, for example, we do date the Yahwist to the first part of, or even somewhat later in, the tenth century,[83] then Abraham was being interpreted fairly early on, in his significance for the people of God. We are not wholly dependent on the assumption of a Yahwist source for the idea of pre-exilic reflection on the figure of Abraham. Ezekiel 11:15–16 and especially 33:24 (both to be placed early after 587 BC)[84] point, to some extent, in this direction, even if this particular reflection was based on a selfish reasoning. Indeed, Flury-Schölch himself thinks that perhaps in the time of Josiah Abraham was used as a figure of integration for north and south in Josiah's vision and hopes,[85] though defenders of the Yahwist source could make the same claim for the Davidic Solomon era.

Of course, even once Genesis had reached its present form, these streams of tradition may not have ceased to exist forthwith, but presumably they would fade out of existence eventually, and the people of Israel would hear/read Genesis as we know it.

Abraham is mentioned in the remaining chapters of Genesis (26–50). We may briefly summarize these occurrences. His name is mentioned when God introduced Himself to later descendants as the God of Abraham, to Isaac (26:24); or as the God of Abraham and of Isaac, to Jacob (28:13) or is referred-to in this way by Jacob (31:42 [here along with a reference to the Fear of Isaac], 53 [here along with a reference to the God of Nahor, the God of their father]; 32:9; cf. 48:15–16), or when God renewed the promises, first made to Abraham, to Isaac, and to Jacob (26:2–4; 28:4; 35:11–12) or when Joseph referred to the oath sworn to the three patriarchs (50:24). Of these references, those in chapters 26 (within the Isaac cycle of stories), 28, and 35 (in the Jacob cycle) deserve special mention.

After the reference to Isaac's marriage to Rebekah, her childlessness, the eventual conception of twins, the oracle from Yahweh to Rebekah about their rivalry and the superiority of the younger, the narrative leaps over to the incident when Jacob induced Esau to sell him the birthright of the elder son (25:19–34). The next episode is when a famine occurred in Canaan, as

---

83. Rejecting the much later date proposed, for example, by van Seters, *Abraham*; Thompson, *Historicity of the Patriarchal Narratives*. See Dever, *What Did the Biblical Writers Know?*, for trenchant criticism, from the point of view of an archaeologist, of a minimalist approach to OT history.

84. Eichrodt, *Ezekiel*, 143, 461–63; Allen, *Ezekiel 1–19*, 132–33, 163–64.

85. This is linked to a particular development of the tradition of Abraham, Isaac, and Jacob. See, e.g., Flury-Schölch, *Abrahams Segen*, 311–13. This view accords priority to the Jacob/Isaac tradition and sees the figure of Abraham introduced as an integrating figure for unity between north and south, perhaps in the time of Josiah.

a result of which Isaac moved to Gerar, in the territory of the king of the Philistines (26:1). At this point, Yahweh appeared to Isaac and commanded him not to go to Egypt but to stay in Gerar. By implication, Canaan is to be the land where he should live. God promised to be with Isaac, to bless him, to give him the land, to establish the oath which He had sworn to Isaac's father, Abraham,[86] to multiply Isaac's descendants like the stars of heaven, and that "all the nations of the earth will pray to be blessed as they are blessed"[87] (NEB).[88] All these promises were made "because Abraham obeyed my voice and kept my charge, my commandments, my statutes, and my laws" (v. 5). This wording is anachronistic and reflects Deuteronomic language.[89] Abraham's obedience is emphasized here; it is in the context of what God had promised him on oath.

As the story progresses, the narrator made the comment that when Isaac sowed, he reaped a hundredfold "and Yahweh *blessed* him" (v. 12). After a period of strife between the herdsmen of Gerar and Isaac's men, Isaac moved to Beersheba. Then Yahweh appeared to Isaac during one night and said to him: "I am the God of your father Abraham: do not be afraid, for I am with you, and I will bless you and multiply your seed for the sake of My servant, Abraham" (v. 24). Presumably, it is Abraham's obedience which underlies this promise of blessing "for Abraham's sake" (v. 24).[90] There are references in the context both to Abraham's obedience (v. 5), and the oath/promise made to Abraham (v. 3e), but perhaps the reference to Abraham as God's servant in verse 24 tilts the balance in favor of a reference to Abraham's obedience. There is a case for saying that what is in mind in the references to Abraham's obedience is cumulatively the references to his obedience to God's call, his belief in God's promise, his obedience to the command to circumcise himself and his household, and his obedience to the command to sacrifice Isaac.[91] The motif of Abraham's obedience and his crucial signifi-

---

86. There may be a consecutive sense in the statement about establishing the oath made to Abraham: "*And so/so that* I may establish the oath which I swore to your father, Abraham" (v. 4e). So Westermann, *Genesis 12–36*, 421, 424; Flury-Schölch, *Abrahams Segen*, 171.

87. The hithpael of *brk* is used, as at 22:18, with a reflexive sense. The REB altered the NEB translation, substituting "wish" instead of to "pray."

88. Of these promises, that to bless occurs in 12:2b; 22:17a; that to multiply descendants like the stars of heaven in 15:5; 22:17b; and that of land (the plural is actually used here) at 12:7; 13:15; 17:8.

89. Westermann, *Genesis 12:36*, 425.

90. In agreement with Westermann, *Genesis 12–36*, 428. On the other hand, von Rad, *Genesis*, 267, interprets it as "for the sake of the promise given to Abraham."

91. So Yeung, *Faith in Jesus and Paul*, 237. Levenson, *Death*, 1141, points to the stress on this obedience of Abraham to God's commands in verses 2-5 over against the

cance as a source of benefit for his descendants is thus emphasized. At the same time, this obedience is a response to God's initiative in calling him and making promises to him.

Later, Abimelech approached Isaac in Beersheba with a request for a covenant with him, openly giving his reason because he had seen that Yahweh was with Isaac (v. 28) and that he was *blessed* by Yahweh (v. 29). This supports the reflexive use of the hithpael of *brk* in verse 4c, and illustrates the idea of others seeing the blessing given by God to the fathers of Israel and longing for it for themselves.

Finally, we turn to Genesis 28:3-4, 13-15, both of which figure within the story of Jacob's flight from the anger of his brother Esau when he had robbed him of Isaac's blessing. The idea of getting away from Esau and going to Haran to Laban (Rebekah's brother and Jacob's uncle) was suggested by his mother, Rebekah (27:41-45), who disguised her real motive by expressing to her husband her disgust at Esau's marriage to Hittite women and her fear lest Jacob should do the same (27:46).[92] The suggestion of going to Haran/Paddan-aram was endorsed by his father Isaac, who charged Jacob to get a wife from among his kinsfolk (28:1-2). Then Isaac blessed Jacob with these words: "God Almighty bless you, and make you fruitful, and multiply you, that you may be a company of peoples, and give you the blessing of Abraham, to you and your seed with you; that you may take possession of the land where you now live as an alien—the land which God gave to Abraham" (28:4). On a linguistic level, there is an echo of the command to humankind to be fruitful and multiply in the story of creation in Genesis 1:28, while also this is the only occurrence of the phrase "the blessing of Abraham" in the Hebrew scriptures (Paul was to use it). How Jacob and his descendants would take possession of the land is unspecified, though presumably some form of military action would be in mind. The prayer for descendants and the land reinforces major motifs of the Abrahamic promise. Isaac sees Jacob as the heir of that Abrahamic promise.

Jacob left Beersheba (28:10). At night as he slept at a place called Luz, which he subsequently called Bethel (vv. 11, 19), he dreamed that he saw a ladder set between earth and heaven with the angels of God ascending and descending upon it (v. 12). Yahweh appeared to him and spoke to him. He introduced Himself as "Yahweh, the God of your father Abraham and the God of Isaac" (v. 13ab). Promises follow. Firstly, Yahweh promised to give him and his descendants the land on which he lay (v. 13c), and then,

---

way Christian and Jewish thinkers have tended to stress his faith.

92. On the traditional source theory, these two reasons for Jacob's departure are due to J (27:41-45) and P (27:46-28.9). See Westermann, *Genesis 12-36*, 443, 446, for details.

secondly, to multiply his descendants as the dust of the earth-and through those descendants he would spread to the four points of the compass. Thirdly, through him and his descendants all the families of the earth would be blessed (v. 14). Fourthly, God promised to be with him and protect him, and, fifthly, to bring him back to the land which he was just about to leave. Finally, there is the promise: "I will not leave you, until I have done what I have spoken to you about" (v. 15). The first two promises, land and descendants, reiterate key motifs in the patriarchal narratives. The third promise agrees verbatim with Genesis 12:3b, with the addition of "and through your descendants (seed)."[93] The fourth and fifth promises refer to the particular situation of Jacob as a fugitive on a journey facing possible dangers and leaving the land which he had come to regard as home. The last promise embraces all the previous five.

If at 28:2-4, Isaac had recognized Jacob as the heir of Abraham, now that was enunciated by God Himself. God took the deceiver and cheat into the line of promise. God chose Jacob without reference to his worthiness.[94]

After Jacob had return from Paddan-aram to Canaan, God told him to go and live at Bethel and make an altar there, and God appeared to him there (35:1, 7, 9). After God gave him the name Israel, He told Jacob-Israel to be fruitful and multiply, and promised that a nation and company of nations and kings should descend from him. "I will give the land which I gave to Abraham and to Isaac, to you and your seed after you" (35:11-12). Here we have echoes of both Genesis 1:28 transferred as it were to the descendants of Jacob-Israel, and of the promises made to Abraham at Genesis 17:5-6. In addition, his descendants are incorporated into the promise of the Land of Canaan. These points are reiterated when Jacob-Israel talked with his son Joseph in Egypt, and told him about this appearance of God to him (48:4) and assured him that God would bring him to the land of his fathers (later Joseph repeats these sentiments to his brothers at 50:24, mentioning specifically the oath to Abraham, Isaac and Jacob).

At the end of Genesis, there are references to the burial ground which Abraham purchased at Hebron (49:30-31; 50:13).

---

93. In particular, the niphal of *brk* "will be blessed" and *kl mšpḥt hʾdmh* "all the families of the earth" are used in both passages. For details see Flury-Schölch, *Abrahams Segen*, 176-77.

94. See von Rad, *Genesis*, 282: "As for Jacob, his human nature, i.e., any worthiness he may perhaps possess, no art of empathy can succeed in making the incomprehensible comprehensible, namely, that the fleeing deceiver received such a word of grace." A not dissimilar point is made by Henton Davies, *Genesis*, 220. Brueggemann, *Genesis*, 242, says: "The miracle is the way in which this sovereign God binds himself to this treacherous fugitive."

1.1.2 The Book of Exodus

The book of Exodus opens by linking the story of the Exodus about to be told with the previous accounts of the patriarchs. The Hebrews in Egypt are identified as the sons of Jacob-Israel (1:1-5). The narrator says that they increased and multiplied. While the language used is reminiscent of the command in Genesis 1:28, it also cannot but evoke recollection of the promise of numerous descendants made to Abraham (Gen 15:5, repeated at 17:4-6) and reiterated to Jacob (Gen 35:11).[95]

Further references to the numerical increase of the Hebrews, despite measures taken to curb it, occur at 1:12 and 20. These measures were enslavement and extremely harsh working conditions in building cities for the reigning Pharaoh. The narrator tells us that the Hebrews groaned under their burden and their cry came to the attention of God, who heard them and "remembered His covenant with Abraham, Isaac and Jacob" and "took note of them" (2:24, usually regarded as a note from P). The attentive reader of the Pentateuch as it now stands would recall that God predicted such enslavement to Abraham at the time when He made a covenant with him recorded at Genesis 15:13, and would expect some divine resolution of the problem given the promise in Genesis 15:14 that the descendants would come out of the enslaved condition. The covenant with the fathers, beginning with Abraham, has decisive importance and is the key to the story which will unfold.

The instrument of God's deliverance of the Hebrews from their slavery is to be Moses, whose call is narrated in chapter 3 (usually regarded as mainly J, with additions from the E stream of tradition). The initiative for this call lies with God. He broke into the life of Moses without prior intimation. God appeared to him in the burning bush[96] in the wilderness after his flight from Egypt and his settling among the Kenites. God introduced Himself:

"I am the God of your fathers, the God of Abraham, the God of Isaac, and the God of Jacob" (3:6), and then proceeded to say that He had heard the cry of the people and He had come down to deliver them, and to bring them to the land of Canaan (vv. 7-8). In verse 10 comes the commission: "Come now, I will send you to Pharaoh that you may bring forth my people, the Israelites, from Egypt" (v. 10).[97]

---

95. Henton Davies, *Exodus*, 59, also points out that Joseph is the geographical and biological link as indicated in Genesis 45:5-7. See Childs, *Exodus*, 2.

96. Childs, *Exodus*, 74, describes the phenomenon of the bush which does not burn as "a visible sign of God's power which breaks through human experience."

97. For the correlation of (hidden) divine action and (visible) human agency, see the brief but helpful comment in Brueggemann, *Theology of the Old Testament*, 364.

Moses countered this commission with a series of objections, one of which was how should he answer the people in Egypt when they asked what was the name of the God of the fathers. To be able to give the name of God would legitimate his claim to be sent. He was told: "I will be what I will be."[98] Thus you shall say to the children of Israel: 'I Will Be[99] has sent me to you ... Yahweh, the God of your fathers, the God of Abraham, the God of Isaac and the God of Jacob, has sent me to you.' This is my name forever"[100] (v. 15). Moses was told to gather the elders and to say to them: "Yahweh, the God of your fathers, the God of Abraham, of Isaac and of Jacob, has appeared to me, saying I will bring you up out of the misery of Egypt to the land of Canaan" (vv. 16-17).

A number of assertions seem to be made through this divine speech. In the first place, *the identity of the God of Moses and the God of the patriarchs is firmly established and emphasized.* The God of the coming Exodus and Settlement is the same God who was the God of Abraham, Isaac, and Jacob. At the same time, secondly, the passage in its present form, with the assertion that "This is my name forever," implies that *this name for God superseded all other designations and was linked with the call and commission of Moses, and so, thereafter, became a crucial part of Israel's experience of God.*[101] Thirdly, the passage contains a reflection (as it were) on the meaning of the name. What exactly is the actual significance of this name, which we have reproduced as "I will be what I will be"?[102] To discuss the problems concerning the meaning and translation of the Hebrew *'hyh 'šr 'hyh* in verse 14a would go far beyond our particular interests. I have opted for what I think is the best sense: viz. God indicated to Moses that the people *will discover God's character in the unfolding situations of their story.* He will prove Himself to be entirely appropriate to these situations.[103] There is mystery about God which cannot be tied down, and He preserves, as it were, His

---

98. Or "I Am Who I Am" (Hebrew of v. 14a is *'hyh 'sr 'hyh*).

99. Or "I Am has sent me to you" (Hebrew of v. 14b is: *'hyh slhny 'lykm*).

100. "This is the name which will then be cultically remembered by his people throughout the generations. The revelation of the name in Israel is not to satisfy curiosity but to be the medium of continuous worship" (Childs, *Exodus*, 76-77).

101. "The main testimony of the E tradition has been preserved which marked the introduction of the new name to Israel through Moses, while at the same time preserving the continuity of God's history of revelation" (Childs, *Exodus*, 68-69).

102. So RV mg; NEB mg; GNB (TEV) mg; NIV mg; REB mg; NRSV mg.

103. "Yahweh declares himself in what he does" (Zimmerli, *Old Testament Theology in Outline*, 21); cf. "The people also will experience God's purpose by what he does in their future. . . . Who he is and what he does will emerge in the history which yet lies ahead" (Childs, *Exodus*, 76, 88).

freedom to act in a way which He sees fit;[104] hence the aura of indefiniteness about the name.[105] At the same time, there is the assurance of His presence and help in the future[106] (note how God promised to be with Moses when he went to Pharaoh [v. 12] and the promise that God would be with the mouth of Moses [4:12, 15]). Fourthly, the goal of the deliverance is to bring the Israelites to the land of Canaan (vv. 8, 17). Given God's proclamation of Himself as the God of Abraham, Isaac, and Jacob, the previous promises of the land to them and their descendants are implicitly being recalled.[107]

When Moses expressed his fear that the Israelites would not believe him, he was given miraculous powers "that they may believe that Yahweh, the God of their fathers, the God of Abraham, the God of Isaac, and the God of Jacob, has appeared to you" (4:5). Again, we meet the two concerns, both to establish the identity of the God of the patriarchs and the God who has appeared to Moses with a view to delivering the Hebrews from slavery, and to assert the authority of Moses as one sent.

After the refusal of Pharaoh to let the Israelites leave Egypt and his imposition of even harsher working conditions upon them, the stream of tradition known to scholars as P is taken up in chapter 6.[108] What originally was probably the story of Moses' call in the P stream of tradition, now becomes in its present context in the book of Exodus a confirmation and/or reassurance of Moses by God.[109]

In the section 6:2-8, God is depicted simply as addressing Moses and revealing His intentions. There is nothing about the reaction of Moses, and even in the immediate sequel (6:9-13) there is nothing like the extended dialogue between God and Moses as in 3:1-4:17. We read:

---

104. Zimmerli compares the form of the saying with Exodus 33:19, and continues: "In this figure of speech resounds the sovereign freedom of Yahweh, who, even at the moment when he reveals himself in his name, refuses simply to put himself at the disposal of humanity or to allow humanity to comprehend him" (Zimmerli, *Outline*, 20).

105. Brueggemann comments: "Not only will this God show no form, but even God's name is given so that it is not accessible to Moses and Israel. Thus, not only is the eye prohibited access to God, but even the ear is given only partial entry into inscrutability" (Brueggemann, *Old Testament Theology*, 121). See also Noth, *Exodus*, 45, who states that "it is the kind of indefiniteness in which something definite is envisaged but is not meant to be expressed ('I am something, but it will only turn out later what I am'). Most likely, however, that kind of indefiniteness is expressed which leaves open a large number of possibilities ('I am whatever I mean to be')."

106. See the paraphrase by Eichrodt, *Theology of the Old Testament*, 1:190, "I am really and truly present, ready to help and to act, as I have always been"; and Vriezen, *Outline of Old Testament Theology*, 235, "I Myself am there, count on Me!"

107. See Halpern-Amaru, *Rewriting*, 13.

108. Noth, *Exodus*, 58.

109. See Noth, *Exodus*, 58; Childs, *Exodus*, 114.

"God spoke to Moses and said to him: I am Yahweh. I appeared as El Shaddai [God Almighty] to Abraham, Isaac, and Jacob. I did not make myself known to them by My name, Yahweh.[110] Also I made My covenant with them to give them the land of Canaan, the land they lived in as strangers" (6:2–4). God promised "I will bring you to the land which I swore that I would give to Abraham and Isaac and Jacob, and I will give it to you for your own; I, Yahweh, will do this" (6:8).

While this story in Exodus 6:1–8 shares with the account of Exodus 3 a concern to identify the God of the fathers and the God now appearing to Moses, it also emphasizes more strongly, firstly, that whereas God had made Himself known to the patriarchs as El Shaddai, now He was revealing the personal name of Yahweh to Moses (6:2–3),[111] and mentions, secondly, that He had made a covenant with Abraham, Isaac, and Jacob which entailed the promise of the land of Canaan (vv. 4, 8) and which also was the basis for His present intervention to rescue the Hebrews from slavery (vv. 5–6).

That the Covenant to be made at Sinai is fundamentally a renewal or continuation of the Covenant with the fathers, or perhaps we should say that it is an extension of the covenant with the fathers, is implied by the statement in verse 7: "I will take you as my people and I will be your God." Now, formally, their descendants, the people about to become the nation Israel, are embraced within the covenant relationship.[112] God had promised Abraham that He would make a great nation of him (Gen 12:2; 18:18; cf. 17:6). That promise is beginning to be fulfilled in the imminent Exodus, Covenant at Sinai, and Settlement in the Land.

The huge amount of priestly material in the book of Exodus once the covenant had been made at Sinai justifies Vogel's assertion that the event at Sinai and the establishment of the sanctuary for worship is understood by P as the fulfilment of the covenant made with Abraham, in the horizon too of the covenant with Noah.[113]

---

110. Within the P stream this agrees with Genesis 17:2, where God announced Himself as El Shaddai. In Genesis as we now have it, however, it is said that people began to call on the name of Yahweh in the time of the children of Adam and Eve (4:26), while Abraham had addressed God as "Lord Yahweh" at Genesis 15:2 (cf. 18:14; 22:14, 16).

111. Note how "I am Yahweh" ('ny yhwh) occurs at vv. 2, 8, and frames the speech of God to Moses, and within it the phrase occurs also at vv. 6–7.

112. In agreement with Childs, *Exodus*, 115, and pace Henton Davies, *Exodus*, 83, who describes the Sinai covenant as "distinct from that with the fathers."

113. Vogel, *Heil*, 112, in dependance on Weimar, *Sinai und Schöpfung*, 337–85, argues for a verbal link between Exodus 26:30 and Genesis 6:18; 9:9–17, and between the chronological notes at Genesis 8:13 and Exodus 40:17.

While the worship of the Golden calf and the sexual orgy associated with such worship was going on (32:1-6), God told Moses to go down to the people. He would let His wrath blaze out to destroy them, but He would make a great nation of Moses. That is, Moses would become the ancestor of a replacement nation, a new "Abraham" (vv. 7-10).

An editor appears to have placed an intercession by Moses in verses 11-14 (by implication he refused the offer of becoming the head of a new nation). Moses pointed out to Yahweh that the Israelites were His people and that He had brought them out of Egypt and that if God were now to destroy them, He would be "playing into the hands" of the Egyptians who could say that God brought the Israelites out of Egypt only to destroy them. This would do God's reputation no good. God should remember what He had sworn to Abraham, Isaac, and Jacob, the promise to make their offspring like the stars of the heavens and to give land to those descendants forever.[114] It is as if the reminder of the oath and promise to Abraham, Isaac, and Jacob is the clinching argument. Yahweh cannot go back on His own word. He cannot set aside His own oath.[115] Yahweh acceded to this intercession (32:14)

In the story as we have it, Moses returned to the top of the mountain and offered another intercession, including his willingness to be blotted out of Yahweh's book for the people to escape obliteration. Yahweh ordered Moses: "Leave this place, with the people you brought out of the land of Egypt and go to the land which I swore to Abraham, Isaac, and Jacob I would give to their descendants . . . a land flowing with milk and honey" (33:1-2). He promised that His angel would accompany the people on their journey but that He Himself would not go with them (vv. 2-3).

The importance of the promise of the land made to the patriarchs thus figures near the beginning (Exod 3; 6) and near the end (Exod 32-34)[116] of the book.

---

114. Genesis 12:7; 13:15; 15:7,18; 26:4; 28:13; 35:11-12; 48:16.

115. Fretheim, *Abraham*, 145, makes the following comment on the way in which Moses appealed to the promise to the ancestors: "Israel's future is thus grounded by Moses, not in their keeping the law or maintaining loyalty to the Sinaitic covenant, but in the promises of God to the ancestors. In other words, Moses gives the promises of God to the ancestors a higher priority for the future of the people of God than obedience to the law" (cf. 147).

116. Chapters 35-40 report the work done to carry out the instructions about the sanctuary mentioned in chapters 25-31

1.1.3 The Book of Leviticus

Leviticus 26 sets before Israel two possible choices. Either to obey God's commands and receive His blessing on crop and land, the gift of peace, prosperity, and liberty (vv. 3–13); or, to disobey these commandments and endure Yahweh's just punishment, viz. exile, forfeiture of the land, and subjugation under enemies (vv. 14–45).[117] But even in this latter situation, if Israel will humble themselves, God said "I will remember my covenant with Jacob and also my covenant with Isaac and I will remember my covenant with Abraham, and I will remember the land" (v. 42; cf. v. 45).

If this chapter reflects an awareness of the exile, there is at verses 42 and 45 a note of hope. The nation may still have a future. God's promises to Abraham, Isaac, and Jacob remain valid. God will remember the covenant with the ancestors of the people (v. 45).

1.1.4 The Book of Numbers

In the midst of a speech of Moses to the members of Reuben and Gad who wished to remain east of Jordan and rear cattle there, he said that such an action would discourage their fellow Israelites. They would be like those at Kadesh who were not for going on and possessing the land of Canaan, and were disqualified by Yahweh from seeing that land which God had sworn to give to Abraham, Isaac, and Jacob (32:5–11; cf. 11:12, where Moses referred to the land which God had sworn to give to the fathers). The Reubenites and Gadites promised to join in the fight to possess Canaan. They would then return to the land east of the Jordan.

Once again, Yahweh's oath to Abraham, Isaac, and Jacob is the charter of Israel's right to the land.

1.1.5 The Book of Deuteronomy

The original core of Deuteronomy may well have been some of the legal and other traditions of the northern Kingdom, Israel,[118] and been brought

---

117. For the latter theme, see also 20:22 where the Israelites are warned to obey God's statutes, lest the land (virtually personified) to which God was bringing them would vomit them out. In verse 24, the promise that the Israelites should inherit the land as a gift from Yahweh is reiterated, and Yahweh described Himself "I am Yahweh your God, who have separated you from the peoples." This is repeated in verse 26 with the summons to be holy "for I Yahweh am holy and have separated you from the peoples that you should be Mine."

118. I use the phrase "legal traditions" rather than "Law Code," since the laws

south to Judah by those who fled from the Assyrian invasion and conquest of Israel in 721 BC. We may reasonably assume that those from the northern Kingdom who had fled to the south and brought these legal traditions had a theological stance of their own. They must have come eventually to the conclusion that the future lay with the state of Judah, and may have felt agreement with Hezekiah's attempts at reform, in respect of at least two aspects: national independence and purity of worship. They drew up their own programme over time. During this period, their approach was modified, adapted, and supplemented, and what we may broadly call the Deuteronomic theological position as discernible in the canonical Deuteronomy + the Deuteronomist History developed.[119] Clearly, as it now stands, Deuteronomy contains much that "points to familiarity with, and concern for, the political and cultic traditions of Jerusalem."[120] In other words, while Deuteronomy may contain elements of theological thinking from within the old Northern Kingdom,[121] it is not now a purely northern document.

A copy of it could have been deposited eventually in the Temple archives,[122] and been the book discovered in the Temple during the early part of the reign of King Josiah (see 2 Kgs 22).[123] It is reasonable to suppose

---

within Deuteronomy 12–26 are presented in a preaching or rhetorical or paraenetic style. See von Rad, *Studies in Deuteronomy*, 15; Clements, *Deuteronomy*, 18; Weinfeld, *Deuteronomy and the Deuteronomic School*, 3; Patrick, *Old Testament Law*, 101–3, 257; McConville, *Deuteronomy*, 212.

119. This sort of sketch is a position widely held, e.g., Nicholson, *Deuteronomy and Tradition*, 1–16, 58–59; Clements, *God's Chosen People*, 18–23; Weinfeld, *Deuteronomy*, 7, 57, 158, 161, 166; Lohfink, *Höre, Israel*, 18–21; Braulik, *Studien zur Theologie des Deuteronomiums*, 164–67. Any link with Josiah's reforms is denied by McConville and Millar, *Time and Place in Deuteronomy*, 141; and individually, McConville, *Grace in the End*, 45–64; *Deuteronomy*, 21–38; Millar, *Now Choose Life*, 99–101.

120. Clements, *Chosen People*, 20. One example would be that, according to Deuteronomy 31:26, a copy of it was to be placed by the side of the Ark of the Covenant. David had brought the Ark into the Tabernacle in Jerusalem and then it was placed in the Temple built by Solomon. Deuteronomy 17:16–17 could have King Solomon in mind (so Braulik, *Deuteronomium* 2:129, but to the contrary, Mayes, *Deuteronomy*, 272; McConville, *Deuteronomy*, 294, both of whom point to Isa 2:7–9; Mic 5:10—southern prophets!).

121. A clear example of this would be chapter 27, which reflects a covenant renewal ceremony at which the tribes were stationed on Mount Gerizim and Mount Ebal, representing the blessings and the curses of the Covenant respectively.

122. If that was the case, it suggests that the circle behind Deuteronomy would include some priests faithful to Yahweh during the years of Manasseh. See Clements, *Chosen People*, 22–23.

123. See Clements, *Deuteronomy*, 72, 74–76, who expresses a growing hesitation about identifying it with the book discovered in the temple, and suggests that Deuteronomy may have been more the product rather than the basic presupposition of Josiah's

that the section of laws (Deut 12-26) had an introduction which comprised an address by Moses.[124]

At the time of the discovery, the stress in the legal section on the need for worship to take place only in the place where Yahweh had placed His name[125] (Deut 12:1, 14) was taken to refer exclusively to the Jerusalem Temple,[126] and this either led to, or was an important factor in, the so-called Josianic reformation with the destruction of all shrines in Judah apart from the Jerusalem Temple (2 Kgs 23).

In the way in which the book of Deuteronomy is now arranged, it is cast in the form of addresses by Moses to the Israelites. The occasion was after God had made a covenant with them at Mount Horeb (so Deut 1:1-5; 5:2-3),[127] and they were on the east side of the Jordan in the land of Moab and on the brink of entering the promised land. There is thus a covenant setting to the work, with Moses as the mediator of the Law of Yahweh which Israel is expected to observe as the people whom Yahweh has delivered and made into His people.[128]

The first two addresses include historical reviews which set the background for the covenant which Yahweh has made with the Israelites. The first address extends from 1:1 to 4:40.[129] Within the second one (4:44-28:68),

reform.

124. E.g., Nicholson, *Deuteronomy*, 19-22. Lohfink, *Väter Israels*, 104, attributes chapters 1-3, 5, 9-10, 31, and 34 to the Josianic text of Deuteronomy (see note 135] below). While chapter 5 has the Decalogue with its stress that Israel should have no other gods beside Yahweh, it does not prescribe where Yahweh worship should take place. Presumably Lohfink would include the Laws of chapters 12-26.

Clearly Moses is a vitally important figure in the estimate of Deuteronomy, as 18:17 amply shows.

125. For a corrective to the view, very much associated with von Rad (*Studies*, 37-44), that this concept was a way of correcting the assumption that Yahweh's presence was located in the Temple, see Wilson, *Out of the Midst of the Fire*.

126. Originally, this may have been the sanctuary at Shechem. We need not go into the issue of whether originally the curtailment of worship was to any Yahweh sanctuary as opposed to the Canaanite sanctuaries, with Deuteronomy 12:1-7 deemed a secondary addition, as Welch, *Code of Deuteronomy*, argued.

127. According to Deuteronomy 29:1, 10-15, Yahweh commanded Moses to make a covenant with the people in the land of Moab in addition to the covenant made at Horeb. Nowhere else in the OT is such a covenant mentioned. Deuteronomy 29-30 reflects the situation of exile and the hope for the future of a return to the land.

128. Clements, *Chosen People*, 28. Weinfeld, *Deuteronomy*, 151, 157, believes that Deuteronomy adopted the combination of law code and treaty which existed in Israel before him.

129. Deuteronomy 4:41-41, which deals with the setting up by Moses of three cities of refuge, apart from being narrative, seems oddly placed, and is considered to be a late addition by, e.g., von Rad, *Deuteronomy*, 51; Mayes, *Deuteronomy*, 159 (he suggests

there is an exposition of the laws and statutes which God had commanded them to obey as His people (12:1–28:68). The third address, which envisages the situation—future from the standpoint of Moses—of exile, covers 29:1–30:20. The book concludes with instructions for the future, including the appointment of Joshua as his successor (Deut 31);[130] the so-called Song of Moses (Deut 32); the Blessing of Moses (Deut 33); and an account of the death of Moses (Deut 34).[131] We shall assume that the original edition of Deuteronomy consisted of 4:44–28:68, to which at a later date additions were made (1:1–4:40; 29:1–30; 31–33; 34), not necessarily at the same time. For example, the third address (29:1–30:20), which presupposes the exile, must accordingly be set in the exilic or early post-exilic era.

There are seven passages which refer by name to Abraham, always in conjunction with Isaac and Jacob.[132] But, within the addresses, there are also frequent references to "the fathers," "their fathers," "our fathers," "your[133] fathers."[134] What is the referent contained in these passages?[135] Statistically, there are 19 references to "father" in the singular, of which 17 refer to a literal, biological father (as in the fourth commandment at 5:16), one to Jacob as an ancestor (26:5), and one to God as Israel's father (32:6). There are 44 instances of "fathers" in the plural. Seven refer to the three patriarchs by name; three refer to the Exodus generation (5:3;[136] 8:3, 16); one refers to Jacob's extended family which went down into Egypt (10:22); seven to all previous ancestors (13:6; 28:36, 64; 30:5 bis; 31:16; 32:17); and one to

that the person responsible thought that Moses must have appointed these cities after the area east of the Jordan had been conquered). The issue is dealt with also at Deuteronomy 19:1–13.

130. While the MT assumes that chapter 31 is a continuation of the third address, the LXX and the Dead Sea Scrolls start 31:1 with "and Moses finished speaking." Mayes, *Deuteronomy*, 372–73, accepts their reading as original, and assumes that the alteration into the reading of the MT took place when further material was added.

131. See the commentaries on Deuteronomy for a more detailed discussion.

132. There are seven specific references to Abraham. Significantly, six of these refer to the oath which God had sworn to Abraham, Isaac, and Jacob, with the land being specifically mentioned, or, in all probability, presupposed.

133. Both singular and plural forms are found.

134. Lohfink, *Väter*, 9, has pointed out that "father" is an appellative as is the plural "fathers," i.e., it refers to a class; it has not become a title or fixed concept. The semantic range covers a literal father, the immediate preceding generation, distant ancestors, and the founding fathers of the nation.

135. The suggestion that originally "the fathers" referred to the Exodus generation was put forward by Römer, *Israels Väter*, and criticized by Lohfink in a series of articles which he worked up into a book, *Die Väters Israels im Deuteronomium*.

136. Here the Hebrew idiom "not . . . but" is probably best rendered in English as "not only . . . but also."

Moses' being gathered to his fathers (31:16). Space forbids detailed discussion of the remaining 25 instances, but they will receive mention as we turn to consider how significant a figure Abraham and the other two patriarchs were within the theological thinking of Deuteronomy.

The first address is introduced by setting the scene in the land of Moab, east of Jordan. Moses passed on the command of God that the people had spent long enough in the land of Moab and should go and possess the land which He had sworn "to give to your fathers, to Abraham, Isaac and Jacob, and their seed after them" (1:8). This is a crucial placing of the mention of Abraham and the other two by name at the beginning of the address, and is intended to serve as a control of how the hearer/reader should take subsequent references to "fathers." A little later (1:10) Moses went on to say that God had multiplied the people like the stars of heaven (echoing Gen 15:5) and hoped that the God of their fathers would bless them and increase them even more. Then at 1:20 when the people are at Kadesh-barnea, there is a repetition of the command to possess the land "which Yahweh the God of your fathers had spoken to you about." At 1:35–36, God's exclusion of all but Caleb and Joshua from entering "the land which I swore to give to your fathers" is mentioned. Then at 4:1, Moses commanded the people to listen and obey all the laws and statutes which he was passing on to them "in order that you may live and go and possess the land which Yahweh the God of your fathers is giving you" and at 4:31 he promised that Yahweh "will not forget the covenant of your fathers which He swore to them." Finally, at 4:37, "Because Yahweh loved your fathers, He therefore chose their seed after them and brought you . . . out of Egypt."[137]

The second address begins with the Decalogue and a rehearsal of the events surrounding its being given. Then Moses encouraged the people to keep these laws and statutes. He warned them against forgetting Yahweh their God once He had brought them "into the land which He swore to your fathers, Abraham, Isaac, and Jacob, to give you" (6:11). This would reverberate back on how to understand verse 3, where the Israelites were encouraged to observe God's commandments "that it may go well with you and that you may multiply greatly in a land flowing with milk and honey, as Yahweh, the God of your fathers, has promised you." It exercises influence forwards on 6:18: "Do what is right and good in the sight of Yahweh, that it might go well with you and so that you may go in and occupy the good land which Yahweh swore to your fathers to give you" and also on 6:23 which is part of instructions what to tell sons when they asked what was the meaning

---

137. See below for the importance of this passage for the case against the Exodus generation as the referent.

of these laws and statutes: they should be told about the deliverance from Egypt and the mighty signs and wonders which accompanied this momentous event. "He brought us out from there in order to bring us in, to give us the land that He promised on oath to our fathers."

In the continuation of the second address, there are several references to the fathers (7:8; 8:1; 10:11, 15; 11:9), plus two which refer to the three patriarchs by name. The first of the latter is at 9:5, where Moses bluntly told the Israelites that it was not because of their righteousness or uprightness of heart that they were going in to occupy the land. Rather it was because of the wickedness of the existing inhabitants and to "fulfil the promise that Yahweh made on oath to your fathers, to Abraham, to Isaac, and to Jacob." Lohfink has suggested that the mention of the three patriarchs by name would serve as a "refreshment" of the memory in view of the length of this second address. Perhaps the same could be said of 9:27 which comes at the end of a long rehearsal of the rebelliousness of the people towards God, including the molten calf episode at the foot of mount Horeb. Moses appealed to God not to destroy the people but "Remember your servants, Abraham, Isaac, and Jacob; do not look on the stubbornness of this people nor on their wickedness nor on their sin. . . . Yet they are your people and your inheritance whom you brought out by your great power and by your outstretched arm."

The section of Laws (Deut 12–26/28), which is part of the second address, opens with the command that the people should observe the laws and statutes "in the land which Yahweh, the God of your fathers, has given you to possess" (12:1). By this time, cumulatively, the "fathers" would surely convey to hearers/readers the three patriarchs. This would hold true of further references to the fathers in 13:17; 19:8 bis; 26:3, 7; 27:3; 28:11.

The final address is framed by references to Abraham, Isaac, and Jacob, at 29:13 and 30:20. Thus, there could be no doubt who was in mind at 29:25. The immediate context is the reaction of people (unspecified) to what Yahweh did in imposing the curses of the covenant on the land and in exiling the Israelites from it. People will say, "Because they forsook the covenant of Yahweh, the God of their fathers, which He made with them when He brought them forth out of the land of Egypt, and they went and served other gods" (vv. 25–26). The covenant idea picks up what was said at 7:12: the people should keep God's laws and statutes "so that Yahweh your God may keep with you the covenant and mercy[138] which He swore to your fathers and He will love you and bless you and multiply you."

---

138. Probably a hendiadys–His covenant mercy or covenant lovingkindness.

In the later additions, chapters 31, 32–33, and 34, there are references to "their fathers" at 31:7 and 20 (both times with reference to Yahweh's oath and the land). Finally, in chapter 34, which reports how God showed Moses all the promised land from Mount Pisgah before he died, Yahweh said to him, "This is the land which I swore to Abraham, to Isaac, and to Jacob, saying, I will give it to you seed" (v. 4). It may be that the final redactor intended this mention of the three patriarchs by name to balance 1:8, and thus frame the whole book with references to them.

After this survey, we may make two points. Firstly, in the passages which mention the three patriarchs by name, especially the three key verses of 1:8; 6:10; and 29:13, there are a cluster of ideas: Yahweh swore an oath to them (1:8; 6:10; 9:5; 29:13), promising them numerous descendants (6:3) who would become His people (9:27; 29:13), and land, especially the latter (1:8; 6:10; 9:5; 34:5). Now precisely this cluster of ideas appears also in references to the fathers without any specific names: oath (7:12; 8:1; 10:11; 13:17; 19:8; 26:3, 15; 31:20); descendants (6:3; 13:17); land (7:1; 13; 12:1; 19:8; 26:3, 15; 27:3; 31:20), plus the idea of covenant (7:12; 8:18).

The parallelism is striking, and supports the assumption that in these verses "the fathers" is a term which has Abraham, Isaac, and Jacob in mind.

The second point could be regarded as the clinching argument. There are three passages where God's attitude towards the fathers is mentioned. According to 4:37, Yahweh loved the fathers and, therefore, chose their seed and brought those descendants out of Egypt, while in 10:15 Yahweh had a delight in the fathers and loved them and chose their seed out of all the nations. Then, at 29:9, in the final address which envisages Israel in exile repenting and returning to its allegiance to Yahweh, it is said that when this happens, "Yahweh will again rejoice over you for good as He rejoiced over your fathers." Now it is impossible to apply these statements to the Exodus generation, who are branded on numerous occasions as evil, disobedient, and rebellious.[139] Only Abraham, Isaac, and Jacob could have been in the author's mind.

We now draw together the threads of our discussion:

Firstly, there are 9 instances in the canonical Deuteronomy, where Abraham is mentioned by name along with Isaac and Jacob. Some of these seem to occupy strategic positions near the beginning of the addresses of Moses. They would thus exercise a control over how any reader/hearer of Deuteronomy might understand occurrences of "fathers" where no specific names are mentioned (so emphatically Lohfink in respect especially of 1:8).

---

139. 1:26–36, 41–45; 2:14–15; 4:3; 9:7–16, 19–20, 22–29; 10:16.

Secondly, the terms "father" or "fathers" in Deuteronomy remain an appellative, and have not become a title or fixed concept. There are some instances where "fathers" refers to those who were in Egypt before the Exodus; or who left Egypt under Moses but who were sentenced by Yahweh to die in the wilderness and not enter the promised land; or the entire past generations of Israelites.

Thirdly, the majority of references to "fathers," however, is linked to concepts like an oath or promise made by Yahweh, relating especially to the land, but also increase of descendants or some other idea. In Deuteronomy, there can be no doubt that the promise given with an oath by Yahweh to Abraham and renewed to Isaac and Jacob is the ground, basis, and focal point of the hope which Deuteronomy has for Israel.[140]

In the fourth place, we looked at these references with a view to seeing whether they referred to Abraham, Isaac, and Jacob, without their names being specified, or whether they referred to the Exodus generation, with the references to the three fathers being later additions. The references to God's delight in or love for the fathers (4:37; 10:15; 30:9) seemed crucial, because they absolutely excluded the Exodus generation who were sentenced to die in the wilderness because of their lack of faith, rebelliousness, and ingratitude towards Yahweh who had delivered them from slavery in Egypt.

Fifthly, other references like the oath to give the land or to multiply descendants or covenant making the patriarch's descendants Yahweh's people seemed to refer to the Genesis narratives, without its being necessary to assume knowledge of traditions traditionally referred to as J and E, though we do accept the existence of these, and, in particular, the nearness of Deuteronomy in some of its theology to E, a tradition originating in a northern Israelite provenance.

Finally, there are a few references within the Legal Code to the "fathers." These are best taken as referring to Abraham, Isaac, and Jacob, although the probable reference to Jacob as the wandering Aramean in the Credo of chapter 26 is striking and points to early tradition (whether linked to a shrine associated with Jacob like Bethel, or, if the view of some scholars is right,[141] to a period before Abraham and Isaac were acknowledged along with Jacob).

We must emphasize that Deuteronomy stresses the faithfulness of God. He is the God who "keeps covenant and mercy" (7:9). His faithfulness is to His word, His promise, the oath made to the fathers, beginning with Abraham (cf. 7:9), grounded in the mystery of His love for and delight

---

140. See, e.g., Braulik, *Mittel*, 58.

141. For a recent statement of this, see Flury-Schölch, *Abrahams Segen*, 311–13.

in them. But Israel had obligations. She must keep Yahweh's commands, but even where she is disobedient, there is hope of restoration because of Yahweh's love and mercy.

Summary

If the Pentateuch received its final form either during the exile or in the fairly early post-exilic period, it is easy to understand the stress on the promise to Abraham and the other patriarchs, in particular concerning the land. It would act as a reassurance and give hope to a nation suffering from the shock of the Babylonian conquest and the destruction of the structures of its nationhood, or to a small state struggling to make its way back in the land but facing an uncertain future.

The stress on Abraham's obedience is likewise understandable. The founding father of the nation is a model of one who takes God's commands seriously and carries them out. Ego suggests that Abraham embodies "ideal Israel."[142] *Here is the canonical foundation for the stress in early Judaism on the obedience of Abraham.*[143]

The identification of God as the God of Abraham, Isaac, and Jacob/Israel (sometimes abbreviated to "of our fathers") figures prominently in the books of Genesis, Exodus, and Deuteronomy (once in Lev 26), and serves to remind later readers/hearers of the roots of their religion. The God of the Exodus and the Conquest was the same God who appeared to the patriarchs.

1.2. Abraham in the Former Prophets

1.2.1 The Book of Joshua

With Deuteronomy as its introduction, the book of Joshua is the opening work of the so-called Deuteronomist History (Joshua–2 Kings).

Abraham is only mentioned by name (twice) in chapter 24. There, at the beginning of Yahweh's speech through Joshua to all Israel gathered at Shechem,[144] He stated that long ago Israel's ancestors, Terah and his sons Abraham and Nahor, lived beyond the Euphrates and served other gods (v. 2). "Then I took your father, Abraham, from beyond the River and led him through all the land of Canaan and made his offspring many. I gave him

---

142. Ego, *Abraham*, 36.

143. See Ego, *Abraham*, 38–39.

144. "And Joshua said to all the people, Thus says Yahweh the God of Israel" (Josh 24:2).

Isaac" (v. 3). The divine review continues with the sojourn in Egypt, the plagues, the exodus, and the conquest of Canaan (vv. 2–13). Then Joshua took over (as it were) and appealed for a wholehearted commitment to Yahweh, to which the people agree and a covenant is established between Yahweh and the people (vv. 14–28).

In this speech there is a frank admission of Abraham's polytheism before Yahweh took him and led him to Canaan (this idea figures in later Jewish writers, as we shall see), while it is emphasized that Isaac was God's gift to Abraham and through Isaac Abraham's descendants increased.

There may be the hint that as God brought Abraham from "Beyond the River," so He is able to bring exiles back to the homeland.

In addition, there are three references to the oath which Yahweh had sworn to give the land of Canaan to "the fathers." The first of these comes at the beginning of the book, in Yahweh's speech to Joshua after the death of Moses. Yahweh promised to be with him as He had been with Moses; He would not fail or abandon him (1:5). He would ensure that Joshua caused the Israelites "to inherit the land which I swore to their fathers to give them" (1:6). This phraseology clearly picks up that of Deuteronomy, and so we may be confident that Abraham, Isaac, and Jacob are in mind.

The next occurrence is at 5:2–9,[145] in the rather strange account of a mass circumcision of the Israelite men by Joshua at Yahweh's command after the company had crossed over the river Jordan and was poised (as it were) for battle to take possession of the land. We need not discuss the details here;[146] suffice to say that at verse 6b,[147] there is a reference to the fact that, because of their disobedience, the warriors who came out of Egypt were prevented from entering the land which Yahweh had sworn to the fathers to give to their descendants ("to us," v. 6). We may have no hesitation in seeing here a reference to the three patriarchs, as there is a clear distinction between them and the (disobedient) Exodus generation.

The account of the distribution by lot of the cities for the Levitical priests in chapter 21 ends with a summary which states that Yahweh gave to Israel all the land which He had sworn to give to their fathers, and they possessed it and dwelt in it (v. 43). Yahweh gave them "rest" (i.e., freedom from

---

145. The MT and the LXX vary considerably in vv. 2b, 4–6a. The LXX has a shorter text. See Nelson, *Joshua*, 72, where the two versions are set out in English translation, and Lohfink, *Väter*, 77, for discussion. Happily for our purpose, there is substantial agreement in the crucial verse 6b.

146. For details, see the discussion in Blaschke, *Beschneidung*, 34–43. He discusses the LXX alterations on 114–16.

147. We may accept that verses 4–7, in both versions, bear the marks of Deuteronomist editing.

attacks by enemies) "according to all that He had sworn to their fathers" (v. 44). Then the author states that all that Yahweh had promised to the house of Israel had come to pass (v. 45).[148]

Turning to 22:28, the context shows quite clearly that there the phrase "our fathers" refers to the ancestors of the tribes of Reuben, Gad, and the half of Manasseh who, after participating in the conquest of the land, had settled east of the Jordan. In the story as we now have it in chapter 22, the question whether these tribes had committed a breach of Yahweh's law by erecting an altar for sacrifices was raised by the other tribes. The two and a half tribes defended themselves against the charge and suggested that if ever in the future the membership of their descendants in Israel might be challenged, they would say that the altar erected by their ancestors was not for the purposes of sacrifice but as a witness to the rest of the Israelite tribes that they were in no way intending to rebel against Yahweh, but intended to serve Him (vv. 28–29). In the end, the altar which had been a source of friction to start with becomes a means of agreement.[149]

1.2.2 The Book of Judges

Abraham is not mentioned by name in the Book of Judges, but there are a number of references to "fathers." We may leave on one side 6:13, where, in his lament to the angel of Yahweh who had appeared to him, Gideon asks why had the Midianites been allowed to oppress the Israelites if Yahweh was with them: "And where are all his wonderful works which our fathers have told us about, saying Did not Yahweh bring us up from Egypt?" The reference to "our fathers" is most naturally taken as their literal fathers whose job it was to instruct their sons in the facts of the faith of Israel.[150]

There is a cluster of references in chapter two which is widely acknowledged as part of the Deuteronomist editing. After the death of Joshua, the

---

148. There are further references to Yahweh giving Israel the land without specific reference to the oath sworn to the fathers: 2:9, 24; 24:13; while 3:10; 10:42; 23:4–5, 12–13, 15–16, all make it clear that it was Yahweh who had driven out the existing inhabitants before the Israelites.

149. Nelson, *Joshua*, 243–53, has a full discussion of the various issues of sources, final shape, and themes which are being handled. He points out that the primacy of the law about the central sanctuary seems presupposed, while there are also priestly concerns (e.g., the possibility of the danger to the whole community through a breach of cultic regulations; whether land east of Jordan is cultically clean or unclean). He suggests that the story illustrates the issue of "separation versus solidarity," and intends "to promote an awareness of and commitment to national unity in the face of opposing attitudes and circumstances" (Nelson, *Joshua*, 247, 249).

150. Similarly, at 21:22, there is a literal use of fathers—the biological parents.

Israelites forsook Yahweh, the God of their fathers, who had brought them out of the land of Egypt, and they followed other gods (2:12). In the light of our discussion of Deuteronomy, we may take this as a reference to the three patriarchs. As a punishment for this disobedience, Yahweh handed them over to their enemies. Even when He raised up judges to save them, they still forsook Him: "they soon turned aside from the way in which their fathers had walked, who had obeyed the commandments of Yahweh; they did not follow their example" (2:17). This description of "their fathers" fits the three patriarchs; it does not fit either the Exodus generation nor those who entered the land and who outlived Joshua. The assessment of the behavior of the Israelites continues with the indictment that once a judge had died, the same old habit of disobedience asserted itself and "they behaved worse than their fathers, following other gods, worshipping them and bowing down to them" (v. 19). Here the reverse is true! This does not fit the patriarchs, but it does fit the Exodus generation and/or those who lived in Israel in the post Joshua era. Yahweh's anger was aroused against them. "Because this people have transgressed my covenant which I commanded their fathers and have not obeyed my voice, I will no longer drive out before them any of the nations that Joshua left when he died" (v. 20). His purpose in doing this was to test Israel to see whether the people would walk in His ways as their fathers had (v. 22). Here the reference to covenant in verse 20 could be the Horeb-Moab covenant, though even the covenant with Abraham and renewed with Isaac and Jacob is not impossible, since once again the fathers who walked in the ways of Yahweh (v. 22) can only be the three patriarchs.

The author gives a list of the nations whom Yahweh allowed to remain in the land to test the Israelites (3:1–3). "They were for the testing of Israel, to know whether Israel would obey the commandments of Yahweh, which He commanded their fathers by Moses" (v. 4). This reference suggests either the ten commandments, or, perhaps, more likely, the further commandments which Moses received on Horeb and which he was instructed to pass on to the people (Deut 5:31–6:3).

There is, thus, no monochrome usage of the term "fathers" in Judges. The Deuteronomist author exhibits considerable flexibility in its use in chapters 2–3 and 6.[151]

151. There are no references to Abraham in 1 and 2 Samuel. The term "fathers" occurs five times in 1 Samuel, all in chapter 12, which is Samuel's defense of his conduct as spokesman for Yahweh. He mentioned that Yahweh had brought their fathers out of Egypt (v. 6), and, in an endeavor to move the people to obedience when he has died, he referred to the righteous (i.e., saving) acts which Yahweh had done for them and their fathers (v. 7). Putting the people first underlines that they were beneficiaries of what Yahweh had done in the past. Samuel then reminded them of how the fathers had cried out to Yahweh when oppressed in Egypt and He had sent Moses and Aaron who

1.2.3 1 and 2 Kings

On the occasion of the contest between Elijah and the prophets of Baal on Mount Carmel, Elijah opened his prayer to Yahweh: "O Yahweh, God of Abraham, Isaac, and Israel, let it be known this day that You are God in Israel" (1 Kgs 18:36). This is probably a deliberate reminder of the "true" past as opposed to the Baal religion which was being promoted in the nation by the queen, Jezebel.

During the period when Hazael, king of Aram oppressed Israel (the northern kingdom), Yahweh had compassion on the people. He turned to them "because of His covenant with Abraham, Isaac, and Jacob" and would not let them be destroyed, nor did He banish them from His presence until now (2 Kgs 13:23).[152] The mention of Yahweh's grace to the northern kingdom may come as a surprise in view of the general Deuteronomist position, but it is an all the more striking illustration of the significance of the covenant with Abraham and the ancestors—it availed even to postpone the fate of the northern kingdom!

Excursus on the Use of "Fathers" in 1 and 2 Kings.

The term occurs 31 times in 1 Kings and 38 times in 2 Kings. We classify the occurrences in 1 Kings as follows:

- The phrase that a particular individual slept or slept and was buried with his fathers accounts for the majority of occurrences—sixteen times (1:21; 2:10; 11:21, 42; [13:22]; 14:20, 31 bis; 15:8, 24bis; 16:6, 28; 22:40, 50 bis).

- Next come references to ancestors of previous generations six times (8:57; 14:22; 19:4) or specific ancestors (15:12, King Asa's predecessors; 21:3, 4, Naboth's ancestors)

---

brought them forth and made them dwell in the land (v. 8). He warned the people that if they rebelled against Yahweh, His hand would be against them as it was against their fathers (v. 15). This probably embraces the previous generations who had lived in the land but had forsaken Yahweh (as indicated in vv. 9–12).

There is one occurrence in 2 Samuel. At 7:12, Nathan passes on the promise of Yahweh that when he died ("When your days are fulfilled and you shall sleep with your fathers"), one of his "seed" would succeed him on the throne.

152. Gray, *I & II Kings*, 544, treats "until now" as a later gloss, but it would have been part of the text received when 1 and 2 Kings became authoritative Scripture.

- There are four references to the fact that Yahweh had given the land to their fathers (8:34, 40, 48; 14:15). Here we may assume that the three patriarchs are in mind.
- Twice, the Exodus generation is mentioned (8:53; 9:9).
- Twice, the events associated with Horeb-Moab were evoked in Solomon's prayer of dedication of the Temple (the covenant made with the fathers, 8:21, and the commandments and statutes which Yahweh commanded the fathers, 8:58).
- Once there is a reference to "the leaders of the ancestral (houses) of the Israelites" at 8:1. Here the author is endeavoring to indicate that all Israel was representatively present at the dedication of the Temple, and so mentions that Solomon assembled the elders of Israel, all the heads of the tribes, and the leaders of the ancestral (houses) of the Israelites to Jerusalem for the special occasion.

The occurrences in 2 Kings fall into the following categories:

- Once again, by far the majority of occurrences is in the reference to sleeping with one's fathers or sleeping and being buried with one's fathers or being gathered to them—22 times (8:24 (bis); 9:28; 10:35; 12:21; 13:9, 13; 14:16, 20 (bis), 29; 15:7 (bis), 22, 38 (bis); 16: 20 (bis); 20:21; 21:18; 22:20; 24:6).
- It is just possible that there is an implied reference to the three patriarchs in 21:22, where Ammon, King of Judah, is said to have forsaken Yahweh, the God of his fathers, but more probably the reference is to his ancestors in general and this should go in the next category.
- There are five instances where the reference seems to be to the immediate ancestors (12:18; 15:9; 20:17; 23:32, 37)[153] and three to the disobedience of previous generations of ancestors (17:14 [an indictment of both Israel and Judah], 41[the sins of Israel]; 22:13[the sins of Judah]) and once that Ammon had forsaken the God of his fathers (21:22). Total—nine times.
- In 21:15, the fathers are those who came out of Egypt. In 17:13, 15, the Law was given to the fathers and the Covenant was made with the fathers respectively, both of which probably have those involved in the events of Sinai/Horeb-Moab in mind. The word from God to David

---

153. Apart from 15:9, where the reference is to the way Zechariah, King of Israel, copied the sins of his father, Jeroboam, the other passages refer to the Kings of Judah (this would be apart, of course, from Hezekiah and Josiah).

contained the promise not to cause the Israelites to wander from the Land which He had given to their fathers (21:8): in all, four times.[154]

1.3. Abraham in the Latter Prophets

1.3.1 The Book of the Prophet Isaiah[155]

At 41:8, God addressed Israel as "my servant," and, in parallel, Jacob, as the one "whom I have chosen." Israel-Jacob is described as "the seed of Abraham, whom I loved [or, who loved me]."[156] In the person of Abraham, God had chosen and called his descendants from the ends of the earth to be His servant.[157] There follows an oracle of reassurance that God had not cast Israel-Jacob off, but, rather, will help her and hold her right hand.[158] What God had done in the past to Abraham, He could do again for the exiles in Babylon. Exile is not God's last word; the exiles have a future.

Later on the prophet appeals to those who pursue righteousness, who seek Yahweh:

> Look to the rock from which you were hewn,
> and to the quarry from which you were cut.
> Look to Abraham your father,
> and to Sarah who bore you,

---

154. We exclude 19:12 (the reference to the ancestors of Sennacherib of Assyria) and the reference in 14:6 to the law promulgated in Deuteronomy 24:16 that fathers should not be put to death because of the sins of their children nor children for the sins of their fathers.

155. We cannot here go into questions about the division of Isaiah 1–66 in any detail. Clearly, once the book had been put together in its entirety, it would be read and heard as the message of "Isaiah" (see Clements, *Unity of the Book of Isaiah*, 93–104). However, it is rather significant that the references to Abraham are all within portions assigned to the exilic or post-exilic periods by modern scholarship, i.e., Second Isaiah (chs. 40–55), Trito-Isaiah (chs. 56–66) and Isaiah 29:17–24 (on which, see note 163).

156. *BDB*, 13, classified *'hbî* under "friend," and this is the rendering of RSV/NRSV, NEB/REB, JB, and NIV. Westermann, *Isaiah 40–66*, 70, pointed out: "In the Hebrew there is an active verb in the perfect with a suffix, i.e., 'who loves, or loved, me,'" and comments that this construction expresses the element of activity in the relationship, yet in his translation has "whom I loved." The LXX has ον ηγαπησα. See also Mühling, *Blickt*, 95–96, for discussion.

157. Westermann, *Isaiah 40–66*, 70–71, says that there may be an amalgam of the call of Abraham and the deliverance from Egypt.

158. Westermann, *Isaiah 40–66*, 70, deduces from this that Deutero-Isaiah knew of the Yahwist traditions as contained in Genesis. Mühling, *Blickt*, 93–94, in her comment on Isaiah 51:2 doubts this.

> For he was one when I called him
> But I blessed him and made him many.
> For the LORD will comfort Zion
> and restore her ruins. (51:2-3)

The reference to Abraham is intended as an encouragement to the exiles soon to return to Zion. As Yahweh blessed Abraham and Sarah with many descendants, so He can transform the situation of Zion (cf. the message of the oracles in chapter 54). As He created Israel out of Abraham and Sarah, so He can create Israel anew out of the band of exiles.[159]

The last reference to Abraham in the Isaiah corpus sequentially comes at 63:16, which is part of a larger unit, embracing 63:7–64:11.[160] It occurs in a prayer of penitence and an appeal to Yahweh to remember His people in their affliction. Their enemies have trampled down and burned His holy and beautiful sanctuary (63:18b; 64:10–11).[161] Yahweh was withholding His heart's yearning and compassion from them (v. 15).

> Do not let Your compassion go unmoved. (15)
> For you are our father, though Abraham does not know us
> and Israel does not acknowledge us.
> You, Yahweh, are our father; our Redeemer from of old is
> Your name (16).
> Why, O LORD, do You make us stray from Your ways and
> harden our heart, so that we do not fear you?
> Turn back for the sake of Your servants, for the sake of the
> tribes of Your heritage. (17)

---

159. Mary Callaway, *Sing, O Barren One*, 62, has suggested that Deutero-Isaiah was answering the kind of question recorded in Ezekiel 33:10, where the exiles are reported as lamenting: "Our transgressions and our sins weigh upon us, and we waste away because of them; how then can we live?" It looks as if in Isaiah 54:1 Deutero-Isaiah has fused the barren woman motif with that of Zion (standing for the nation), which had already in the tradition been portrayed as a woman. There may be a hint that the renewal of Zion/Israel from her situation of desolation was prefigured in the birth of Isaac to the barren Sarah (so Callaway, *Barren One*, 71).

160. Westermann, *Isaiah 40–66*, 390–92. Hanson, *Dawn of Apocalyptic*, 92–93, believed that this unit originated from a group excluded by the Zadokite community. He is criticised effectively by Schramm, *Opponents of Third Isaiah*, 152–54, 174–82, who sees Trito-Isaiah as representative of former Babylonian exiles who had returned to the homeland and who defined the people of God as those who abstained from various kinds of traditional syncretistic cultic acts.

161. This would point to the original composition shortly after the destruction of the temple and city by the Babylonians in 587–86. The composition was retained and used subsequently as a communal lament in the period after the return, when circumstances were difficult and far from the rosy future predicted by Second Isaiah (the same would be true of compositions like Psalms 44; 79; 89; and Lamentations).

This passage makes some remarkable assertions. Verse 15 is a plea for renewed help addressed to God, which, together with a questioning of God's mysterious ways (v. 17a, "Why?"), is resumed in verse 17b. Verse 16 gives the reason for this plea for help. It imagines that Abraham and Jacob (Isaac is not mentioned), the ancestors of the nation, no longer acknowledged them because of their sinful behavior. God alone is the father of the people. He knows them; He acknowledges them. He is the One who long ago redeemed the nation from Egypt. All this is by way of seeking in verse 17 to motivate Yahweh to move from apparent inactivity to a compassionate intervention on behalf of His people.

Such was the despondency of those who framed this lament and plea for help that they imagined that the link with Abraham and Jacob was no longer operative, but they nevertheless clung to the conviction that Yahweh had not really abandoned them totally and they hoped that He would intervene speedily on their behalf.[162]

Finally, Abraham is mentioned in a section which deals with the coming age of salvation (29:17-24).[163] In a message for the house of Jacob, Yahweh is described first as He who redeemed Abraham (v. 22), which is unique.[164] Various explanations have been offered: either Yahweh rescued him from the paganism of Ur of the Chaldees,[165] or rescued him from Pha-

---

162. Westermann, *Isaiah 40-66*, 393-94, suggests that the message is that tradition, while important, has its limitations and can become a source of perversion; God is the present reality. However true in general, this interpretation seems somewhat abstract. Hanson, *Dawn*, 93, takes "Abraham" and "Israel" as indicating the central Israelite community of the contemporary period under the leadership of the Zadokite priests. Schramm, *Opponents*, 152-54, points out that Yahweh had sided with the nations against His own people, and the speaker wants to know if this is permanent and pleads for God to take action on behalf of His people. Mühling, *Blickt*, 101-2, summarizes some older interpretations (she was not aware of Schramm's work). She herself refers to Ezekiel 33:23-29 and suggests that our verse reflects a controversy between those who had remained in the land and those who returned from exile. That, in fact, broadly agrees with Schramm's position, although the Ezekiel passage is dealing with a different issue (what does the exile mean for the question to whom the land of Israel belonged ?).

163. Clements, *Isaiah 1-39*, 240-41, assigns verses 17-24 to the post-exilic age and maintains that its affinities are with chapters 24-27, the so-called Isaiah-Apocalypse. Wildberger, *Isaiah 28-39*, 109-110, also sees this section linked with the Isaiah Apocalypse, but to be dated a little earlier than the oldest levels of its material and so still within the fifth century. Kaiser, *Isaiah 13-39*, 278-79, assigns it to the Hellenistic period, before the conflict between Judaism and the Seleucid kings. For a defense of Isaiah 1-39 (with the exception of chapters 34-35) as emanating from Isaiah of Jerusalem, see Hayes and Irvine, *Isaiah*, 7.

164. The LXX differs from the MT in having Yahweh refer to the house of Jacob ον αφωρισεν εξ Αβρααμ ("whom He set apart from [the descendants of] Abraham").

165. Clements, *Isaiah 1-39*, 242.

raoh and Abimelech (Gen 12; 20),[166] or saved him from the fiery furnace into which he was thrown after destroying the idol of Nimrod,[167] and called him into His service and began the process of the emergence of the people of Israel, the House of Jacob (v. 22). In the use of the idea of "redeem" à propos Abraham, it looks as if language used of Israel (God redeemed her from the land of slavery) has been transferred to the patriarch, with the result that God's action towards Abraham in the past becomes a sign of hope for the renewal of the community addressed. When this age of salvation dawns, Jews will no longer be ashamed or frustrated, but will reverence God and worship and obey Him.

1.3.2 The Book of the Prophet Jeremiah[168]

There is one specific reference to Abraham in the book of Jeremiah. It occurs in a unit, 33:23–26,[169] which seeks to answer a question in the hearts and minds of some people. These, whether renegade Jews or other nations, were assuming that, in the light of the events of 721 and 586 BC, Yahweh had cast off Israel and Judah, and consequently they despised Him. God compared the reliability of His covenant with the offspring of Jacob and David to that of His covenant with the day and night. As the latter is absolutely certain, so is the former. It is inconceivable that Yahweh should not choose descendants of David to rule over the offspring of Abraham, Isaac, and Jacob (v. 26).

---

166. Wildberger, *Isaiah 28–39*, 115.

167. Bloch, "Midrash," 44. Wildberger, *Isaiah 28–39*, 115, does not think that the author of this section would have known this sort of legendary embellishment. Kaiser, *Isaiah 13–39*, 280, does not decide which sense is likely.

168. The study of the book of Jeremiah is complicated by the fact (generally agreed among scholars) that it has undergone considerable editing by someone within the Deuteronomic circle, plus the fact that there are wide differences between the MT and LXX, both in terms of order and content. As there is only one reference to Abraham in the book, the issue is thereby eased for us.

169. This section is missing from the LXX. Nicholson, *Preaching to the Exiles*, 91–92, assigns our passage to the Deuteronomic editing stage, i.e., late exilic. Clements, *Jeremiah*, 199–201, also assesses it as a late addition to the corpus of Jeremiah. This means that there is no overt reference to Abraham in Jeremiah's own preaching, even if canonically 33:23–26 is now part of the Jeremiah tradition. Diepold, *Israels Land*, 204–9, accepts that it does not come from Jeremiah, but neither does he assign it to the Deuteronomic editor (though he does not explain its origin, he presumably would assign it to "the second hand within the Deuteronomic circle," whose message he summarizes as "Repentance towards Yahweh and new obedience to the Deuteronomic Law will move Yahweh to gather His people again and bring them back to the promised land").

This note stands in some tension with assumptions elsewhere in the Jeremiah corpus that the covenant with Israel has been irretrievably broken.[170] At 14:20-21, the people are portrayed as appealing to God not to break the covenant in spite of the sins of their ancestors and their own sins. They assume that such a breaking is a possibility. In the famous New Covenant passage, Yahweh announced that His people had broken the covenant. There is no mention of the covenant made with Abraham, Isaac, and Jacob. What God proposed is a new covenant (31:31-34; 38:31-34 LXX), and this can only be described as based on His grace.[171]

There is a general reference to the promise of the land made to the fathers in Jeremiah 3:18. "In those days the house of Judah will walk with the house of Israel, and they shall come together out of the land of the north to the land which I gave for an inheritance to your fathers." Other allusions to the Abrahamic story have been detected in Jeremiah 3-4. Firstly, Jeremiah 3:16—"and, in those days, says the LORD, when you have multiplied and increased in the land"—may pick up the command to multiply and be fruitful made to Jacob in reiteration of the previous promise to Abraham of a multitude of descendants (Gen 35:11).[172] Secondly, some scholars detect an allusion at Jeremiah 4:2. God has appealed to Israel to return to Him and promised that He would cure them of their backsliding (3:22a). In response, Israel promised to return, acknowledging that they and their fathers had sinned, that the idolatrous gods were a deception, and that Yahweh alone was the salvation of Israel (3:23b-25). God's response to Israel's promise of repentance followed in 4:1-2. He laid down certain conditions. If they put away their abominable idolatry, and took seriously His will for truth, justice, and righteousness, then there would be two consequences: "the nations will pray to be blessed in Him and they shall glory in Him."[173] Here the hithpael of *brk* is used, i.e., a reflexive sense is intended. In the translation offered, the "in Him" (*bô*) refers to God. Some scholars wish to refer it to Israel. Against a direct application to Israel is the fact that we would expect an "in you" of

---

170. The messages of hope and comfort in Jeremiah 33 stand "in amazing and profound tension with the main claims of the Jeremiah tradition and with the threat of the exilic experience. These promises do not resist or deny the reality of discontinuity, but are voices of hope after the breaking point" (Bruggemann, *Commentary on Jeremiah*, 320).

171. See Gross, *Erneuerter oder Neuen Bund?*, 41-66.

172. So Lee, *Blessing*, 105. "God said to him, I am God Almighty: be fruitful and multiply; a nation and a company of nations shall come from you, and kings shall spring from you" (Gen 35:11).

173. The translation is from the REB; cf. GN (TEV); NRSV mg.

direct speech if that were the case.[174] The same type of objection might be registered against assuming a reference to God ("in me" might have been expected, as in 4:1 Yahweh says "If you will return, O Israel, return *to me*."). However,[175] verse 2cd occur in the context of an oath which would be sworn in the third person "As Yahweh lives!" and this may have influenced the use of "in him" in verse 2cd, as Flury-Schölch has suggested.[176] Furthermore, in the immediate context, the conditions laid down about Israel's return focus very much on God, while the larger context contains a vision of a future when Israel had returned in obedience (3:15–16), and then "all nations will gather to [Jerusalem], to the presence of Yahweh in Jerusalem and they shall no longer stubbornly follow their own evil will" (3:17). The phrase seems, therefore, to refer in the first place to Yahweh,[177] not to Israel nor to Abraham, concerning whom there has been nothing said in the context.[178] God is the ultimate source of blessing, but the action of the repentant Israelites and their renewed relationship with Yahweh prompts the nations to seek a similar blessing for themselves as Israelites enjoy, and they will also glorify Him. To that extent, then, there may be some picking up of the Abrahamic promise, but the case is not very strong.

We will round off this section on Jeremiah by a brief mention of the use of the term "fathers." Whereas for Deuteronomy the term "fathers" clearly refers on many occasions to the three patriarchs, Abraham, Isaac, and Jacob, that is never the case in the book of Jeremiah. Of passages where there is a probability of authentic Jeremianic material, "fathers" refers to all Israelites of the past, or perhaps sometimes the immediate preceding generation, and those addressed by the prophet in his day (2:5; 3:24–25; 14:20). These references are entirely negative: Israelites of the past together with the present generation have consistently refused to obey Yahweh's commands.[179]

---

174. Leslie, *Jeremiah*, 43, assumes a reference to Israel and without discussion and justification has altered the Hebrew in his translation to read "you."

175. See Flury-Schölch, *Abrahams Segen*, 185–92, esp. 187–92, who denies any reference to Abraham.

176. Flury-Schölch, *Abrahams Segen*, 188.

177. Flury-Schölch, *Abrahams Segen*, 185–92.

178. Those who see a reference to Abraham include Welch, *Jeremiah*, 72n2; Bright, *Covenant and Promise*, 160; Brueggemann, *Jeremiah*, 49; Wisdom, *Blessing for the Nations*, 39–40; Lee, *Blessing*, 105–7 (The main focus of the monographs by Wisdom and Lee is what Paul said in Galatians 3). The RV margin reference for Jeremiah 4:2 is Psalm 72:17, where it lists Genesis 12:3; 18:18; 22:18; 26:4.

179. See the discussion in Diepold, *Land*, 117, 158–59. The same is true for passages usually assigned to the Deuteronomic editor (3:18; 7:7; 9:14; 11:4–5, 7, 10; 14:22, 25–26; 16:11–13, 15; 17:22; 19:4; 23:27, 39; 24:10; 25:5; 30:3; 31:32; 32:22; 34:13–14; 44:3, 9–10, 17, 21; 50:7): Israel's history has been marked by a constant refusal to obey

1.3.3. The Book of the Prophet Ezekiel

Following on a report by a survivor that Jerusalem had fallen (33:21-22), Ezekiel received a word from the LORD (vv. 23-29) intimating that those still left in the Judea[180] were claiming that they formed the remnant of Israel and that national renewal would come through them. "Son of Man, the inhabitants of these waste places in the land of Israel keep saying, Abraham was only one man, yet he got possession of the land, but we are many; the land is surely given to us to possess." (33:23-24). Allen aptly comments: "Those still in the land saw themselves as religious pioneers, typologically reliving not the occupation achieved by Israel under Joshua, but Abraham's earlier occupation."[181]

This claim was then roundly rejected. Yahweh proclaimed further judgment on its propounders and announced that the land would be made desolate. "Then they will know that I am Yahweh" (v. 29).

Here a claim based on the story of Abraham is branded as illegitimate. The claim assumed that Abraham was called and promised the land by Yahweh (he hardly got possession of it—contrast Acts 7:5!). The claim was illegitimate because it did not rely totally on Yahweh's promise and gift, but assumed that because they were many, they could possess the land. They appealed to the Yahweh's promise, but in the wrong way.[182] In the prophet's

---

the commands of Yahweh. The concept of Yahweh's oath, prominent in Deuteronomy, occurs only at 11:5 in a passage from the Deuteronomic editor (and there could refer to the promise made by Yahweh to Moses at the burning bush [Exod 3:8]). The concept of "inheritance" (*nhlh*), and/or verbs "to cause to inherit" (*nhl* or *yrs*), again prominent in Deuteronomy, occurs four times in authentically Jeremianic passages: at 2:7 (where the land is referred by Yahweh as His inheritance); 3:19 (the land as the most beautiful inheritance among the nations); 12:7-9 (where Yahweh says that He has abandoned His inheritance to foreign nations); and 17:4 (Yahweh states that the people will lose the inheritance which He gave them). The concept also occurs at 3:18; 10:16 (=51:19); 12:14; 16:18, in passages widely attributed to the editor of the book. Diepold, *Land*, 117, thinks that over against Deuteronomy, Jeremiah stressed that the land was Yahweh's inheritance and property which He gave to Israel, whereas Deuteronomy emphasized the land as Israel's, but since Deuteronomy also stressed that Yahweh had given the land to the Israelites (which Diepold himself recognizes), it seems difficult to sustain this alleged difference (see Clements, *Chosen People*, 50-58, esp. 52, for the land as a gift of God in Deuteronomy).

180. See 2 Kgs 25:12; Jer 39:10 for allocation of land to those left in Judah.
181. Allen, *Ezekiel 20-48*, 153.
182. See Eichrodt, *Ezekiel*, 462. In this claim "there survived something of that obstinately wilful self-assertion which tries to force even God himself to serve it, and which replaces pure trust in God by a fanatical belief in a divine election which retains its validity under all circumstances." See also Allen, *Ezekiel 20-48*, 153.

estimate, their lifestyle contradicted any claim to be the inheritors of the promise to Abraham (vv. 25–26).

1.3.4 The Book of the Prophet Micah

The book ends with what has been considered a kind of liturgy in which the community confessed its guilt and its trust in God's salvation (7.8–10, 11–12, 13, 14–17, 18–20). The final unit is an affirmation of Yahweh's mercy and compassion: "Who is a God like You, who pardons iniquity?" God delights in mercy (v. 18). He will cast the people's sins into the depths of the sea (v. 19). "You will show faithfulness (*'mt*) to Jacob and unswerving loyalty (*hesed*) to Abraham, as You have sworn to our ancestors from of old" (7:20).

The names of the ancestors are used for the people as the corporate object of Yahweh's faithfulness, in accordance with the oath which He swore to those ancestors back in the beginnings of their national story. Hope for the future rests in the character of God—in His unswerving faithfulness to what He has promised. At the heart of the oath is the promise to give the land. God will graciously forgive their sins and restore them to the land. "The land will become a sacrament of His forgiveness."[183]

If we assume a post-exilic date for this passage,[184] then the appeal to the oath sworn to Abraham and the patriarchs is significant. In the dark days of the exilic era, when the monarchy and temple had disappeared, the call of and promise to Abraham were held on to tenaciously as a ground for hope, and the same held true even when the Temple was rebuilt after the exile and it seemed a poor substitute for the Temple built by Solomon (Zech 4:10).

1.4. Abraham in the Writings

1.4.1 The Psalms

How did Abraham figure in the hymns of ancient Israel? Did they mention him as they sang their songs to Yahweh? Perhaps surprisingly, there are only four specific references to the patriarch, and three of these occur in Psalm 105, while there is one allusion to the promise made to Abraham and renewed to Isaac and Jacob.

---

183. Mays, *Micah*, 169.

184. Mays, *Micah*, 21, dates it to the fifth century BC. Wolff, *Micah*, 26–27, 218–20; Mason, *Micah, Nahum, Obadiah*, 43–53, place it in the post-exilic period.

Psalm 47[185] celebrates the kingship of Yahweh and may have been sung to accompany the progress of the ark into the temple:[186]

> God has gone up with a shout,
> the LORD with the sound of a trumpet . . .
> God is seated on His holy throne. (vv. 5, 8)

The Psalm opens its first section (vv. 1–5) with the command to all peoples[187] to sing praises to God for He is the King of all the earth and over all nations (vv. 1–2). Then comes a reference to the fact that Yahweh had subdued peoples under the Israelites[188] and settled them in the land (vv. 3–4), which recalls the early history of the nation as a demonstration of Yahweh's power. Whether these verses were an original part of the hymn or a later addition is disputed. They are in the first person plural format and are a congregational affirmation about their past story. From a form-critical point of view they do not quite fit,[189] though they are not out of place theologically in a pre-exilic setting.

The Psalm announced that God had gone up to the sound of the trumpet (v. 5: presumably a reference to the taking of the ark inside the temple building).

A second section of the Psalm (vv. 6–9) again sounds out a call to worship and praise God, for He is King of the whole world (vv. 7–8a). God has sat down on His throne (v. 8b) and "the princes of the peoples gather as[190] the people of the God of Abraham" (v. 9).

185. There is a useful review of scholarly discussion of Psalm 47 in Zenger, *Der Gott Abrahams und die Völker*, 413–30.

186. So Johnson, *Sacral Kingship in Ancient Israel*, 75. The occasion may have been the New Year Festival at which the Covenant was renewed. Cf. Mowinckel, *Psalms in Israel's Worship*, 3, 115, 121–22, 171; Zenger, *Gott Abrahams*, 425; *Psalm 1–50*, 290, who dates the original core of the Psalm (two strophes, EV verses 1–2a, 5 and 6–7a, 8, each strophe containing a noun clause statement about Yahweh—verses 2a and 7a) to the pre-exilic era, specifically to the eighth century BC, while the additions 2b–4 and 7b, 9 are best set in the post-exilic period. Since Zengler, *Psalmen 1–50*, 293, attributes verse 9 to a post-exilic redaction, it is the Festival of Tabernacles as celebrated then.

187. The suggestion that the plural "peoples" refers to Israelites is unconvincing.

188. The criticism that non-Israelites could hardly be expected to rejoice at being subject to Israel (going as far back as Duhm) has a modern ring about it. It could be argued that the benefits of being under Yahweh's beneficent rule would outweigh the loss of independence. In any case, verse 3 refers to the period of the Conquest in the past.

189. See Gerstenberger, *Psalms*, 1:197.

190. There is a certain difficulty of interpretation here. The Hebrew simply juxtaposes "the princes of the peoples gather" and "the people of the God of Abraham." The verb *'sp* (here in the niphal) has no preposition nor is there an "as" accompanying the noun "people." The LXX has rendered ἄρχοντες λαῶν συνήχθησαν μετὰ τοῦ Θεοῦ

The psalmist envisages the rulers of the nations (representatively or with their people) as part of the people of Israel and worshipping the King of all the earth. But in what sense do the nations become part of the people of God, the people of the God of Abraham? Gerstenberger sees the concept of the world-wide pilgrimage towards Israel and Mount Zion expressed here.[191] Weiser sees a joyful acceptance of the Gentiles and thinks that this surpasses even the idea of the pilgrimage of the nations to Zion, for here the nations themselves become "the people of the God of Abraham,"[192] though other scholars dissent. Leslie envisaged the nations as vassals of Israel.[193] The text, however, does not say that the nations become vassals of Israel; rather, they are servants of Yahweh and, therefore, become part of His people. R. Martin-Achard is cautious about any missionary aspect.[194] Zenger believes that the post-exilic redaction had transformed an End Time event into world history, when the nations give up their previous gods and recognize the God of Abraham as their God. Insofar as they do this, they become or are the people of the God of Abraham.[195]

A number of scholars believe that this is an indication that the blessing promised to Abraham has found its fulfilment.[196] However, Zenger has pointed out that there is not so much as a remote echo of Genesis 12:3b. There is nothing about Abraham's being the mediator of blessing in Psalm 47. Nor is there any echo of Genesis 17:4–6 or 14:18–20.[197] This raises the question of when it is right or when illegitimate to detect an echo or intertextual reference. If we applied the seven tests set out by Richard Hays who

---

Αβρααμ ὅτι τοῦ Θεοῦ οἱ κραταιοὶ τῆς γῆς σφόδρα ἐπήρθησαν ("The rulers of the peoples have assembled with the God of Abraham, because God's mighty ones of the earth have been greatly exalted"). Hence, some translations supply a "with" (GNB [TEV]; REB; cf. JB), while others supply an "as" (NIV; NRSV). The latter sense would indicate a conviction that Yahweh was the God of all the world and that, therefore, the praise of all nations belonged to Him, and a hope that they might be brought into the company of those who worship the true God of the world (Zenger, *Psalm 1–50*, 293).

191. Gerstenberger, *Psalms*, 1:198.

192. Weiser, *Psalms*, 378–89. Among other scholars to assume this interpretation we may mention Wolff, who quotes Schreiner, "Segen für die Völker," 13; Kraus, *Psalmen*, 135.

193. Leslie, *Psalms*, 67; Rowley, *Missionary Message of the Old Testament*, 34. Both opt for the translation that the princes of the peoples gather *with* the people of the God of Abraham.

194. Martin-Achard, *Light to the Nations*, 54–59.

195. Zenger, *Gott Abrahams*, 427; *Psalm 1–50*, 293.

196. Weiser, *Psalms*, 378; Wolff, *Vitality*, 63. Leslie, *Psalms*, 67, sees this as an implicit reference to Genesis 12:3.

197. Zenger, *Gott Abrahams*, 427–29; much more briefly in *Psalm 1–50*, 293.

was one of the first to pioneer the idea of intertextuality in Pauline studies, we might well endorse Zender's negative verdict that here there is no echo of, in particular, Genesis 12:3b. Hays did say, however, that there may be exceptional occasions when the tests fail to account for the spontaneous power of particular textual conjunctions. This might be one such occasion, but that will probably become a subjective judgment.

Even if we reject an echo of any specific Genesis text, we would still have to explain why the Psalmist chose the unusual phrase "the people of the God of Abraham." Zenger himself has put forward an interesting explanation of why Abraham is mentioned here. He suggests that it picks up the tradition of how God took Abraham from Ur of the Chaldees and removed him from the worship of strange gods to become "the first monotheist," a tradition first present at Joshua 24:2-3 and later developed in early Judaism. He sees this verse as part of a post-exilic working over of the psalm.[198] How those who reject his traditio-historical analysis and hold to a pre-exilic origin for the whole psalm react to this idea may depend on how far one believes that the theologians of pre-exilic Israel were monotheistic or monolatrous in their thinking.

The Psalm concludes with another affirmation of the sovereignty of Yahweh: "For the mighty ones[199] of earth belong to God, and He is exalted on high" (v. 9cd).

Granted that in the worship the Israelites re-experienced the reality of the kingship of God,[200] outside of worship there must have been some sense of dislocation between what was being proclaimed in worship and in the real world. The nations were not in reality becoming part of the people of God and were not experiencing the blessing promised to Abraham. Worship and affirmations made in it helped to keep alive this hope and sustain faith.

Psalm 105 deals with the revelation of God in the history of Israel. The Psalm opens with a summons to make known Yahweh's deeds among the peoples and to worship and praise Him. They must remember His wonderful works, His miracles, and His judgments (v. 5). This is addressed to the "offspring of His servant, Abraham, children of Jacob, His chosen ones" (v. 6). In verse 7, there is a combination of Israel's sense of relationship with God and God's universal authority and power: "He is Yahweh our God; His judgments are in all the earth." Yahweh, Israel's God, is mindful

---

198. He sees an original, pre-exilic core of two strophes (Grundschrift), verses 1-2a, 5 and 6-7a, 8 (Hebrew vv. 2,3a, 6, 7-8a, 9), later expanded probably in the post-exilic era with verses 2b-4 and 7b, 9 (Hebrew vv. 3b-5, 8b, 10).

199. Literally, shields—metonymy for those who carry them into battle.

200. As Mowinckel, *Psalms*, 115, emphasizes.

of the covenant which He made with Abraham, His oath to Isaac, which He confirmed to Jacob as a statute, to Israel as an everlasting covenant (vv. 8-10), saying "To you I shall give the land of Canaan as your portion for an inheritance" (vv. 10-11).[201] There may be an allusion to the promise to multiply the descendants of the three patriarchs in verses 12 and 24. In verse 12 the Psalm said that they were few in number when they sojourned at first in the land, but then God made His people very fruitful and made them too numerous for their foes (v. 24).

The Psalm reviews the early nomadic wanderings, the career of Joseph, the time in Egypt, the plagues, the Exodus under Moses and Aaron, and the time in the wilderness when Yahweh fed them and gave them water from the rock (vv. 12-41), "for He remembered His holy promise, and Abraham His servant" (v. 42). Throughout this review there is considerable emphasis on what Yahweh did for His people to protect and to care for them. Thus the "for" clause of verse 42 encompasses the whole review section. The concluding verses refer to the possession of the land by God's people, His chosen ones. "He gave them the lands of the nations, and they took possession of the labor of the peoples, in order that they might keep His statutes and observe His laws" (v. 44-45). The plural "lands of the nations" refers to the idea that God drove out seven nations before the Israelites (see Gen 15:19-20; Deut 4:38; 7:1; 9:1, etc.), while the idea that the Israelites entered into the labors of those nations whom they dispossessed is reminiscent of Deuteronomy 6:10-11 and Nehemiah 9:25. Füglister rightly points to the note of prevenient grace in the sequence that God gave the land into the hands of the Israelites in order that they might keep His statutes and Laws: God's deed precedes the human action.[202]

The psalm closes with the responsive cry "Hallelujah" (v. 45).

So, the psalm at its beginning and end recalls the promise to and the covenant with Abraham.[203] For the psalmist, the classic period of Israel's history is from Abraham to the entry to Canaan.[204]

At least these two psalms witness to the importance of the covenant with Abraham and the promise of the land.

We now turn to one of the royal psalms to examine a possible reference to the promise of blessing in connection with the nations. Psalm 72 has been described as a psalm praying for God's blessing on the new king

---

201. The allusions are to Genesis 15:18-21; 26:2-5; 28:13-15. Note how in verses 8-10, covenant, word, oath, and statute seem to be synonymous.

202. Füglister, *Psalm 105*, 59.

203. Füglister, *Psalm 105*, 49, notes that Abraham receives the main emphasis in Psalm 105.

204. Leslie, *Psalms*, 164.

at his coronation, but more recently this view has been challenged and such a specific Sitz im Leben rejected.[205] However exalted the king might be, he is regarded as dependent ultimately on God. He is expected to ensure that righteousness and justice prevail throughout the land for all members of society. He must especially ensure the protection of the weak and vulnerable (vv. 2, 12-14). He should bring about peace (v. 7), not just in the sense of the absence of war but of wellbeing for all his subjects. A just and upright reign will have as its corollary bounty and productiveness in nature (vv. 6, 16). A long and blessed reign is sought from God for him (vv. 5-6, 15a). His rule, it is hoped, will be universal and all nations will serve him and bring him tribute (vv. 8-11). The psalm draws towards its close with the prayer-wish that the king's name and fame may endure forever (v. 17ab), and:

> all nations shall bless themselves by him *wythbrkhû bô* hithpael of *brk*
> (= wish that they had such blessing as he has)
> And shall call him blessed[206] (v. 17cd). *yšrûhû* piel of *'šr*

The two lines dovetail into each other. The nations observe how blessed the king is and wish for this type of blessing for themselves (v. 17c), and this observation also leads them to praise the king (v. 17d).

Is there an allusion or intertextual reference to Genesis 12:3 here or not? Several scholars do see such a reference.[207] Zenger, who attributes v. 17cd, along with 8-11 and 15, to an expansion of the original core of the Psalm which he dates to no earlier than the fourth century in the light of its dependence on Micah 7:8-20, believes that there is an allusion to Genesis 12:1-3 especially (but also 22:18; 28:14).[208] By contrast, Flury-Schölch does not think that there is.[209] He sees Genesis 12:1-3 as a post-exilic composition dependent upon but reacting against the kind of ideology of royal power expressed in Psalm 72 (which he sees as originating during the reign of Josiah). If, however, one does not postulate a post-exilic date for Genesis

---

205. Mowinckel, *Psalms*, 224; Johnson, *Sacral Kingship*, 8; Leslie, *Psalms*, 94; Weiser, *Psalms*, 502. Against this view, see Hossfeld and Zenger, *Psalms 2*, 207, who points out that there are no references to the royal investiture and that the programme of petitions need not be limited to enthronement celebrations.

206. Translation from Weiser, *Psalms*, 501; Hossfeld and Zenger, *Psalms 2*, 202, is not dissimilar; cf. REB: "Then all will pray to be blessed as he was; all nations will tell of his happiness."

207. Leslie, *Psalms*, 97; Weiser, *Psalms*, 504; Hossfeld and Zenger, *Psalms 2*, 218. Westermann, *Genesis 12-36*, 151-52, speaks about a parallel.

208. Hossfeld and Zenger, *Psalms 2*, 208-9. Since Genesis 12:1-3 is God's first word in the history of Israel, the king who puts into practice the justice and compassion outlined in the programme serves the history of God and Israel begun with Abraham.

209. Flury-Schölch, *Abrahams Segen*, 222.

12:1–3, the way is open for seeing the idea of blessing for the nations as a theologoumenon in pre-exilic Israel which different writers could develop. Whoever composed Psalm 72 believed that this idea could be tied in with the royal ideology of the Davidic House. Their ideal king would be a sign of how blessing might come to the other peoples of the earth. While the idea of enemies licking the dust is distasteful to modern ears (even Deutero-Isaiah used the imagery at 49:23 as does the redactor responsible for Micah 7:17), the concern for social justice, peace, and improvement of the lot of the poor represents a noble ideal. If realized in practice, it would be an attractive society to others.

1.4.2 *1* and *2* Chronicles and Ezra-Nehemiah

Purely statistically, there is an increase of references to Abraham in 1 and 2 Chronicles, but this is mainly due to the genealogy at the beginning of 1 Chronicles (1:27, 28, 32, 34) and to 16:16 = Psalm 105:42.

In the prayer of David in 1 Chronicles 29, on the occasion when he had completed gathering the material for the future construction of the temple and Solomon was about to be proclaimed the future king, Yahweh is first addressed as "Yahweh, the God of Israel our father" (v. 10) and then later this description is widened to "the God of Abraham, Isaac, and Israel our ancestors" (v. 18). It is as if the Chronicler begins with Jacob as the father of the heads of the tribes (cf. 1 Chr 2:1, even if in what follows the Chronicler concentrates on the line of Judah because of his interest in David)[210] and then extends beyond him to Abraham as the very beginning of the nation.

Yahweh was asked to keep forever in the hearts of His people their joyful willingness to give to Him all that was necessary for the enterprise and to direct them always toward Himself.

In yet another prayer of a king, this time that of King Jehoshaphat in 2 Chronicles 20, we come across another reference to Abraham. "Did You not, O our God, drive out the inhabitants of this land before Your people Israel and give it forever to the descendants of Your friend,[211] Abraham?" (v. 7). The reference to Abraham as God's friend may pick up the similar reference in Isaiah 41:8.

The promise made to Abraham concerning the land is regarded as definitive for all time.

---

210. For the Chronicler's interest in David, see Welch, *Chronicler*, 11–41; Noth, *Chronicler's History*, 100–102; Johnstone, *1 & 2 Chronicles*, 1:44–59; Japhet, *Ideology*, 445–78.

211. Literally, "who loves you." See earlier (45n16) the discussion of Isaiah 41:8.

Finally, in 2 Chronicles 30:6, in Hezekiah's letters to all Israel and Judah to celebrate Passover, we read: "O people of Israel, return to Yahweh, the God of Abraham, Isaac, and Israel, so that He may turn again to the remnant of you who have escaped from the hand of the kings of Assyria."[212] There is here a double use of "turn," as in v. 9: the people must turn to Yahweh, they must repent and return to Him. As a result, that will mean that God will turn to them (cf. 1 Chr 28:9; 2 Chr 15:2; Jer 29:13-14; Isa 55:6-7).

Whether or not the Chronicler wrote Ezra-Nehemiah need not be discussed here. A number of scholars have in recent years veered away from common authorship, but this issue does not concern us.

There is one reference to Abraham in Nehemiah (9:7). Nehemiah 8-9 discussed the work of Ezra in reading from the book of the Law of Moses, with the Levites giving the sense of what Ezra read, and in celebrating the Festival of Tabernacles. Three weeks later, another assembly was held with confession of sins and separation from all foreigners. A prayer of confession, which used historical recollection as a powerful motivation, was led by Ezra (Neh 9:6-37). This led to a rededication to obey the Law, to ban marriage with foreigners, to keep the sabbath, and to pay a yearly sum for the upkeep of the Temple (9:38-10:39).

Ezra's prayer opened with an acknowledgement of Yahweh as creator of heaven and earth and the seas (Ezra 9:6). He, the Creator, is the God who chose Abram and brought him out of Ur of the Chaldees and gave him the name Abraham (v. 7). He found Abraham faithful and made a covenant with him to give him the land of Canaan inhabited by various ethnic groups, a promise which He had fulfilled because He is righteous (v. 8d). The wording of these two verses suggests that beyond Genesis 12:1 the author had Genesis 15:6 and 17:5 in mind,[213] or was he thinking of Abraham's willingness to offer up Isaac, or, indeed, both Genesis 15 and 22?[214] Though it looks as if the writer knows of Genesis 15 and 17, the list of nations mentioned at verse 8 differs from that in Genesis 15:19-21. He may have been drawing on a different tradition.[215]

---

212. The deportation of the north by the Assyrians is here assumed.

213. Both Williamson and Blenkinsopp assume the writer's knowledge of Genesis 15 and 17 (Williamson, *Ezra, Nehemiah*, 313; Blenkinsopp, *Ezra-Nehemiah*, 304). Oeming, *Glaube*, 23, speaks of the reception of Genesis 15:6 in Nehemiah 9:7-8. See Mauren Yeung, *Faith*, 239.

214. So Schliesser, *Abraham*, 162; Mühling, *Blickt*, 109. Oeming, *Glaube*, 24, believes that a reference to Genesis 22 is possible.

215. Oeming, *Glaube*, 23-24, believes that the Chronicler was not summarizing Genesis 15.

Schliesser believes that while the stress is on God in this prayer, it marks the beginning of a shift from Abraham's faith to his faithfulness leading to constant obedience under testing, which was to be characteristic of the interpretation of the figure of Abraham in early Judaism.[216]

The prayer constantly stressed the initiative and faithfulness of God towards His people, in spite of which the people were stubbornly disobedient. Despite all that God had done for Israel, she had continually disregarded His will (see, e.g., the contrasts drawn in vv. 16–17b, 17cd, and vv. 18, 19–21).

Interestingly, there is no mention of the covenant with David. This could be due to the fact that the monarchy had long since ceased to exist. Hope now centered on the Abrahamic covenant. God will fulfil what He has covenanted because He is righteous.

In summary, we may say that there is, compared with the earlier Deuteronomist history, more emphasis on Abraham in 1 and 2 Chronicles and Ezra-Nehemiah. God chose him, made a covenant with him, and promised him the land forever. The relevance of this promise to the post-exilic people is obvious. The renewed emphasis on the fathers may in part be explained by the demise of the Davidic monarchy.

Summary

Before we set out what our survey of the material about Abraham in the OT has revealed, it will be well to recall our earlier comment that interpretation of the figure of Abraham is discernible in the three streams of tradition designated J, E, and P. Probably long before the Pentateuch reached its final shape, the figure of Abraham had been interpreted and applied to the situation in which the framers of these traditions lived. The figure of Abraham was always an "interpreted" Abraham.

It may well have been that the Abrahamic tradition suffered some eclipse in the south because of the ideology of the supporters of the Davidic dynasty, though even the comparatively meagre literary attestation to him outside the Pentateuch shows that it was never totally forgotten. Certainly in the exilic and post-exilic eras, the promises of God to Abraham came to the fore again as offering encouragement and hope after the catastrophe of the destruction of the Judean state in 587–86.

We now turn to gather together the main results of our survey.

---

216. Schliesser, *Abraham*, 162; cf. Oeming, *Glaube*, 24 (Abraham is a model Israelite, a model of trusting obedience); Mühling, *Blickt*, 109.

(a) One passage makes reference to Abraham's polytheistic past when he lived in Ur of the Chaldees. This occurs in Joshua's speech to the Israelite tribes gathered at Shechem in Joshua 24.

(b) After Genesis 25, we meet descriptions of God which link Him with Abraham in various forms: "the God of your father Abraham"; together with Isaac, "the God of your fathers Abraham and Isaac"; and together with Jacob as well, "the God of Abraham, Isaac, and Jacob" in the early chapters of Exodus. These are addressed to Moses to ensure that he realized that the God who was confronting and commissioning him was identical with the God of his ancestors.

Interestingly, the phrase (with "Israel" in place of Jacob) is put on the lips of Elijah in his address to the Israelites on Mount Carmel, where its occurrence clearly functions as a reminder of the true roots of Israel's faith as opposed to the innovations of Baal worship (1 Kgs 18:36). In the post-exilic work of the Chronicler, God is referred to as the God of Abraham, Isaac, and Israel (1 Chr 29:18) in David's prayer of thanksgiving at the end of his life. Here the use helps to link the Chronicler's generation with the patriarchal age and that connection which God had established with the fathers. The other occurrence in the Chronicler's work is in Hezekiah's letter to the remnant of the northern tribes inviting them to the Passover in Jerusalem (2 Chr 30:6): there is a reminder of their common history and what connects them. It is possible that Psalm 105 is to be placed in the post-exilic period, if it is accepted that it presupposes the completion of the Pentateuch, but it could contain material used in one of the great festivals to recall God's acts on Israel's behalf and Israel's lack of a proper response. At any rate, it appeals to the congregation as "the seed of Abraham" (v. 6).

(c) The covenant with Abraham, renewed with Isaac and Jacob, has what has been called soteriological consequences. That is to say, that covenant accompanied by Yahweh's oath has continuing beneficial consequences for the descendants of Abraham.

In the story of the conflict between Isaac's herdsmen and those of Abimelech, King of the Philistines, God appeared to Isaac in the night and spoke a word of assurance to him. Isaac was not to fear, because God would bless him and multiply his "seed" "for the sake of My servant Abraham" (26:24).

In Deuteronomy, God through Moses reminded the people that God chose them not because they were mighty or populous, for they were the fewest of all peoples. "It was because the Lord loved you and because He kept the oath which He swore to your fathers, that He brought you out with a mighty hand and redeemed you from the house of slavery, from the hand of Pharaoh king of Egypt" (7:8). In recalling the appalling incident of the golden calf and his intercession for the apostate people, Moses said that he appealed to God "Remember Your servants, Abraham, Isaac, and Jacob; pay no attention to the stubbornness of this people, their wickedness, and their sin" (9:27). When Moses passed on the words of the covenant commanded him by God, he urged the people to enter wholeheartedly into the covenant which God was making with them, that He might establish them as His people and be their God, "as He swore to your fathers, Abraham, Isaac, and Jacob" (29:13).

We may also refer to the comment by the Deuteronomic editor of 2 Kings: during the reign of king Jehoahaz, the northern kingdom suffered from the raids of King Hazael of Aram, "but the Lord was gracious to them and had compassion on them; He turned towards them, because of His covenant with Abraham, Isaac, and Jacob, and would not destroy them, nor has He banished them from His presence until now" (13:22-23), If the phrase "until now" is to be omitted as a later gloss,[217] the sentence would be a remarkable indication of the significance of the patriarchal covenant, given that the Deuteronomic editor was no friend of the northern kingdom.

In Jeremiah 33:14-26,[218] which consists of a series of seven oracles of hope, the final one tackles a question of whether Israel-Judah continues to be God's people or whether they have been rejected (v. 24). Whoever had stated the latter conclusion (other nations or a group within Israel itself?) was wrong. God pointed out that just as He was faithful to His covenant establishing day and night, so both His election of "the seed of Jacob" and His promise that a Davidic descendant should rule over "the seed of Abraham, Isaac, and Jacob," were unalterable (vv. 25-26). God would cause His people to return from exile and would have mercy on them (v. 26). Although the question of the continuance of Davidic house is uppermost, the mention of Abraham, Isaac, and Jacob contained a reminder of the election of the nation back in the time of Abraham, his son, and his grandson. God will not go back on His word to Abraham.

(d) Of the two major promises made to Abraham in Genesis 12, 15, and 17, it is especially that of the land which is frequently mentioned later;[219] that of descendants somewhat less so. These are too numerous to reiterate, but as an example we might mention how Deuteronomy begins and ends with references to this promise of land. At the beginning of the book. Moses reports how at length God commanded the Israelites to depart

---

217. Gray, *I & II Kings*, 544.

218. Attributed by many scholars (Volz, Rudolph, Leslie, Clements, and Brueggemann) to the post-exilic period—it is absent from the LXX.

219. See Westermann, *Promises*, 130, 148-49.

from Kadesh-barnea and to proceed to the land of Canaan: "See, I have set the land before you; go in and take possession of the land which I swore to your fathers, Abraham, Isaac, and Jacob, to give to them and to their descendants after them" (1:8). Then, in the final chapter, when on the eve of his death, Moses was given a sight of the land of Canaan, God said: "This is the land of which I swore to Abraham, to Isaac, and to Jacob, saying, I will give it to your seed" (34:4).

(e) Qualities of Abraham, such as his obedience, his trust in God's promissory word, his faithfulness, are not so much the subject of reflection within the Hebrew scriptures. That comes to the fore in the inter-testamental literature. Of course, Abraham's obedience is implied when he responded to the divine command and left his native land and his kinsfolk, and when he was prepared to carry out the command to sacrifice Isaac. Subsequently, we do come across a reference to Abraham's obedience, when God appeared to his son, Isaac, and renewed to Isaac the promises which He had made to Abraham. God promised to bless him, increase his descendants, and give him the land. This was "because Abraham obeyed my voice and kept my charge, my commandments, my statutes, and my laws" (26:5). Isaac benefits from his father's obedience.[220]

In the book of Ezekiel we have a wrong sort of an appeal to Abraham. Survivors of the devastation of Jerusalem and the Judean countryside were claiming that they and not those exiled to Babylon were the ones favored by God. They cited the example of Abraham who was only one man, a landless nomad, and yet he received the promise of the land of Canaan from God. They, by contrast, number far more than he. They say "We are many" (33:23-24). The prophet is authorized by God to reject this reasoning. Their behavior is so reprehensible[221] that it rules out the idea that they are the objects of God's favor and should possess the land. Their lifestyle belies their claim (33:25-26)! There seems to be an implied contrast between the way Abraham behaved and the way they are behaving.[222]

It cannot be said that within the canonical OT Abraham is held out as a model to be followed and imitated, with the possible exception of Nehemiah 9:7-8. Again, that was something which emerged later in the inter-testamental literature.

---

220. Von Rad, *Genesis*, 266, considers this stress on the merit of Abraham to be a new note in the patriarchal stories.

221. See the comment of Eichrodt, *Ezekiel*, 463: "This gives us a glimpse of a class of the nation who have grown depraved and disciplined during the long war years, and who no longer know or want to know of the unconditional moral ordinances of the people of God."

222. As later this argument appeared in John 8:39-40.

(f) The divine soliloquy before the dialogue with Abraham about the fate of Sodom reveals the standing of Abraham in Yahweh's sight. "Shall I hide from Abraham what I am about to do, seeing that Abraham shall become a great and mighty nation, and all nations of the earth shall be blessed in? No, for I have chosen him" (18:18–19). It is as if Abraham is partner with God in His world-wide designs and, therefore, deserves to be a confidante. It is really a development of the germ of this idea when Second Isaiah reports that God called Abraham "my friend" (41:8) and the Chronicler has King Jehoshaphat saying "Did not you, O our God, drive out the inhabitants of this land before your people Israel, and give it forever to the seed of your friend, Abraham?" (2 Chr 20:7).

(g) What appears to be absent is any widespread influence of the idea that in Abraham all the nations of the earth will be blessed. We do know that some of Israel's thinkers did find a place for Gentiles, as the idea of the pilgrimage of the nations to Zion to worship shows (Isa 2:2–4/Mic 4:1–4; Zech 8:20–23).[223] Yet the language of Genesis 12:3 cannot be said to have been taken up extensively outside Genesis. There are possible allusions in Psalms 47 and 72 and in Jeremiah 4:2 and Isaiah 19:24–25, but it cannot be said that these allusions are beyond doubt.

---

223. See also Isaiah 19:23, 24–25 (regarded by most scholars as post-exilic, though when precisely is almost impossible to pin down). Here a future is envisaged when Egypt and Assyria will be reconciled and will come into the same covenant relationship with God as Israel, though Israel remains a means of blessing to the nations, which is a possible echo of Genesis 12:3 (so Kaiser, *Isaiah 13–39*, 111, without discussion). The LXX "backs off" this suggestion and translates: "In that day Israel will be third among the Assyrians and the Egyptians, blessed in the land which the Lord of Hosts has blessed, saying 'Blessed be my people who are in Egypt and who are among the Assyrians, My possession, Israel.'"

Part II

Abraham in Early Judaism

2

Abraham in Early Jewish Literature

We turn now to the Jewish writings which were produced from ca. 200 BC (possibly a little earlier) to ca. AD 100+ (possibly a little later) and which were not admitted to the Old Testament canon. These will give us glimpses of how the figure of Abraham was being regarded within the various streams of thought in the Judaism of this period. There is a noticeable increase in the number of references to Abraham and the significance accorded to him over against the Old Testament seen as a whole. This continues a trend that was beginning in the post-exilic period and was to be observed in writings usually dated in that era.

2.1 Ecclesiasticus

The Book of Ecclesiasticus or *Wisdom of ben Sirach* was originally composed in Hebrew, probably ca. 200–175 BC, and then, sometime later, translated into Greek in Egypt by his grandson.[1]

---

1. See the Preface composed by the grandson and 50:27 for the grandfather's open declaration of his name. For discussion, see Nickelsburg, *Jewish Literature*, 64–65; Skehan and di Lella, *Wisdom of Ben Sira*, 8–16; Sauer, *Jesus Sirach/Ben Sira*, 22; Wright III, *Book of Ben Sira*, 436–38.

As we would expect, Abraham figures in the long section in praise of the heroes of Israel's past (44:1–50:21). This encomium is preceded by a lengthy section (42:15–43:33) praising the Lord for His mighty works in creation, ending with the statement "The Lord has made everything and has given wisdom to the godly" (v. 33). There is thus a juxtaposition of God's mighty works in creation and what He has done through certain figures in history, especially the history of Israel. This verse 33 functions as a transition to the Praise of the Fathers, whom, we are to bear in mind in the light of 43, 33, even if it is not overtly stated in chapters 44–50, God has endowed with wisdom.[2]

In the general introduction to the encomium (44:1–15), the author stated that the Lord established His renown and revealed His majesty in each succeeding age through the heroes of the Israelite nation (v. 2). This should be borne in mind when Sirach stresses the virtues and accomplishments of Abraham and the others. Even if he focuses on these, he has not forgotten what God did through or for them or gave to them.

Abraham is the third person (after Enoch and Noah) to be praised, verses 19–21.

> 19 Great Abraham was the father[3] of a multitude of nations,
> And no one has been found like him in glory.[4]
> 20 He kept the law of the Most High,
> And entered into a covenant with him;
> He confirmed the covenant in his flesh,
> And when he was tested he proved faithful.
> 21 Therefore the Lord assured him with an oath
> That the nations would be blessed through his seed;
> That he would make him as numerous as the dust of the earth,
> And exalt his seed like the stars,
> And give them an inheritance from sea to sea

---

2. For the importance of the juxtaposition of the praise of God's glory in creation and His glory in history, see Mack, *Wisdom and the Hebrew Epic*, 12, 161, 191–92. Mack also maintains that the proems to both pieces, viz. 42:15-25; 44:1-15, provide a theological lens through which the subsequent descriptions are to be read. For 43:33 as a means of binding God's work in creation with His work in the history of Israel, see Marböck, *Weisheit im Wandel*, 68, 70–71, 145; Skehan and di Lella, *Ben Sira*, 496.

3. Or, Abraham was the great father (JB; NRSV).

4. The Hebrew differs. "Kept his glory without stain" is the translation offered by Skehan and di Lella, *Ben Sira*, 503, while "an seiner Ehre gab es keinen Makel" ("there was no stain on his reputation") is offered by Sauer, *Jesus Sirach*, 303, who in his brief comment thinks that the absence of cultic transgressions was in mind.

And from the River [Euphrates] to the ends of the earth.

22 To Isaac also he gave the same assurance for the sake of his father Abraham.

In this section on Abraham, many phrases are picked up from Genesis and used—the father of many nations, the nations to be blessed through his descendants, the latter as countless as the dust of the earth and to be raised as high as the stars (vv. 19a, 21b-d), and there are references to his being circumcised (as a mark of the covenant with God, v. 20bc) and to his proving faithful when tested (v. 20d). The area of the land to be possessed extends from the Great River (Euphrates) "to the ends of the earth," which considerably exceeds what is said in Genesis 15:18-21. There is, however, no specific reference to Genesis 15:6.

The section opens with the description of the patriarch as great and the father of many nations. He is the origin both of Israel and also of numerous other nations.[5] He is then described thus: "No one has ever been found to equal him in glory" (v. 19a). The founding father of the nation stands preeminent in fame. Such is the stress on Abraham that he is said to enter upon a covenant with the Most High[6] (v. 20b), whereas in the accounts of Genesis it is always God who takes the initiative.[7] Circumcision is emphasized in the phrase that Abraham "confirmed the covenant in his body" (v. 20c). It is clearly constituent of the covenant.[8]

Sirach asserted that Abraham "kept the law of the Most High" (v. 20a).[9] Anachronistic as this may be, it probably reflects the concern of the author.

---

5. Sauer, *Jesus Sirach*, 304, seems to go too far when he asserts that "the whole story of humanity takes its starting point from him. That is why he is described as the 'father' of all men."

6. The text runs και εγενετο εν διαθηκη μετ' αυτου. Those who take Abraham as the subject of the verb εγεντο include JB, NEB, and NRSV; Skehan and di Lella, *Ben Sira*, 503; Sauer, *Jesus Sirach*, 303; Hansen, *Abraham*, 180; Schnabel, *Law and Wisdom*, 34; Vogel, *Heil*, 245-46; Yeung, *Faith*, 250; Schliesser, *Abraham's Faith*, 172; Mason, *Divine and Human Agency*, 37-39. If, however, it is felt that God must be the giver of the covenant, then it would seem to be a reward for Abraham's keeping the Law—so Jeremias, "Αβρααμ," *TWNT* 1:8; VanLandingham, *Judgment and Justification*, 36.

7. Most references in Sirach to covenant are to the covenant made at Sinai at which the Law was given (17:11-12; 24:23; 28:7; 39:8; 42:2; 45:5). At 45:7, the covenant of priesthood made with Aaron is mentioned, and the covenant of kingship with David occurs at 47:11.

8. See Hansen, *Abraham*, 180; Vogel, *Heil*, 247.

9. Abraham's motivation for keeping the Law is not specified. Schnabel, *Law*, 55-57, has helpfully drawn up a list of the motives for obedience to be found throughout Sirach (gaining merit is not to be found!).

It chimes in with the affirmation "When he was tested, he proved faithful," an allusion to the willingness of Abraham to sacrifice Isaac (v. 20d).

We note that it is *because of* all his qualities enumerated in verse 20 (δια τουτο, v. 21) that God assured him with an oath that the nations would be blessed through his descendants (seed), that He would multiply him like the dust of the earth and exalt his descendants like the stars, and that they would inherit (the land) from sea to sea and from the River (Euphrates) to the ends of the earth (v. 21).[10] Sirach can also go on to say that it was because of Abraham that God made the same promises to Isaac as to his father (v. 22) and, according to the Hebrew text, "He gave him the covenant of each of his ancestors," which presumably is a reference to Noah and Abraham.[11] Beyond Isaac, the promises were then transmitted to Isaac's son, Jacob, while the twelve tribes (i.e., the descendants of Jacob's sons) were in turn allotted portions of the promised land (v. 23).[12] There is here, then, a pattern of faithfulness/obedience followed by reward, along with a stress on genealogical continuity from Abraham to the twelve tribes of Israel. If, however, the total teaching of the book is borne in mind, it is clear that a stress on one's own personal moral performance is not the primary emphasis of Sirach. "Fear of God" is a key concept in the book, and at the heart of this concept is the personal surrender to and trust in God.[13]

We need to bear in mind the purpose behind the Praise of the Fathers. The whole encomium could help to bolster pride in their identity and history among the addressees. In particular, the assertions that Abraham kept the Law and was faithful imply that the ancestor of the nation should be followed by the author's contemporaries who should resist the lures of Greek culture and the Hellenizing proclivities of the ruling classes, for God will bless those who are faithful to Him amid testing. We might say that

---

10. Middendorp, *Die Stellung Jesu*, 73, follows the Sinaiticus MS which does not have verse 21cd, and thus it is the nations who will inherit the world, and Middendorp sees this as an indication of the consideration which Sirach had towards the nations of his time. But S could have omitted verse 21cd because of homoiteleuton. The Rahlfs-Hanhart Septuaginta includes the two lines, while the Anchor Bible commentary, by Skehan and di Lella, does not even mention the variant reading. It seems unlikely that Sirach would expand the promise to Abraham's descendants contained in the Law to the nations. There may well be influence from Psalm 72:8 (cf. Zech 9:10), as Skehan and di Lella, *Ben Sira*, 505; Sauer, *Jesus Sirach*, 305, suggest.

11. So Skehan and di Lella, *Ben Sira*, 502, 505; Vogel, *Heil*, 116.

12. Vogel, *Heil*, 116, points out that the continuity of the generations since Noah is based on the successive covenants made by God.

13. Haspecker, *Gottesfurcht bei Jesus Sirach*, esp. 232–80. This thorough, careful, and detailed study has established the importance of fear of God, in the sense mentioned above, for Sirach, even if its claim that it is the main theme should be rejected, with Marböck, *Weisheit*; Sanders, *Paul and Palestinian Judaism*, 332.

Abraham is being utilized to bolster the position that Sirach himself espoused in the period before the crisis precipitated by Antiochus Epiphanes in the 160s BC.

2.2. The Book of Tobit

The Book of Tobit, the date of which is difficult to determine,[14] is a didactic or wisdom novella. It tells the story of the trials and recovery of a devout Jew, Tobit, in exile in Assyria, and also the story of the successful marriage of his son, Tobias, to a young Jewish woman despite the opposition of a demon. Tobit is clearly the example of someone whose lifestyle of loving one's neighbor and doing good works, and of praise and prayer to God (1:3, 6-8, 11-12, 16-18; 2:2-4), is pleasing to God, and so he is a model of how a devout Jew should live in the Diaspora. At the same time, there is the problem of Tobit's blindness, and how one copes with this apparent contradiction with the conviction that God will bless the righteous. Linked with this is the conviction that God can intervene and that He does help His people even in the Diaspora (e.g., Tobit's initial business success in Nineveh 1:13; his recovery from blindness; and the successful consummation of his son's marriage 3:16-17; Tobias's guidance by the angel Raphael in chapters 5-12). There is a strong emphasis on endogamy: Tobit urged his son not to contemplate marrying anyone outside the Jewish people (4:12-13).[15] The setting of the story and its major themes suggest a provenance of the book in the Diaspora, but there is no agreement among scholars concerning its provenance.

The first reference to Abraham occurs at 4:12-13. The statements contained in these verses are part of Tobit's instructions to his son, Tobias, when he sent him to reclaim a loan made to a fellow Jew called Gabael, who lived at Rages in Media (4:1-2). They read almost like a testamentary speech of a dying man. Tobias should give his father a decent burial, respect his mother, and obey all the commandments of the Lord, for He will guide and give

---

14. Nickelsburg, *Jewish Literature*, 35, contents himself with stating that it was written before the persecution by Antiochus Epiphanes. Moore, *Tobit*, 40-42, cautiously opts for a date no earlier than ca. 300 BC. Mühling, *Blickt*, 132-34, adopts the position of a core composition in the third century with a working over in the second century before the persecution by Antiochus Epiphanes. Jacobs, *Book of Tobit*, 1314, posits a consensus of 225-164 BC. There is no consensus about where the writing originated, whether in Israel or the Diaspora.

15. Following the text of B A against the Sinaiticus text, which does not have verses 6b-18. See Rahlfs and Hanhart, *Septuaginta*, 1012-13.

prosperity to those who obey Him (4:3–6a). Tobit further urged his son to be generous to those in need (vv. 6b–11).[16]

Then Tobit bade his son not to marry any foreign woman but to marry within the tribe of his father, "for we are descendants of the prophets. Remember, my son, that Noah, Abraham, Isaac, and Jacob, our ancestors of old, all took wives from among their kindred. They were blessed in their children, and their posterity will inherit the land" (v. 12). Probably the author envisaged the four individuals mentioned as prophets: Noah had been forewarned about the flood and in some later writings was seen as a preacher of judgment and the need for repentance.[17] Abraham was described as a prophet in Genesis 20:7, while the patriarchs collectively are so designated in Psalm 105:15. Presumably the reference to marriage has in mind Genesis 11:27–32 and 20:5 for Abraham and Sarah's relationship to Abraham, together with the way that Abraham ensured a wife for Isaac from within his own kin (Gen 24). The issue of mixed marriages could have been a constant one faced by Diaspora Jews. It is easy, therefore, to see why this figures as a theme in the book. Endogamy was a way of maintaining Jewish identity surrounded by pagan idolatry.

In the Sinaiticus text of 14:7[18] there is another reference to Abraham. If it is not original, it could be part of the working over of the text which Mühling has suggested,[19] and still fall very much within the timeframe with which we are dealing. After the successful business trip and marriage, the angel Raphael, who had accompanied Tobias as an apparently fellow Jew, revealed himself to Tobit and Tobias. He stressed that the two men should praise and thank God and live a devout and generous life. Immediately after Raphael's departure to heaven, Tobit broke forth in just such a hymn of praise and thanksgiving to God (13:1–18). This hymn also expressed the hope of the rebuilding of the Temple and a glorious destiny for Israel, while at the same time it envisaged a "pilgrimage of the Gentiles" to the restored city and sanctuary. Following this hymn of praise, the author noted that Tobit died, but included the dying Tobit's testamentary instructions to his son (14:3–11). The father urged Tobias to go and live in Media for the prophetic message about the fall of Nineveh would come true. Both Israel-Samaria and Jerusalem will be destroyed, but God will have mercy on the exiles and

---

16. This section concludes with the assertion: "For almsgiving delivers from death and keeps you from going into the darkness. Indeed, almsgiving, for all who practice it, is an excellent offering in the presence of the Most High" (vv. 10–11).

17. See 2 Pet 2:5; 1 Clement 7.6; 9.4; *Sib. Or.* 1.125–29; cf. Josephus, *Ant.* 174.

18. See Moore, *Tobit*, 53–60, for a discussion of the textual problems associated with the Greek text of Tobit. Moore uses the Sinaiticus text for his commentary.

19. See Rahlfs and Hanhart, *Septuaginta*, 1037.

bring them back to the land. All faithful Israelites will be led back to Jerusalem "and they will take possession of the land of Abraham and live there for ever in safety" (14:7). In the meantime, Tobias should seek to please God by doing good and maintaining the giving of alms, and by being mindful of God and praising Him at all times (14:8-9). The importance of the land, the description of it as "the land of Abraham" (which presumably means the land promised to Abraham by God and, therefore, rightfully his), would be meaningful for those Jews living in the Diaspora.

2.3. The Book of Jubilees

The Book of Jubilees was composed in Hebrew, then translated into Greek, and from Greek into Ethiopic. It survives in its entirety only in the Ethiopic. Suggestions about the date of the composition vary within ca. 175-100 BC.[20] VanderKam, who has made a special study of Jubilees, suggested limits of 164-100 BC, and then narrowed it down to 160-150 BC;[21] Schwarz argued for composition during the crisis provoked by the Hellenizing programme promoted by certain Jews and preceding the formation of the Qumram community,[22] while Boccaccini believes that it was written after the Maccabean crisis.[23] The book is basically a rewriting of Genesis, which, it is claimed, was dictated to Moses on the second occasion of his ascent of mount Sinai.[24]

Interestingly, the Angel of the Presence informed Moses that God had told him and his fellow angels on the seventh day of creation, the day of rest, that He intended to separate for Himself a people from among the nations,

---

20. E.g., Nickelsburg, *Jewish Literature*, 78-79; Wintermute, *Jubilees*, 44, postulated 161-140 BC, while Charles, *APOT*, 2:6, opted for 109-105 BC. More recently, Segal, *Book of Jubilees*, 319-22, has argued that a number of sources lay behind the composition, none of which offers sound bases for individual dating, and that a final redaction occurred after the formation of the Esssene sect or stream, and it reflects the beginnings of the internal rift in the nation, which reached its full expression in the sectarian literature preserved at Qumran. See also Segal, *Book of Jubilees*, 843-46.

21. VanderKam, *Book of Jubilees*, 21.

22. Schwarz, *Identität durch Abgrenzung*, 99-129. Mühling, *Blickt*, 180, suggests that it may reflect the situation after Antiochus Epiphanes's prohibition of the Jewish religion.

23. Boccaccini, *Beyond the Essene Hypothesis*, 86.

24. See van Ruiten, *Abraham in the Book of Jubilees*, for a very comprehensive picture of the treatment of Abraham in the book of Jubilees. As to date, van Ruiten contents himself with somewhere in the second century BCE (8n23). van Ruiten's interest is primarily in the way the author has utilized the material in Genesis rather than the picture of Abraham per se.

who would keep the sabbath. He would sanctify them and bless them. This people would be the seed of Jacob whom God described as His first born son (2:18–20). The reference to the seed of Jacob rather than Abram is no doubt due to the sheer fact that it was Jacob's sons who were the heads of the individual twelve tribes of Israel. Furthermore, the result of this comment by the Angel of the Presence is that the election of Israel has been traced back to a pre-cosmic decision of God.[25]

The author of Jubilees seems to want to draw a close link between Noah and Abram. Thus, after the flood, God made a covenant with Noah. Noah was assigned all animals, fish, and vegetation, but he and his descendants received the commandment that they must on no account consume blood (6:1–3, 4–10).[26] A little later, the author indicated that after Noah died, his sons broke this commandment and they did consume blood. "But Abraham alone kept it," as did Isaac and Jacob (6:18–19). Then, at 14:20, we read "And on that day we made a covenant with Abram just as we had made a covenant in that month with Noah."

Near the end of his life, Noah divided the earth between his three sons by lot (8:10–11). The portion of land assigned to Shem (from whom Abram was descended) included the land of Eden, Mount Sinai, and Mount Zion (8:12–21). "And Noah rejoiced because this portion was assigned to Shem and for his sons" (8:18). Later we are told that Noah loved Shem much more than he loved his other sons (10:14b).

The division of land was documented, each son receiving a copy. Noah made his sons swear an oath calling down a curse on anyone who seized any portion of land not assigned to them by the lot (9:14–15). In the eventuality, Canaan did just this and seized a portion of Shem's land (10:29–34). The result of this was that when the Israelites later possessed the land of Canaan, they were in fact taking what was really theirs.[27]

We have mentioned above that Abraham was descended from Shem.[28] The author indicated that both on his father Terah's side and his mother Edna's side Abram was descended from Shem (11:14), while his eventual wife, Sarai, was "the daughter of his father" (12:9).[29] The combination of

---

25. See Halpern-Amaru, *Rewriting the Bible*, 25.

26. This prohibition figures prominently in Abraham's instructions to all his sons and, in particular, to Isaac and his grandson, Jacob.

27. Halpern-Amaru, *Rewriting*, 26, calls this a return rather than a claim to a land inhabited by others.

28. The line of descent goes from Shem to Arpachshad (9:4), Shelah, Eber, Peleg (10:18), Reu, Serug (11:1, 6), Nahor (11:7–8), Terah, Abraham.

29. van Ruiten, *Abraham*, 35, argues that the author has obviated any possible conclusion from Genesis 11:29 that Sarai was the daughter of Haran, who for him was the

these two factors means that any offspring of the marriage of Abram and Sarai had a "pure pedigree." The author also omitted the reference to Sarai's barrenness (Gen 11:30), and so he did not make this a Leitmotif of the Abram story.

The author said that while still a child in Ur of the Chaldees, Abram began to realize the errors of idolatry, and, on this point, when fourteen years old, separated from his father, Terah, to avoid idolatry (11:16). Abram prayed to the Creator-God to keep him from error and uncleanness (11:17). Immediately after this, the author recorded how he, still a fourteen year-old, caused a flock of ravens to cease eating corn seed and to fly away. These birds had been sent by Mastema to spoil the earth and so rob mankind of food. His fame spread and other people from Chaldea secured his help against the birds which had invaded their fields also (vv. 18-22). The author intended his addressees to note the sequence: Abram's prayer to the Creator to be saved from the errors and pollutions around him, followed by the success against the forces sent by Mastema. As Werrett has said, "For the Jews of the Second Temple period, the Jubilean image of the solitary Jew worshipping the one, true God of Israel and doing battle with the forces of evil in a Gentile society that was exclusively polytheistic must have provided great comfort and joy."[30]

Abram also added to his fame by inventing a vessel to hold the seed and let it fall on the ground while ploughing (vv. 23-24).[31]

Abram sought to persuade his father to turn from idolatry, but Terah feared that such a step would incur persecution and indeed death. Terah advised his son to keep quiet lest he should be killed (12:1-8). Eventually Abram burned the house of the idols,[32] at which point Terah and his sons, including Abram, left Ur and settled in Haran. The author then recorded Abram holding a night's vigil in an effort to determine from the motion of the stars what the rainfall that year might be. He received a word in his heart: "All of the signs of the stars and the signs of the sun and the moon are all in the hand of the LORD. Why am I seeking?" (12:17). This may be the author's way of suggesting that observation of God's handiwork in nature as a guide to Him ("natural revelation") needs to be supplemented by direct revelation from God.[33] In response, Abram prayed to God and

---

epitomy of an idolater and the complete opposite to Abraham.

30. Werrett, *Salvation through Emulation*, 222.

31. Meyer, *Aspekte des Abrahamsbildes*, 125, has pointed out that the Latin poet, Tibulus (ca. 55-19 BC), praised the Egyptian god Osiris as the inventor of the plough.

32. One of Abraham's brothers, Haran, rushed into the burning building to save the idol but was killed by the fire.

33. So Mühling, *Blickt*, 195-96. Meyer, *Aspekte*, 124, however, suggests that the

acknowledged God Most High as his God and sought help to resist evil spirits and to keep loyal to God (vv. 19-20). Abram had thus offered ample proof of his abhorrence of idolatry.[34] Abram was in this way depicted as the first Gentile proselyte, a convert from idolatry.[35]

Abram's prayer continued with a request for guidance as to whether he should return to Ur or continue to dwell in Haran. Then, in God's response to this prayer, the author recorded the words of God from Genesis 12:1-3, mediated to Abram by the Angel of the Presence, with the promises of blessing and a great name and that God would be his God. The last mentioned point is an addition over against the Genesis wording. It runs "And I shall be God for you and your son and for the son of your son and for all of your seed. Do not fear henceforth and for all the generations of the earth. I am your God" (12:24).

In other words, the author has filled in the gap in the Biblical story of Abram's life before his call recorded in Genesis 12. How Abram has conducted himself in Ur of the Chaldees shows why God chose him.[36] As a result, therefore, what God promised Abram appears as a reward for his dedication to God and dependence on him.[37] Furthermore, as a result of this prayer, the initiative in Jubilees lies with Abraham rather than with God as in the Genesis account.[38] In addition, the promises in Jubilees climax in the stress on the everlasting relationship between God and Abram and his seed.

The Angel of the Presence enabled Abram to learn and speak Hebrew, described as "the tongue of creation" (vv. 25-26). The study of Hebrew must have been important to the author of Jubilees to make this addition.[39] Then

---

author of Jubilees was here expressing some reserve towards the idea of Abraham as an astrologer.

34. He would thus be a model for those seeking to resist the inroads of idolatrous Hellenism (cf. Sandmel, *Philo's Place in Judaism*, 49; Niebuhr, *Heidenapostel aus Israel*, 94n7; VanderKam, *Jubilees*, 140-41; Calvert-Koyzis, *Paul*, 7-18; VanLandingham, *Judgment & Justification*, 25; Mühling, *Blickt*, 196).

35. That Abram emerged from an idolatrous background is asserted in Joshua's speech at Shechem (24:2, 15), and is also mentioned in the book of Judith 5:6-9 in the comment of Achior, the leader of the Ammonites, to Holofernes, leader of the Assyrian forces, explaining why the Israelites were prepared to resist the advance of the Assyrians. The author of Judith was using Achior "to express his own understanding of the sacred history of the Jewish nation" (Moore, *Judith*, 158).

36. Evans, *Abraham in the Dead Sea Scrolls*, 150-55, sees the author of Jubilees trying to answer the question why did God choose Abraham? So, too, Mühling, *Blickt*, 196.

37. Grindheim, *Crux of Election*, 45.

38. See Halpern-Amaru, *Rewriting*, 31-32

39. Earlier (11:16), the author said that Terah had taught Abram to write. In the

we are told that Abram took his father's books which were written in Hebrew and copied them and began to study them. The Angel of the Presence enlightened Abram about anything which he did not understand (12:27). These books referred to a written tradition which went back, according to Jubilees, to Enoch, from whom it passed down through Methuselah and Lamech to Noah and eventually to Abram (see 4:17-19; 7:38-39). Later, it will be said that Jacob inherited these books from his grandfather (see 32:21-26, referred to below).[40]

The author followed the narrative of Genesis 13-16. Having told the reader that Sarai was the daughter of Abram's father at 12:9,[41] the writer thus had Abram not being economical with the truth about his relationship to Sarai when he told Pharaoh that Sarai was his sister (according to Gen 12:13, 18-19). The reference to Pharaoh's taking Sarai by force and the subsequent punishment from God clearly pins the blame on Pharaoh. Although it is not expressly said so, it is probable that the author intended the reader to deduce that no sexual intercourse took place,[42] since God plagued Pharaoh with some illness immediately after he had abducted her.

In Genesis 12:6-7 God appeared to Abram at Shechem and promised him the land of Canaan, whereupon in response Abram built an altar. It is not said that he actually sacrificed on the altar. Westermann denies that he did so and maintains that the erection of the altar is more a sign of later possession of the land.[43] When Jubilees narrates the episode, the author has

---

references at 11:16 and 12:25-27, Mühling, *Blickt*, 197, sees Abram emerging as the prototype of a Jewish scribe.

40. Boccaccini, *Beyond*, 89, links this with the idea of heavenly tablets in which the Angel of the Presence was commanded to write the history of the world from creation to new creation, and which he revealed to Moses on mount Sinai and told him to copy (1:29–2:1). Boccaccini maintains that "the heavenly tablets became the center of a complex history of revelation involving several revealers (Enoch, Noah, Abraham, Jacob, Moses). The heavenly tablets were shown to them; the revealers saw, recalled, and wrote; and their work generated a written tradition eventually handed down by Levi and his sons 'until this day.'" Actually, it is never specifically said that Abraham had a direct vision of the heavenly tablets, but, rather, he studied his father's books, whereas Jacob actually does have a heavenly vision in which he was shown the heavenly tablets (32:21-26).

41. Mühling, *Blickt*, 185, points out that such a marriage is condemned by Leviticus 18:9, though Abram was a "Gentile" when he married Sarai.

42. Van Ruiten, *Abraham*, 79, says that such was "not imaginable" and refers to Deuteronomy 24:1-4 (cf. Jer 3:1).

43. Westermann, *Genesis 12-36*, 155. The same pattern occurs at verse 8 when Abraham reached Bethel: he built an altar there and called on the name of the LORD. Nothing is said about the offering of a sacrifice.

the same sequence of a promise from the LORD ("To you[44] and to your seed I will give this land") and Abram's response in building an altar, but the author said expressly that Abram offered up a burnt offering to the LORD (13:4). Abram did the same when he got to Bethel. "He called on the name of the LORD; "You are my God, the eternal God." And he offered up a burnt offering to the LORD upon the altar so that He might be with him and not forsake him all the days of his life" (13:9). Thus Jubilees presented Abram carrying out priestly duties, while he also had Abram making a personal confession that God was his God, and he stressed the concern of Abram to ensure God's presence with him throughout his life (13:9).[45]

While there is a lacuna in the text where we would expect an account of the war against the five kings and the meeting with Melchizedek, there is a reference to tithe for the Lord, which was ordained forever to be given to the priests (13:25b–27), and this seems to presuppose some prior incident as a precedent for the tithe.[46] In any case, Abram is shown as one who followed the practice of tithing.

In telling the story of Genesis 15, the author emphasized Abram's instant obedience to the command to look at the stars (Jub 14:4–5). Following the statement that Abram believed God's promise of descendants and that this was credited to him for righteousness, God stated that He had brought Abram from Ur in order to give him "the land *of the Canaanites to possess forever and (so that I might) be God for you and for your seed after you*" (14:6–7).[47] The italicized section is the addition of the author of Jubilees over against Genesis 15. Here, then, the two promises of Land and the relationship of God with Abram and his descendants receive emphasis.

---

44. Halpern-Amaru, *Rewriting*, 32, calls this a minor change, but sees it as a way of stressing Abram as the link between what had been foredetermined and what would be realized in the future. She maintains that this appears with various degrees of emphasis in the rewriting of the subsequent covenantal encounters.

45. Mühling, *Blickt*, 197, makes the comment that the author anchors cultic rites in the first ancestor. He does not seem to be bothered that Abraham offers sacrifices outside Jerusalem.

46. VanderKam, *Jubilees*, 2:82, tentatively restored the Hebrew text as: "Upon returning he took a tithe of everything and he gave it to Melchizedek. This tithe was." Koch, *Der König als Sohn Gottes*, 24, reconstructs it rather boldly by reproducing the Pirke of R. Elieser 27, to the effect that a slave of Abraham paid the tithe to the Lord as atonement for defilement incurred in the waging of war, but the Lord commanded it to be given to the priests and that it should remain like this forever.

47. "Thus, Abraham's faith finds its counterpart in God's declared faithfulness" (Schliesser, *Abraham*, 178).

Two weeks later (14:10),[48] God made a covenant with Abram. He said to Abram: "To your seed I will give this land from the river of Egypt to the great river, the Euphrates River" (Gen 15:18). This is declared to be a renewal of the covenant previously made with Noah (14:20). We are told that Abram rejoiced at God's statement and believed that he would have descendants (14:21).

The story of Sarai's giving Hagar her servant for Abram to get an heir is mentioned briefly (14:21-24).

The author comes to the story of Genesis 17 in chapter 15. Abram celebrated the feast of the first fruits of the harvest,[49] i.e., he obeyed the Law even before it was formally given on Sinai through Moses. During this celebration, God appeared to Abram and promised that Abram would be the father of many nations; changed his name from Abram to Abraham; declared that His covenant with him and with his seed would be an eternal one so that He should be his and their God; promised to give them the land of Canaan where currently he was a sojourner as a possession forever; commanded that the sign of this covenant should be circumcision; and indicated that Abraham would have a son by his wife, whose name henceforth would not be Sarai but Sarah (15:6-16).[50] Abraham fell on his face and rejoiced, though the author retains Abraham's internal question whether a son would be born to him who was a hundred years old, and whether Sarah, who was ninety years old, would bring forth a son (v. 17). As in the Genesis 17 account, the author stressed that God's covenant would be with Isaac, the son to be born of Sarah, and that it would be an eternal one (15:19, 21).

To God's speech the author added a long section on the absolute necessity of circumcision, and that on the eighth day after birth, for all subsequent generations (15:25-32). Through circumcision, the descendants of Abraham would be like the angels in the presence of God, who had circumcised

---

48. Jubilees appears to separate Genesis 15:1-9 and 15:10-21 into two scenes, the first taking place on the first day of the third month and the second in the middle of this month.

49. Throughout, the author stressed that Abraham observed the festivals. Compare the earlier reference in the section on Noah: Noah observed the feast of weeks, but his sons corrupted it "until the days of Abraham.... But Abraham alone kept it. And Isaac and Jacob and his sons kept it until your days" (6:18-19a).

50. Jubilees takes over the promises recorded in Genesis 17, including the promise of the land of Canaan. Halpern-Amaru, *Rewriting*, 31, believes that Jubilees has shifted the focus in the covenant-making scenes from the promise of the land to the special relationship between God and Israel. She is right to have drawn attention to this latter emphasis. She may have overemphasized the alleged *shift* of focus. Even in the intertestamental period, the land retained significance.

them on the day of their creation (15:27).[51] He also pointed out that God did not choose Ishmael or Esau,[52] but He chose Israel to be His people, over whom He would exercise direct rule, and had not entrusted rule over her to an angel or a spirit. His aim was that He "might guard and bless them and that they might be his and he might be theirs henceforth and forever" (15:30–32).[53] There will be no forgiveness for those Israelites who do not observe circumcision, however. They will count as sons of Beliar. Their sin is an eternal error (vv. 33–34).

The birth of Isaac was again announced to Abraham (16:1). Sarah overheard and laughed, and was rebuked by the angel. The birth took place at Beer-sheba at the time of the Festival of Weeks at the Well of the Oath [Beer-sheba], and Abraham duly circumcised Isaac on the eighth day, the author noting "He was the first one circumcised according to the covenant which was ordained forever" (16:2–4, 10–14). The author alluded to Abraham's future sons (without specifically mentioning Abraham's marriage to Keturah after Sarah's death), but said that they were to be counted as Gentiles (16:16–17a), whereas his line should be traced through Isaac: "from the sons of Isaac one should become a holy seed." It should become a kingdom and priests and a holy nation (16:17b–18).[54] The author of Jubilees takes over the concept of Israel as a "holy seed" from Ezra.[55]

The rejoicing of Abraham and Sarah was mentioned (v. 19). Then Abraham was depicted as observing the festival of Tabernacles (16:20–31). The author stressed that there was no foreigner or uncircumcised with Abraham in this celebration of the feast (16:25). He blessed his Creator, "for he knew

---

51. In 15:28, the translation of *OPT* 2.87, reads that the Israelites would not be uprooted from the *land* because of circumcision. Segal, *Jubilees*, 240, has "from the earth." Historically, in view of the events of 587–86, the author of Jubilees could hardly have intended "Land" (Canaan); whereas despite those traumatic events, the descendants of Abraham had survived. On the other hand, since many of the exiles had come back to the land, perhaps the author of Jubilees could maintain that they had not been uprooted from the land permanently. See Halpern-Amaru, *Rewriting*, 147n77, for a discussion.

52. Cf. what Paul said in Romans 9:6–13.

53. Again, here is the theme of the relationship of God and Israel stressed by Halpern-Amaru.

54. See Hayes, *Gentile Impurities and Jewish Identities*, 68–81, for a discussion of the concern on the part of the author of Jubilees for the preservation of the genealogical purity and sanctity of Israel, based on the idea of Israel as holy seed which should not suffer adulteration by intermarriage with Gentiles who are profane seed. In particular, she focuses on 16:17–18; 30:7–15. In 16:18 the author used the language of Exodus 19:5–6 because he believed that basically all Israelites were priests and that, therefore, the rules governing priestly purity (Lev 18:21; 20:3; 21:9, 15) were applicable to lay Israelites as well.

55. Hayes, *Gentile Impurities*, 73–81.

and perceived that from him would arise a plant of righteousness for the eternal generations, and from him a holy seed, so that it should become like Him who had made all things" (16:26). The "plant of righteousness" is the people of Israel as God's people.

With chapters 17-18 we come to the story of the banishment of Hagar and Ishmael and the story of the offering of Isaac. Jubilees did not edit the story of the banishment in any way significant for our purpose, so we turn to his treatment of the binding of Isaac. He reported that in heaven different opinions were expressed about Abraham. Some said that he loved the Lord and that in every affliction he had been faithful, but the prince Mastema proposed that God should ask Abraham to offer Isaac as a burnt offering, and then God would know that he was faithful in everything by which he might be tested (17:15-16). But God knew that Abraham was faithful, because He had tried him through many circumstances previously (six times, according to 17:17). In all of these tests, Abraham had proved himself "faithful and a lover of the Lord" (17:18).[56] But the only way to silence Mastema was for God to order Abraham to sacrifice Isaac, which He did (18:1). Then follows the account how Abraham was preparing to offer Isaac but was stopped at the last minute and received the reward of his obedience in the renewal of God's promises to him. The renewal of the promises is prefaced by the acknowledgment that Abraham had not denied his first born son (18:11, a phrase repeated at v. 15) to God. By the use of "firstborn," Ishmael was ignored and the primary significance of Isaac was emphasized.[57] The promises were the multiplication of his seed, their possession of the cities of their enemies, and the blessing for the nations through the seed (18:15-16). The author mentioned that prince Mastema was put to shame (18:12).

The concluding words of God to Abraham run: "Because you have obeyed my voice, and I have shown to all that you are faithful to me in all that I have said to you, Go in peace" (18:16). The notion that God had thus shown to others that Abraham was faithful to Him is an elaboration of the Genesis text.[58]

---

56. Jubilees seems to be the origin of the haggada tradition that God imposed ten testings on Abraham. The tenth was the death of Sara (19:3).

57. Hapern-Amaru, *Rewriting*, 34, suggests an allusion to 2:20, where God calls the Israelites, the seed of Jacob, His first-born son.

58. Oeming, *Glaube*, 26, believes that Jubilees represents Abraham's faith as a constant basic attitude which has proved itself again and again under different circumstances. Faith proves itself as that which continuously defines the relationship to God.

Probably the author intended his addressees to follow the example of Abraham's obedience and faithfulness, and so secure protection against and victory over Mastema and his forces of evil and secure God's blessing.[59]

The death of Sarah was the occasion of another testing of Abraham by God (described as the tenth trial, v. 8).[60] He was tested to see whether he would be patient under the pain of the loss of his wife, and he proved just that (19:3, 8-9). "He was found faithful and was recorded on the heavenly tablets as the friend of God" (v. 9).[61]

According to Jubilees 19:11, Abraham married after the death of Sarah. The author mentioned that Keturah was "from the daughters of his household servants." In other words, she was not a foreigner, for marriage of an Israelite with a foreigner was anathema to the author.[62]

Interestingly, in chapter 19 it is said that of Isaac's two sons, Abraham loved Jacob (v. 15) and that he gave instructions to Rebecca to take special care of Jacob "for he shall be in my stead on the earth . . . for I know that the Lord will choose him to be a people for possession unto Himself, above all peoples that are upon the face of the earth" (vv. 16b-25), thus showing Abraham to be in line with God's intentions concerning the two brothers. Indeed, Abraham summoned Jacob and gave him his blessing (19:26-29). This is one of those points at which the author supplements Scripture with his own composition. In Genesis the blessing promised to Abraham was reiterated by God to Isaac and Jacob; in Jubilees Abraham himself extended the promised blessing to Jacob.[63]

The same is true of chapters 20-22 which are dominated by the theme of Abraham's farewell in view of his approaching death. Abraham summoned Ishmael and Isaac and their children and the six sons of Keturah,

---

59. So Werrett, *Salvation*, 226. Sprinkle, *Paul & Judaism Revisited*, 213, also believes that the author wished his audience to follow Abraham's example of obedience and withstand the demonically charged power of sin (Later, at 48:2-18, Mastema's attack on Moses is mentioned). Certainly, in Jubilees 15:25-32, the angel stressed that failure to circumcise one's children would lead to extirpation from the earth because such would have broken the covenant. By being faithful to God and His covenant demands, Israelites will obtain divine help against evil spirits who lead people astray.

60. See note 56.

61. Endres, *Biblical Interpretation in the Book of Jubilees*, 20, believes that the author has shifted the focus from acquiring at least some part of the promised land, to the character of Abraham and his fidelity.

62. Prohibition against marriage with foreigners is a Leitmotif of Jubilees (20:22; 25:1-10; 41:1). See Hayes, *Gentiles Impurities*, 73-81.

63. In Genesis there is no indication that Abraham lived to see the birth of Jacob. Endres, *Jubilees*, 27, comments that the author of Jubilees' contribution is to have transformed an interpretation into a story.

and warned them all to avoid idolatry, to eschew fornication and intermarriage with the Canaanites, to observe circumcision, and to live righteously (Jub 20). These instructions were repeated to Isaac on his own in chapter 21. Abraham said that he himself had hated idols and had sought to do the will of the living God, who was holy and faithful and righteous. Isaac must on no account copy the behavior of the surrounding nations or else he would forfeit God's blessing. He must avoid idolatry and the consumption of any blood, he must sacrifice in the proper manner; and he must keep the commands of God (see esp. 3-5, 21-24).[64] Abraham concluded by pointing to the reward for performing God's will (vv. 23-25).

At his last celebration of the Feast of the First Fruits, Abraham summoned Jacob and once more gave him his blessing and repeated some of the instructions which he had given to Isaac previously (Jub 22). Once again, there is an emphatic warning to separate from the Gentiles (to avoid eating with them and to eschew their idolatrous practices, vv. 16-19) and a renewed prohibition against taking a wife from the Canaanites (vv. 20-22).

Thus, at 16:17-18; 20:1-11; 22:16, 20, Abraham is associated with strict warnings against marriage with foreigners, by which the holy seed of Israel would not only be profaned but also defiled. Christine Hayes believes that Jubilees has transformed Abraham into "the original champion of strict endogamy." "Ironically, Abraham, the progenitor of diverse peoples (Israelite and non-Israelites, see Jub 16:17), becomes the earliest separatist and righteous protector of the holy seed."[65]

There is also a strong emphasis on God's election of Jacob's descendants as His people and inheritance (vv. 10, 11-13, 15, 24). The role of Jacob at the time of Abraham's death is highlighted.[66] Indeed, at Abraham's request, Jacob slept with his grandfather who died peacefully by his side. It was Jacob, not Isaac, who discovered that Abraham had passed away.[67]

---

64. Wisdom, *Blessing for the Nations*, 98-99, points to the influence of Deuteronomic language and covenant structure in these farewell addresses of Abraham. Endres, *Jubilees*, 30-39, stresses that this speech contains several of the concerns of the author, especially in the realm of cultic and ritual purity: sin pollutes the land and the people, and it needs to be eradicated.

65. Hayes, *Gentiles Impurities*, 80. She also illustrates the theme of Israel as the holy seed in Jubilees' treatment of the rape of Dinah, noting how the author had altered the account in Genesis 34 in pursuance of his theme (Hayes, *Gentiles Impurities*, 75-79). But to discuss this would take us beyond our specific interest in Abraham.

66. So, e.g., Endres, *Jubilees*, 48; Grindheim, *Crux*, 45.

67. The importance of Jacob was actually highlighted near the beginning of the book in the section on the significance of the Sabbath (2:17-33). In a divine speech to Moses, God said that He had separated for Himself a people from the nations to keep the sabbath. "I have chosen the seed of Jacob from among all that I have seen. And

There are other references to Abraham in Jubilees which we shall look at, but it is worth noting at this stage that in fact far more space is devoted to the story of Jacob than to that of Abraham. Endres has pointed out that the Jacob traditions span approximately 45 percent of the entire work, and has suggested that in the estimate of the author Jacob is the central and pre-eminent character of the book, with Abraham subordinated to him.[68] At the same time, the importance of Levi should not be overlooked either, since Jacob handed over his own books and those of his fathers to Levi for him to preserve and renew "until this day" (45:16; cf. 30:11-17, 18-19, where Levi is blessed before Judah by the dying Jacob, and his zeal for righteousness is praised in a fulsome way.).[69]

After recording his peaceful death, the author said of Abraham: "Abraham was perfect in all his deeds with the Lord and well-pleasing in righteousness all the days of his life" (23:10). At the same time, the author noted an anomaly. In spite of his perfection, Abraham did not, in fact, live four jubilees. The earlier ancients in the pre-Flood era had lived nineteen jubilees, but after the Flood people began to live for a considerably shorter period because of the evil of their ways, except Abraham. The author offers no explanation of this anomaly. Perhaps we are meant to conclude that the general wickedness affected Abraham.[70]

In summary, it is obvious that the author of Jubilees stressed Abraham's perfect obedience to the will and command of God. He sought to be loyal to God and rejected the idolatry prevalent in his home area of Ur of the Chaldees; and he strongly urged his descendants to have nothing to do with the idolatrous practices of the Gentiles and emphatically warned against intermarriage with non-Israelites, which would adulterate the holy seed of Israel. Throughout all the trials of his life, he emerged faithful, and his righteousness was pleasing to God. He was depicted as observing festivals which God ordained for the future people of Israel.[71] Through the multiple farewell addresses allocated to Abraham, the author set out the main themes

---

I have recorded him as my firstborn son, and have sanctified him for myself forever and ever. And I will make known to them the sabbath day so that they might observe therein a sabbath from all work" (2:20).

68. Endres, *Jubilees*, 18-19; cf. 228. Schwarz, *Identität*, 90, had already noted the importance of Jacob, and assumed that it was because he was the father of the heads of the twelve tribes. Schwarz also pointed to many OT passages in which it is stated that God chose Jacob.

69. See Schwarz, *Identität*, 20, 83, 110, 127.

70. As Endres, *Jubilees*, 53, suggests.

71. Jubilees advocated the solar calendar of 364 days, which the author traced back to Noah after the Flood (6:32-37).

of his policy in the struggle between Judaism and Hellenism: true Jews must be loyal to the God who chose Abraham and Isaac, his son by Sarah; avoid contact with Gentiles, especially their idolatrous worship and intermarriage with them; observe God's laws, especially circumcision and the prohibition of blood, and practice righteousness.

Abraham was, then, a model of piety and obedience to God, for his descendants through the line of Isaac and Jacob, and, in particular, for the contemporaries of the author of Jubilees who were faced with the pressure to assimilate to, or the temptation to adopt, the practices of Hellenism.[72]

As mentioned, there are a few references to Abraham in the rest of the work.[73] Isaac followed in the steps of his father as regards worship of God (24:23). When Isaac gave his patriarchal blessing to Jacob, he said "And may all the blessings with which the Lord blessed me and Abraham, my father, belong to you and to your seed forever" (26:24).

Later, after Jacob's return from working for Laban and the (temporary) reconciliation with Esau, he made his way to Bethel to fulfil his vow to pay a tithe to the Lord, made at the time of his vision there. He intended to build a wall round the court there and sanctify it (31:26; 32:1a, 2). But, on the second night there, he was granted a vision of the Lord who gave him the name of Israel (32:16-19). Then an angel gave him seven tablets from heaven. These revealed to him what would happen to him and his descendants down the ages (32:20-21). Jacob was ordered not to build an eternal sanctuary at that place. The time had not yet come for that to be built. He was to go to the house of Abraham and live with his father, Isaac, until Isaac's death. Jacob himself would die in Egypt but would be buried along with his ancestors, Abraham and Isaac (32:23-26). Clearly Jerusalem is to be the place of the eternal sanctuary. This suggests that for the author of Jubilees the Temple at Jerusalem was divinely appointed, even if the priests of his day were deserving of heavy criticism.[74]

When the author records the death of Jacob, he said that Jacob had been buried in the cave of Machpelah in Hebron "near Abraham his father,"

---

72. See Konradt, *Die aus Glauben*, 31; Werrett, *Salvation*, 227. "The book of Jubilees and the Qumran community understood the patriarch Abraham as the quintessential example of piety and obedience." Mühling, *Blickt*, 209-210, sees Abraham in Jubilees as a symbolic figure for a new beginning, based on the knowledge of the one, true God.

73. For the sake of completeness we include them, though they do not really add anything of major significance. It is perhaps not surprising that Mühling, *Blickt*, does not pursue these references to Abraham after Jubilees 23:1-7.

74. Endres, *Jubilees*, 168, discusses the suggestion whether there had been a resurgence of religious interest in Bethel in the second century. He suggests that the reference to "Abraham's house" meant Mount Zion = Jerusalem, but this is by no means compelling.

and then recorded that Jacob had given "his fathers' books to Levi, his son, so that he might preserve them and renew them for his sons until this day" (45:13-15). These books went back ultimately to Enoch, and had been handed down through the generations since him (4:17-22; 7:38; 10:14; 12:27; 45:15). Thus Levi, and the priests descended from him,[75] became the guardians and interpreters of these ancient ancestral traditions. These traditions thus passed on were not only Abrahamic, but, beyond Abraham, Enochian.[76]

Before leaving Jubilees, we need to return to the question of why Jacob seems to be given even greater prominence than Abraham.[77] This may be linked to the fact that with Jacob the election is decisively settled, whereas Abraham had a number of sons—Isaac, Ishmael, and the sons of Keturah, and Isaac himself had two sons, Esau and Jacob. With the choice of Jacob his twelve sons became the heads of the tribes of Israel.

2.4. The Additions to the Book of Daniel and the Book of Esther in the LXX

One of the *Additions to the Greek Book of Daniel*, inserted between 3:23 and 3:24 is *The Prayer of Azariah*[78] *and the Song of the Three*. The former, with which we shall be concerned, may have existed before its insertion into the book of Daniel: it does not concern the fate of the three friends, but the fact that the Temple worship can no longer be carried on (v. 15). It seems to assume the situation created by the persecution of Antiochus Epiphanes with the support of Hellenophile members of the ruling class (v. 9).[79]

---

75. White Crawford, *Rewriting*, 67, 75-78, lists a concern for the priestly line through Noah and Abraham culminating in the choice of Levi as priest as one of the major concerns of Jubilees.

76. See Boccaccini, *Beyond*, 88-89.

77. See the discussion in Endres, *Jubilees*, 228-31, who assesses the earlier treatment of this issue by Mihaly, *Rabbinic Defense*, 103-163.

78. The verse enumeration is that of the NRSV. For a discussion, see Steck et al., *Das Buch Baruch*, 229-36. Kottsieper is responsible for the commentary on the additions to Esther and Daniel.

79. So Nickelsburg, *Jewish Literature*, 28. The references to "a wicked king, the vilest in the world" and to "no burnt offering, no sacrifice, no oblation, no incense, no place to make an offering before You and find mercy" could fit the situation during the persecution by Antiochus Epiphanes. So also Vogel, *Heil*, 45n71; Kottsieper, *Zu Ester und Daniel*, 231-32.

This Prayer of Azariah[80] is basically a national confession of sins, for which the nation is justly suffering God's judgment (vv. 3-10). Azariah then appeals to God: "For your honor's sake do not abandon us forever; do not annul your covenant. Do not withdraw your mercy from us, for the sake of Abraham, your beloved, for the sake of Isaac, your servant, and Israel, your holy one. You promised to multiply their descendants as the stars in the sky and the sand on the seashore" (vv. 11-13). The prayer asks God to accept their repentance in lieu of sacrifices (vv. 16-17). All three patriarchs receive mention, Abraham being described as "your beloved," Isaac "your servant," and Israel (=Jacob) "your holy one" (v. 12). The reference to Jacob as Israel provides a lead in to the state of the people who are now something of a remnant compared with former days.[81]

Because of God's own character and His reputation, and because of that covenant made with the patriarchs, the prayer hopes that God would show mercy to the present generation (v. 19). The appeal to the promise of increase in descendants made to Abraham is a reminder to God that He should keep His word, and, therefore, not destroy the nation. The appeal for God's mercy is made from within membership of the covenant which God made with the patriarchs. The prayer ends with the hope of a change in the contemporary power structures and the hope that God's worldwide sovereignty will be recognized by those who now are the enemies of those who seek to follow God's ways and serve Him (vv. 20-22).

There is also an addition of a prayer by Mordecai and one by Esther to the Greek text of Esther 4:17.[82] They are inserted at Esther 4:17, and pick up the fasting of Esther and the Jews which Esther had called for in the light of the impending threat.

Mordecai acknowledged the greatness and majesty of God; and explained his refusal to bow down to Haman as due to his desire not to give

---

80. The Jewish name of Abed-nego, the friend of Daniel (see Dan 1:6).

81. As suggested by Kottsieper, *Zu Ester*, 235.

82. These are printed as Addition C and enumerated as 13:8b-17; 14:1-19, respectively, in the *NRSV with Apocrypha* (37-38), while the Greek text appears in Rahlfs and Hanhart, *Septuaginta*, 960-61. Dating these additions is far from easy. Nicholsburg, *Jewish Literature*, 175, dates the addition of them to the book to the introduction of the feast of Purim. Mühling, *Blickt*, 168, is prepared to say that they might go back to popular laments at the time of the persecution of Antiochus Epiphanes. Kottsieper, *Zu Ester*, 160, believes that at the base of both there are community laments which an editor has utilized for the Esther narrative. He believes that the community lament within Esther's prayer comes from the Maccabean period, and since the one in Mordecai's prayer shows agreements with that of Esther, it may stem from the same context also. Fox, *Greek Version of Esther*, 604, suggests that the composition probably occurred between late second century and the middle of the first century BC in Ptolemaic Egypt.

to a human being the glory due to God (13:9–14).[83] Then comes the prayer-request. Mordecai appealed to God: "And now, O Lord God and King, God of Abraham, spare your people, for the eyes of our foes are set upon us to annihilate us, and they desire to destroy the inheritance that has been Yours from the beginning. Do not neglect Your portion, which You redeemed for Yourself out of the land of Egypt. Hear my prayer, and have mercy on your inheritance, turn our mourning into feasting that we may live and sing praise to your name. O Lord, do not destroy the lips of those who praise you" (13:15–17). Thus, Mordecai is pictured as appealing to God's election of Abraham and his descendants and His act in liberating them from Egypt, as the basis for God to intervene in the situation of distress and crisis in which Mordecai and his fellow Jews find themselves. Kottspieler believes that the phrase about God's inheritance as "from the beginning" (εξ αρχης) does not refer to the election of Abraham nor to the Exodus, but to the pre-history division of the peoples and compares this with both Deuteronomy 32:8–10 and Psalm 74:2 (where απ'αρχης occurs).[84] He may be right, although the specific reference to God as the God of Abraham and to the Exodus would place these points very much to the fore.

As with Mordecai's prayer, Esther's comprises a communal lament plus Esther's personal justification of her conduct, viz. how she has remained a loyal Jew even though a queen at a pagan court.[85] After an introduction describing how Esther took off her royal robes and covered herself with ashes (14:1–2), Esther's prayer follows (vv. 3–19). She also appealed to the fact that God elected her ancestors from among all the nations so that Israel might be an eternal inheritance for Him and had fulfilled all His promises (14:5). Israel's enemies planned to destroy God's inheritance and annihilate those who praise Him, and this for the glory of their idols and to magnify a mortal king (vv. 8–10).

Esther appealed fervently for divine help in her predicament, for she was on her own and had no helper but God (v. 14). Though queen, she has had no pleasure in her position and her relations with her pagan husband. She had abstained from the king's feasts and not consumed the wine of libations.[86] She has had no joy "except in You, O Lord God of Abraham" (v. 18).

---

83. Kottspieler, *Zu Ester*, 161–62, points to the fact that in verses 12–14 Mordecai speaks of himself, whereas it is the people who speak in the surrounding verses. This suggests that verses 12–14 are the work of the redactor.

84. Kottspieler, *Zu Ester*, 165.

85. For details see, Kottspieler, *Zu Ester*, 169–70.

86. We need not discuss whether these verses (vv. 25b–29), while dealing with the issue of the conduct of a Jew/Jewess within a non Jewish context, also contain an implied defense of the Hasmoneans against the charge that they had given up Tora piety in

She concluded with a plea to hear her cry and save her and the Jewish people from the hand of evil-doers (v. 19).

Whereas the original book lacked any reference to God, the additions help to remedy that deficiency. The author of these additions clearly wished to emphasize that God was the author of the rescue and used His servants to that end. At the same time, by referring to God as the God of Abraham, the author linked the scene of the book, and his own present, with the election of Israel in the beginning with Abraham, and perhaps the pre-history election of Israel.

2.5 The Dead Sea Scrolls

There are not all that many references to Abraham in the *Qumran Writings,* and several of these occur in fragments whose condition is so poor that reconstruction is very uncertain. These will not be mentioned.[87]

We turn first to the so-called *Damascus Document.*[88] The author began at 2:14 to exhort his addressees to follow ways that please God and not to follow the evil inclination and what the eyes lust after. Through these, many even heroic people went astray in the past. He mentions the fall of the Heavenly Watchers and their offspring, the giants, who perished in the flood, and then (3:1) described how the descendants of Noah went astray.[89] By contrast, Abraham "did not walk in it [viz. the way of disobedience characteristic of his predecessors] and he was accounted a friend of God because he kept the commandments of God and did not choose his own will. And he handed them down to Isaac and Jacob, who kept them, and were recorded as friends of God and party to the Covenant for ever" (3:1-3). In the idea that Abraham surrendered his own will the author may be thinking in general terms, or he might have been thinking of his willingness to sacrifice Isaac, or possibly uprooting himself from his family in obedience to God's

---

pursuit of pagan magnificence. See Kottspieler, *Zu Ester und Daniel*, 175-77.

87. Mühling, *Blickt*, 220-29, 233-48, mentions all these.

88. It is so called because of the references to the making of the New Covenant in the land of Damascus. Two incomplete medieval copies were found in a storeroom in a Cairo synagogue in 1896-97, and subsequently extensive fragments have been found in three of the caves at Qumran. Vermes, *Complete Dead Sea Scrolls*, 127, suggests a date about 100 BC, with Nickelsburg, *Jewish Literature*, 124, opting for 100-75 BC. Blanton IV, *Constructing a New Covenant*, 22, dates the final form of this composite document between 150 BC and 50 BC. For an overview, see Hempel, *Damascus Document*, 510-12.

89. The history of Israel from Kadesh to the exile as one of disobedience is given in a highly compressed account in 3:4-12 (so Knibb, *Exile in the Damascus Document*, 109).

call recorded in Genesis 12:1.[90] The obedience of Abraham and the other patriarchs is obviously held up as a model to be imitated by both the full and prospective members of the community.

The tale of disobedience continued, but God made a covenant with a remnant who held fast to His commandments, and He revealed to them "the hidden things in which all Israel had gone astray" (3:13-14).[91] They received the forgiveness of their sins: "According to the Covenant which God made with the forefathers, forgiving their sins, so shall He forgive their sins also" (4:9-10). It is as if there was a gap between the patriarchs and the community, who become the heirs of the covenant made with the three patriarchs.[92] At 5:20-6:2 it is said that "in the time of desolation" God remembered the covenant with the fathers and raised up men of discernment from among the priests ("Aaron") and men of wisdom from the laity ("Israel") and He caused them to hear (this is supported by a midrash on Num 21:18). A little later (8:14-18), Deuteronomy 9:5 and 7:8, which together reminded Israel that God had intervened on their behalf not because of any righteousness of theirs but because He loved the fathers and wanted to keep His oath to them, are applied to the converts of Israel who depart from the way of the people: "Because God loved the first (men) who testified in His favor, so will He love those who come after them, for the Covenant of the fathers is theirs." Over against what it considered apostate Israel, the group was the inheritor of the covenant with the fathers, Abraham, Isaac, and Jacob (cf. 1:4; and in the War Scroll, 1QM 13.7-8; 14.8-9).

Later, in the context of what a Hebrew person should not sell to a Gentile, a person is prohibited from selling his man or maid servant to a Gentile because "they have been brought by him into the Covenant of Abraham" (12:11). Here there seems to be an allusion to the story of the covenant with Abraham in Genesis 17, when he was ordered to incorporate his servants within that covenant by having them circumcised. Presumably, the assumption here is that servants who were formerly male Gentiles had been circumcised in compliance with Genesis 17, and, therefore, would stand

---

90. It is quite possible that the Teacher of Righteousness had fled Judah and gone to Damascus in order to escape from his enemies in Jerusalem, with others accompanying him — see CD 6.5, assuming the reference to Damascus is to be taken literally, with Blanton IV, *Constructing*, 86-98. Other scholars see the reference to Damascus as symbolic and based on Amos 5:27.

91. According to 1:3-12, the group came into existence 390 years after Nebuchadnezzarr had captured Jerusalem and deported the people to Babylon. After 20 years of their existence, God raised up for them the Teacher of Righteousness to guide them in ways that pleased Him.

92. This implies that the covenant with Israel first took exclusive shape through the existence of the group behind the Damascus Document, as Vogel, *Heil*, 300, maintains.

within that covenant made with Abraham[93] (If they were Jews, they would have been circumcised already before their purchase as slaves). Circumcision is seen as a sign of membership of the archetypal covenant, which God made with Abraham.[94]

Finally, it is said (in a reference to the book of Jubilees) that when a person swears to return to the Law of Moses, the Angel of Persecution[95] shall cease to follow him, provided that he fulfils his word: "for this reason Abraham circumcised himself on the day that he knew" (16:6).[96] In the writer's mind, there is a link between circumcision and protection against the Angel of Persecution.

The first of these references certainly and the last by implication basically emphasize Abraham's obedience. The second underlines the importance of the Abrahamic covenant.

The Genesis *Apocryphon*[97] was discovered among the manuscripts at Qumran. The beginning appears to have been lost, and may have dealt with the creation of the world and human history up to Enoch and Noah. After dealing with the birth of Noah (columns 2-5) and then the words of Noah (columns 6-17), it turns to Abram in columns 19-22.[98] It expands

---

93. In support of the fact that former Gentiles are in mind, we may refer to 14:4-5, where it states that, when there is an assembly, members gather in a prescribed order, namely, firstly the priests, secondly the Levites, thirdly the Israelites, fourthly the proselytes. "Thus shall they sit and thus be questioned on all matters." If this is a correct interpretation, then the Damascus Document is more open than Jubilees (15:11-14, 25-26) which stressed that only eighth day circumcision is valid for entry into the covenant with God. On the other hand, the Midrash on the Last Days (4 Q174.1-4) excludes the foreigner and the stranger among others from entering the sanctuary which God will build in the last days.

94. Christiansen, *Covenant*, 112, boldly asserts that "covenant with Abraham is synonymous with circumcision." Vogel, *Heil*, 254, prefers to say that circumcision has "identity forming function. . . . Circumcision is not the content of a confessional demand, but the legal basis for a privileged status of belonging to the people of God."

95. So the translation of Vermes, *Dead Sea Srolls*, 139; Vogel, *Heil* 251, translates as the Angel of Hostility (Feindschaft).

96. Jubilees 15:32 speaks of the fact that God did not entrust Israel to any angel or spirit but He alone was their ruler and would guard them and bless them.

97. "The Genesis Apocryphon appears to have been composed in Aramaic around the turn of the era" (Nickelsburg, *Jewish Literature*, 265); "Paleographical date of the Scroll falls between 25 BCE and 50 CE" (White Crawford, *Rewriting Scripture in Second Temple Times*, 106). Both Nickelsburg and White Crawford rely on Fitzmeyer. While agreeing, Vermes, *Dead Sea Scrolls*, 481, suggests "at least as early as the first half of the second century BCE" for a pre-Qumran version. For an overview, see Eshel, *Genesis Apocryphon*, 664-67.

98. Column 18 is lost. It may have contained some of the material now contained in Genesis 11-12, as Column 19 starts with Abram in Canaan. See White Crawford,

on Genesis 12–14 as an account in the first person. Abram was in Canaan, and resided in Hebron for two years. Because of famine, Abram travelled to Egypt. On entering Egypt, he had a dream about a cedar tree and a palm tree (19:14). Men came and tried to cut down and uproot the cedar tree, while leaving the palm tree standing. The palm tree objected and as a result the cedar tree was spared. The cedar tree stands for Abram and the palm tree is Sarai, while those who try and cut down the cedar tree are Pharaoh's men. Abram shared the dream with Sarai and interpreted it as an indication that the Egyptians would try to kill him, while sparing her. He asked her to say that he was her brother and then his life would be spared.[99] After five years, three members of the Egyptian royal family visited Abram (19:14–17).[100] On their return to Pharaoh, they praised Sarai's beauty and attractiveness in superlative terms (20). Pharaoh took Sarai as a wife and tried to kill Abram, but Sarai's pleas saved him. That night Abram, together with his nephew Lot, wept and prayed to God, addressing Him as "Lord and King of all things and who rules over all the kings of the earth and judges them all," and imploring help to preserve Sarai's purity (20:10–15). Thus, in his turmoil, Abram turned to God in prayer. In response, God sent an evil spirit to scourge Pharaoh (the severity of the scourges sent by God is somewhat more emphasized than in Genesis). This lasted for two years, at the end of which Pharaoh restored Sarai, rebuking Abram for his deception. Then Abram not only prayed for Pharaoh but he also laid hands on him and the scourge (unspecified, unless sexual impotence is being indicated) departed from him. Thus, Abram is portrayed as possessing healing properties and superior to the Egyptian healers and magicians who had been unable to cure Pharaoh (20). Clearly, this section was so shaped as to try and exonerate Abram for his deception. This deception was sanctioned by the dream-vision, which will have been assumed to have been sent by God.[101] Abram appears as a righteous and God-fearing person.[102]

Rewriting Scripture, 116.

99. "In mortal danger, Abraham had no choice but to deceive Pharaoh" (Evans, *Abraham*, 157).

100. According to the translation of Machiela, *Dead Sea Genesis Apocryphon*, the Egyptian nobles "asked erudition and wisdom and truth for themselves," and Abram read and expounded the contents of the book of the Words of Enoch (19:25) (van Ruiten, *Abraham*, 95–109, quotes Machiela's translation of 1QapGen 19:8–21:26 in its entirety). This would seem to be a very early indication of that tradition about Abram which depicted him as a wise person who enlightened others and revealed truths hidden from them (see Ps.-Eupolemus, Artapanus, and Josephus below).

101. Cf. "Such a dream would have been interpreted as a warning from God" (Evans, *Abraham*, 157).

102. For this prayer and other links with the book of Jubilees, see White Crawford, *Rewriting*, 116–27.

Abram returned to Canaan and retraced his steps and visited places he had previously stayed at. He built a second altar at Bethel and offered prayer to God, praising Him and thanking Him for His favor and guidance. The author then recounted briefly the separation of Lot from Abram, to the latter's great dismay. Abram was generous to Lot as they separated and added to his flocks. Next comes a reproduction of the Genesis account of how the patriarch received assurance from God that the land which he could see from where he was standing would be given to him and his descendants for ever, to which the author added a reference to the fact that subsequently Abram climbed to the top of mount Ramath Hazor. Over against the Biblical account which simply says that "the LORD said to Abram," the author says that "God appeared to me in a vision at night and said to me." After having seen the land from mount Ramath Hazor, Abram travelled through it, as if symbolically staking a claim to it, until eventually settling at Hebron (21:8-14).

The rest of column 21 and column 22.1-26a describe Abram's participation in the fight against the five kings in order to rescue Lot, Abram's successful defeat of the enemy, and the meeting with Melchizedek. The author recorded the prayer with which Melchizedek blessed Abram, and then stated "And Abram gave him the tithe of all the possessions of the king of Elam and his companions." This may be due to avoid the impression that Abram tithed his own possessions.[103] Then comes Abram's refusal to take a share in the spoils of the war.

The divine word to Abram at the beginning of Genesis 15 is expanded by a reference to the way in which God had materially prospered Abram in the ten years since he left Haran. His wealth had doubled in this period, and it would be multiplied in the future (22:26 to the end). Abram raised the question of an heir, but at this point unfortunately the text ends, just short of the crucial 15:5-6!

If we may assume that the Genesis Apocryphon represented a priestly-levitical tradition which emerged in Palestine in the third century BC or even earlier,[104] then the picture of Abram which emerges in it becomes significant. It is evidence that Jewish scholars and writers of that era were reshaping the story of the great founding figure of the Jewish nation and adapting it to the needs of their own generation.[105]

---

103. So Koch, *Der König als Sohn Gottes*, 24.

104. White Crawford, *Rewriting*, 127

105. This also has implications for the dating of the compilation of Genesis, but that is an issue far beyond our remit.

In the 4Q252 I,[106] 2.8, Abraham is called God's beloved, to whom God promised the land.[107]

Some fragments in Hebrew of the book of Jubilees or of a writing akin to Jubilees have been found at Qumran. Into the latter category falls 4Q225 II.[108] This mentions God's promise and Abram's believing response in Genesis 15.5-6. This fragment has replaced the perfect consecutivum of the MT with an imperfect consecutivum.[109] Then follows the reference to Abraham's begetting a son whom he named Isaac (Col.I, lines 8-9), and to the story of how prince Mastemah impugned Abraham's loyalty and God commanded Abraham to sacrifice Isaac (Col.I, lines 9-14). When Abraham said to his son that God would provide the lamb for sacrifice, Isaac told Abraham to tie him well[110] (Col.II line 4). The holy angels are mentioned as weeping, while the angels of Mastemah were rejoicing that Isaac would be destroyed because then Abraham's loyalty would be found to waver. God intervened to stop the proceedings,[111] and He blessed Isaac all his life (Col.II lines 5-11). This fragment has condensed the story of Abraham as recorded in Genesis 15-22. Oeming calls this telescoping "the most impressive evidence hitherto for the combination of "faith" and "readiness to sacrifice." "[112]

There is a fragment of a corporate confession of sins in 4 Q393.[113] The appeal is made to God not to forsake the people which is His inheritance, for God chose the fathers long ago. God had caused the community, which represents the fathers in the present as a remnant, to receive the covenant which God established with Abraham for Israel, that she should possess the land.[114]

---

106. Described by Vermes, *Dead Sea Scrolls*, 492, as a fragment of a "non-continuous paraphrase of Genesis."

107. In line 9, it is said that Abraham lived in Haran for five years. The length of the stay is not mentioned in the biblical record.

108. Vermes, *Dead Sea Scrolls*, 540, "Palaeographically, 4Q225 is dated to the turn of the era."

109. Oeming, *Glaube*, 29.

110. Vermes, *Dead Sea Scrolls*, 540, describes this as the earliest (pre-Christian) evidence for the rabbinic story of Isaac's voluntary self-sacrifice.

111. The text is defective. Vermes's conjectural translation (*Dead Sea Scrolls*, 542) runs: "Now I know that (it was a lie that?) he (Abraham) will no longer be loving." In another small fragment (4Q226.7), the first line states that Abraham was found faithful to [*conjecture* God] (Vermes, *Dead Sea Scrolls*, 542).

112. Oeming *Glaube*, 30. Mühling, *Blickt*, 241, points out that Ishmael is not mentioned because he is unimportant as far as the writer is concerned.

113. "The script is dated to mid-first century BCE" (Vermes, *Dead Sea Scrolls*, 396).

114. Vogel, *Heil*, 42, believes that in 4DibHam (Q504), which is also a corporate confession of repentance—with an appeal to God for help on the basis of His

We may briefly mention that in two fragments the priestly aspect of Abraham receives mention. In 4 Q214b, fragments 2–6, the Aramaic Testament of Levi,[115] Levi said that he saw Abraham taking care how he sacrificed, and that Abraham told him what types of wood should be burned on the altar.[116] While there is no regulation in the Bible about what types of wood should be burned, in the book of Jubilees 21:12–15 Abraham gave detailed instructions to Isaac about what types of wood might be burned and what their condition should be before they would be acceptable for burning.[117] It would appear, therefore, that the author ascribed priestly functions to Abraham (as in the book of Genesis), and depicts him as transmitting rules for sacrifices by priests to the generations to come after him.[118]

4Q 464 (4Q Exposition on the Patriarchs), a badly preserved series of fragments,[119] refers to Abraham and other patriarchs, and seems to express ideas akin to the statement in Jubilees 12:25–27 that the angel taught Abraham Hebrew, the language of creation (cf. Jub 3:28). In fragment 3, lines 8–9, there seems to be an allusion to Zephaniah 3:8–9: here there is a promise that, after God's judgment on the nations, He will change the speech of peoples to a pure speech, so that all of them might call on the name of the Lord and serve Him with one accord. 4Q464, fragment 3 (according to the editors) reads, "I will make the peoples pure of speech." We might assume that the author of this fragment believed that after God's judgment,

---

covenant—there may be an allusion to Abraham in the reference to Moses' atoning for their sins after the golden calf apostasy at 2:9 (he refers to Exodus 32:13, where Moses does ask God to remember His oath to Abraham, Isaac, and Jacob in the context of his appeal for mercy. Exodus 33:1 also mentions the patriarchal covenant, while 34:10 promises a covenant in the context of God's mercy). Vogel may be right, but the matter is far from certain. The writer appealed to God to remember His past wonders (2:13), His election of them (3:9), and His past maintenance of the covenant (5:11), to ensure that a limit should be placed on the execution of His wrath because of Israel's apostasy, so that the destruction of the people would be averted, and to evoke a renewed turning of God to Israel in saving activity. Vogel, *Heil*, 43, remarked rightly that "From the unbreakable nature of the covenant, those who prayed 4QDibHam drew the hope of God's mercy," but the covenant in the author's mind seems to be pre-eminently the covenant at Sinai.

115. Vermes, *Dead Sea Scrolls*, 560.

116. See van Ruiten, *Abraham*, 288–89. For a discussion about the possible relationship between the book of Jubilees, Aramaic Levi, and the Testament of Levi, see van Ruiten, *Abraham*, 282–83, 289.

117. The author of 4 Q214b may be drawing on a tradition known also to the author of Jubilees, the priestly-Levitical tradition which may go back to the third century BC and possibly earlier, which White Crawford has advocated.

118. See Mühling, *Blickt*, 236.

119. For details, see *DJD*, 19.215–30; Mühling, *Blickt*, 221–24.

the curse of Babel would be reversed and everyone would speak the pure language, Hebrew, again.[120]

In 4Q542, the Testament of Qahat,[121] the priests were commanded to preserve the heritage which they have received: "So hold to the word of Jacob, your father, and seize the laws of Abraham and the righteousness of Levi and mine." They should be holy and avoid fornication, and in this way they will "give me a good name, among you, and a rejoicing to Levi, and joy to Jacob, delight to Isaac, and glory to Abraham."[122] This link of Abraham with the laws which priests should follow is again not dissimilar to the picture in Jubilees 21:5-20, while in T. Levi 9:5-14 it was Isaac who instructed Levi in such matters.

In summary, we may say that the Qumran writings, where they do mention Abraham, reveal that members of the Qumran community believed themselves to be the heirs of the covenant made with Abraham, Isaac, and Jacob. In penitential prayers, appeal was made to God to remember this covenant so that He should put a limit on His wrath and not destroy Israel. Abraham appears as a priest in some fragments, and there is a link between him and the laws appertaining to priestly duties. The Genesis Apocryphon, as a work congenial to but not originating at Qumram, may well indicate that this priestly emphasis goes back into the third century BC and possibly earlier.

All in all, Abraham does not figure a great deal given the extent of the material found at Qumran. In view of the importance of Enoch in the Essene tradition, perhaps this is not surprising.

2.6. The First Book of Maccabees

First Maccabees[123] was written to defend the legitimacy of the Hasmonean dynasty, which had combined the royal and high priestly roles. For some, both these aspects were illegitimate: royal sovereignty belonged to the Davidic dynasty, while the high priesthood was vested in the Levitical-Aaronic line. In chapter 2, Mattathias, who had led the revolt against Antiochus Epiphanes and whom the author had compared to Phinehas in his militant

---

120. See VanderKam, *Greek at Qumran*, 176.

121. NIV; REB; NRSV print as Kohath at Gen 46:11; Num 3:17; 26:57.

122. Vermes, *Dead Sea Scrolls*, 568-69.

123. Goldstein, *First Maccabees*, 14-16, 63, maintains that the book was originally composed in Hebrew and is to be dated between 100 and 63 BC; followed by Nickelsburg, *Jewish Literature*, 117. Rappaport, *First Book of Maccabees*, 904, suggests the last decade of the rule of John Hyrcanus, i.e., 114-104 BC, as the most probable date.

zeal for the Law (2:26), was now near to death and gave a testamentary address to his sons (2:49-68). He exhorted them to be zealous for the Law, to be ready to give their lives for the covenant of their fathers, and to recall their deeds. If they do these things, they would have great glory and eternal fame (vv. 50-51). He asked: "Was not Abraham, when tested, found faithful and it was counted to him for righteousness?"[124] (v. 52). Here, while clearly Genesis 15:6 is being quoted, it is being interpreted in the light of Genesis 22 (the offering of Isaac). It is as if Genesis 15:6 is being treated as a proleptic declaration of the *faithfulness* which would be proved by Abraham's willingness to sacrifice Isaac at God's command. It is significant that the επιστευσεν of Genesis 15:6 has been replaced by εν πειρασμω πιστος. The stress is on faithfulness and fidelity. Other examples of loyalty to God in Israel's history are also recounted briefly. The sons should follow their example also. "No one who trusts in Heaven shall ever lack strength" (v. 61b). They should not fear the threats of a wicked man (a reference to Antiochus Epiphanes), whose success would only be temporary (v. 62). "But you, my sons, draw your courage and strength from the Law, for by it you will win great glory" (v. 64).

Thus, Abraham and others from the distant past, but also from the not too distant past, Mattathias himself (as shown by his deeds in 1:23-28, 45-48), were treated as models for the resistance to the efforts of Antiochus Epiphanes to obliterate faith in the God of Israel. In the contemporary situation of the author, he and his readers needed to be as vigilant against the influence of Greek culture and religion which were inimical to the Jewish faith.[125] This stress on the need to be faithful is, from a rhetorical point of view, entirely natural. At the same time, the author indicated Mattathias's conviction that the Israelite people were the recipients of a covenant which God had made with their fathers and of the Law which accompanied it. From chapters 1-2, it could also be said that Mattathias proved himself to be a true son of Abraham and to be the worthy founder of the Hasmonean dynasty.

In the account of how Judas defeated the detachment of the opposing army under Gorgias,[126] Judas rallied his men with a stirring speech which

---

124. Αβρααμ ουχι εν πειρασμω ευρεθη πιστος και ελογισθη αυτω εις δικαιοσυνην.

125. There are, so to speak, three levels: firstly, the story from centuries past of Israel's history and its heroes; secondly, from the fairly recent past, the stirring example of Mattathias and his sons in the struggle to defend the faith of Israel against Greek rulers and renegade Jews; thirdly, the contemporary situation of the author and readers, when the Hasmoneans were under criticism from some sections of the Israelite nation.

126. Antiochus IV had gone to Persia and entrusted the campaign against the Jews to Lysias, a member of the royal family. Lysias had divided his army under three

included "Let us cry now to heaven to favor our cause, to remember the covenant made with our fathers, and to crush this army before us today. Then all the Gentiles will know that there is One who saves and liberates Israel" (1 Macc 4:10-11). The covenant made with Abraham and renewed with Isaac and Jacob has soteriological significance. God will remember it and come to the aid of His people.

The author's handling of Jonathan's correspondence with the Spartans is revealing. Both his letter to the king of the Spartans (12:5-18) and a previous letter from a Spartan king in response to a letter from the high priest Onias (12:19, 23) referred to the fact that the Spartans were also descended from Abraham (cf. 2 Macc 5:9). In his letter, Jonathan made it clear that he did not regard an alliance with Sparta as a necessity (12:9). He stated that in recent years Israel had been attacked on every side but "In the course of these wars we had no wish to trouble you or the rest of our allies and friends; we have the aid of Heaven to support us, and so we have been saved from our enemies, and they have been humbled" (12:14-15). It is not descent from Abraham that necessarily matters. Only God's covenant with Israel was the foundation of Israel's unique position, and Sparta had no share in that Covenant.[127]

We need not spend time discussing whether this correspondence is genuine or not.[128] Whether genuine or not, it clearly shows that at the time of the writing of 1 Maccabees the idea that there might be other peoples of the world descended from Abraham would not have appeared strange, or else the writer would not have introduced the correspondence into his story. Gruen has pointed out that the invention of a genealogical tree represented the kind of propaganda tactic quite commonly practiced in Hellenistic milieux. He has called the idea of a kinship between Jews and Spartans the "kinship connection," and sees it as constituting another facet of attempts by Jewish intellectuals to embrace Hellenism.[129] Presumably, the reference in Genesis 17:5 to Abraham's becoming the father of many nations could be in the minds of those who pursued this approach.[130] For other Jews the divine

---

generals, Ptolemaeus, Nicanor, and Gorgias (1 Macc 3:31-41).

127. Arenhoeval, *Die Theokratie*, 33.

128. The discussion of Goldstein, *I Maccabees*, 449-59, concentrates on the issue of the historicity of the correspondence and the likelihood of knowledge of Abraham on the part of the Spartans.

129. Gruen, *Jewish Perspectives*, 77-80.

130. Meyer, *Aspekte*, 123, has listed this reference in 1 Maccabees 12 under the motif of trying to assert the universal fatherhood of Abraham over against the criticism that the Jews were nationalistic and hostile to other peoples.

insistence that Abraham's line was to be traced through Isaac recorded in Genesis 17:19-21 would be the determining factor.

In conclusion, we might say that the main significance of Abraham for readers of this book would be that they, the present generation of his descendants, must prove themselves as faithful and obedient to God as Abraham was in his day.

2.7. The Third Book of Maccabees

Third Maccabees[131] was probably written in Egypt and for Jews there. The limits within which it may have been composed are 217 BC (the date of the battle at Raphia, referred to at 1:1-5) and AD 70 (the temple is presupposed as still in existence).[132] On the basis of its affinities with certain other literature, Anderson narrows it down to the early first century BC as a reasonable hypothesis.[133]

There is one reference to Abraham in the book. This occurs within the prayer of an Eleazar, a priest. The Pharaoh Ptolemy IV, who is portrayed as a cruel and arrogant tyrant, had been baulked of his desire to enter the Holy of Holies of the Jerusalem Temple by divine intervention following the prayer of the High Priest, Simon. Ptolemy IV returned to Egypt, determined to exact revenge on the Jews and to kill those who were resident in Egypt. They were assembled in the hippodrome in Alexandria, and the plan was for elephants to attack them.

At this point, the devout Eleazar is recorded as turning to God in prayer (6:1-15). "King, great in power, Most High, all-conquering God, who governs the whole creation with mercy, look upon the seed of Abraham, upon the children of Jacob whom You sanctified, the people of Your sanctified inheritance who are perishing unjustly as strangers in a strange land" (6:1-2). He recalled instances of divine intervention to help in the Exodus, the deliverance from Sennacharib of Assyria, the three Jewish youths and Daniel in Babylon, and Jonah (vv. 3-8). Then followed an impassioned plea for deliverance from their present plight at the hands of insolent and godless

---

131. The title is really a misnomer, as the contents do not concern the Maccabean struggle for independence.

132. Anderson, "3 Maccabees," 510.

133. Anderson, "3 Maccabees," 512. Johnson, *Third Book of Maccabees*, 907-8, mentions the division between proponents of a date in the late Ptolemaic period and one in the early Roman period (27 BC-AD 49), with the balance of scholarly opinion titling slightly to the Hellenistic period.

idolaters so that it might be made clear that God had not turned His face away from His people (vv. 9–15).

In the eventuality, the elephants turned on the friends of Ptolemy, and the Jews were not harmed (6:15–29). As a result of this divine rescue, their status was reassured. They had cause for celebration and held a great feast to mark their deliverance (6:30–41).

We see that the Jews consider themselves to be descendants of Abraham and of Jacob, set apart as a special inheritance for God. It was important for them to know that God had not turned His face away from them and abandoned them to their foes. The story of this deliverance would act as an encouragement to Jews facing hostility, in the Diaspora in general and especially in Egypt in particular.

2.8. The First Book of Enoch (or The Ethiopic Enoch)

There is no reference to Abraham by name in the corpus of *1 Enoch*,[134] but he is alluded to in two sections. There is an allusion to him in the *Apocalypse of Weeks*,[135] in 1 Enoch 93. Enoch recounts the history of the world in seven weeks, of which four have already past, three are yet to come. During the second week, iniquity increased and an end (of the world) is brought about, but one man (a reference to Noah) would be saved. Iniquity still continued and a law was given to hold it in check (a reference to the prohibition of shedding of blood, recorded in Gen 9). The author then said that at the end of the third week (the continuation of violence and iniquity is presumed), "a

---

134. 1 Enoch 1–36 and 92–105 (or parts of 92–105) may have formed the earliest part of the Enoch corpus, with chapters 81–82, 91 serving as a narrative bridge between these two complexes, and may go back to the late third century BC. Chapters 83–90 may have belonged to the testament of Enoch or been a later addition. Later, at different times, this core was expanded with chapters 106–7; 72–80 (which in origin may also go back into the third century BC, so Nickelsburg and VanderKam, *1 Enoch 2*, 345); 37–71; and finally, 108. See Nickelsburg, *Jewish Literature*, 150–51; *1 Enoch 1*, 25; Nickelsburg and VanderKam, *1 Enoch 2*, 337–38, 346–47, 360–61. In *1 Enoch 2*, 58–63, Nickelsburg dates chapters 37–71 to between the latter part of Herod's reign and the early decades of the first century AD. Rowland, *Open Heaven*, 250–52, 255, 266, tentatively suggests as a general guide the third century BC (250) for 1 Enoch 1–36 and the second century BC for 1 Enoch 83–90 (ca. 165) and 91–105 (ca. 140). Stokes, "Book of the Watchers," 1332–34, reports a scholarly agreement to a date sometime during the third century, while Knibb, "Similitudes of Enoch," 585–87, thinks of the end of the first century AD in response to the fall of Jerusalem for the Similitudes, though he also mentions that a good case has been made for a date around the turn of the era.

135. Stuckenbruck, "Epistle of Enoch," 584, suggests a date between 175 and 170 BC when some Jews were supporting the Hellenizing reforms of Antiochus IV Epiphanes.

man shall be elected as the plant of righteous judgment, and after him will go forth the plant of righteousness forever and ever" (93:5). Abraham was chosen to begin the process of instilling in the world "the righteousness... that had been lost with the removal of Enoch at the end of the first week."[136] Abraham's descendants, the people of Israel, were also to continue his role of establishing righteousness in the world.

At the close of the sixth week, the temple would be destroyed and the exile in Babylon would occur: "the whole race of the chosen root shall be dispersed" (v. 8). The "chosen root" is probably a reference to Abraham.[137] The seventh week embraces the period from the exile to the writer's own day and will be a period of apostasy. At its completion, however, at the End, God would choose the elect righteous ones from within Israel, "from the eternal plant of righteousness." They would be given sevenfold wisdom and knowledge (vv. 9-10). They have an unspecified role in establishing righteousness and uprooting the foundations of violence (see 91:11-12). These elect represented the community to which the author belonged. They regarded themselves as the true descendants of Abraham, who himself is "the eternal plant of righteousness."

Within what is entitled *The Dream Visions* (1 En 83-90), in the section regarded as a second dream vision (1 En 85-90),[138] the author allegorized human beings as animals. Abraham is alluded to as a white bull (a good person) amidst a series of other animals, all unclean in Jewish eyes and many of them fierce predators (89:10). These other animals represented Gentiles whose violent and rapacious characters boded ill for the Israel living in their midst.

All that is said about Abraham is that he begat a wild ass/boar [= Ishmael] and a white bull [=Isaac] (89:11). The white bull=Isaac begat a black wild boar=Esau and a white ram of the flock=Jacob, who begat twelve sheep=twelve patriarchs of Israel (89:12). The author made a clear distinction between the descendants of Abraham.[139] Ishmael and Esau were excluded from the chosen people; the line of God's people went from Abraham to Isaac and then to Jacob and his twelve sons. Matthew Thiessen maintains that "the author does not in any way suggest that the differences between Ishmael and Isaac, Esau and Jacob . . . lie within the actions of these

---

136. Nickelsburg, *1 Enoch 1*, 444.

137. Unless the genitive is in apposition—"the whole root, the chosen root, shall be dispersed." This is listed as a possibility in Nickelsburg, *1 Enoch 1*, 447.

138. Nickelsburg, *Jewish Literature*, 93, dates to 164-60 BC, while Nickelsburg and VanderKam, *1 Enoch 2*, 360-61, refines this to 165-63 BC. Assefa, "Book of Dreams," 552, states "usually dated to 165-164 BCE."

139. See Thiessen, *Contesting Conversion*, 89-94.

characters; rather their nature is imparted to them at birth and is immutable regardless of their actions."[140] He also maintains that the author was hostile to links between Jews and Idumeans in the period before John Hyrcanus converted and absorbed the Idumeans into the Jewish Kingdom.[141]

Obviously, Enoch plays the supreme role in 1 Enoch; so it is perhaps not so surprising that we do not find many references to Abraham. Enochian Judaism saw itself as the inheritor of the role for which Abraham was elected, to bring righteousness to a world dominated by evil. It saw itself as "a plant of righteousness."

We may ask why it was that Enochian Judaism looked to Enoch more than it did to Abraham, and that at a time when the stature of Abraham in Jewish thought was increasing? Although sparse,[142] the information which Genesis 5:21-24 offered is intriguing and must have fascinated many within the Jewish community. If we leave aside the reference to those whom he fathered (v. 21a-22), we can say that there are some very important things said of Enoch. In the first place, there is the highly significant statement that he "walked with God"(v. 21, repeated at v. 24). Secondly, it is said that "he was not, for God took him"[143] (v. 24). Thirdly, he lived 365 years (v. 23).

Let us compare this with the picture of Abraham in Genesis. While twice in the Hebrew Scriptures it is said of Abraham that he was the friend of God, he is never described with the words "he walked with God."[144] Indeed, on at least a number of occasions, it could be claimed that his behavior was lacking. His assertion that Sarah was his sister was far from being the whole truth; at 17:15-18, he clearly felt that the promise of a son by Sarah was laughable; it could be said that he—and Sarah—tried to take the matter of descendants into his own hands and fathered a child by Hagar.

Abraham died and was buried. Here was a striking difference between him and Enoch. From the fact that Enoch existed in the realm of heaven, those who pored over the scriptures could deduce that he would be in possession of all sorts of celestial and cosmic mysteries.

---

140. Thiessen, *Contesting*, 91.

141. Thiessen, *Contesting*, 94, in agreement with Kasher, *Jews, Idumaeans, and Ancient Arabs*, 27, 75.

142. "The passage . . . gives the impression of being only a brief reference to a much more extensive tradition" (Von Rad, *Genesis*, 70) and raises the question whether much of the apocalyptic Enoch tradition preceded the Priestly narrative.

143. Von Rad, *Genesis*, 70, points out that the verb *laqah* is a theological term for translation into otherworldly spheres of existence (2 Kgs 2:10; Ps 49:15).

144. Von Rad, *Genesis*, 69, contrasts the fact that Enoch walked *with* God, whereas Abraham walked *before* God.

The huge difference in the length of their lifetimes—Enoch 365 years, Abraham 175 years (Gen 25:7)—could also be interpreted as a further pointer to the superiority of Enoch.

In view of these points, it is not difficult to understand that for some Jews Enoch could become a revered figure, around whom there could become attached various speculations about the mysteries of heaven and the cosmos and of history.

2.9. Fragments of Jewish Writers

There is some interesting material contained in the *Fragments of Jewish Writers* which have been preserved in either Jewish writers like Josephus, Christian writers such as Clement of Alexandria and Eusebius of Caesarea, or pagan writers like Alexander Polyhistor.[145] It would appear that most of these writers were Jews who lived in the Diaspora, many in Egypt.

We begin with *Demetrius the Chronographer*, who may have written in the reign of Ptolemy IV of Egypt (221–204 BC).[146] Fragment 3 of his writing is concerned with Moses, but what interests us is the fact that he connected Zipporah, the wife of Moses, genealogically with Abraham via Midian, one of the sons whom Abraham had by Kenturah after Sarah's death (Gen 25:1–4). In this way he legitimized Moses' taking a Midianite wife (according to Num 12:1, Aaron and Miriam had criticized their brother for marrying a Cushite woman). This illustrates the importance of preserving a pure descent from Abraham.

Artapanus, who may have been an Egyptian Jew and may have written towards the end of the third century BC or the beginning of the second century BC,[147] or even the middle of the second century,[148] wrote of Abraham as the ancestor of the Jews and claimed that it was he who taught the Egyptians astrology during a twenty-year residence there. Behind this claim lies the conviction of the superiority of Jewish faith and culture over against Egypt.[149]

---

145. These fragments have been conveniently gathered together in translation with discussion in Charlesworth, *OTP*, 2:775–918 ("Supplement: Fragments of Lost Judeo-Hellenistic Works"), on which we have relied. For a discussion of the picture of Abraham in these fragments, see Meyer, *Aspekte*, 118–27.

146. See Hanson, *Demetrius the Chronographer*, 843–54, esp. 844, 852–53 (Fragment 3); Adler, *Demetrius the Chronographer*, 530–31.

147. See Collins, *Artapanus*, 889–903, esp. 890–91, 897 (Fragment 1).

148. Bowley, *Artapanus*, 386–87.

149. In a much larger fragment dealing with Moses, preserved by Eusebius (see Collins, *Artapanus*, 898–903), Artapanus claims that Moses, who was called Musaeus

Another writer who may have written at the turn of the third and second centuries BC was *Philo the Epic Poet*,[150] who wrote a work entitled *On Jerusalem* in verse. In a panegyric on Abraham, he weote that Abraham's prayers were loved by God and full of wondrous counsels. When Abraham was about to sacrifice Isaac, God (described as the praiseworthy thunderer) quenched the pyre and made His promise (presumably a reference to descendants) immortal. From that moment on, the descendants of Isaac (described as "that awesome born one") have won praise from distant people.

Ezekiel the Tragedian[151] wrote about the Exodus in the form of Greek tragedy. In the scene of the Burning Bush, God identified Himself as the God of Abram, Isaac, and Jacob, and said that it was because of His promises to them that He was about to intervene to save the Hebrew people whose cries He had heard (lines 104–8).

We turn now to *Hecateus/Pseudo-Hecateus*.[152] Both Josephus (*Ant.* 1.159) and Clement of Alexander (*Strom.* 5.113) state that Hecateus wrote a book about Abraham. There seems to be agreement that this should be ascribed to a Pseudo-Hecateus.[153] Other statements by Josephus in Against

---

by the Greeks, was the teacher of Orpheus, thus making Moses the father of Greek poetry and prophetic traditions. In addition, he was an inventor of many useful artefacts and weaponry together with philosophy. On this, see Gruen, *Jewish Perspectives*, 71–72.

150. See Attridge, *Philo the Epic Poet*, 781–84, esp. 781, 783 (Fragments 1–2); Collins, *Philo the Epic Poet*, 1080, opts for sometime before Alexander the Great.

151. See Robertson, *Ezekiel the Tragedian*, 803–819, esp. 804, with hesitation in default of hard evidence, suggests a date in "perhaps the first part of the second century BC." Van der Horst, *Ezekiel the Tragedian*, 620, suggests probably the middle of the second century. Niehoff, *Philo on Jewish Identity*, 23, points out that Ezekiel the Tragedian assumed that Moses could choose to marry even a dark-skinned Ethiopian, which fits with Ptolemaic times but not under Roman administration. Since the Romans took control of Egypt after the battle of Actium, this does not actually help to pin down the date more closely than Robertson's suggestion.

152. There was a Greek historian called Hecateus of Abdera who wrote under Ptolemy I about 300 BC, who appears to have thought highly of the Jewish constitution to judge by reference to it in Diodorus Siculus. The pro-Jewish slant of other fragments attributed to him has caused some scholars to attribute them to another writer (or writers) given the title Pseudo-Hecataeus (I and II). Doran, *Pseudo-Hecataeus*, 905–918; Mühling, *Blickt*, 274–77, discuss the arguments for and against authorship by Hecateus. While Mühling, *Blickt*, 276, in dependence on the study of N. Walter, adheres to Pseudo-Hecateus, Doran (*Pseudo-Hecataeus*, 907) defends the authenticity of fragments 1–4, rejects the references to Hecateus in Josephus, *Ant.* 1.159, and Clement Stromateis 5.113, as incorrect, and accepts that they are references to a work by a Pseudo-Hecateus. For brief reviews, see Bethelot, *Hecateus of Abdera*, 718–19; Collins, *Pseudo-Hecateus*, 718.

153. So even Doran, "Cleodemus Malchus," 907, 909; Collins, *Pseudo-Hecataeus*, 718.

Apion are regarded as problematic.¹⁵⁴ The fragment in Clement says that Hecateus in his book quoted a strong affirmation of monotheism and a sharp criticism of idolatry by the Greek poet Sophocles. From this, it is assumed that Pseudo-Hecateus must have discussed Abraham's monotheistic beliefs. Walter goes further and claims that this work is behind the material which Josephus used in his section on Abraham and which he did not get from the biblical Genesis, viz. Abraham's visit to Egypt to discuss the nature of the gods/God.¹⁵⁵

Of the other fragments attributed to Hecateus, none of them actually mention Abraham, and so for our purpose need not be discussed.

Pseudo-Hecateus might well have been an Egyptian Jew responding to his environment and asserting the superiority of Jewish religious and cultural beliefs.¹⁵⁶

The Greek historian Alexander Polyhistor quoted from the work of a Jewish historian called *Eupolemus*. Both Clement of Alexandria and Eusebius of Caesarea give excerpts from these quotations. The latter seems to be quoting verbatim, whereas Clement summarized the contents. There are in all six fragments, of which the sixth is only preserved by Clement. This Eupolemeus has been identified with the ambassador of that name sent by Judas Maccabeus to Rome (1 Macc 8:17-18; 2 Macc 4:11), a member of a priestly family. Since Abraham is not specifically mentioned, we may pass over these passages without further comment.

There are, however, two further fragments within Eusebius's discussion of Abraham in his Praeparatio Evangelica. One of these is said to come from Alexander Polyhistor who assigned it to Eupolemus, while the other is said to be anonymous. Scholars disagree whether in fact the first is from Eupolemus or another writer given the nomenclature of *Pseudo-Eupoleus*.¹⁵⁷ In the first of these excerpts, Abraham is said to have originated in Babylon, surpassed all in nobility and excellence, and possessed knowledge of astrology and the Chaldean craft. He was pious and well pleasing to God. At God's command he went to Phoenicia and passed on his knowledge of

---

154. Collins, *Pseudo-Hecateus*, 718.

155. For Walter's arguments, see Doran, "Pseudo-Hecataeus," 906-7, 909; Mühling, *Blickt*, 274-77. For a very general discussion of the way Jewish writers sought to find theological ideas of the Hebrews in Greek writers, see Gruen, *Jewish Perspectives*, 74-77.

156. See the characterization in Mühling, *Blickt*, 275-77. Collins, "Pseudo-Hecateus," 718, characterizes the work as belonging "to the corpus of pseudepigraphic works supposedly written by Gentile authors" designed to promote "the glory of Judaism and its teachings."

157. See Doran, "Pseudo-Eupolemus," 873-82; "Eupolemus," 611-12; "Pseudo-Eupolemus," 612-13. Doran, "Pseudo-Eupolemus," 873-82, esp. 874-76, denies that there was a Pseudo-Eupolemus.

the heavenly bodies there. The author described Abraham also as a courageous fighter who did not seek his own personal gain, released the prisoners of war, and only financed his own soldiers. The meeting with Melchizedek took place on Mount Gerizim (which could suggest the Samaritan origin of the author) and, contrary to Genesis 14, Abraham received gifts from Melchizedek (not the other way round), and there is no mention of the tithe paid to Melchizedek. Then Abraham went to Egypt where the Pharaoh married Sarah, but, as he was unable to have intercourse with her, restored her to Abraham. Abraham explained astrology and other sciences to the priests. He himself attributed the discovery of astrology to Enoch whom the author identified with the Greek Atlas. The author said that Methuselah was the son of Enoch, and he learned everything through the angels of God and so "knowledge came to us."

A second, short fragment preserved in Eusebius may originally have comprised disparate elements brought together by Alexander Polyhistor. The first half linked Abraham with Babylon, and stated that he was descended from the giants who were destroyed because of their wickedness. The second half could be a brief summary of the longer fragment just summarized above, since it refers to Abraham's knowledge of astrology and how he passed it on to the Phoenicians, and then he went to Egypt.

Eupolemus/Pseudo-Eupolemus evinced a clear desire to show the antiquity of Jewish culture and its superiority to Egyptian culture. Abraham was important in this propaganda warfare, in the fragment which we have.[158] The fact that Abraham received gifts from Melchizedek and did not tithe on behalf of Melchizedek may also be due to the desire to enhance the dignity of the forefather of the nation.

Finally, we come to *Cleodemus Malchus*, who may have lived in Carthage and who wrote before Alexander Polyhistor who utilized him, i.e., before 50 BC.[159] Cleodemus mentioned that two of the sons whom Abraham had by Kenturah, Afera and Iafra, fought with Heracles in his campaign in Libya. They joined him in the attempt to bring civilisation to a barbarous land. Heracles married a daughter of Afera. The city of Afra and the region of Africa were named after Afera and Iafra respectively.

---

158. In one of the fragments from Eupolemus (Fallon, *Eupolemus*, 865), Moses is credited with handing on knowledge of the alphabet to the Jews and the Phoenicians received it from them, and subsequently the Greeks received it from the Phoenicians. Gruen, *Jewish Perspectives*, 71, commented that this made the Greeks indirect beneficiaries of the Hebrews, not their antagonists.

159. So Doran, *Cleodemus Malchus*, 883–87. Bowley, *Cleodemus Malchus*, 476, describes him as a second-century BCE Hellenistic author.

On this reckoning, Abraham would be the grandfather-in-law of Heracles and so the ancestor of those who lived in Mauretia.[160] Since Abraham was older than Heracles who was regarded by the Greeks as the bringer of culture, by implication, it was Abraham who actually had this role. Gruen sees this as a combination of what he calls the "kinship connection," and the idea of the indebtedness of Greek culture to Hebrew culture (a kind of cultural aggrandizement).[161]

Although not characteristic of every writers discussed in this section, we may say that *the theme of the superiority of Jewish culture and religion is quite prominent*, and this is often linked with the figure of Abraham and how he taught other nationalities certain branches of knowledge. This was part of the Jewish need to establish their identity and place within the Hellenistic milieu of their day. Gruen has shown how the picture of Jewish attitudes to Hellenistic culture was not one sidedly antagonistic and that in the same writer can be found criticism of idolatry and these more positive attempts to reach out to Greek civilisation.[162]

2.10. The Psalms of Solomon

Abraham does not figure prominently in the collection of psalms known as *The Psalms of Solomon*, which are generally dated to the middle years of the first century BC and located in Jerusalem.[163]

In Psalm 9, the writer referred to the expulsion from the land and the Babylonian exile. He accepted that the people were responsible for their actions, and acknowledged that God judges fairly and with complete

---

160. See Meyer, *Aspekte*, 122–23, who sees here a desire to combat the idea that the Jews were hostile to other races.

161. Gruen, *Jewish Perspectives*, 71–83.

162. See Gruen, Jewish Perspectives, 62–93.

163. Gray, *APOT*, 2:628, dates to the middle of the first century BC; Maier, *Mensch und freier Wille*, 264–80, between 63 and 40 BC; Nickelsburg, *Jewish Literature*, 203, the middle decades of the first century; Wright, *Psalms of Solomon*, 641, about 70 to 45 BC; Winninge, *Sinners and the Righteous*, 13, posits 70 to 40 BC; and Atkinson, *Psalms of Solomon*, 1238–40, suggested that the collection was edited and possibly expanded to include new poems, between 48 and 42 BCE, following Pompey's death, which is referred to at 2:26–27. These psalms have been linked with the Pharisees in the past, and Nickelsburg, *Jewish Literature*, 203; Winninge, *Sinners*, 141–80, still hold to this position, but some scholars are hesitant about the view that the *Psalms of Solomon* originated from within Pharisaic circles. See Wright, *Psalms of Solomon*, 642, where the general editor (Charlesworth) suggests that it is unwise to label them either Pharisaic or Essene. Yinger, *Paul, Judaism, and Judgment*, 75, classified them as an expression of early Palestinian hasidism.

knowledge. He appealed to God for compassion because "we are the people whom You have loved . . . for we are yours . . . for You chose the descendants of Abraham above all the nations and You put Your name upon us, Lord, and it will not cease forever." He then went on to say "You made a covenant with our fathers concerning us" (9:9-10). The relevance of the covenant with the fathers for the generation of the writer is clear. Hope is based on the fact of God's election of His people (v. 10). The group behind these psalms believed that "if they remain within the covenant, by acknowledging their sins and accepting divine punishment, then God would carry out justice in the resurrection if it is not administered in this world."[164]

There is a further reference to Abraham in Psalm 18, where we read "Your love is for the descendants of Abraham," and this is followed by the assertion "Your discipline for us (is) as (for) a firstborn son, an only child" (vv. 3b-4a). God's fatherly love and discipline are reserved for the descendants of Abraham; they are like (ὡς) an only son.

It should be pointed out that the covenant with David is also of crucial importance for the author as can be seen in Psalm 17. That is the basis of his opposition to the Hasmonean dynasty. But there is no need to set the Davidic covenant against the patriarchal one,[165] especially since David was a descendant of Abraham.

The author clearly believed that God had chosen Abraham and his descendants forever, though equally Israelites needed to walk in His ways in response.

2.11. The Book of Judith

The *Book of Judith* could be the product of a rewriting of a story from the Persian period. The story has been recycled for the Hasmonean period.[166]

Chapters 1-7 describe the crisis facing Israel: the approach of the armies of Nebuchadnezzar under his general, Holofernes. We learn of the

---

164. Atkinson, *Enduring the Lord's Discipline*, 163. Atkinson points out (161) that the group believed that it was necessary to be within the covenant, yet because of their conviction that the temple was defiled, they had separated from it, and believed that frequent prayer, fasting, and daily acts of piety merited salvation from God.

165. As does Wright (and Schwartz), *Psalms of Solomon*, 645, who believes that the covenant which was central to the writer's thought was the Davidic one.

166. See Nickelsburg, *Jewish Literature*, 109. He comments that it is generally agreed that the Greek form of the book is a translation from a Hebrew archetype. Moore, *Judith*, 67-68, dates to the reign of John Hyrcanus (ca. 135-104 BC); followed by Bird, *Waiting for His Deliverance*, 17. Halpern-Amaru, *Book of Judith*, 856, speaks of a scholarly consensus of the Maccabean-Hasmonean era, a more precise dating remaining elusive.

advice given to Holofernes by the leader of the Ammonites, Achior. Referring to the Israelites, Achior said that they were descended from the Chaldeans. They had refused to worship the ancestral gods of Chaldea and embraced the worship of the God of Heaven whom they now acknowledged. The Chaldeans drove them out, and they settled in Mesopotamia, from where their god had ordered them to leave and settle in Canaan. There they have acquired great wealth in gold, silver, and cattle (5:6–10).

That here we have a reference to Abraham can hardly be doubted. Mühling goes so far as to see here a corrective of the tradition contained in Joshua's speech in Joshua 24:2, 14.[167] It certainly represents an alternative tradition.

Holophernes rejected the advice of Achior, and set up a blockade of the town of Bethulia with the resultant dismay among the ranks of the Israelites and their decision to surrender the town. Judith, a wealthy widow, summoned the elders of the town and reprimanded them for the decision to surrender. She accused them of putting God to the test and arousing His anger. As a people, the Israelites have acknowledged no god but the Lord and they could be confident that He would not spurn them.

> We have every reason to give thanks to the Lord our God; He is putting us to the test as He did our ancestors. Remember how He dealt with Abraham and how He tested Isaac[168] and what happened to Jacob in Syrian Mesopotamia when he was working as a shepherd for his uncle Laban. He is not subjecting us to the fiery ordeal by which He tested their loyalty, or taking vengeance on us; it is for discipline that the Lord scourges His worshippers. (8:26–27)

In general, the story of the patriarchs is exploited for the idea of God's putting them to the test and saving them. In the particular case of Abraham and Isaac, some scholars think that the story of Genesis 22 may be in mind, when God tested Abraham and asked him to sacrifice Isaac, his only son. The phrase οσα επειρασα τον Ισαακ is striking, and hardly fits the text of Genesis 22 as it stands. Other possibilities are that the story of Isaac in Gerar of the Philistines in Genesis 26:1 may have been in mind, or indeed his entire life.[169]

---

167. Mühling, *Blickt*, 123.

168. Does the author here reveal an acquaintance with an interpretation of Genesis 22 in which the role of Isaac had become a more active rather than a passive one? Neither Vermes nor Levenson mention this passage from Judith in their studies of the Aqedah.

169. So Mühling, *Blickt*, 26. Moore, *Judith*, 183, suggests that Isaac's whole life was

PART II — ABRAHAM IN EARLY JUDAISM

The author intends the same message for his contemporaries. In the struggle for independence against Antiochus IV, the Jews need to display the same faithful obedience as Abraham, Isaac, and Jacob displayed in their time of testing. If they do so, they, like their forebears, will know God's saving power.[170]

12. The Testaments of the Twelve Patriarchs

How the *Testaments of the Twelve Patriarchs* arose is a matter of considerable debate. Long before the discovery of the Qumran material, Charles believed that the original writing had been expanded by Jewish editors, and then subsequently Christian editors also added material. He dated the original to between 137 and 107 BC, and narrowed it still further to 109-107 BC.[171] Kee contented himself with the Maccabean period as the date of origin of the Testaments.[172] The discovery of a Testament of Naphtali in Hebrew and a Testament of Levi in Aramaic (considerably longer than the extant Greek version) at Qumran raises a number of possibilities. For some scholars, these works have suggested that there might have been an original Jewish collection of Testaments, which was probably expanded by Jewish editors and was certainly interpolated by Christians, or the two found in Qumran may have been the beginnings of what became a full-scale collection of twelve testaments, later interpolated by Christians.[173] On the other hand, members of the so-called Leiden school under the leadership of M. de Jonge have argued that the Testaments should be interpreted as they

---

something of a test — he did not have an easy life. See previous note.

170. Moore, *Judith*, 183; Mühling, *Blickt*, 127-28, point to similar coloring between Ozias's praise of Judith and the language used by Melchizedek when he went out to meet Abraham in Genesis 14:19-20. Mühling speculates on the relationship between Judith and Genesis 14 in view of the fact that Genesis 14 was a late addition to the Abraham stories.

171. Charles, *Testaments*, 288-291.

172. Kee, "Testaments," 777-78.

173. See the brief discussions in Nickelsburg, *Jewish Literature*, 233-34; Kee, "Testaments," 776-80, and the more detailed survey in Kugler, *Testaments of the Twelve Patriarchs*. Rost, *Judaism Outside the Hebrew Canon*, 144-45, points out that the two testaments found at Qumran are of a different genre to our present testaments and are dependent on two visions which prefigure the future. He thought that the Aramaic Levi reflected the assumption of the high priesthood by Jonathan in 153 BC and the Hebrew Naphtali came later, as the Maccabean kingdom pressed northwards, and contains a warning against union with the Samaritans. The present collection of twelve testaments came afterwards.

stand in their present form and that they aimed at a Christian audience.[174] We cannot enter into this debate here. Suffice to say that while we may accept that the Testaments, in the form in which we now have them, did aim at those who were Christians or interested in the Christian faith, it remains true that a substantial amount of Jewish material has been taken over in the Testaments. It is, therefore, not illegitimate to include them in this survey of early Judaism.[175] That said, the amount of material on Abraham is not that substantial, and no great loss would ensue if this section were to be omitted. The material basically reinforces themes already present in the other literature surveyed.

The *Testament of Levi* records a vision granted to Levi of the divine throne room. He was informed that he would be a priest (2:6-10; 5:1). He was given a commission to avenge the rape of his sister, Dinah (5:3). Levi said that he had wished to avenge his sister without involving the Shechemites in the rite of circumcision, but his father had not listened. In the eventuality, he had avenged his sister to the anger and sadness of his father (6:3-7). But Levi knew that the Shechemites were guilty in the sight of God, and alleged that they had wanted to do the same to Sarah and Rebecca, but God had prevented them (6:8). He continued "They persecuted Abraham when he was a nomad, and they harassed his flocks when they were pregnant, and they grossly mistreated Eblaen, who had been born in this house" (6:9). This tradition is not otherwise known, and does not depend on Genesis. It seems as if the author has identified Hamor and the Shechemites with Abimelech and the people of Gerar (Gen 20), though Genesis 20 and 21:22-34 indicate peaceful relationships between Abraham and Abimelech.

Levi had a second vision in which he was invested with the insignia of the priesthood.[176] There is a reference to one of his posterity who would be beloved, as a prophet of the Most High, a descendant of Abraham, our father (8:15). Exactly who is in mind is difficult to determine;[177] suffice to say for our purposes that Abraham is regarded as the father of the nation.

---

174. See the survey in Kugler, *Testaments*, 31-38, 99, and the recent defense of this methodology in de Bruin, *Great Controversy*, 27-35, 47-48. See de Bruin's bibliography for a list of the numerous publications of de Jonge and also of Hollander, de Jonge's pupil, colleague, and collaborator in a commentary on the Testaments.

175. See the approach of Kugler, *Testaments*, 1296.

176. Jubilees 30:17-23 also links the conferral of the priesthood on Levi as a result of his zeal in avenging the rape of Dinah.

177. Opinion varies between three figures being in mind (Moses, Aaron, and John Hyrcanus), and three offices (priests, judges and scribes, and guardians of the sanctuary).

The writer seems to refer in chapter 15 to the desecration of the Temple and the persecution at the hands of Antiochus Epiphanes, and interpreted this as the just judgment of God (vv. 1–3). "And unless you had received mercy through Abraham, Isaac, and Jacob, our fathers, not a single one of our seed[178] would be left on the earth" (v. 4). Probably, what is in mind here is the covenant which God made with Abraham and renewed to the other patriarchs. This is indicative again of how much the patriarchs are part of Jewish thinking and how soteriologically significant the covenant with them was for Israel.[179]

Later, in the description of the eschatological High Priest from the tribe of Levi, the writer said that sanctification would come upon him from heaven, together "with a fatherly[180] voice as from Abraham to Isaac" (18:6). This seems to mean that God would acknowledge the eschatological Levitical High Priest as His messianic son (as Abraham acknowledged Isaac as his son). After a description of the blessings which this messianic High Priest would bring, it is said "Then Abraham, Isaac, and Jacob will rejoice" (v. 14). Naturally, they will participate in the joys of the age to come.

The final reference is to the fact that after his death Levi was buried in Hebron with Abraham, Isaac, and Jacob (19:5).

In the *Testament of Judah*, Judah claimed that he was blessed by both Abraham[181] and Jacob as one destined to be the king in Israel. Thus, he knew that through him the kingdom would be established (17:5–6). Isaac seems to be ignored and Abraham is described as the father of Judah's father (17:5). It is possible that there is an allusion to Abraham in chapter 24, the prophecy of a messiah to come. The Messiah is called "the shoot of God" (v. 4) who "will arise from your root" (v. 5). Abraham may be intended by the phrase "your root."[182]

Belief in the resurrection of the three patriarchs emerges in this Testament at 25:1: "After this [viz. the arrival of the messiah and the establishment of justice and peace] Abraham, Isaac, and Jacob will be resurrected

---

178. So Charles, *Testaments*, 313. Kee, "Testaments," 793, has "your descendants."

179. The view of VanLangingham, *Judgment & Justification*, 53, that underlying this kind of reference to the covenant made with Abraham and the other patriarchs is "the conviction that if God allowed Israel to be destroyed, he would be either faithless, or unrighteous, or forgetful. God's mercy and grace, then, is not simply free and unmerited, but the rightful and faithful fulfilment of his obligation to Abraham," runs the risk of imposing alien categories into the assessment of this Jewish work. For a general criticism of VanLangingham, see Dunn, *New Perspective*, 66–68.

180. So Kee, "Testaments," 795. Charles, *Testaments*, 314, "With the Father's voice."

181. Charles, *Testaments*, 321, preferred the reading Isaac in d A. Would that not be the easier reading?

182. So Hofius, *Das Evangelium und Israel*, 186–87n42.

to life and I and my brothers will be chiefs (wielding) our sceptre in Israel." Beliar's spirit of error will be destroyed and Israel will be "one people of the Lord with one language."[183] At the resurrection Israel will be reconstituted as of old. She would be incomplete without the founding fathers. Those who died in sorrow, those who died in poverty for the Lord's sake, and those who died for the Lord's sake, are among those also specifically mentioned as enjoying the future resurrection.[184]

There is a reference to all three patriarchs in the *Testament of Asher*. Asher predicted to his sons that in the future their descendants would sin and be scattered, but the Lord would gather them together through His tender mercy and "on account of Abraham, Isaac, and Jacob" (7:7). Charles bracketed verses 4-7 as a first century BC addition.[185] Whether this is a correct verdict or not, the passage as we have it shows once again the standing of Abraham and the other patriarchs in the pre-Christian era. For their sake, God will gather the scattered Israelites and return them to their land.

The patriarch *Dan* is said to have been buried with Abraham, Isaac, and Jacob (T. Dan 7:1-2).

In the *Testament of Naphtali*, he said that his mother, Bilhah, was the daughter of Rotheos, who was of Abraham's tribe, a Chaldean. She honored God. She was free and well-born, but was taken captive and sold to Laban (1:10). The aim was to show that Bildad was descended from Abraham, even if she was a concubine of Jacob. The Hebrew version of the Testament of Naphtali found at Qumran mentions that whereas the seventy nations worship the guardian angel appointed over them by God, Abraham chose the one God and Creator as Guide and Protector for him and his descendants.

Mention should be made of the reference in the *Testament of Joseph*, when he is describing how he was able to withstand the attempt by Potiphar's wife to seduce him. Initially, he refused to eat the food with which she sought to entice him. But after praying aloud "May the God of my fathers and the angel of Abraham be with me," he did eat, in order to show her that those who trust in the living God are enabled to exercise self-control (6:7). Where in the Genesis story the angel who appears to Abraham is a circumlocution for God, here the angel seems to be given an independence (as it were).[186]

---

183. Since Israel is in mind, the language is probably Hebrew. Israelites from the dispersion will be fluent in Hebrew!

184. See Nickelsburg, *Resurrection, Immortality, and Eternal Life*, 50.

185. This position is not shared by Kee, "Testaments," 818.

186. Cf. the note in Kee, "Testaments," 820.

Finally, the *Testament of Benjamin* opens with the statement that just as Isaac was born to Abraham in his old age, so Benjamin was born to Jacob (1:1). When Benjamin was dying, he said to his sons that he bequeathed to them the Law and its commandments rather than an inheritance, and urged them to pass them on to their children for an eternal possession, for this is what Abraham, Isaac, and Jacob did. They said "Keep God's commandments until the Lord reveals his salvation to all nations" (10:2–5). At this revelation of God's salvation, which coincides with the general resurrection and the final judgment, they would see Enoch, Noah, Seth, Abraham, Isaac, and Jacob raised to life at God's right hand with great joy (10:6).[187]

Summary

What emerges from these references to Abraham and the other patriarchs is chiefly the soteriological significance of the covenant which God made with them for their descendants, and the conviction that the three patriarchs will share in the general resurrection and in the blessings of the age to come. The idea of Abraham being persecuted by the Shechemites seems unique, while in the case of Naphtali the demonstration that his mother was a member of the Abrahamic group could reflect concerns about endogamy.[188]

2.13. The Wisdom of Solomon

The *Wisdom of Solomon*[189] evinces a combination of the wisdom traditions of Israel and Greek philosophical thought. The work is usually divided into

---

187. See the brief discussion in Nickelsburg, *Resurrection*, 176–77.

188. Baltzer, *Covenant Formulary*, 144–46, argued that in the Testaments, the place of the Acts of God ("antecedent history") in the covenant formulary has been replaced by "Example" (the lives of the patriarchs as examples of virtue or warnings against vice).

189. Based on the severe criticism of especially Egyptian idolatry, together with an emphasis on the judgment of God on Egypt at the time of the Exodus, Nickelsburg, *Jewish Literature*, 184, suggests that the work not only was written to strengthen the faith of Egyptian Jews but also to try and convince non-Jews. Although dating is not easy, he thinks that the work was probably composed in the early decades of the first century AD. Winston, *Wisdom of Solomon*, 20–25, 59, narrows the date of composition down to AD 37–41. This is unlikely in the opinion of Harrington, *Saved by Wisdom*, 182, who thinks that a first-century BC date is very likely, though any date from the second century BC to the first century AD is possible. Hubner, *Die Weisheit Salomons*, 19, considers a date in the reign of Augustus after his capture of Alexandria (30 BC–AD 14). McGlynn, *Divine Judgment*, 13, opts for a date in the early years of Roman occupation of Egypt, viz. about 30 to 40 years after the battle of Actium (31 BC). Barclay, *Paul and the Gift*, 195, contents himself with "sometime in the period c. 20 BCE and

three parts, but there is often disagreement over the exact limits of the divisions: 1:1–6:21 (which contrasts the fate of the godless and the godly); 6:22–9:18 or 10:21 (praise of Wisdom by Solomon); and 10:1–19:22 or 11:1–19:22 (God's dealings with His people through Wisdom, especially at the Exodus). For our purpose the disagreement is immaterial. The work[190] aims to strengthen the conviction of the superiority of the Jewish way of life and to underline the need to be faithful to it among its addressees. This is achieved by a criticism of practical atheism, which is marked by a pursuit of one's own pleasures and which does not take God into consideration; by a stress on the gift of immortality to those who faithfully follow God and His Wisdom as the source of all virtue (1:1–6:11); by an emphasis on Wisdom as the guiding principle behind the cosmos and, therefore, by the conviction that people, kings as well as others, should shape all aspects of human life and conduct in accordance with Wisdom which leads to immortality (6:12–9:18); by a scathing criticism of idolatry and the way it leads to immoral conduct (Wis 13–15); and by emphasizing the role of Wisdom in the story of the salvation of Israel (10; 11:1–14; 16:1–19:22).

Recently, through the work of Barclay and his pupil, Linebaugh, the way in which the author holds together divine gift and human worthiness has been demonstrated.[191] Divine saving activity is for the worthy. While human worthiness is the condition, it is not the cause of divine saving action. This divine grace is an expression of the cosmic order established by Wisdom from the very beginning.

The events around the Exodus set up a paradigm of the exercise of divine judgment and mercy which is applied by the author in chapter 10 to the events recorded in Genesis.[192] To that chapter, where an allusion to Abraham occurs, we are now in a position to turn. Chapter 10 describes the activity of Wisdom in the lives of people from Adam onwards. There is a reference to Abraham without his name being specified: "Wisdom also, when the nations in the unanimity of their evil had been put to confusion,[193]

70 CE," while Chesnutt, *Wisdom of Solomon*, 1243, also believes that internal evidence precludes a more precise dating than sometime in the early Roman period (ca. 30 BC–AD 40).

190. The author builds on the identification of wisdom and the Torah already carried through by Sirach (24:1–23). See Winston, *Wisdom*, 35–38.

191. Barclay, *Unnerving Grace*, 91–110; *Gift*, 198–211; Linebaugh, *God, Grace, and Righteousness*, 48–52, 55–60.

192. See Watson, *Hermeneutics of Faith*, 389–91; Linebaugh, *God*, 56–57.

193. This may be an allusion to the scattering of the nations at the time of the erection of the tower of Babel (Gen 11), if we take the sense of εθνων συγχυθεντων to be that the nations were confused by God (divine passive). Hübner, *Weisheit*, 136, prefers the sense of falling out among themselves, which, he thinks, fits better the ironic idea

recognized[194] the righteous man and preserved him blameless before God, and kept him strong in the face of his compassion for his child" (10:5). Here Wisdom both recognized Abraham's righteousness and equally helped to preserve his blameless conduct (αμεμπτον Θεω), in particular giving him the strength to carry out the order to sacrifice his son, a command which must have been agonizing for a father in respect of his only son.[195] There is a reciprocity of agency between the divine and human, between the activity of Wisdom and that of Abraham.[196]

Of the survey of the examples from Genesis from Adam to Joseph, Linebaugh comments: "At points where Genesis knows only of human agency, *Wisdom* detects the unnamed actions of σοφια," and he goes on to say "Wisdom, it seems, both saves the righteous and, at least co-operatively, establishes the righteous as such."[197]

At 10:15, Wisdom is said to rescue "a blameless race." The rescue was a gracious intervention, a gift; but it was a fitting gift, because Israel, like Abraham, was blameless (αμεμπτον). Israel continued in the steps of its ancestor. Later, while discussing that God had given the possibility to the heathen to repent, the author says that this should teach God's people that they should behave humanely towards others and that there was always the possibility of repentance for sins committed. If God displayed such towards His enemies, with what exactness (μετα ποσης ακριβειας)[198] did God pass

of the unanimity of their planning evil (εν ομονια πονηριας). The main point of Wisdom's election of Abraham is not affected.

194. For the sense of recognize, acknowledge, see Bauer, *Lexicon*, 161. The NEB renders εγνω as "picked out." Bauer, *Lexicon*, 160, lists "to find out" as one of the nuances of γινωσκειν. Perhaps behind this verb, whichever nuance is preferred, lies the idea of Wisdom's search as we find it in Sirach 24. If the MS B reading ευρεν is preferred, there would be no doubt (McGlynn, *Divine Judgment*, 128, accepts B and sees a reference to Wisdom's search).

195. McGlynn *Divine Judgment*, 48, thinks that Abraham's compassion is contrasted with the conduct of Canaanites who murdered children and even parents killed defenceless infants in secret rites (12:3-6).

196. Hübner, *Weisheit*, 137, draws attention to the fact that the author makes no mention of God's promises to Abraham. Of the other examples—Lot, Jacob, and Joseph—all are described as being δικαιος (vv. 6, 10, 13), and Wisdom, in various ways, helped all three of them. Lot was saved from the destruction of Sodom; Wisdom guided Jacob on his flight from Esau's anger, and subsequently in his dealings with Laban and gave him victory in the hard struggle (with the unknown assailant at night as recorded in Gen 32); Wisdom preserved Joseph from sin, was with him in prison, brought him to a position of authority, and gave him everlasting renown.

197. Linebaugh, *God*, 58,59.

198. The author continues "So we are chastened by You, but You scourge our enemies ten thousand times more" (12:22).

judgment "on His sons to whose fathers You gave oaths and covenants (ορκους και συνθηκας) full of good promises"[199] (12:21). The use of the plural here presumably refers to the confirmation of the original covenant with Abraham to his son and grandson.

There is probably a reference to God's oaths to the patriarchs in the section on the night of the Passover in Egypt. The writer said that the Israelites had advance knowledge of the impending event of the death of the firstborn, in order that they might rejoice[200] because they had a sure knowledge of the oaths in which they had placed their trust (18:6). Later the author goes on to say that at the time of the wanderings in the wilderness, Aaron succeeded in limiting the execution of God's wrath by reminding Him of the oaths and covenants made with the fathers (18:22). This reference to the oaths and covenants made with the fathers is all the more striking as there is no such reference to these in the passage at Numbers 16:41-50 (17:6-15 LXX) to which the author is indebted for the story.[201] There are, thus, no less than three references to the oaths or oaths and covenants made with the patriarchs (12:21; 18:6, 22).

While the stress is on the activity of Wisdom, nonetheless, when the ancestor of the nation is mentioned, he is recognized in respect of his righteous conduct. He becomes, by implication, an example to be imitated.

2.14. The Writings of Philo of Alexandria

Philo[202] was a major figure of Hellenistic Judaism, in Alexandria,[203] and Abraham is often mentioned in his voluminous writings.[204]

---

199. Following the translation of Winston, *Wisdom*, 243, and NRSV. The NEB translates "the promise of good."

200. Wisdom 18:6 is the only entry listed in *LSJ*, 619, for επευθυμεω meaning rejoice at + dative.

201. See Vogel, *Heil*, 43-44.

202. See Sandmel, *Philo's Place*; Borgen, *Bread from Heaven*, 124-27; Barclay, *Jews in the Mediterranean Diaspora*, 158-80; Watson, *Hermeneutics*, 238-58, 267-69; Calvert-Koyzis, *Monotheism*, 19-24, 40; Sterling, *Philo*, 1063-70. For the importance of setting Philo in the context of Roman Alexandria, see Niehoff, *Jewish Identity*, esp. 6-13. The best treatment of Abraham in Philo is the outstanding work by Böhm, *Rezeption und Funktion*. She covers Isaac and Jacob as well as Abraham, as her title indicates.

203. For Egyptian Judaism, see Borgen, *Judaism in Egypt*, 71-102; Barclay, *Jews*, 17-228; Böhm, *Rezeption*, 38-59. Niehoff, *Jewish Exegesis and Homeric Scholarship*, sheds new light on the spectrum of Jewish exegetical engagement with the Scriptures in Alexandria, and the variety of reaction to the literary and text-critical activity of Homeric scholarship in Alexandria.

204. Philo often referred to Abraham even when not mentioning his actual name.

2.14.1 Body and Soul

Philo assumed that a person was composed of body and mind/soul,[205] the latter being a portion or fragment of the heavenly world, a copy of the Logos who was the model on which the human mind was formed.[206] The mind/soul is imprisoned in the body, but it can attain to God, or what can be known of the utterly transcendent God, by freeing itself from all ties to the material world. The journey of the soul from the material world to God is regarded by Philonic specialists as the hermeneutical key to Philo. He called this the royal highway,[207] along which Abraham sought to travel.[208]

Along with this stress on human effort, Philo can also stress the grace or graces of God to assist the mind/soul on this journey.[209] God generously pours out His grace on the created order and meets the mind/soul to help it. A corrolary of this concept of a journey is that the mind/soul which strives to attain knowledge of God will be rewarded, while the mind/soul which lets itself be dominated by passions and the pleasures of the material world will be punished.

In his handling of Scripture, Philo operated on two levels: the literal and the spiritual which he extracted by allegorical interpretation.[210] While not neglecting the literal meaning, Philo's interest is in the spiritual meaning.

---

205. Strictly speaking, Philo envisaged two types of souls (ψυχαι). He said that the first type inhabited the area between earth and heaven. They were immortal and incorruptible, mind of the very purest kind (νους ο καθαρωτατος), and were servants of God. Moses called them angels. Some like stars have a corporeal form. The second type had a yearning for things human and descended to earth and took on a human body. Of these some were wholly captivated by human passions, but others, longing to return to their former habitation, sought the wisdom of philosophy, by which Philo meant the Jewish faith, in order to regain what they had lost and return to their former existence (see *Opif.* 143–44; *Gig.* 6–8, 12–16; *Plant.* 14; *Somn.* 1.135–40).

206. For αποσπασμα used of the soul, see *Op.* 146; *Leg. All.* 3.161; *Det.* 90; *Mut.* 223; *Somn.* 1.34. For similar idea, see also *Gig.* 60; *Immut.* 45–46; *Her.* 85; *Somn.* 1.146; *Spec.* 4.123. For the idea of a copy of an original, μιμημα του παραδειγματος, see *Op.* 139; *Plant.* 18 (Allegorical); *Decal.* 134; *Praem.* 163; *Spec.* 1.81; 3.207 (Exposition). In *Op.* 146, Philo used three terms: εκμαφειον (casting, or imprint); αποσπασμα (fragment or portion); and απαυασμα (ray, beam). Strictly speaking, the first of these belongs within the model/copy conceptuality, but Philo was not concerned to differentiate, as Runia, *God and Man*, 345, observes, because the context did not require it.

207. Philo took the phrase from Numbers 20:17, and used it in his own way for the journey of the soul.

208. E.g., *Gig.* 62–64.

209. See Zeller, *Charis bei Philon und Paulus*; Barclay, *By the Grace of God*, 140–57; *Gift*, 212–38, 310–11; Linebaugh, *God*, 52–55.

210. See Christiansen, *Die Technik*. She has shown how Philo proceeded according to certain rules of exegesis current at the time, and that he was far from being capricious

One further introductory point should be made, a point stressed by Martina Böhm, is that Abraham is one of a trio: himself, Isaac, and Jacob. Philo allegorized this patriarchal trio into types of acquiring virtue.[211] Abraham represented virtue acquired by means of instruction and learning; Isaac is self-taught and reached perfection without labor; Jacob acquired virtue by practice and discipline. Philo seems to have taken over a commonplace idea in antiquity that nature, teaching, and practice were necessary in the formation of a mature person, and used it for his own purpose.

With these few preliminary remarks we now turn to what Philo said about Abraham.

2.14.2 Questions and Answers on Genesis

We turn first to consider the work *Questions and Answers on Genesis* (hereafter *QG*).[212] A number of Philonic specialists consider this, with the work on Exodus (*QE*), to come from an early stage of Philo's work as an interpreter

and arbitrary in his work as an exegete. See also Früchtel, *Die Kosmologischen Vorstellungen*, 119–26; Niehoff, *Jewish Exegesis*, for discussions of the influence of the allegorical techniques of exegetes of Homer on Philo.

211. Böhm, *Rezeption*, 123–32, 252–318. See also Noack, *Gottesbewusstsein*, 166–68.

212. *QG* has survived only in an Armenian translation from the last third of the sixth century AD and in quotations in the works of some Christian authors. Though Marcus, the editor of it in the Loeb series, expressed the view that the Armenian translation had faithfully preserved Philo's meaning, Hay is rather dismissive: "An ancient Armenian translation remarkable for its stiffness and indications that the translator or translators were often baffled by the original Greek" (Hay, *Both Literal and Allegorical*, viii). It has not received a great deal of scholarly attention. However, there is now a collection of essays on it and *Questions and Answers on Exodus*, under the title *Both Literal and Allegorical*, edited by D. M. Hay. Böhm, *Rezeption*, 336–39, 342–45, suggests that the *Questions* may have been a study book or exercise book, cataloguing various interpretations and intended for young men acquainted with the literal and allegorical interpretative techniques and at the beginning of their study of Jewish philosophy. Somewhat similar is the view of Niehoff, *Jewish Exegesis*, 8, who suggests that they appeal to a less sophisticated readership, possibly Philo's own students. Borgen, *Philo*, 80–101, esp. 100–101, considers that the setting of the technique of questions and answers was that of learned circles within Judaism, quite possibly within the context of the synagogue, as well as in the wider Hellenistic context. Birnbaum, *Judaism*, 19, considers that the *QG* and *QE* may have been intended as a collation or digest of interpretations reflecting the opinions of a broader community of Alexandrian Jews than just those who shared Philo's interest in allegory and in the journey of the soul.

of Scripture.²¹³ Other Philonic scholars consider that *QG* and *QE* come in between the Allegorical Commentary series and the Exposition series.²¹⁴

The section covering Genesis 10:10–15:6 is unfortunately no longer extant. Our *QG* 3 covers Genesis 15:7–17:27, while *QG* 4 exegetes Genesis 18–20; 23–25:8; 25:20–26; 27; 28:9 but, again unfortunately, lacks Genesis 21–22.

Philo speaks of the literal sense of a passage and of the allegorical interpretation (e.g., 3.1, 15, 16, 18, 23, 24, etc.). There is a significant declaration by Philo in 4.137, which is very revealing about his approach: "For the inquiry of the theologian is about characters and types and virtues, and not about persons who were created and born."

Sometimes, he referred to the opinions of others (e.g., 3.8, 11, 13, 43, 52, 53). He interpreted numbers (e.g., 3.38–39, 49, 56) and place names (e.g., 3.36) symbolically. The content seems to go beyond the stage of initial catechism, and assumed awareness of both literal and allegorical techniques of interpretation; but does not go into the depth of allegorical interpretation found in the later Allegorical Writings.²¹⁵

---

213. Of contributors to Hay, *Both Literal and Allegorical*, see Terian, "Priority of the Quaestiones," 29–46; Sterling, "Philo's Quaestiones," 99–123, who argue that the Quaestiones were the first of Philo's series of writings, though not necessarily notes in preparation for the Allegorical series. Runia, *Secondary Texts in Philo's Quaestiones*, 47–79, argued that in the Quaestiones Philo quoted secondary passages as short, illustrative material, whereas in the Allegorical treatises the secondary texts have an explanatory role and the exegesis is often as extensive as on the main text. Böhm, *Rezeption*, 363, considers that these two works represent Philo at an early stage of his interpretative practice. She argues that in them Philo does not interpret "Moses by Moses"—the practice of undertaking primary exegesis with the help of secondary exegesis is lacking—while Philo often mixed the literal and allegorical interpretation in a manner not typical of the other works. She also argues that Philo took over the typization of the three patriarchs from the exegetical tradition in Alexandria, but only developed it in the later two series.

214. According to Niehoff, *Jewish Exegesis*, 158, Cohn suggested in 1899 that the two *Questions & Answers* came after the Allegorical Commentary. This view was followed by Royse, *Works of Philo*, 60–61. Niehoff herself, *Jewish Exegesis*, 152–58, 167–68, 187, also places them at a later stage in Philo's career than the Allegorical Commentary. She considers that *QG* and *QE* assume a basic knowledge of the biblical stories and were written for Jews who were now ready for further instruction. In them, as opposed to the treatises in the Allegorical Commentary, Philo displays a greater confidence in his own views over against the academic methods of colleagues more critical of scripture than he was. He also no longer addresses literal readers of scripture. She alleges that Philo considered that he was an authentic interpreter of Moses and that he stressed "our" group identity vis-à-vis "other" critical readers and also literal ones. These two works indicate a mature teacher speaking to a convinced following, committed to Philo's more conservative approach to biblical studies.

215. See Böhm, *Rezeption*, 342–43, 345.

We meet broadly the criticism of Chaldea and its astrology (3.1) and the identification of Egypt with corporeal and external blessings (3.16).

Abraham is regarded as a wise man (4.53); a virtuous man (3.8; 4.8, 29, 73), humble before God (4.28); a man of piety before God and love of humanity (4.2); a lover of peace (3.8), opposed to wrong doing and greed (3.8); hospitable (4.8, 20); and a faithful husband (3.21). Philo spoke of his marriage with Sarah as a union of two people joined in harmony through heavenly love, while he explained the intercourse with Hagar as solely to beget an heir and not for pleasure (3.21).[216]

At the begininng of book 3, Philo started to expound Genesis 15:7. After stating that the literal meaning was clear, Philo moved to his allegorical interpretation of "the land of the Chaldeans" and "this land." God honored Abram with two gifts. In the first place, He called him out of Chaldea with its idolatrous worship of the created things rather than the Creator, which is the cause of great evils and impiety. Secondly, God granted him fruitful wisdom (symbolized by "this land"). In this way, God showed that wisdom and virtue are unchanging, because He would not have revealed that which changes (3.1). Philo then turned to Abram's question "Lord. What shall I be informed that I shall inherit it?" (Gen 15:8). Here Philo distinguished between what can be discerned with the mind and what with the outward senses. The mind is able to trust God in accordance with what He has said, but Abram wanted also to have a sign which could confirm to the outward senses that the promise had been fulfilled (3.2).[217]

Philo allegorized the action of Abram in driving off the birds from the animal and bird sacrifices mentioned in Genesis 15:11. The birds represent the afflictions and passions which enslave the soul. Abram who is the virtuous person and lover of people "is a healer of our race[218] and is a genuine and true apothecary and dispeller of evils. Now all these are allegories of the soul" (3.10).

---

216. This is the literal interpretation according to Philo. On the allegorical level, interpreting Genesis 16:3, the union with Hagar was the use of encyclical studies. Training in these branches of learning "has the force of a concubine, but the form and rank of a wife." Furthermore, Philo endeavored to exonerate Sarah's treatment of Hagar (see QG 3.23-24).

217. See pages 189-92 for a discussion of the same passage from Genesis 15 in Her. 243-48, where Philo dealt with a criticism that had been levelled at Abraham for what was regarded as an expression of unbelief. Pages 184-92 below also deal with other criticisms levelled at Abraham.

218. Früchtel, *Kosmologischen Vorstellungen*, 170, takes this to mean the human race.

We meet the concept of the immortality of the soul. It has come from its mother city[219] and resides in a mortal body. The earthly body is only a colony, a temporary abode. "The soul of the wise man is truly a sojourner in a land not its own, for the earthly nature of the body is alien to the pure mind and subjects it to slavery" (3.10). It will return to its original home (3.11).[220] God endues the virtuous mind with the power to ensure that it is not governed by the body but rather the body is its servant (3.45). So, Philo can say that the virtuous man begets good and useful things in distinction to the wicked person (3.13).

Hagar is interpreted as the handmaiden of Virtue (symbolized by Sarah), in the capacity of intermediate or encyclical study (3.20).[221] On this allegorical level, Sarah's suggestion that Abram should have sexual relations with Hagar is an indication that Abraham was not yet ready to beget children by virtue. He needed to embark on the intermediate studies. Once these were completed satisfactorily, he would then be ready to beget a child with virtue (3.20).

That Hagar fled to the wilderness was given a positive slant in Philo's allegorical interpretation, because the wilderness represents an escape from all the pressures and passions which assault the soul and becomes a means of recovering the equilibrium of the soul (3.27). The command of the angel (Philo takes the angel to be the Logos) to Hagar to return to obey her mistress Sarah indicated the limits of encyclical study and the need to submit to Virtue/Wisdom (3.28-31).[222]

219. Philo uses fatherland of the soul's true origin in 3.45.

220. Here, Philo allegorized God's words that Abraham should be gathered to his fathers recorded in Genesis 15:15. This refers to the immortality of the soul which returns to its mother city. Philo took "fathers" to mean the incorporeal Logoi (= angels) of the divine world (and not, as other allegorists had asserted, the elements into which the body will be dissolved).

221. Cf. scattered references in 3.21, 25, 35 to this idea; by extension Ishmael also in 3.59.

222. Sandmel, *Philo's Place*, 155, maintains that "Philo sees in the flight of Hagar (Gen 15:6) the experience of Abraham's mind at the level of encyclical knowledge," but to import Abraham into the figure of Hagar seems to confuse matters unnecessarily. Böhm, *Rezeption*, 369, is more correct to see Hagar as embodying both encyclical study and also the soul familiar with many branches of learning, but which cannot bear the greatness of virtue and wisdom and flees from them as embodied in her mistress. The angel of the Lord commands the soul to return to wisdom.

We may agree that the implication of this is that after the encyclical studies, the soul striving for virtue will press on to have children by Virtue (Sarah), but so far as I can see that is nowhere *expressly* said in QG 3. In his comment on Sarah's statement about her barrenness (Gen 16:2), Philo said that Sarah had not abandoned hope that one day she would bring forth offspring. Later, in 54, in the comment on God's promise to give Abraham children "from her" (Gen 17:16), Philo indicated that once Sarah had

The promise of the angel that she would conceive a son (Gen 16:11) meant for Philo that her offspring would not be perfect (this was indicated by the fact that Ishmael means "the hearing of God" and hearing is inferior to sight),[223] for only the perfect soul can produce perfect offspring, consisting of words and works (3.32).

The fact that God appeared to Abram in Genesis 17 is explained in 3.39-42. Philo believed that what Abraham experienced was in fact God's two powers, His creative and ruling powers, as is indicated by the use of God and Lord respectively in the text of Genesis (3.39). This is an indication of the greatest blessing which He can confer on the wise person: "He not only carried him off and brought him up from earth to heaven, or from heaven to an incorporeal and intelligible world, but also (brought him) from here to Himself, showing (Himself) clearly, not as He is, for this is impossible but (in so far) as the eyes of the beholder are able to attain to the genuine and intelligible power itself" (3.42).

Philo also pointed out that the mind must exercise sovereignty over the variety of inclinations in the soul, for which purpose it receives help from God's powers,[224] "the beneficent and the destructive:" "beneficence toward those who wish to obey, reproof toward those who are out of hand and refractory, since some profit from praise, others from castigation" (3.42).

The change of name from Abram to Abraham[225] was interpreted as indicating a change in Abram from one who pursued a study of the heavens and the stars to Abraham as "the elect father of sound," which means that the mind is the father of the uttered word, which Philo took as a definition of the wise man whose wisdom, received from God, included a knowledge of invisible, divine things above (3.43).[226]

We meet the idea of Abraham as the benefactor of the nations through his wisdom, based on "I will set you among the nations" in Genesis 17:6. Through his wisdom he was deemed worthy to be "foundation and base and firm support of the nations and of mankind," since the wise man was "the savior of nations and an intercessor with God and one who seeks forgiveness for his countrymen who have committed sins"[227] (3.44). His act

received a share in the divine virtue, she began to conceive.

223. See notes 238, 253.

224. Cf. 3.45.

225. For a study of Philo's etymologies, see Grabbe, *Etymology*. On Abram/Abraham specifically, 126-28.

226. In addition Philo explained the change from Sara to Sarra in 3.53, just as in Genesis 17:15 LXX.

227. Philo may have had in mind Abraham's intercessions concerning Sodom and Gomorrah, or Genesis 20:7, or both.

of circumcising even those members of his household whom he had purchased from strangers was interpreted as a humane act, sharing the value and significance of this religious rite with those of foreign birth (3.62). Earlier, commenting on Genesis 17:4, Philo said that one explanation of the verse was that the lover of God was also a lover of mankind and would devote himself to helping not just people of his own nation but of others as well (3.42).

At 3.54-58, Philo dealt with Abraham's unbelief when promised that he would have a son with Sarai and that God would bless him and that he would be for the peoples and that kings of the nations would come from him (Gen 17:17-19). In Genesis, Abraham is said to have fallen on his face and laughed and thought how could such an event happen when he was a hundred years old and Sarah ninety years old? He asked God that Ishmael might in fact count as his heir, a request which God firmly rejected, though promising blessing for Ishmael. Philo, however, interpreted the laughter as joy over the promise and hope of its being fulfilled (55), and then went on to say that, as it was a case of a thought not expressed verbally, Abraham was not guilty of doubt. "Perhaps too he is not in a state of doubt but was struck with amazement at the excessiveness of the gift" (3.56). Philo has God at first ignoring Abraham's request about Ishmael and reaffirming His assertion about Sarah and a son: "Yes, be it so: behold, Sarah your wife will bear you a son" (58). God then affirmed Abraham's faith: "Your faith is not ambiguous but is unhesitating, and partakes of modesty and reverence. Therefore, what you have received before as destined to come about because of your faith in me, shall certainly be done, for this is shown by the 'Yes'" (58). This seems to be a reference back to God's promise and Abraham's response of faith to it in Genesis 15:5, which was now reaffirmed. Then Philo went on to consider God's promise to bless Ishmael (59).

By this combination of Genesis 15:5 and 17:19, Philo stood within a tradition of Jewish exegesis and presented Abraham as a man who trusted in God.

In 4.8, dealing with Genesis 18:6-7, Philo allegorized Abraham and Sarah as "ideas:" Abraham as the most pure mind, while Sarah stands for "the perfection of virtue."

Later (4.17), Philo sought to explain why Sarah was rebuked for laughing at the promise of a son (Gen 18:13-14), while Abraham escaped censure for laughing at a similar promise earlier (Gen 17:17). Philo maintained that the rebuke seems to indicate praise rather than blame, "for she wonders that . . . a new act should be sown by God in the whole soul for the birth of joy and great gladness."[228] He then went on to refer to Abraham's "unswerving and inflexible conviction of faith, for to him who has faith in God all uncertainty is alien" (4.17).[229]

2.14.3 Exposition of the Law

We turn now to look at *the picture of Abraham presented in the treatises contained in his Exposition of the Law*, especially the work *Concerning Abraham*.[230] In it, Philo stated that Moses' intention in portraying the lives of virtuous men was to show that the written laws agreed with nature and that it was not difficult for people to live according to God's laws because these virtuous men had obeyed the unwritten laws before any were written down, and so were living embodiments of the Law.[231] They had obeyed the promptings of their own nature (5-6). After discussing Enos, Enoch, and Noah (7-47), he mentioned a trio from the same family, obviously Abraham, Isaac, and Jacob (48-59), all of whom were lovers of God and beloved by God because of their virtues. Because of their virtues, God was content to be called by a name which linked Him and them, viz. The God of Abraham, the God of Isaac, and the God of Jacob (50-51). Philo interpreted the three of them as symbols of types of soul, of persons who acquire virtue:[232] Abraham through instruction; Isaac through nature; and Jacob through

---

228. This reflects the way Philo tended to remove any short comings from his portrait of those who function as models to be imitated, especially the patriarchs and their legitimate wives.

229. Possibly a reference to Genesis 15:5-6. A similar positive explanation of Abraham's laughter occurred in, e.g., *Leg. All.* 3.218; cf. *Mut.* 154, 166-67. On the other hand, in *Abr.* 111-113, Philo seemed to postulate a development in Abraham from an initial unbelief expressed by the laughter to a gradual perception of the nature of his visitors. In *Mut.* 175-88, Philo also said that Abraham's doubt existed in the mind but was not expressed in words, and went on to say that it was only temporary, and illustrated the fact that Abraham was a man and not on the same level with God. See the discussion on Abraham's faith in Philo in this volume, 170-75.

230. It is well to state at the outset that Philo only infrequently used the actual name Abram/Abraham (four times in all) but referred to him by phrases like this wise man, beloved of God (or if active, lover of God), or even the man. We may also mention here that Abraham figures, but to a much lesser extent, in *Concerning Virtues*, viz in the closing part of this treatise (212-19); in a passing reference in *Mos.* 1.7; and occasionally in conjunction with Isaac and Jacob in other Exposition works (*Mos.* 1.71-76; *Spec.* 4.18; *Praem.* 24-51, 166).

231. At the very end of the treatise, Philo described Abraham as "himself unwritten law and statute" (νομος αυτος ων και θεσμος αγραφος) (276).

232. Philo used συμβολον. A few sentences later, he said that God's eternal name "is meant to indicate the three said values rather than actual men" (54).

practice (52).²³³ He hastened to add that all three were endowed with all these qualities but one predominated, though they had mastered the others (53). God had bestowed on our race these three virtues (nature, instruction, and practice) in order to produce perfection of life (52–54).²³⁴ The three of them became the parents of a special part of the human race, called Israel, which means "The one who sees God" (56–57).²³⁵ Then Philo went on to say that whereas the sight of the eyes was the most excellent of the senses, the sight of the mind (διανοια) which is the ruling part of the soul (ψυχη) far surpassed all other faculties, and it was only through this that one could obtain a sight of the Father and Maker of all and advance to the crowning point of happiness (58). While Philo was generalizing here about the soul/mind, it seems reasonable to assume that the three patriarchs were not far from his mind, for he had just discussed them and he was about come on to Abraham very shortly, and he would use the phrase the eye of the soul when describing Abraham's conversion from reliance on Chaldean astronomy to belief in the true Creator God (see 70).

Then Philo came to Abraham as an individual (60), initially describing him as filled with zeal for piety (ευσεβεια) and as someone who was eager to follow God and to obey Him. Abraham's piety will occupy the greater part of the remainder of the treatise (60–207). *What follows was adduced by Philo to illustrate Abraham's ευσεβεια: that is the thrust of the flow of Philo's exposition.* He selected a few episodes to support his assert that this was the supreme quality of the patriarch.

The first selected theme was the migrations of Abraham, and included both the migration from Chaldea to Haran and that from Haran to a desert countryside. Philo mentioned the oracle which commanded Abraham to depart from his country and family and Abraham's prompt obedience to it (61).²³⁶ Philo described this journey as if Abraham were travelling from a foreign country back to his own country (62). Then, a little later, he remarked "He set out for another country in his soul before he started with his body, because his love for heavenly things overpowered his desire for

---

233. For a similar interpretation, see *Mos.* 1.76.

234. If Philo was aiming to reach interested Gentiles, then the references to "our race" in 54 and "the nation" in 57 would serve as commendation of the Jewish people to Gentiles.

235. Birnbaum, *Judaism*, 122, has commented that here and at *Praem.* 44, where the etymology of Israel is discussed, "we cannot conclusively identify the referent." The same might justly be said about the following paragraph here where we might wonder whether Philo was thinking of the soul of anyone or of Abraham and the other two patriarchs as symbols of the soul aspiring to see God.

236. Bohm, *Rezeption*, 152, aptly describes this as "the beginning of the biography of inner-salvation" (*der inner Heilsbiographie*)

mortal things" (66). Philo drew a distinction between the literal expressions of scripture and the laws of allegory: the migration was, according to the latter, a journey of the soul devoted to virtue and occupied with the search for the true God (68). So when Abraham realized the errors of the Chaldean astronomers in equating the created world with God, it was as if his soul had awakened from a deep sleep. Philo described it in terms of Abraham's opening the eye of his soul and his beginning to see a pure beam of light instead of deep darkness. He followed that beam and discerned what he had not seen before. With the eye of the soul[237] he saw[238] the One who had created the world standing above it and guiding it with powerful care[239] (69–70). This is an important element of faith in Philo's portrait of Abraham. Philo gave a speech to the holy Logos[240] ordering Abraham to depart from the contemplation of this world, which is described as the greatest of cities, and turn to the lesser. In this way, he would be able the better to apprehend the Overseer of the All (71).[241] By "lesser" the soul/mind is meant.[242]

So then Abraham left Chaldea and went to Haran (72). Philo interpreted Haran as meaning holes which are a symbol of the bodily orifices used by each of the sense perceptions to apprehend what belongs to it, but

237. The thought here is based on the belief that the soul is related to the Logos, who mediates between God and humanity.

238. For Philo, sight was superior to hearing. See notes 223, 253; Mühling, *Blickt*, 282n537. Elsewhere, Philo interpreted the change from Jacob to Israel as the movement from hearing to sight (*Ebr.* 82; *Migr.* 38–40).

239. "A charioteer and pilot presiding over the world and directing in safety His own work" (69).

240. Böhm, *Rezeption*, 140, sees this as adding vividness to the account while also exhibiting a great deal of literary freedom over against the biblical source.

241. "Friend, the great is often known by its outlines as shown in the smaller, and by looking at them the observer finds the scope of his vision infinitely enlarged. Dismiss, then, the rangers of the heavens and the science of Chaldea, and depart for a short time from the greatest of cities, this world, to the lesser, and thus you will be able to apprehend the overseer of the All" (71). There may possibly be a hint that all this was not solely Abraham's achievement because Philo says that in order to establish more securely the sight revealed to him, the holy Logos spoke to him. The move from astrological speculations to self-knowledge as a further step to knowledge of God was the result of divine guidance.

242. For a similar description of the movement of Abraham's thinking, see *Mut.*15–17 in the Allegorical treatises, where Philo also drew a distinction between Scripture's use of Lord and God in Genesis 17:1–2, in respect of Abraham's relationship to the Deity. Initially, Scripture said the Lord appeared to Abram (Gen 17:1), but when God said "I am your God" (Gen 17:2), that was an indication that Abraham had advanced and improved. God is called the Lord and Master of bad men, but the God of those who are advancing and improving, and Lord and God of the most excellent and perfect (*Mut.* 19).

these need the invisible mind to direct them (72–73).[243] As the invisible mind needs to control the body, so the invisible God controls the world. The world was not God, but was the work of the God and Father of all things (74–75). God appeared to Abraham in Haran. That God appeared to Abraham was important to Philo. It was both an indication that Abraham had not known God while in Chaldea (77) and also an illustration of the fact that God goes out to meet the soul and reveals Himself, so far as one could receive such a revelation. It is impossible for anyone to comprehend by his own unassisted power the true living God unless He revealed Himself to him (78–80). There is a blend of human and divine involvement. There followed Philo's thoughts on the difference between an astrologer-meteorologist and the wise man, and the superiority of the latter. Abraham advanced from Chaldean astrology to receiving "the vision of Him who had so long lay hidden and invisible" (79). Philo tied this advance by Abraham into the change of name from Abram (which Philo interpreted as sublime father, that is, one who contemplates the sublime bodies in the sky) to Abraham (Philo took this as "the elect father of sound," meaning the mind as father of uttered speech) (81–82). "Now to the meteorologist nothing at all seems greater than the universe, and he credits it with the causation of what comes into being. But the wise man with more discerning eyes sees something more perfect perceived by the mind, something which rules and governs, the master and pilot of all else" (84).[244]

Next, Philo mentioned another migration[245] undertaken by Abraham (85).[246] Again, Philo drew a distinction between the literal sense (Abraham wandered around in what Philo calls a desolate country without settling down) and the allegorical sense (the soul loves solitude because this brings it nearer to God the creator and ruler of all and through reason it leaves behind the visible world and soars upwards to behold that which is invisible, the one who is Creator) (85–88). Philo commented "Therefore, having now given both explanations, the literal one concerning the man, and the allegorical one relating to the soul, we have shown that both the man and the mind are deserving of love, inasmuch as the one is obedient to the sacred oracles, and because of their influence submits to be torn away from things

---

243. Grabbe, *Etymology*, 218.

244. Philo did not make use of the idea that Abraham had introduced astrology to the Egyptians. Meyer, *Aspekte*, 124, thinks that this is a conscious rejection of the idea.

245. Philo called this a second migration.

246. I.e., the journeys mentioned in Genesis 12:6–9, which referred to a move to Shechem and then to near Bethel, and concluded with the note that Abram was moving southwards. This southward direction was continued, for Genesis 12:10 then mentioned that Abram went to Egypt because of a famine in Canaan.

from which it is hard to part;[247] and the mind deserves to be loved because it has not submitted to be deceived for ever or to stand rooted permanently to the material world perceptible to the outward senses" (88).

For his second episode, Philo paraphrased the account of Abram's stay in Egypt (89-98), initially forced on him because of famine in Canaan (91-92), recorded in Genesis 12:10-20. He depicted Pharaoh as a licentious and cruel despot who was determined to satisfy his lusts on Sarah. Philo said that both Abraham and Sarah turned in petition to God for His help in their desperate predicament (95). God took pity on the couple and inflicted unbearable pains on Pharaoh. By this means, God preserved Abraham's marriage, safeguarding Sarah's chastity from Pharaoh's intentions towards her. The episode is so told that it also illustrates Abraham's excellent piety! "Thus the chastity of the woman was preserved, while God considered it fitting to demonstrate the nobility and piety (την καλοκαγαθιαν και ευσεβειαν) of the man by conferring on him a very great reward," viz. the preservation of his marriage (90).[248] Philo mentioned an allegorical interpretation of this story which he rejected (99). These interpreters took Abraham to be a symbol of the mind, while Sarah stood for virtue. Philo disagreed, because for him virtue is a masculine attribute, and he, therefore, preferred to interpret Abraham and Sarah in the reverse manner as representing virtue and thought respectively (102),[249] while Pharaoh represented the mind devoted to the body (103).[250]

The third episode is when Abraham entertained the three visitors (107-132). Abraham's instant response of warm hospitality to the three strangers was rewarded by the promise of a son, which neither he nor Sarah at first believed but he began to perceive the true nature of his visitors (107,

---

247. If Philo was aiming at interested Gentiles, this aspect of Abraham's life would underline the social cost of adhering fully to Judaism.

248. *Abr.* 98. Philo omitted any details of the story which might detract from the excellence of his ideal types–for full details, see Böhm, *Rezeption*, 133-36, 171.

249. Elsewhere, Philo takes Sarah to symbolize virtue and Abraham as the one who wishes to be united to her. See *QG* 3.20; 4.8, 11; *All. Leg.* 3.218, 244; *Cher.* 5, 9; *Det.* 59; *Cong.* 2-6, 63, 180; *Mut.* 78; *Abr.* 206.

250. Philo began by saying that he had heard (ηκουσα) some natural philosophers (φυσικων ανδρων—see Colson, *Philo*, 6:597-98, for this meaning) who took the passage allegorically (αλληγορουντων). Although Philo rejected their interpretation, he did say of it that it was "not without good reason" (ουκ απο σκοπου. *LSJ*, 1614, gives for απο σκοπου the literal meaning "away from the mark"). They maintained that Sarah stood for virtue, on the basis that her name in Greek meant princess and what is more royal than virtue (*Abr.* 99). For Philo (101-2), virtue was masculine by nature, while it is thought (ο λογισμος) which is feminine, it being "moved and trained and helped, and in general belonging to the passive category" (102). So, in the marriage of Abraham and Sarah there was a union of virtue and thought.

111–13). Philo commented that Abraham's hospitality to the three strangers was a by-product of the virtue of his piety (η αρετη θεοσεβεια 114), and went on to ask how it was that these angels, holy and divine beings, deigned to receive his hospitality, since the visitors gave the appearance of eating and drinking (118). Philo said that it was because they recognized that Abraham was "their kinsman and fellow servant who had sought refuge with their master" (116). They assumed human form to do kindness to the good man (προς τον αστειον) and to show that the Father recognized his wisdom (118).[251]

Then Philo turned to the figurative meaning of the story (119). The three persons are God the Father of the Universe surrounded on either side by His creative and royal (= governing) powers (121), being His beneficent and chastising powers respectively (145). They are rather like bodyguards. The mind received a vision at one time of one being and at another time of three. Ultimately, however, it was the former which was what the soul should strive for, viz. the vision of the true and living God Himself (122, 125).

Philo also mentioned, fourthly, the destruction of Sodom literally (138–141) and allegorically (147–66). As regards the latter, he took the five cities of the plain of Sodom to represent the five outward senses (147). While taste, smell, and touch represent the worst sides of human nature, sight and hearing, especially the former,[252] have something philosophical and pre-eminent about them (149–50), though in the end Philo placed hearing with the other three as slaves to the flesh and its passions (164). That God destroyed four of the five cities but preserved one (Gen 19:20) is an indication for Philo that sight was the most important because it could look up and find sources of pleasures superior to bodily passions (164–66).[253] Abraham was not mentioned.

Finally, the demand to sacrifice Isaac was next handled by Philo (167–207). He responded to some criticism that Abraham's action was by no means unique (178–83) by arguing that Abraham did it neither through custom (Chaldean), nor fear of other men nor a desire to receive praise from

251. Niehoff, *Jewish Identity*, 223, commented, "Philo himself emphasized elsewhere that table fellowship presupposes congeniality, especially if celestial participants are involved."

252. "Sight has been created to be an exact image of the soul" (*Abr.* 153).

253. The superiority of sight over hearing also figures in the Allegorical Writings–see Sac. 78; *Immut.* 45; *Plant.* 20–23; *Ebr.* 82; *Conf.* 148; *Mig.* 38–40 (in *Plant.* 20–23, Philo indicated that the human ψυχη, which shares in the divine Logos, is able with the help of the eyes to grasp the existence of God. The eyes can observe the marvels of the heavens and so provide the "material" for the mind to reflect on and move from the visible to the invisible, from creation to its Creator).

others (188-91). Rather, Abraham sought to obey God (192), and he deserved praise because Isaac was the child of his old age (194-96). In return for the piety which he had shown, God rewarded Abraham by returning the gift (203). This episode also afforded an illustration of reason conquering the outward senses and the passions. Abraham overcame the natural feelings of a father (195-96). Likewise, when Sarah died, Abraham was not overwhelmed by inordinate grief but controlled his feelings (256-58). It is not surprising, therefore, to find that on several occasions Philo described Abraham as a perfect man, a just man, a pious man.[254] Philo said that an unprejudiced person must be overwhelmed by admiration for Abraham's extraordinary piety (ευσεβεια). No action of this wise man was small but showed the greatness and loftiness of his soul (199).

Philo then devoted a section to discuss the etymology of Ισαακ = laughter and the gift of laughter/joy to the souls of the wise (201-7).

Philo concluded this major section by saying that what he had written so far (i.e., 60-207) must be sufficient to demonstrate *Abraham's piety* (ευσεβεια).

Then he turned to consider Abraham's dealings with fellow human beings, "for the same nature which is pious is also kindly, and the same person will exhibit both qualities, holiness to God and justice to men" (208).[255] Once again, he indicated that he would mention two or three illustrations. As a result, he backtracked to illustrate the gentle disposition of Abraham by mentioning how he gave his nephew, Lot, the choice of where he wished to settle, in order to end the disputes between their two sets of servants. Abraham did not relish a life characterized by dissension and strife, but one marked by peace and tranquillity (209-216). Then Philo allegorized the story in terms of older and younger standing for different qualities (older = every type of virtue; younger = wealth, authority, glory and external things) (219). The soul must detach itself from adherence to external things (223-24).[256] He went on to discuss the battle with the five kings recorded in Genesis 14, first literally (225-35) and then allegorically (236-44). The literal sense showed Abraham to have been a courageous, resourceful, and noble military leader,

---

254. *Abr.* 208; *Virt.* 216, 218; *Decal.* 38; *Praem.* 27 (Exposition); *Immut.* 4; *Migr.* 130; cf. *Leg. All.* 3.203 (Allegorical Commentary).

255. These two qualities — holiness towards God and right conduct towards one's fellow human beings (sections 207-261 deal with this second theme) — implied that Abraham kept the Law, and such behavior would be rewarded with immortality (cf. *Opif.* 155).

256. If this story illustrated that the truly pious person renounces material advantages, it is nevertheless true, as Böhm, *Rezeption*, 160, points out, that Abraham remains a rich and powerful man in Philo's presentation.

who trusted in God, while allegorically the story illustrated the soul fighting an alliance of passions and outward senses.

Philo commented on Abraham's wife, Sarah[257] (245–54), and then on his reaction to her death—how he conquered his natural grief through reason[258] (255–59), such that the local inhabitants of Hebron were astonished, admired his way of life, and described him as a king (Βασιλευς) from God among them (260–61).[259]

This praise led Philo to his final section which is his praise of Abraham (262–76).[260] He quoted the words that Abraham believed God (Gen 15:6). Philo asked, on whom else can we believe? To believe in human authorities and things like honor, glory, riches, noble birth, personal qualities, health, beauty, and vitality, is unstable. "Trust in God is the only real and true and lasting good, the comfort of life, the fulfilment of good hopes, the absence of evils and the source of blessings . . . the improvement in every respect of the soul, which has relied for support on Him who is the cause of all things, who is able to do everything but who wills only to do what is best." (263–68).[261] This faith was directed to the One who is. It was described by Philo as "the queen of the virtues" (270). Philo pointed out that Abraham is the first person in Scripture to be called an elder[262] because of this, for an elder is so regarded not because of the length of his days but because of the praiseworthiness of his life (270). Philo went on to say that the wise

257. See Böhm, *Rezeption*, 132, 135–36, 156, 164–68, 180–82, 226, 228, 234, for discussions of how and why Philo eulogized Sarah.

258. According to Philo, Abraham believed that at death the soul returned to the region from which it had come, i.e., God (258).

259. Böhm, *Rezeption*, 151, comments: "The seeking soul has already come to the climax of its striving and to the goal of its biography of salvation." Mühling, *Blickt*, 283, sees the episode as revealing Abraham as fulfilling the Stoic ideal of the wise person who lets reason control all their conduct.

260. Böhm, *Rezeption*, 350, points out that here Philo had systematically gathered together statements honoring the patriarch, whereas in *QG* they appear scattered throughout. See *QG* 4.84 for a similar interpretation of elder.

261. Böhm, *Rezeption*, 162–63, says that this faith is unshakable trust on the basis of rational conviction and observation of the world, an attitude which one practices permanently in obedience over against the One who is (cf. Konradt, *Die aus Glauben*, 35).

262. Philo is dependent on Genesis 24:1 LXX, which reads και Αβρααμ ην πρεσβυτερος προβεβηκως ημερων. Here, the comparative sense has faded completely. Sandmel, *Philo's Place*, 139n197, thinks that Philo was interpreting the word as meaning "honorable," but in *Abr.* 270 Philo had also used the reference to Abraham's being described as πρεσβυτερος in Genesis 24:1 and then commented that though others before him had actually lived longer, they were not accounted "worthy of this title" (αξιωθεντα ταυτης της προσρησεως. *LSJ*, 1525, give "naming" and "designation" for one category of the meanings of προσρησις). So Böhm, *Rezeption*, 359n148, is surely correct to suggest that Philo is interpreting the term as a *title* of honor.

man (Abraham) was the first man in the human race, being what a pilot is in a ship, a governor in a city, the soul in the body or the mind in the soul, the heaven in the world and God in the heaven (272).[263] God so admired Abraham's faith (πιστις) that He gave him a pledge (πιστις) in return, viz God's oath[264] to confirm the gift which He had promised (273, a reference to Gen 22:16). The purpose of the oath was to establish Abraham's mind more firmly and immovably than before (273). Then Philo added that God conversed with him not as God might with man, but as one friend to another (273).

In the light of this passage, it is clear that Philo took Genesis 15:6 to be a comment on the whole of Abraham's life.[265]

As a concluding tribute to Abraham, Philo quoted God's commendation of him to his son Isaac (Gen 26:5): "God added to the multitude and magnitude of the praises of Abraham, the wise man, by saying "This man fulfilled the divine law, and all the commandments of God," and this, though he had not been taught to do so by written books, but in accordance with the unwritten law of his "nature" (275). Thus, faith and obedience go together.[266]

The way in which Philo described Abraham in this tractate means that he was the embodiment of piety towards God and considerate kindness towards others. He was one who achieved the perfection of virtue. Everything was made to serve this end. Thus, for example, his spiritual journey from the polytheism of his background to the knowledge of the existence of the God who is the creator of all things and who sustains the world providentially, illustrated the journey of the soul; it is not a defense of monotheism per se. Add to this his excellent ethical virtues and this meant that he not only embodied the ideal wise man but that he was a model for any potential

263. Cf. *QG* 3.44 on Genesis 17:6, particularly on the phrase, "I shall set you among the nations."

264. It maybe useful to mention in a footnote, in view of the parallel with the Letter to the Hebrews, that Philo emphasized God's oath in Genesis 22:16-18, confirming His promise to Abraham after Abraham's willingness to offer Isaac, and thus affording the patriarch greater reassurance (*Abr.* 273; *Leg. All.* 3.203-7). Although in *Sacr.* 91-96, Philo actually rejected the notion that God can be said to swear an oath, here, however, the discussion is about the legitimacy of using anthropomorphisms in talking about God. Philo suggested that Moses' words are a concession to human weakness (Moxnes, *Theology*, 141-46, discusses these passages. See also *Immut.* 60-69, for another discussion on the use of anthropomorphisms).

265. As Watson, *Hermenutics*, 250-52, rightly points out. This is preferably to limiting it only to Abraham's sacrifice of Isaac, as Yeung, *Faith*, 252-53, does.

266. Cf. Watson, *Hermeneutics*, 251-52: "Faith itself is the supreme and primary act of obedience to the unwritten law taught by nature."

proselyte contemplating conversion to Judaism.²⁶⁷ The would-be proselyte could also see something of the social and economic cost of conversion in the story of how Abraham was uprooted from his family and social background, though Abraham does seem to remain a wealthy person in Philo's presentation.²⁶⁸ Furthermore, the nobility of Abraham's character could be an answer to those who attacked the Jewish people.²⁶⁹

Some of the closing paragraphs of the treatise *Concerning Virtues* are also devoted to "the most ancient member of the Jewish nation" (212-19).²⁷⁰ Philo never actually used the name Abraham in these paragraphs, but, after the initial reference to him as the ancestor of the Jews, he referred to him as "this man" (214, 218-19). Abraham was a Chaldean by birth.²⁷¹ His father was one of the Chaldean astronomers. They regarded the stars, the entire heaven, and the cosmos as gods, and believed that there was no originating cause outside the things that we perceive with our senses (212). Abram left his homeland due both to what his own mind had worked out²⁷² and to divine inspiration.²⁷³ He realized that as long as he stayed in that

---

267. So also, e.g., Böhm, *Rezeption*, 123, 151, 154; Konradt, *Die aus Glauben*, 34, 37; Mühling, *Blickt*, 284. In *Mos*. 1.7, Moses was descended from the one (Abraham) who is described as επηλυτης and the founder of the whole Jewish nation. LSJ, 620, describe επηλυτης as synonymous with επηλυς and give the meaning as "one who comes to (a place)," and so "incomer, stranger, foreigner." Yonge, *Philo*, 459; Colson, *Philo*, 6:279, translate with "settler." Birnbaum, *Judaism*, 198n17, thinks that either "sojourner" or "proselyte" or both could fit here. Böhm, *Rezeption*, 220, 222, translates "als Hinzugekommener" (literally, one who has come in addition [to others]) and sees in the term a signal to outsiders that Judaism has been in principle open to επηλυται from the very beginning.

268. Böhm, *Rezeption*, 154, 159-60, points out both aspects.

269. What Böhm, *Rezeption*, 232, says of the three patriarchs is true for the portrait of Abraham on its own—it guaranteed the noble origin of the Jewish people and diverted any defamation of it.

270. For an introduction, translation, and commentary, see Wilson, *Philo of Alexandria*. Noack, *Gottesbewusstsein*, 40-103, exegetes these paragraphs in a detailed manner.

271. If Philo was aiming at interested Gentiles, this reference to Abraham's Chaldean origins would be an indication that the accident of birth is not the main criterion for true nobility of a person, but rather a virtuous life (e.g., *Virt*. 189-91).

272. The phrase εννοιαν λαβων indicates forming an idea of something or someone, and so indicates Abraham's own intellectual effort. In 215, Philo spoke of Abraham's intense desire to know the One who Exists and in 216 how he came to an unswerving and firm understanding that there was one Cause above all. Noack, *Gottesbewusstsein*, 48-49, correctly observes that it is Abraham's decision which is to the fore. Divine inspiration supports reason, not replaces it.

273. Philo uses επιθειαζειν here, at 214(επιθειασας) and also at 217 (επιθειαζων). See also note 280.

polytheistic country[274] he would not make progress in his quest to discover the eternal God, who is Father of all things, the supreme cause, and the overruling providence of all things. He needed to leave his native land in order to change his false opinions into true belief (214). At the same time, he received divine oracles which further stimulated his search for the one God and guided his steps on this quest, and he arrived at a distinct perception not of God's essence (which is impossible) but of His existence and His overruling providence (215).[275] Thus, Abraham found that there is one supreme cause who governs the world by His providence. So, indeed, Abraham was "the first person of whom it was said that he believed in God, since he was the first who had an unswerving and firm comprehension of God, apprehending that there is one supreme cause and that He it is who provides for (προνοει) the world and everything in it" (215-16).[276]

Faith here is the intellectual conviction of the existence of God as the supreme Cause of everything and His providence. There seems somewhat more stress here on monotheism than in the treatise on Abraham.[277] While the focus is on what Abraham did, we also have an indication of the encouragement and stimulus provided by God. Philo seems to want to indicate that Abraham did not get to where he did purely by his own intellectual efforts. At the same time, Philo went on to say that Abraham, having acquired trust (in God), that most steadfast of virtues (πιστιν την των αρετων βεβαιοτατην), also acquired all the others (216).

Due to his magnanimity and greatness of soul, those who received him thought of him as a king (216),[278] while his own servants observed the greatness of his nature and disposition. The divine Spirit took possession

274. *Virt.* 212-13 contains a negative evaluation of Chaldean astrology and its polytheism.

275. See *Leg. All.* 1.35, where Philo generalized and stated that we have received an idea of the existence from His works. On the other hand, at *Praem.* 44, Philo said that Jacob learned of God's existence by direct instruction from God.

276. In another of the Exposition treatises (*Praem.* 27), Philo referred to Abraham as the first to lead the way to the God-loving viewpoint, to pass from vanity to truth, who received faith in God as his reward. Because of the innate goodness of his natural disposition and his acquiring of virtue through instruction he was given joy.

277. Noack, *Gottesbewusstsein*, 51, comments that truth finds its center in monotheism. He also made the observation (70) that in this description of Abraham, faith means to be rational through orientation on God alone.

278. Noack, *Gottesbewusstsein*, 70-77, has a helpful discussion of the link between the wise philosopher, kingship, physical beauty, and divine qualities in Plato and Hellenistic writers, and he goes on to state (81) that Abraham did not lose consciousness but inspiration deepened his ability to communicate rationality (at the start of his monograph, 1-2, Noack is critical of Hans Jonas's theory that Philo thought that in inspiration the human consciousness was replaced by the divine Spirit).

of him and both endued him with physical beauty and endowed his words with persuasiveness,[279] enabling also his hearers to understand him (217).[280] This man, then, aimed at making himself a kinsman, disciple, and friend of God (218). He was justly regarded as in the highest category of prophets because he trusted in the Uncreated God who is Father of all things. He was honored as king by those who met him, not because of any military prowess but because he was chosen by God. By his life he benefited others (218). This man was the standard of nobility to all proselytes,[281] who had given up ignoble customs such as paying honor to stocks and stones and all sorts of inanimate things as if they were gods and who had come over to a commonwealth full of vitality and life, with truth as its director and president (219). He was indeed a standard not only for men but also for women (220). With proselytes in mind, Philo in this passage was holding up Abraham as a model to be imitated and a model who can be imitated.[282] Another aspect to be noted is that Philo's description has no traces of Jewish ethnicity but is phrased in universal terms: for example, he ended the treatise by saying that the law assesses a person on the basis of their own conduct and not on the basis of the virtues or vices of their ancestors when it awards praise or punishment (227)[283] Neither in this passage nor elsewhere in his writings did Philo actually discuss whether a proselyte had to embrace circumcision,

---

279. Noack, *Gottesbewusstsein*, 79, points out that rhetorically convincing powers are part of the theory of the philosopher-king.

280. Again, Philo uses ἐπιθειάζειν of this inspiration. Isaacs, *Concept of the Spirit*, 47n39, may be right in mentioning *Virt.* 217 under prophetic inspiration (in *Her.* 259, Philo said that every good man is a prophet and that the prophet speaks only that which is prompted by one other than himself), but, strictly speaking, Philo's main concern seems to be the search for the one true God and becoming a kinsman and friend of God, and it is in this context that he referred to Abraham's ranking with the greatest of the prophets. Aune, *Prophecy in Early Christianity*, does not discuss *Virt.* 217. For Philo's own experience of the inspiration of the Spirit when in contemplative reflection, see *Somn.* 2.250–52.

281. Colson, *Philo*, 8:297; Wilson, *On Virtues*, 88, both translate ἐπηλύταις in this way. See also note 283. Kuhn, προσήλυτος, 731–32, has shown that Philo preferred ἐπιλύτης, ἐπίλυτος, and ἔπηλυς to προσήλυτος, and thinks that this is because these terms would be more familiar to pagan readers. This explanation would fit if the Exposition writings were aimed at a wider audience than just Jews. See *Spec.* 1.51–52, 309, where Philo described the change of mind and conduct which characterizes the proselytes.

282. In 220–222, Tamar is held up as a model for female proselytes.

283. Cf. Noack, *Gottesbewusstsein*, 102–3; Böhm, *Rezeption*, 195–96. See Birnbaum, *Judaism*, 195–219, 220–30, for a general discussion of Philo's attitude to proselytes. She comes to the conclusion that in Philo "Israel" is a class which represents the ideal of seeing God and occurs most frequently in the Allegorical Commentaries, and denotes a relationship potentially open to all and is not limited to those born into the historical nation.

but since a proselyte accepted the obligations of the Law and since Philo declared in *Migr.* 92 that even if circumcision had a symbolic significance, that was no reason to do away with the law which imposed it, one might assume that he did expect a proselyte to be circumcised.[284]

Much of this basically repeats what we have summarized from *Concerning Abraham*,[285] though we notice that in *Concerning Virtues* Philo referred to Abraham's inspiration by the Holy Spirit, a point not made in *Concerning Abraham*.

In the treatise *Praem.*, Philo said that Abraham was the first to pass from vanity to truth. He used the virtue which comes through instruction as a means towards perfection, and chose as his reward faith in God (27; cf. 49, 58). On this interpretation, faith is the climax of the quest and not the starting point. It becomes the reward for prior effort to acquire virtue.[286] Philo commented "What can any one conceive to be either more useful or more respectable than to believe in God and throughout one's whole life to be continually rejoicing and beholding the living God?" (27). To believe in God is not to believe in all created and perishable things (including the outward senses and even reason which can at times be erroneous, 28–29). The person to whom it has been given to see and examine thoroughly all corporeal and incorporeal things, and to lean upon and to found himself on God alone, with firm and steadfast reason and unalterable and sure confidence, is truly happy and blessed (30). Faith here seems to be a conviction which penetrates beyond things perceivable with the senses to the existence of the one supreme Being.

2.14.4 Allegorical Commentary

We turn now to consider the picture of Abraham which emerges from the *Allegorical Commentary*. Of the 21 tractates assigned to Genesis in this series, five deal with passages to be found in Genesis 12:1–17:22. Of these five, four deal with Abraham, viz. *Migr.*, *Her.*, *Congr.*, and *Mut.*, while *Fug.* deals

---

284. See the careful discussion in Birnbaum, *Judaism*, 199–200. For a general defense of circumcision by Philo, see *QG* 3.46–47; *Spec.* 1.1–11.

285. See Böhm, *Rezeption*, 192n340, where she suggests that *Virt.* 211–19, paraphrases material from *Abr.*

286. A somewhat similar line of thought is found in *On the Migration of Abraham* 44. The warning of Barclay must at this point be heeded—while God's gifts are congruous with the quality of the recipient, "a *congruous* gift is still a gift: it has not been 'debased' into a form of payment, 'earned' by the good works of the recipient" (Barclay, *Gift*, 237).

with Hagar.[287] Unlike the Exposition treatises, the Allegorical ones, while starting from a text in Genesis, range well beyond the passage, so that it is not possible actually to adopt a chronological approach from the departure from Chaldea to Abraham's death. Of course, Abraham figures in many of the other Allegorical treatises and many of these references[288] will also be drawn upon to furnish us with the kind of information which we seek, but on the whole *Migr.* will provide the initial starting point[289] (hence references with a number only are from it), with this then being enlarged with material from other tractates.

On several occasions, Philo described Abraham as a wise man,[290] as a philosopher, dedicated to contemplating the Sublime. The wise man is dedicated to pursuing the path of virtue.[291] Comenting on "Abraham journeyed even as the Lord spoke to him" (*Migr.* 127–29, on Gen 12:4), Philo said that "as God speaks, so the good man does everything, blamelessly keeping the path of life straight, so that the actions of the wise man are nothing else than the commands[292] of God" (129).

Precisely because he is a wise man, Abraham is a royal figure, he (or sometimes the wise man) is a king, or, one might say, he is the philosopher-king.[293] Philo exploited the statements of the people of Hebron in Genesis 23:6 LXX, when they said of Abraham, "You are a king before God among us."[294] Depicted in such glowing terms, it is not surprising that Abraham becomes a model worthy of imitation.

Certainly, in the Allegorical Commentary, once again "the journey of the soul, its struggles against the passions, and its quest for God,"[295] is a

---

287. *Migr.* deals with Genesis 12:1–4, 6; *Her.* handles Genesis 15:2–18; *Congr.* expounds the meaning of Genesis 16:1–6a; and *Mut.* discusses Genesis 17:1–5, 15–22.

288. Abraham is mentioned in other tractates of the Allegorical Writings, whether by name or under such phrases as the wise man, this man, etc.

289. *Migr.* expounds Genesis 12:1–4: verses 1–3 is expounded in para. 2–117, verse 3 in para. 118–127a, verse 4a is expounded in para. 127b–147, and verse 4b in para. 148 on, though actually Philo ranged forth over the Pentateuch without any special order, far beyond the story of Abraham and referred to a considerable number of OT characters.

290. E.g., *Migr.* 13, 122; *Congr.* 48, 92, 109, 119; cf. *Cher.* 45.

291. When the mind pursues the path of virtue, this is described by Philo as the same as "to live in agreement with nature" advocated by the best philosophers (128).

292. Literally, "words," but here legitimately rendered "commands," in view of the context.

293. *Agr.* 41; *Sobr.* 57; Mig. 272; *Mut.* 128, 151–53; cf. *Somn.* 2.243–44.

294. *Mut.* 151; cf. *Somn.* 2.244. Genesis 23:6 LXX runs: Βασιλευς παρα Θεου εν ημιν. The MT has "You are a prince of God among us."

295. Birnbaum, *Judaism*, 19. Früchtel, *Kosmologischen Vorstellungen*, 104, states

dominant concern. Through the allegorical interpretation of the text, the story of Abraham becomes an illustration of one aspect or possibility of the progress of the soul in its journey to God[296]—the journey to wisdom and perfection through instruction and learning (just as the other patriarchs illustrate other aspects or possibilities, while the wives of the three patriarchs—Sarah, Rebekah, and Leah—illustrate certain virtues).[297]

We shall draw together certain themes which pertain to and illustrate this journey of the soul:

(a) We meet *the concept of the rational and the irrational parts of the soul* (66–68, 205–6).

Opening his treatment of Genesis 12:1–3, Philo interpreted the terms land, kindred, and father's house which Abraham must leave, allegorically. While "Land" stands for the body which is mortal and which will decompose back to the earth (*Migr.* 3) and "Father's House" stands for speech (the beauty of whose phrasing could entice the soul from true beauty (12),[298] "Kindred" stands for sense perception, which is closely related to understanding, "the irrational with the rational, for both these are parts of one soul" (3). When the mind comes to know itself, it will thrust from itself that part of the soul which inclines to the objects of sense perception (13)

Desire and anger stir the whole of the irrational part of the soul and seek to destroy the mind (66). The foolish person follows them and thus discards reason as pilot and judge (67), whereas the opposite type of person eliminates anger and desire and lives under divine reason (67). The rational

---

that for Philo, "the few verses in Genesis 12:1–3 were seen as code for the journey of the soul. . . . This journey of Abraham is the prototype for the journey of the soul of the true wise person." The Old Testament confirms "the general validity of Abraham's experience for those who have attached themselves to the company of virtue-loving souls" (Früchtel, *Kosmologischen Vorstellungen*, 105). Here, the word used by Früchtel for company is *thiasos*, a transliteration of the Greek θιασος, which Philo used when contrasting the company of those who love virtue and those who are captives to earthly desires, as symbolized by Sarah/Isaac and Hagar/Ishmael respectively in, e.g., *Cher.* 7-8; *Post.* 38; *Sobr.* 8-9.

296. An example of the way in which Philo can pass from talking about Abraham to talking about the soul is afforded by *Mut.* 52–53. Philo had been commenting on the covenant which God made with Abraham as recorded in Genesis 17 and God's command for him to be blameless. He asserted that a covenant is for the advantage of those who are worthy of it and is a symbol of grace which God had placed between Himself as the One who offers it and the person who receives it. And this is the extravagance of kindness that there is nothing between God and *the soul* except His own virgin grace.

297. See Böhm, *Rezeption*, 255–64.

298. Colson, *Philo*, 4:134, explains that while the mind has a wider range, its most intimate home is speech.

part can turn its free and noble impulses towards everything that is beautiful without anything pulling in the opposite direction (67–68).

The irrational parts are drawn to the outward senses. Philo allegorized the daughters of Salpaad[299] who appealed to Moses for their right to inherit the property of their father who had died without any son (Num 27).[300] They belonged to the tribe of Manasseh, which means "forgetfulness." Forgetfulness loses its reasoning power and has female offspring, who are assumed to be inferior to males. Philo concluded that the daughters in the story stand for the outward senses, and "The outward senses are the daughters of the irrational part of the soul" (205–6).[301]

(b) *The dualism of body and soul means that the soul must seek to distance itself from the body.*

Philo can urge: "Depart, therefore, out of the earthly matter that encompasses you: escape, man, with all your might and main from the foul prison-house, your body, and from its pleasures and desires which act as its jailors" (*Migr.* 9).[302] This note, enunciated early on, recurs in various ways throughout the treatise. Lot is allegorized as the inclination to the outward senses (13; cf. 150). Abraham's departure from his nephew was explained as follows: "it is impossible for a man who is overwhelmed with the love of the incorporeal and imperishable objects to dwell with one, whose every inclination is towards the mortal objects of the outward senses" (13). Later, Philo returned to the theme of Abraham's distancing himself from Lot (whose name Philo interpreted as meaning turning aside or inclining away, in this instance from the good, 148).[303] He said that Lot went with Abraham not to unlearn ignorance and derive improvement, but with a view to leading him astray with counter attractions and allurements (149). But Abraham took care to live at a distance from him (150).[304]

299. So the LXX. The MT has Zelophehad.

300. They won their appeal, and legislation was enacted, but with the proviso that any daughter inheriting should not marry outside her own tribe.

301. As daughters they are the inferior product as compared with sons. Forgetfulness, the slumber of reason, produces females, for it is destitute of reason (206).

302. Cf. Plato's dictum σωμα σημα. *Her.* 68 refers to the prison of the body. In *Leg. All.* 2.58–59, Philo can say that when Abraham heard God's command recorded in Genesis 12:1 he was "naked," i.e., in the light of 2.54, he must have been free from all vices and passions.

303. See Grabbe, *Etymology*, 181–82, for a discussion on the etymology.

304. Further examples of this are: Egypt is a symbol of the pleasures of the flesh, and hence there is need to remove the soul of the people from Egypt or the house of the body (14, 20–21, 23, 151); Joseph stands for the person who is attracted to the body and external things (159–63, 263), and his son, Manasseh, illustrates forgetfulness which arises from the slumber of reason (205).

According to *Det.* 159, Philo said that when Abraham left his country, his kindred, and his father's house (= the body, the outward senses, and speech) according to God's command in Genesis 12:1, he began to be acquainted with the powers of the living God. Then, the statement that God appeared to him in Canaan (Gen 12:7), was taken to show that God was seen by him who had abandoned mortal things and had taken refuge in the incorporeal soul. We may quote also *Gig.*53: the divine spirit dwells with one class of persons (μονω δε ανθρωπων ειδει ενι), viz. those who have put off the things of this creation and the veil of false opinion and who come to God with the spirit bare and naked.[305]

It fits in with this conceptual framework, when, in a comment on Genesis 25:8 about Abraham's death (being gathered to his fathers), Philo said that Abraham left mortal things and became equal to angels (*Sacr.* 5).

(c) *As the mind (νους) is part of the divine in a person, a person should ensure that it controls that person's actions and that the mind must war incessant war against the passions.*

That Philo's interest is in the soul and not really so much in the historical Abraham is revealed straightaway. God wished to purify the soul of man, and impelled it to a change of abode in order to quit the three regions which consist of the body, the outward senses, and speech.[306] Here, in accordance with the biblical text, Philo stressed the divine initiative: God had the purpose of cleansing the soul in issuing the command to leave Chaldea. Thus, that command to depart from his country, family, and father's house

---

If one cannot fight unreasonable passions, then it is best to flee to escape them. Jacob was right to leave Laban's employment (26) in Haran, which stands for the external senses (27; cf. 212–13). So, when perfect, he quit the abode of the outward senses. Jacob's question, "When shall I make myself a house?" (Gen 30:30) is interpreted to mean "When shall I dwell in mind and intellect?" (214). Simeon and Levi's action in massacring the inhabitants of Shechem is taken as destroying those devoted to pleasure and indulgence. These two are, therefore, friends of wisdom (224). Philo takes the transportation of Joseph's bones–bones being the only parts of the soul left after the body has dissolved–to be a symbol of taking the imperishable to the cities of virtue (17).

305. In this instance, Moses becomes the illustration of such a class of persons (*Gig.* 54–55).

306. Philo explained that the body was fashioned from earth and dissolves back to the earth; the outward senses are the irrational part of the soul; while speech is merely the abode of the mind and inferior to sight. What was true of Abraham was somewhat similar in the case of Jacob. At *Migr.* 30, 38, Philo said that God told Jacob that he needed to leave the land of which Laban was a symbol (immersion in objects of sense perception), in order to receive the fruits of his victorious struggle against passions, and reside in the land of his fathers, symbol of the Word and Wisdom. There "he obtained the inheritance based on sight, having passed beyond that based on hearing" (και τυγχανει του καθ ορασιν κληρου τον εξ ακοης υπερβας) (38), and was renamed Israel (a reference to the incident at Penuel). He who sees is the wise man.

really meant that a person must not let the body, the outward senses, and speech cling to them, but must stand above them (7). A person must learn to govern them and not be governed by them since a person is a king (8). We meet the maxim, so typical of Greek thought—"Know yourself" (8), and this figures elsewhere in the treatise (137-38, 185, 187, 222).[307] But this should not be taken as an indication that human self-effort is all that is involved, because, later, Philo said that there is a mind in a person and in the universe (186), and these two are linked, the former reflecting the latter. To look within oneself is, therefore, to be brought in touch with the Mind behind the universe. "By observing the conditions in your own individual household . . . you will gain a sure knowledge of God and of His works" (185). As the Mind of the universe governs the world, so the mind in a person should subject everything to itself.[308]

At *Somn.* 1.60, Philo can speak of Abraham's coming to know himself completely and, as a result, renouncing the nothingness of the creature in order to learn to comprehend the living God.[309] Knowing oneself leads to the flight from oneself to God.[310]

(d) *Philo described the way which God has laid out for the soul to go as the "royal way."*

He took this phrase from Numbers 20:17; 21:22, where it describes the trade route through Edom from Damascus to the Gulf of Akaba, and he allegorized it to mean the way the soul must go if it was to attain to God, turning neither to the right or left. This royal road was the way which God had laid down for virtue-loving souls to keep to (146).

This road was the one used by Abraham who did not deviate from it to the left or right (*Gig.* 64; cf. *Immut.* 161-62).[311] This road is the way of

307. Cf. God's advice to Moses (*Spec. Leg.* 1.44). In *Legat.* 69, Philo declared that Macro, the prefect of Egypt who pursued a severely discriminatory policy towards the Jews, had no idea about that great lesson which came from the Delphic oracle, "Know yourself."

308. Cf. the advice given by Rebekka to Jacob when he was about to leave for Haran: he should know the country of the senses, but especially he should know himself so that he might know whether it was the mind in himself or the Mind behind the universe which controlled his actions (*Fug.* 46).

309. In para. 58, Philo had contrasted Socrates with his Know Yourself approach and Terah who represents the principle of knowing oneself in order to gather the fruits of pure morality, but it is in para. 60 that the contrast with Socrates was fully developed through the figure of Abraham and his departure from Haran.

310. Maren Niehoff, *Jewish Identity*, 145, says that Philo here represents Abraham as achieving the philosophical breakthrough in contrast to Socrates who emphasized self knowledge. Jews, therefore, who follow Abraham would be associating with authentic and unchanging values. Their culture was superior to that of the Greeks.

311. Philo here alluded to the concept from Numbers 20:17 without specifically

wisdom, of true philosophy (but not that of the Sophists, as Philo made clear in *Post.* 101-2), of virtue (*Migr.* 146).[312] This royal way leads to the knowledge and understanding of God. The mind/soul must beware of the corrupting influence of the flesh as it journeys on.[313] So Philo encouraged his readers to proceed along this royal road, which alone enables souls to escape to the uncreated God.[314] Even though the earthly Edom seeks to block this way, the divine Logos helps by blocking Edom's road so that it cannot reach the knowledge-seeking soul (*Immut.* 180). In *Post.* 102, Philo can identify the royal road with the Logos.[315]

(e) *Philo allegorizes the various journeys of Abraham.*

Although the treatise bears the title περι αποικιας, Philo spent the bulk of *Migr.* 2-126 on the gifts which God promised Abraham = the wise person. At paragraph 127, he quoted Genesis 12:4 to the effect that "Abraham journeyed even as the Lord spoke to him." Philo allegorized this: to journey in accordance with the commands of God was to live according to nature and was the goal (τελος) praised by the best philosophers. It is attained when the mind (νους) walks in the way of virtue, travels in the footsteps of right reason, and follows God, mindful of His commands and recognizing them as valid for speech and action.

At paragraph 177, Philo reminded his addressees that before Abraham resided in Haran, at an earlier date, he had migrated from Chaldea to

quoting the passage. The same is true of *Immut.* 159-60.

312. For a study of "royal way/King's Highway" in Philo, see the monograph by Pascher, *Der Konigsweg*. See Früchtel, *Kosmologischen Vorstellungen*, 90-91, 112-15, for criticism of Pascher's argument that Philo depended on the Mystery religions for his ideas. rather, the idea was frequent in Middle Platonism, and in Philo the Mystery was a written, not a cultic, one, contained in the writings of Moses. Müller, Χριστος Αρχηγος, 193-207, discusses the concept of God and the Logos as leaders of the soul in Philo's thought and also his use of the concept of the "royal way/King's Highway" from Numbers 20. Mack, *Logos und Sophia*, 133-41; Cox, "Royal Road," 167-80, also discuss the concept. Apart from *Spec. Leg.* 4.168, the references to the royal way occur in the Allegorical treatises.

313. *Immut.* 143-44. That Philo has in mind the passage from Numbers 25, even though he does not specifically quote it, is shown by the fact that he refers to Edom as always fighting those who wish to proceed on this route. He interprets Edom as meaning "earthly."

314. *Immut.* 159-60, 162. Philo can also use the motif of the ascent of the soul: in *Mut.* 179-80, Philo compared the journey of the soul heavenward to the flight of a bird. The soul soars through the air beyond the boundaries perceived by the outward senses and scarcely stops at the boundary of the circle of the stars, while in *Det.* 89-90, Philo said that the soul is eager to advance further to a knowledge of the incomprehensible nature of God, even if only to God's existence (cf. *Conf.* 95).

315. Here Philo has actually quoted Numbers 20:17 about not turning to the right or left.

Haran (177). He then turned to consider the reputation of the Chaldeans. He described the Chaldeans as astrologers and genealogists (178), and so, basically, Chaldea stands for astrology.[316] They saw the universe as displaying a perfect harmony due to affinity between its different parts (178). They believed that this world was the only world in the universe and that this world was either God Himself or that it contained God within itself (i.e., the soul of the universe, 179, 181). They created fate and necessity into gods (179). It was probably these-to Philo-completely erroneous views which occasioned him a little later to describe Chaldea as representing "opinion" (187). Moses, of course, did not subscribe to these views. Rather, God created the world and holds it together by His invisible powers (181), while not being contained by anything (182). It is worth pointing out that, though Philo had assumed monotheism throughout this treatise,[317] it was not until this point that he touched on this topic at any length.[318] The major interest in the treatise is not to defend monotheism or attack polytheism as such, but to reflect on the pilgrimage of the soul.

The way in which Philo interpreted Abraham's departure from Chaldea illustrates the idea of the journey of the soul in its quest for higher things.[319] (In *Ebr.* 94, Philo mentioned some persons like Abraham, who had abandoned Chaldean metereological speculations and passed over to the contemplation of the uncreated God).[320] Earlier, Philo had noted the future orientation to this quest. The soul is seeking that which it does not yet possess, and, therefore, the soul needs to repose trust and faith in God, as Abraham did (*Migr.* 43-44).

Philo appealed to his addressees to come down from astrological research and turn instead to consider themselves, and their reason would show them that as there was a mind in human beings, so there was in the universe who controlled all things (185-86).

From Chaldea Abraham had gone to Haran, and then he departed from Haran, which represented the outward senses (via the explanation

---

316. Cf. *Her.* 96-97.

317. E.g., the uncreated God (157), ruler of the world (169).

318. That is, at para. 176! By para. 184, Philo had returned to the need to reflect inwardly and move from analysing the external senses to contemplate the Mind behind the universe, the Father of piety and holiness.

319. An impassioned illustration of this is the interpretation of God's command to Moses and others to come up Sinai in Exodus 24:1: "Come up, O soul, to behold the God Who Is . . . come . . . willingly, fearlessly, lovingly" (169).

Moxnes, *Theology*, 130, regards this event as one of two events which were more important than others for Philo, the other being the change of name from Abram to Abraham recorded in Genesis 17.

320. Cf. *Abr.* 84.

"holes" which are symbols of openings used by sense-perceptions, e.g., eyes are openings used by sight, 188; cf. 195, 197). A person should investigate their own nature, learning what is "the master in it and that which is in subjection, the living and the lifeless element, the rational and the irrational, the immortal and the mortal, the better and the worse," and this would lead to a sure knowledge of God and of His works (185). One should migrate from outward sense and the corporeal abode (189-194) to attain to the Father of piety and holiness, the Father and Creator of the Universe (193-94).[321] Philo thus returned to a theme which he had enunciated at the beginning of the treatise (cf. 7-14). Abraham looked within at his own soul; he analysed himself.[322] It is the mind/soul which governs the body, just as the Deity governs the universe. When the mind had come to know itself accurately, it would be able to comprehend the nature of God (193-94; cf. 222). By so doing one can see what one ought to obey and what one ought to be master of.

Philo sums up the progress of the mind: it first needed to abandon astrology and the mistaken idea that the universe was God and that the stars controlled human destiny (194); then it considers itself (195). The third stage is to crown the accurate self-knowledge with the knowledge of God Himself (195).

Philo did not deal at length with the journey of Abraham after he left Haran. He stated that Abraham travelled through the country as far as the oak tree at Shechem. This journey indicated that love of learning was by nature curious and inquisitive, possessing an extraordinary appetite for all that is to be seen and heard (216).[323] Then, in an extended passage, Philo mentioned how merchants in pursuit of financial gain travel round the world in all seasons and all sorts of weather, enduring separation from family and country and the amenities of its institutions, and yet how sad it would be to think that men would not do the same in order to acquire the best of possessions, namely, wisdom. The passage culminates in a lyrical appeal to his own soul to travel through land and man, assessing under what influences the body co-operates with the mind; what speech is and how it contributes to virtue; what are pleasure, desire, pain, and fear, and how a person can escape such feelings; what are the destructive vices like foolishness, intemperance, injustice, and how they may be averted; what

---

321. Philo used the difference between Genesis 46:27 LXX (Jacob and his household who entered Egypt comprised 75 people) and Deuteronomy 10 (70 went down into Egypt) to say that Jacob, having gained the ability to behold God, had got rid of the five senses.

322. Cf. also *Det.* 159.

323. Note the difference between this comparatively brief comment and the larger treatment in the treatise on Abraham in the Exposition series.

are justice, prudence, temperance, courage, and deliberate wisdom; what the mastery over passions is and in what way virtue is usually produced (217–19).

This theme occurs in other tractates as well. Thus, in *Who is Heir of All Things*, Philo maintained that the soul must move from worship of things created to the One who has created them, for the stars and planets were not that which controlled events, as the Chaldeans believed.[324] When God said to Abraham that He had brought him from Chaldea to give him the land of Canaan to inherit (Gen 15:7), Philo took this as a confirmation of an old promise, viz. getting him out of the erroneous atmosphere of the Chaldeans, and the bestowal of a new gift, viz. the inheritance of wisdom so that the migration of the soul was a passage "from astrology to real nature study, from insecure conjecture to firm apprehension, and, to give it its truest expression, from the created to the uncreated, from the world to its Maker and Father" (*Her.* 98). Abraham had given his trust "to Him who rides on the heaven and guides the chariot of the whole world, even God" (*Her.* 99). God existed beyond what can be observed with the senses (cf. *Her.* 98).[325]

Philo spoke in a similar way in *On the Change of Names* 16. Having mentioned in the previous paragraph the text which said that the Lord was seen by Abraham (Gen 17:1), Philo proceeded to generalize: When our mind was occupied with the wisdom of the Chaldeans and was studying the sublime things which exist in the world, it made a tour of all the efficient powers as the causes of what exist, but when it migrated from Chaldean doctrines, it then knew that it was moving under the direction of a governor, the appearance of whose authority it perceived (16). Though late in learning the truth, the soul did not continue for ever in ignorance but received an idea that there was an authority and governing power in the universe (17). This gliding over from referring to Abraham to a generalizing mode of speech could be due to the fact that Philo wished to counter the attractions of what one might call the natural philosophical approach to the detriment of revealed truth contained in the Scriptures.[326] Later, still in the context of a discussion on the change of name from Abram to Abraham, Philo moved on to consider the nature of true philosophy. He has God ask those who

---

324. A point which Philo mentions on other occasions: e.g., *Leg.* 3.1; *Migr.* 171–81; and in the Exposition series in *Abr.* 68–70, 79.

325. In *Cher.* 31, Philo allegorized "the fire and sword" taken by Abraham in Genesis 22:6: it indicated that Abraham was eager to slay and burn that mortal element from himself so that he might soar up to God, with the intellect naked and disentangled from the body.

326. Böhm, *Rezeption*, 278, also considers this a possibility, and mentions Calvert, *Philo's Use of Traditions*, 466, as also holding this view.

investigate the movement of the stars and the heavens whether they get any moral advantage from this? Does it help to eradicate the passions which disturb the soul or control base appetites? (72). "As there is no advantage in trees unless they are productive of fruit, so in the same way there is no use in the study of natural philosophy unless it is likely to confer upon a man the acquisition of virtue, for that is its proper fruit" (73). Scholars of older generations had considered that the physical and logical parts of philosophy needed to be conjoined with moral philosophy, by which the moral character is improved and virtue acquired (75). This is the lesson to be learned from Abraham. He did have his name changed, but also in reality changed his nature from a consideration of natural to that of moral philosophy. He abandoned the contemplation of the world itself for the knowledge of the Being who created the world. Through this knowledge he "acquired piety, the most excellent of all possessions" (76). Later, Philo summarized Abraham's attitude when expressing the hope that God might consider Ishmael as his heir (Gen 17:18): faith in God and distrust in the creature/created things (201).[327]

There are some interesting observations on the journey when Philo commented on Genesis 22:4 in *Post.* 17-21. He said that the wise man (= Abraham), who wanted to understand the nature of the Ruler of the universe, proceeded along the road which leads to knowledge and wisdom, and met with the logoi of God, among whom he rested for a while. He saw that the object of his quest was difficult to attain, for God seems to recede. Paradoxically, God, even while standing still, outstrips everything. He is at the same moment both close to us and at a great distance. But it is better to engage on the quest than not at all. Then Philo spoke disparagingly about Cain who was a lover of himself and left his soul without any conception whatsoever of the living God.

Often Philo can speak in very general terms of the wise man in general or Abraham in particular as being a sojourner here (*Ebr.* 100; *Conf.* 77-79; *Her.* 82-83,88; *Somn.* 1.151). In *Agri.* 65, he maintained that the soul of a wise man has heaven for its country with earth as a strange land, or the body as a lodging house in which it proposes to sojourn for a while. The house of wisdom is its true home. In a passage comparing the three patriarchs and what they symbolize, Philo said that Abraham had instruction as his guide along the road which led him to virtue (*Somn.* 1.166-68).

(f) *Philo discusses the various stages on this journey.*

Philo postulated stages for this journey of the soul. He treated this especially in *On Mating with Preliminary Studies*. At the very end of the

327. Philo simply refers to Abraham as the virtuous man.

treatise, Philo said "It is not women that are spoken of here; it is minds—on the one hand, the mind which exercises itself in the preliminary learning, on the other, the mind which strives to win the palm of virtue and does not cease until it is won" (*Congr.* 180). Philo allegorized Sarah as virtue:[328] she was barren as regards evil but prolific in good things, especially wisdom and virtue (1, 5, 63, 180). He allegorized her handmaiden, Hagar, as intermediate instruction or Encyclical Knowledge (9, 72, 155, 180).[329]

The first stage was to be trained in the Encyclia, i.e., the study of grammar, music, rhetoric, arithmetic, astronomy, and dialectic (11, 14–18).[330] In the allegorisation, Sarah's request that Abraham should go into Hagar (Gen 16:2) indicated that it was necessary for Abraham the learner to be obedient to the injunctions of virtue (63). Abraham obeyed Sarah because he longed for knowledge, truth, and virtue. Philo used the analogy of the student listening to the words of his teacher. Encyclical studies were necessary (24),[331] but they were preliminary. They were the road which should lead on to the study of philosophy and virtue (9). The subjects of the Encyclia were stepping stones to the study of the higher knowledge and perfect virtue, to philosophy, by which Philo meant Jewish philosophy which had its primary place in the pursuit of wisdom in the synagogue on the Sabbath, and this wisdom had its basis in nature, in one's capacity to distinguish between right and wrong. This knowledge and wisdom were more admirable than encyclical accomplishments (156).[332]

In terms of the allegory, whereas the encyclical branches of knowledge need bodily organs and faculties (intercourse with Hagar), the qualities of the mistress (Sarah) reach the soul (155). Philo used the analogy of feeding infants with milk (the encyclical stage) and the mature with solid food (philosophy and virtue) (19).

---

328. And also philosophy (cf. Böhm, *Rezeption*, 263n72, referring to *Congr.* 79). For Sarah as φρονησις, see *Migr.* 126.

329. See *Leg. All.* 3.244–45

330. It is after childhood that one is admitted to these studies. Philo indicated this when he allegorized the fact that Sarah gave Hagar to Abraham after they had been in Canaan for ten years (121).

331. Philo thus can be seen as helping upper class Jews to come to terms with Hellenistic culture. He legitimized encyclical education provided it was seen as subservient to the philosophy of Moses. Cf. Böhm, *Rezeption*, 287, 291–92, 295.

332. Borgen, *Bread from Heaven*, 108–111, 121, 124–27, followed by Moxnes, *Theology*, 137, relates this emphasis on the need to go beyond encyclical knowledge to the need to help Jews in Alexandria, especially Jewish youths, to resist the temptation to be drawn into Alexandrian society and lose their Jewish identity. See *Mut.* 253–63, which Borgen, *Bread*, 99–121, isolates as a homily.

One should, then, only be a sojourner in the Encyclical Instruction stage (22), though Philo had known of those who had remained charmed by the handmaiden and neglected the mistress (77).

Sarah stood for virtue and philosophy. Abraham pursued the virtue which came through teaching (η διακτικη αρετη), and this was the fruit of both the encyclical studies and of the union with Sarah (literally, "those born in wedlock which are based on understanding" γνωσιων μεν των κατα φρονησιν 35).[333] Philosophy contributed to the obtaining of wisdom. It was the pursuit of wisdom (επιτηευσις σοφιας), and wisdom was the knowledge of things divine and human and their causes (79). Philo had Abraham addressing Sarah in an elaboration of Genesis 16:6 ("Behold, the servant girl is in your hands. Deal with her as is pleasing to you"): "In the same degree as the mind [διανοια] is more powerful, more active, and altogether better than the hand, I hold knowledge and wisdom [επιστημη και φρονησις] to be more admirable than the culture of the schools and have given them full and special honor" (156; cf. 154)

At *Congr.* 139, Philo began a contrast between the subjects which made up the encyclical studies and philosophy. Encyclical education achieved progress by teaching; philosophy is associated with what is self-taught by nature.[334] While philosophy appropriates the whole nature of existing things (144), it seeks understanding of all things, divine as well as human. What the mind (νους) is to the senses, knowledge which comes through philosophy is to the arts which comprise the encyclical studies (144). One should move from reliance on the perception of outward things, to intuitive wisdom, self-taught by nature, with the climax of the soul's quest being the vision of God, the One who is.[335]

In *Leg. All.* 3.243-44, Philo envisaged the soul being faced with a choice between two women, folly and virtue. We must put our trust in the woman which Sarah was ordained to be, Virtue. The wise Abraham was guided by her. She realized that he was not ready to have children by her, because at that time he was involved in subjects of lofty philosophical speculation (this

---

333. In 74-76, Philo inserted an autobiographical section which described the pattern of his own education. Böhm, *Rezeption*, 290, makes the comment that here Philo identified with Abraham's educational biography, which represents an ideal type.

334. Philo applied to the Encyclia the illustration of bread produced from the earth, while philosophy was compared to the self-grown fruits of the sabbatical year (*Mut.* 253-63). See the discussion in Borgen, *Bread*, 103-7.

335. Philo was very critical of those whom he called sophists, who were skilled in language but blameworthy as regards the quality of their lives. They were powerful speakers but had no ability to do what was best (67). Cf. Früchtel, *Kosmologischen Vorstellungen*, 138-43. See Winter, *Philo and Paul*, 59-93, esp. 72-75, for a discussion of what information Philo can give us on the second Sophistic movement.

was before his name was changed). So she advised him to raise children by her handmaid (encyclical instruction). Afterwards, he would be able to make his approach to perfect virtue.

A somewhat similar chain of thought occurs in *Cher.* 7-8, this time in connection with the change of name from Abram to Abraham. Philo distinguished between the period when the patriarch was an enquirer into natural philosophy and the time when he became a wise man and lover of God and attained to Virtue, having his name changed. Then the encyclical instruction (symbolized by Hagar) and its "Sophistical" offspring (symbolized by Ishmael) will be cast out.

(g) *Philo assumes that faith is necessary for this journey and is also its goal.*

In the treatise *Immut.*, Philo continued to interpret Genesis 6:1-4 begun in *Gig.*, and was starting his interpretation of Genesis 6:2—the angels of God went into the daughters of men and they bore children to them (1). The wise man sees God and His powers so long as the pure rays of wisdom shine forth in the soul, but when the light of the intellect is darkened, then the companions of darkness associate with the dissolute and effeminate passions, which are called the daughters of men, and these bear offspring to them and not to God (3). He allegorized the offspring of the evil angels and the daughters of men as vices, whereas offspring of God are the virtues (6.4). He urged his mind ($\delta\iota\alpha\nu\text{o}\iota\alpha$) to learn from the example of "perfect Abraham" who offered up the only trueborn offspring of his soul ($\psi\upsilon\chi\eta$)—a reference to Isaac who represents self learned wisdom-as a necessary and fitting sacrifice to God. Philo then referred to the fact that Abraham bound Isaac (Gen 22:9), and said that he had done this either because once he had tasted divine inspiration he did not wish to descend to the level of mortal truth,[336] or because he saw that the creature was unstable and moveable, whereas he recognized "the unwavering steadfastness that belongs to the One Who Exists, on whom he is said to have believed," which is a clear allusion to Genesis 15:6 (6.4). To believe is to recognize and live by the fact that God is unchanging. We note also that Philo linked Genesis 15:6 and the intended offering of Isaac of Genesis 22. Here he stood within an early Jewish tradition.

In the *Migr.*, Philo stressed that what God said to Abraham about the land was in the future tense: "Not what I am showing you, but what I will show you" (= Gen 12:1) (43). Philo saw in the fact of the future tense a

---

336. In the *Allegorical Interpretation* 3.228, Philo had said that it was best to trust in God and not in uncertain reasonings or unsure conjectures, and then immediately quoted Genesis 15:6. A little later, he said that the only true doctrine was to believe in God, whereas to trust in vain reasonings was a mere delusion (229).

testimony to the faith with which Abraham's soul believed in God, for Abraham was showing gratitude not for what had already been done, but for what he expected in the future. Through this faith in God who had promised, the soul "found a reward, the perfect good, for in another passage it is said that Abraham believed in God" (= Gen 15:6) (43-44). Here Philo seems to distinguish Abraham's evident trust in what God promised in Genesis 12:1 and what was involved in the statement recorded in Genesis 15:6 that Abraham believed God. What was involved in Abraham's believing God meant an advance in his soul's quest for union with God.[337] Clearly, Genesis 15:6 is very important for Philo's interpretation of the Abraham story.[338]

From the various statements which Philo made about faith, then, it would be understandable if one were to be left with the impression of its intellectual character.[339] Ideally, the soul's journey leads to a conviction that God exists, that He is the Creator or Cause of all things, and that by His providence He guides all things. It is as if faith comes at the end of the journey, rather than being its starting point. Philo said that the wise man (either a reference to Abraham or a generalizing reference) beholds that more perfect Being who rules and governs all things, to whom all things are subject as to a master, and by whom all things are directed, and who *is appreciable only by the intellect*.[340] As Williamson remarks, "One begins to suspect . . . that for Philo . . . πιστις is the crown of intellectual achievement."[341]

At the same time, Philo dealt with texts within the Abraham story which suggest that the patriarch did doubt! Philo interpreted Abraham's complaint to God in Genesis 15:1-2 in a way favorable to Abraham: Abraham did believe the promise, but he was asking for a sign of how the promise would be implemented.[342] Genesis 15:8 is expounded in a similar way. Philo said that some may consider this question to be at variance with perfect faith, but maintained that Abraham was convinced that the promise would take place and was only seeking to know the manner in which the event would take

---

337. See the discussion of this passage in Moxnes, *Theology*, 155-56.

338. Philo said that the comment of the author of Genesis in 15:6 that Abraham believed in God "is a statement brief indeed in words, but of great magnitude and importance when confirmed by action" (*Abr.* 262). Moxnes, *Theology*, 155, considers it to be an hermeneutical principle which determines how Philo discussed the promise made to Abraham in Genesis 12; 15; 17; 18.

339. In *QG* 3.43 Philo stated that philosophy was a sort of college of medicine to the soul and that it was noble to be a philosopher.

340. *Abr.* 84.

341. Williamson, *Philo*, 350, cf. 364-65.

342. *QG* 3.2.

place.³⁴³ On Genesis 17:17, he does speak of Abraham's momentary spasm of unbelief when he laughed after the announcement that Sarah would have a son (this after he had believed—an allusion to his faith mentioned in Gen 15:6). But it did not last long. Philo represented the doubt as extending only to his mind and stopping at the mind. It did not extend to the tongue, i.e., Abraham did not go so far as to express his doubts verbally.³⁴⁴ Philo went on to say that to think of Abraham as in no way afflicted by some doubt would be tantamount to making him equal to God, of whom Deuteronomy 32:4 says "God is faithful [πιστος], and there is no unrighteousness in Him." "It is a great folly to fancy that the soul of man is able to contain the virtues of God, which never vary." Unlike human beings who are compound beings, God is pure and unmixed. Philo drew his conclusion: "Abraham believed in God; but he believed as a man."³⁴⁵ Moxnes makes the comment: "Abraham's faith must not be understood as a threat to God's absolute majesty."³⁴⁶

(h) *Philo mentions that there are difficulties on this journey of the soul but there is Divine help available.*

The mixed multitude who left Egypt (Exod 12:38)³⁴⁷ were interpreted by Philo as an indication of how difficult it is to shake off the enemies in the soul (*Migr.* 150–51), for they impede the speed with which we can depart from Egypt = the body (151).³⁴⁸ The fact that the Israelites spent forty years

---

343. *Her.* 100–101; cf. *QG* 3.2.

344. *Mut.* 175–78, 186; cf. *QG* 3.56. It is worth noting that Philo also transformed Sarah's disbelief at the announcement that she would bear a son, in Genesis 18:12. Philo took "my lord is old" to refer to God and not Abraham: "And Sarah laughed in herself, saying, There has never up to the present time come any good to me of its own accord without care on my part; but He who has promised is my Lord and is older than all creation, and I must of necessity believe Him" (*Mut.* 166; a similar interpretation occurs in *Leg. All.* 3.217). Böhm, *Rezeption*, 301–3, handles how Philo deals with the apparent conflict between the belief of Genesis 15:4–6, and the laughter of Abraham (Gen 17:17) and the laughter of Sarah (Gen 18:12), in her comments on *Mut.* 175–85, 201. That Philo had passed over this in the Exposition writings is an indication of the difference of audience in the Allegorical Writings. In the latter, members of the intended audience are acquainted with Genesis and are aware of some of the problems which the text presents.

345. *Mut.* 176–78, 186.

346. Moxnes, *Theology*, 163. For his discussion of Philo's use and interpretation of Genesis 15:6, see Moxnes, *Theology*, 155–63.

347. Noth, *Exodus*, 99; Henton Davies, *Exodus*, 117, suggest that other elements among forced laborers took the opportunity to escape in similar fashion.

348. Pearce, *Land of the Body*, has examined the way Philo allegorized Egypt as the body.

wandering in the wilderness instead of going directly to the promised land was an indication that not all shared the same viewpoint (151–53).[349]

The supreme good in life is described by Philo as "the perpetual recollection of God and the calling down of the aid that comes from him, to counter the internal, confusing, and continuous warfare of life" (*Migr.* 56). The last phrase indicated the difficulties to be faced in the pilgrimage of the soul, while the assistance of God figured at the same time. Likewise, in a comment on the fact that Abraham accompanied those who visited him in Genesis 18:16, Philo said that "as long as he falls short of perfection, he has the Divine Word as his leader" and substantiated this by quoting Exodus 23:20-21, which was God's promise that His messenger would go before Moses and the people on their journey to the promised land (*Migr.* 173–75).

Philo acknowledged that the soul can be afraid to rise up to the contemplation of the living God. This was why Moses prayed for God to guide him on the road to Him (170, discussing Exod 33:15). Philo stressed that without effort the soul will not attain the objective of its travels (221). It should persevere and not grow weary. The person fond of learning is taken up to the field of Sichem which means a shoulder and indicates labor, since it is on the shoulders that men are accustomed to bear burdens.[350]

Philo spent a fair amount of space listing what he considered to be five gifts of God to the soul: these are an opportunity to contemplate mortal things; improvement in the teaching about virtue; blessing (70–85); a good reputation (86–105); and to be formed by nature (106–8). These were gifts available now and not in some future.

Philo deduced from the action of Cain in attacking and killing his brother that wicked men like him will seek to destroy those who are seeking to cultivate virtue. Like seeks to preserve what resembles it, but seeks to destroy what differs from it (*Det.* 164–65). Philo warned against getting involved in discussion and debate with the Sophists, and applied this to all on the way. He gave his reasons as follows: the beginner because he is destitute of experience; the one who is making progress, because he is still imperfect; and even the perfect, because he is not yet thoroughly practiced in virtue. Just as plaster needs to solidify and become absolutely firm, so it is vital that souls of those who have attained to perfection must become strengthened and established on firmer foundations by continual study and unremittant practice. Interestingly, Philo passed on the opinion of philosophers that it

---

349. Philo said that the mixed multitude stood for the cattle-like and irrational doctrines of the soul (152).

350. Here Philo was alluding to the episode of Genesis 34, and the efforts of Simeon and Levi to avenge the seduction of Dinah.

was impossible for those who have attained perfection to know that they had arrived and that there was an area between the two (*Agr.* 159–61).

This warning had relevant to the situation in contemporary Alexandria, as Bruce Winter has shown.[351]

In a section of *Somn.* 1, beginning at paragraph 60, Philo mentioned that Abraham was among those who made great progress and improved in understanding, a reference to the fact that he renounced knowledge of himself in order to arrive at a comprehension of the living God. Then Philo turned to consider Jacob and his journey to Haran and the LXX rendering of Genesis 28:11 και απηντησεν τοπω. Philo took this as "He met him [Jacob] at the place," (61) and then discussed the meaning of place (62–64). This led him to bring in the earlier reference in Genesis 22:4 to Abraham's seeing afar off the place where he was to sacrifice Isaac. Philo interpreted this to mean that he realized that God was far off, beyond comprehension (65–67). Philo resumed the reference to Jacob, indicating in the light of his discussion about place that Jacob must have met the divine Logos which God had filled with incorporeal powers, and also referred to Isaac who kept to the divine Logos who taught him everything that was suitable (68). God sent His words or angels to help those who love virtue. These attend like doctors the disease of the soul in order to heal them (69). Thus, in the fact that Jacob did not meet God but His Word he was like his grandfather, Abraham, the model of wisdom. To support this statement, Philo quoted the reference to the Lord's departure from Abraham in Genesis 18:33. Then comes the comment that the Divine Word appeared suddenly and supplied an unexpected joy in so far as it was about to travel with the solitary soul (70).[352]

(h) *Abraham is a symbol of the person who made progress on the way and arrived at perfection.*

Genesis 12:4 stated that Abraham journeyed just as the Lord spoke to him. Philo claimed that this was equivalent to what the philosophers called living according to nature. The mind enters the path of virtue, goes along the track of right reason, and follows God, mindful of His commands. Abraham did as God had spoken to him, "so that the actions of the wise man are nothing less than the words of God" (*Migr.* 127–29). (A fuller version of this idea is found in *Her.* 8–9 where also Philo, in support of this, referred briefly to God's commendation of Abraham's obedience to His law in words addressed to Jacob in Genesis 26:5.)

---

351. Winter, *Philo*, 15–108.

352. In a reference to Exodus 19:17, where Moses brought out the people to meet God, Philo asserted that Moses knew that the Word comes invisibly to those souls who long to meet him (71).

In a comment on the fact that Lot accompanied Abraham (Gen 12:4), Philo said that at this point Abraham was just beginning the contemplation of the Divine[353] and his views lacked firmness and stability[354] (*Migr.* 150). After mentioning that Abraham had the help of the Divine Word as long as he fell short of perfection (quoted above), Philo continued "But when he has arrived at full knowledge, he will run with more vigorous effort" and would keep pace with the one who previously had led the way and both become attendants on the all-leading God (175).

Earlier in the work, Abraham was described as having found the perfect good. Philo pointed out that God promised him something in the future ("which I will show you," not "I am showing you"). So, assuming the reliability of the God who promised, Abraham had discovered the reward, the perfect good ("Abraham believed God," 43).[355]

When the mind has attained perfection (τελειωθεις ο νους) it should render its tribute (or its perfection, in the play on the word το τελος) to God who created perfection (τω τελεσφορω) (*Migr.* 139).[356] Philo said that the Law commanded that tribute (το τελος) was owing to the Lord, which is taken as a loose allusion to Numbers 31:28-41. On one level, the idea is that tribute is owing to God; on another, the mind offers its state of perfection brought about by God back to Him. And what in the case of Abraham was his state of perfection? Philo allegorized the proposed sacrifice of Isaac as meaning that Abraham offered back to God "the male offspring of a virtuous soul, the fruit which has blossomed on it," which is a divine growth (139-40).[357] (With this we may compare what Philo said in

---

353. Philo can say that before Abraham became perfect, he gave his attention to subjects of lofty philosophical speculation (*Leg. All.* 3.244).

354. Colson, *Philo*, 4:219, in a free translation renders it "he is but a novice in the contemplation and study of things Divine."

355. Williamson, *Philo*, 370, argues that for Philo faith is the end, not the beginning; it is the reward and the crown of human life and achievement. See the later discussion of Abraham's faith.

356. Colson, *Philo*, 4:211, notes that Philo is playing on the double [sic!] meaning of τελος (the entry under τελος in LSJ, 1772-74, actually reveals an enormous range of meanings for it). I have assumed that Philo in the play on words is taking τελος in the sense of perfection, the state of the consummation. I have preferred "who creates perfection" to Colson's "the consummator."

357. See *Congr.* 63, 71, 78b-79, 81-84, 121-22, 155-56, 180, for how Philo allegorized the relationship of Abraham (the soul seeking virtue) with Hagar (encyclical study). Sarah (virtue) can only bear a son to Abraham *after* he had completed the encyclical studies (Hagar) and had attained such a state of virtue (as illustrated by the fact that he beheld God and His Powers as narrated in Genesis 18—see *Mut.* 270) that he and Sarah can bring forth a child. In *Abr.* 99-103, Philo seems to offer a somewhat different argument. The episode in Egypt over Sara showed that virtue (Sara) and a mind

Immut. 4: Abraham offered up "the beloved and only legitimate offspring of his soul," i.e., the image of self-taught wisdom, called Isaac, as a necessary and fitting offering to God. In *Somn.* 1.194, the willingness to offer Isaac is also described as proof of Abraham's piety.)

Philo referred to the idea of Abraham's making progress elsewhere in his writings.[358] For example, he mentioned "the athletes" of wisdom, who leave behind what can be perceived with the senses and proceed to seek a more accurate knowledge of the living God. Abraham was one such who achieved great progress and improvement in the comprehension of complete knowledge.

We meet the idea that at the moment of acknowledging his own creatureliness, Abraham entered the presence of God. In *Her.* 30, on Abraham's admission that he who was daring to speak to God was but earth and ashes (Gen 18:27), Philo commented "since it is just when he knows his own nothingness that the creature should come into the presence of his Maker." Somewhat similar is the statement that at precisely the moment when he knew himself, he renounced himself, which was in effect a renunciation of the creature in order to comprehend the living God (*Somn.* 1.59-60).

Alongside the attainment of knowledge of God, there is the constant obedience to the will of God and His commands. Philo quoted God's

---

given over to physical pleasures (Pharaoh) are incompatible. Philo rejected the view that in the marriage of souls, the woman represents virtue and the man reason, and that it is "virtue" (the woman) who sows good advice and "reason" (the man) who receives the sacred and divine seed. For Philo, virtue is masculine by nature, while reason is feminine. Böhm, *Rezeption*, 165, thinks that Philo does not feel entirely on safe ground, for he adds a η μηποτε clause.

358. The theme of making progress does not figure in the Exposition writings; it figures in the Questions & Answers but is not developed; it is, however, often handled in the Allegorical Commentaries. In general, Philo divided people into those who have attained perfection (a minority); those who are making progress and are on the way to perfection; and those who have no interest in improvement and have surrendered to the desires and passions of the external senses (the majority) (see *Leg. All.* 3.140-44, 159-60; *Fug.* 213; *Somn.* 2.234-37). Progress and the attainment of virtue were not something human beings can attain by themselves; it is by the help of God through the Logos that humans overcome passions and desires and make progress. For example, *Mut.* 24, discussing the difference between God's being the Lord and the God of people, Philo said that God wills to be Lord of the foolish; to be the God of those who are improving (βελτιουμενων); and both Lord and God of the perfect. The foolish should experience the fear of Him; the man of progress (τον προκοπτοντα) should be helped by Him as God and thus through those kindnesses should reach perfection; and the perfect should be guided by Him as Lord and benefited by Him as God. For, Philo added, through the one he remains free from lapses; through the other he is most surely God's man. Abraham and Jacob were paradigms of those who attain virtue by means of teaching and learning on the one hand and by means of labor and discipline on the other (e.g., *Sacr.* 5-7).

commendation of Abraham in words addressed to Jacob (Gen 26:3-5). God mentioned that Abraham had obeyed His voice and kept His injunctions, commands, ordinances, and statutes. This, said Philo, was the highest praise that can be given to a servant-that he neglects none of his master's commands, that he never hesitates in his labor of love towards him, and that he employs all his powers to accomplish his tasks successfully (*Her.* 8-9).

We may briefly mention that Philo interpreted positively the laughter of Abraham and Sarah, as a sign of joy at the promise of a child (166-67). He also expounded Abraham's request that Ishmael might be regarded as his heir, as a prayer that the divine voice may be awakened in the soul of Ishmael (201, 204, 209b, 216-17). It is an *a priori* principle that no blemish could stain the character of the patriarchs. They are ideal types.[359] There is obviously some tension here between this idea that Abraham attained perfect virtue on the one hand and Philo's acknowledgment on the other that to do no sin is peculiar to God, while to repent is (characteristic) of the wise man; and this latter "is a very difficult thing, and hard to find" (*Fug.* 157), or that it is impossible for the perfect to know that they have arrived-souls who have arrived at perfection need to be established on firmer foundations by continual study and incessant practice (*Agri.* 160-61). It could be that Philo felt the need to safeguard the uniqueness of God and preserve the distance between the God Who alone exists and His creatures.

Abraham is a symbol of the soul which makes progress through instruction and learning and arrives at perfect virtue. The way in which Philo handled Genesis 17 and the change of his name from Abram to Abraham indicates that this event was a symbolic watershed between making progress and having arrived. We, therefore, turn to the treatise *On the Change of Names* to discover Philo's interpretation.

Philo begins by dealing with the biblical statement in Genesis 17:1 that God appeared to Abraham. He was at pains to point out that God cannot be seen by the external sight, but only by the mind/intellect/soul (*Mut.* 3-6). Indeed, the statement does not refer to God Himself but one of His powers, His kingly power (15). Furthermore, when the text said "I am your God," this was equivalent to saying "I am your Creator," for God is self-sufficient and does not need a relationship to anyone or thing (27-29). For Abraham to have received this statement was an indication that Abraham belonged not just to the category "advancing in improvement" but to those who can be described as complete and perfect, truly the man of God (24).[360] To God's

---

359. See Böhm, *Rezeption*, 133-36, 171, 255

360. Cf. *Cher.* 7, where Philo said that Abram changed from being an inquirer into natural philosophy into being a wise man and lover of God, symbolized by the change of name from Abram to Abraham.

demand for blameless living was linked a promise of a gift, God's covenant, a symbol of His grace (51–53). Abraham's gesture in falling on his face showed his humility before the divine. He acknowledged the nothingness of himself and the human race (*Mut.* 54).[361] This gift of the covenant which God offered him (Gen 17:4) stood for God Himself, Philo paraphrasing the divine words with "the beginning and fountain of all graces is I myself" (58).[362] It was indicative of Abraham's worthiness that God did not give him this gift through an intermediary but from Himself (59–60).

Then Philo came to the major theme of the tractate-the change of name from Abram to Abraham. He interpreted Abram = "uplifted father" (μετεωρος πατηρ), as meaning "one who inspects high things, who investigates the heavenly bodies" (66–67). On the other hand, he took Abraham = "elect father of sound" (πατηρ εκλεκτος ηχους) to mean the mind (father) of the wise person (elect), from which flows speech (sound). For Philo, the change of names documented the fact that the erstwhile learner Abram had now attained through God's help to perfect virtue (69–70). As Sandmel has remarked, "The transformed Abraham, then, is no longer the "atheist" of his Chaldean days. He is now completely transformed into the Sage, in possession of archetypal virtue. As a result of the change in his nature, he is now in full possession of piety."[363]

In comparing and contrasting Abraham and Jacob as types of those who achieve perfection through instruction/learning and through practice respectively, Philo said that Abraham understood and did not forget all that he had learned (84). He had an Immortal Monitor and Teacher which was a considerable advantage. Abraham investigated and examined the mysteries of nature with great earnestness and unceasing labor (85). For this reason God altered his name, since he was about to continue in that state of ethical perfection at which he had arrived. Thus, Abraham in his state matches (as it were) God who Himself always stands firm. "Therefore, Abraham in token of the even tenor of his future life received his new name from God, the unchangeable, that the stability of his future might be set on a firm foundation by Him who stands and is ever the same in nature and condition." (87)

---

361. Cf. *Her.* 30, concerning Genesis 18:27, when Abraham approached God to intercede for Sodom.

362. Zeller draws attention to the paradox: "God considers worthy of [perfection of virtues] him who concedes his total inability. The being worthy in the sight of God is the being unworthy in the sight of man" (Zeller, *Charis*, 113).

363. Sandmel, *Philo's Place*, 170. Böhm, *Rezeption*, 296, says that in the story of the change of name, Philo saw the transition to the perfection of Abraham who is the ideal type of soul.

In the very last paragraph (270), Philo commented on the statement of Genesis 17:22 that God finished speaking to him. These words were equivalent to saying that God had made Abraham perfect, "though he was devoid of wisdom before, and He filled him with immortal lessons."[364] When his disciple became perfect, God departed from him. This departure did not mean that God separated from Abraham. But He had given him an example, rather as if God had stamped on him an indelible recollection, and so for the future Abraham can exert himself.

In *Gig.* 62–64, Philo said that Abraham was investigating "the sublime things on high" in a truly philosophical spirit. He was then a man born of heaven. When he became improved (i.e., had moved from the heavenly bodies to contemplate their Creator), he became a man born of God, a fact deduced by Philo from Genesis 17:1 where God declared that He was Abraham's God. He was assigned to God, became His minister, and so made the path of his whole life straight. Philo commented that the change of his name Abram to Abraham was indicative of a change of the pursuits to which he was devoting himself, from the study of creation (astrology) to treading the royal road of the only King who governs all things (*Gig.* 62–64).

Of interest is the way Philo interpreted the statement in Genesis 18:22 that Abraham stood before the Lord. In *Cher.* 18–19, this is an illustration of Abraham's connection or familiarity with God. A further proof of this was that Abraham came near to God and spoke to Him. The episode not only indicated both that he enjoyed familiarity with God but that Abraham had attained to an unchangeable mind close to the power of God Himself, for "the Divinity is unchangeable." Genesis 18:22–23 is handled again in *On the Posterity of Cain*. In *Post.* 27, Philo maintained that it was only the unalterable soul who had access to God and stood near to the Divine Power. He went on (28) to report what God had said to Moses in Deuteronomy 5:31 "But you yourself stand beside me" as illustrating "the lasting good condition and stability of the virtuous man"[365] Philo draws two conclusions: since God was immovable, He moved all else, and He made the virtuous man

---

364. This almost seems to suggest that becoming perfect was an instantaneous transformation, with a once in the past/but now for the future pattern. Taken in comparison with other statements of Philo on Abraham's efforts while in Chaldea and in Canaan to draw near to God, the sharp language of *Mut.* 270 must be taken to be determined by Philo's exegesis of the change of name from Abram, meaning sublime father, to Abraham as the elect father of sound. It is as if on this occasion Philo contracted to one conversion point Abraham's progress to belief in the true Creator and the moral transformation which accompanied it. What God gave was "a renewal of the moral character by means of symbols" (70).

365. In *Migr.* 132, Philo said that piety and faith united the mind (διανοια) to the Incorruptible Being and went on to quote Genesis 18:23.

a partaker in His own tranquil nature. A similar point on Deuteronomy 5:31 was made in *Immut.* 23, while in *Conf.* 30-31 what was said in Deuteronomy was an indication of the honor given by God to the wise man of being related to His steadfast and unwavering power. The two passages in Genesis and Deuteronomy mutually illustrate one another, and indicate the high standing of Abraham and Moses.

Philo made a passing reference in *Migr.* 132 to the fact that after Abraham was said to have believed in God, he came near to God, an obvious allusion to Genesis 18:23. He then went on to generalize with his addressees in mind.[366] If he (probably now any wise or virtuous person) on his journey does not grow weary or turn aside or go astray, but like a good runner, finishes the race of life, he would receive a fitting reward (133).

Once more Philo referred to Genesis 18:22 and linked it with Deuteronomy 5:31 in *On Dreams* 2.226-28. Having quoted Genesis 18:22, Philo asked when would we expect the mind (διανοια) to stand, except when it is standing before God, seeing and being seen? These two aspects are the factors which give the soul its perfect balance. When the mind sees God, it does not give in to the counter attraction of things like itself; while on the other hand God claims for Himself the mind which is worthy to come within His sight. After quoting Deuteronomy 5:31, Philo claimed that that which draws near to God is made akin to God (τω οντι) and is able to stand on its own due to God's immutability (228). When the mind (νους) is at rest, it realizes how great a blessing that rest is. Philo then went on to assert that in this blessed state, the good man was on the borderline: he is neither God nor man, but is connected with humanity by his manhood and with what is immortal through his virtue (230).

Philo drew some significant conclusions from God's statement[367] that He would not hide from Abraham, who was dear to Him, what He intended to do to Sodom, given that He had planned for Abraham to become a mighty nation (Gen 18:17). He declared that this indicated a very special relationship: Abraham alone was nobly born insofar as God was his father and he was His adopted son. Abraham was thus all-wealthy, a king, the only free man (*Sobr.* 55-57).

(i) *There is a tension between statements which assert that the soul can arrive at a vision of God and statements which assert that this is impossible.*[368]

---

366. So, rightly, Böhm, *Rezeption*, 275.

367. In the MT and the LXX it is a question.

368. Früchtel, *Kosmologischen Vorstellungen*, 145-63, has helpfully collected the evidence for both sides of Philo's views. She states that on balance the scales come down on the impossibility of seeing God as He is.

Philo stated emphatically that it was impossible for mortal man to know God as He really is. For example, in *Immut.* 62, in his comment on the sentence that "God is not like man," Philo drew a distinction between God's existence (υπαρξις) and His essence (ουσια). While we can know the fact of God's existence, "beyond that fact, we can know nothing" (cf. *Immut.* 55). In *Mut.* 15, this is applied to Abraham and the statement of Genesis 17:1, "The Lord was seen by Abraham." Abraham did not see the Cause of all things but rather one of His Powers, His kingly Power. This antithesis between "Essence" and "Existence" is also developed in *Post.* 14-18, 167-69, where the discussion involves both Moses and Abraham.

Nevertheless there are places where Philo seems to indicate that the virtuous or wise person does have access to God. Here we need to return to Philo's comments on Genesis 18:22-23 and Deuteronomy 5:31 just considered. When commenting on the Deuteronomic command to fear, serve, and cleave to the Lord, Philo asked what is the "glue" which binds the two together? He mentioned piety and faith (ευσεβεια δηπου και πιστις): they "unite the mind (διανοιαν) to the One who is Incorruptible by nature." Philo quoted Genesis 18:23 in support: "When Abraham believed, he is said 'to draw near to God'" (*Migr.* 132). Philo continued in a generalizing way to speak of the need to continue on the right road without diverting, in order to obtain the crown and prize (133-34).

A slightly different interpretation of Genesis 18:22b, 23, occurs in *Post.* 27-28, where Philo concentrated on the expression that Abraham stood before the LORD, pointing out also that God was standing. Philo asserted that this wording indicated that only the unalterable soul had access to the unalterable God. As such, it stands near to the Divine Power. Philo also drew in the words addressed to Moses in Deuteronomy 5:31: "But you, stand here with me," and proceeded to maintain that this showed that God, who is unchangeable and immovable Himself, moves all other beings, and that He makes the virtuous soul a participant in His own tranquil nature. Thus, we may say that two sides of the coin are both stated here: the stability of the soul is the prerequisite for approaching the unalterable God, but this same unalterable God makes the virtuous person a participator in His own tranquil nature.[369] Philo returned to this passage about Abraham in *Somn.* 2.225-29. After mentioning wise Abraham, Philo glided over into asking when the mind could stand except when it was opposite God, seeing Him and being seen by Him. The mind's stability and tranquillity depend

---

369. See also *Gig.* 49; *Conf.* 30-31. For the idea of the inner calm and stability as a central theme in Philo, see Winston and Dillon, *Two Treatises*, 261-62.

on realizing that there is nothing that can compare with God, so that attractions of things human cease to exercise any pull or create strife within.³⁷⁰

Just prior to this part of the story in Genesis 18, there had been mention of Abraham's hospitality towards the three visitors, interpreted by Philo as God and His two Powers, His creating, sustaining Power and His judging, punitive Power resp. After the meal, Abraham escorted his guests for part of their way. Philo waxed lyrical about this privilege and this indication of the status of Abraham. "The escort is escorted. He gives what he was receiving" (*Migr.* 173).

(j) *Are "those who see" only Israelites or had Philo envisaged non-Israelites as well?*

Philo acknowledged that not all can see things which were endowed with divine attributes. This was permitted only to the purest and most acute-sighted race to whom the Father of the Universe was giving the greatest of all gifts (*Migr.* 46). The question arises whether Philo was thinking of Israelites as a whole or an elite group within the nation? The answer is complicated by the fact that in *Migr.* 54 the nation is described as the race which had the power of beholding the living God, whereas 57–58 speak of God's coming near to help those who are worthy to be assisted (επ ο ωφελεια των αξιων ωφελεισθαι). Who are worthy? All those who are lovers of wisdom and knowledge, wise people and people of knowledge, who are to be distinguished from the rest (57–58, 60; cf. 61) and who are under the leadership of right reason (ο ορθος λογος αφηγειται, 60). Ellen Birnbaum thinks that Philo's vision is potentially universalist.³⁷¹

Interestingly, in commenting on God's promise to bless those who bless Abraham and curse those who curse him, Philo pointed out that God bestowed good things on the rest of mankind for the sake of the wise man (= Abraham, 109), but also in a comment on "In you shall all the nations of the world be blessed," went on to say "The righteous man is the support of all the human race." Such a person "brings all that he has into the common stock and gives it liberally for the advantage of those who can use it" (*Migr.* 121). Abraham, having experienced God's kindness in all matters, believed that, because of even a small fragment of virtue, God would look with pity on the rest and raise up the fallen and quicken dead things (an allusion to Abraham's intercession in Genesis 18:24–32) (122). Philo said that God was accustomed to bestow gifts in response to intercession, from which He does not turn, and he quoted the words to Moses in Numbers, "I am gracious to

---

370. Philo can say that the one who has passed over to the immortal God may justly be called "the dwelling and city of God" (*Somn.* 2.253).

371. See her discussion, Birmbaum, *Judaism*, 115–17. The reference to "potentially universalist" occurs on page 117.

them in accordance with your word" (Num 14:20), which was equivalent to the promise to Abraham "In you shall all the tribes of the earth be blessed" (*Migr.* 122).[372] Philo then gave an extended illustration of how in God's wise providence the smallest goodness can have an enormous influence.

> For as[373] when even the smallest smouldering spark is blown upon, it bursts into flame and sets fire to a large pile of wood, so when the smallest spark of virtue is kindled by good hopes and shines forth, it has opened the eyes previously closed and blind, and caused what had become withered to shoot up again, and brought whatever had become unfruitful and sterile to productive fertility, so by the wisdom[374] of God the scantiest goodness flows forth and becomes vaste, assimilating other things to itself. (*Migr.* 123)

Noah is another such example. A whole crop of wisdom sprang from him: specifically, Abraham, Isaac, and Jacob were descended from him (125).

It will be convenient now to consider the question whether there are differences in emphasis between the portrait of Abraham in the three series of Philo's writings?

The first point to notice is a general one, to do with the fact that all three types of Philo's writings belong to somewhat different genres, and this is linked with the manner in which the Scriptural text is handled. The work *Questions and Answers on Genesis* is like a commentary, taking up phrases from the biblical passage and seeking to elucidate them both on the literal and the allegorical level. Some phrases receive far more detailed comment than others, and not every word or phrase in Genesis is explained. On the whole, Philo does not draw in other passages found in Scripture. He is not dealing with themes and pulling in material from elsewhere. In the Exposition treatises, his technique is to paraphrase scripture rather than quote it directly; to give the literal and the allegorical interpretation of passages; and to discuss matters of etymology at length. Philo does not seem to presuppose knowledge of the Scriptures in his addressees. In the Allegorical Writings, Philo interprets scripture allegorically and discusses matters philosophically. He seems to assume knowledge of the scriptures in these treatises.

---

372. Böhm, *Rezeption*, 274, comments that a historical-theological understanding of the promise of Genesis 12:3 is not present here. All promises are ethically understood prizes of victory, with which each person who strives after wisdom will be presented.

373. I have supplied an implied ὥσπερ to balance the οὕτω which Philo used later at the end of para. 123.

374. Greek επιφροσυνη Θεου is an instrumental dative.

Allowances must be made, therefore, for the different approaches in the different series. Indeed, within a given series, Philo might offer different interpretations of the same passage.

Secondly, we turn to actual content, to what is specifically said about Abraham and what he did and how he behaved. It will be helpful to address two questions.

The first question is: *how critical is Philo about Chaldea, Abraham's place of origin?* In general, he is far less critical of Chaldea than he is of Egypt. Specifically we note:

Firstly, in *QG* 3.1, Philo acknowledged that in the area of mathematical theory, of which astronomy was a part, the Chaldeans had worked diligently and successfully. However, their teaching had made the mistake of attributing the powers of the Creator to what was created and so had persuaded people to honor and worship the works of the world instead of their Creator. This was "the cause of great evils and impiety."

Secondly, in the Exposition, Philo said that the Chaldeans attributed the course of human affairs to the influence of the heavenly bodies and maintained that the world was God, thus likening what was created to the Creator (*Abr.* 69, 95). Abraham for a long time had remained a Chaldean (*Abr.* 70). This state is described as like being asleep (70), in darkness (70), or being enclosed by a great mist (79). Abraham had, at this stage, no grasp of the harmonious and intelligible order of things (ευαρμοστον και νοητην φυσιν) which existed outside of the world and the sphere of sense perception. In *Virt.* 212–13, Philo sounded a more critical note. The ignorance of the true God is horrible and a witness to the lack of nobility of the soul of the Chaldeans.

Thirdly, in the Allegorical Writings, *Migr.* mentioned the reputation of the Chaldeans for astrology and nativities and their belief in the harmony between the different parts of the universe, between heaven and earth, which is like a symphony (178). They held to two other beliefs. In the first place, that the world was God or contained God in itself as the soul of the world, and, secondly, that the heavenly bodies controlled the destinies of everything (179). They thus filled human life with much impiety (179). Moses agreed with the idea of the harmony of the universe, but rejected wholly the other two ideas (180–81), and, indeed, sought to change such views (184).

In *Somn.* 1.52, Philo indicated that the story of the migration from Chaldea to Haran was not to furnish us with a particular historical event, but that a lesson full of wisdom and of the greatest importance for life and relevance for man alone might be given. The lesson was that the Chaldeans were great astronomers, who occupied themselves with subjects related to the external senses. Philo then imagined the biblical account addressing a whole series of questions to those who investigate nature, the celestial bodies, and the heavens, seeking to elicit a reply as to why they bothered with such pursuits. They should rather attend to what is close at hand and examine themselves dispassionately and without flattery (53–54). They should make themselves acquainted with their own soul and mind. In his allegorical interpretation, Terah stands for the principle that each person should know themselves (58). Later, Philo can say that Abraham forsook those who engage in astronomical matters like the Chaldeans, and was brought over to what was suited to a rational being, viz. the service of the great Cause of all things (161).[375]

Summarizing, we may say that the criticism is not expressed with the severity with which it could have been formulated, the most critical note coming in the Exposition. There is unity between the three sets of writings on the inadequacy of Chaldean beliefs about God. In *Migr.*, Abraham himself does not figure much in what Philo said; rather, he invoked Moses and his evidence about Chaldean beliefs and their implications and influence.

The second question is: *Has Abraham's move away from astrology been portrayed in different ways? Specifically, did revelation play any part in this move, or was it entirely due to the exercise of human reason, or did both play a part?*

Firstly, in *QG* 3.1, Philo concentrated on God. He honored the wise man with two gifts. He took him away from Chaldean doctrine and He granted him fruitful wisdom (which is symbolically called land in Genesis 15:7). We may ask whether the description of Abraham as a wise man had prospective force, or did Philo envisage an evolving development, in which, though Abraham was wise, he became wiser because of God's two gifts?

Secondly, turning to the Exposition, Philo said in a general comment that Abraham's migrations were made by a virtue-loving soul in its search for the true God (*Abr.* 68). As to the move away from being a Chaldean, Philo said that Abraham opened the eye of his soul (διοιξας το της ψυχης ομμα) and began to see (βλεπειν αρξαμενος) (70). Philo asserted that this was like awakening from sleep and moving away from deep darkness towards the light, and Abraham perceived (κατειδον) what he had not previously seen (ο μη προτεπον εθεασατο)—God presiding over the world and directing it in safety like a charioteer and pilot (70).

---

375. The context is a comparison and contrast between Abraham and Isaac. Isaac is a symbol of knowledge which exists by nature, which is self-taught; while Abraham is the symbol of knowledge gained through instruction and learning. Hence God called Himself the God and Lord of Abraham, but the God of Isaac. Isaac is a native inhabitant of his country, whereas Abraham is a settler and foreigner (160).

Then, however, Philo said that God (the Holy Word/Logos), in order to establish more firmly in Abraham's understanding the meaning of the sight which had been revealed to him (την φανεισαν οψιν), commanded him to abandon the Chaldean science and to turn to himself in order to have a better apprehension of the Overseer of the All (71). The word φανεισαν (a second aorist participle) suggests an act of revelation given to Abraham.[376] So, God was involved in the opening of Abraham's spiritual eyes! In response to this, Abraham left (71), but, equally, God responded when the soul came to Him, and He revealed His nature, so far as humans can see God (79-80). What Abraham came to know was God as "Maker and First Cause," to use Colson's free rendering of αιτιου του πεποιηκοτης (78). Thus, divine grace continued to be active in the confirmation and the establishing of what Abraham had been assisted to understand.

Philo continued in paragraph 79 by arguing that Genesis 12:7 ("God appeared to Abraham") showed that God had not been revealed to him before (προτερον ουκ ην εμφανης) when in his Chaldean way he was fixing his thoughts on the chorus-like movement of the stars with no apprehension at all of an harmonious and intelligible order of things which existed outside the world and the sphere of sense perception. This suggested that Abraham needed something from outside of himself to move him to change. Philo proceeded "But when he had departed and changed where he lived, he could not help but know that the world is subject but not sovereign, not governing but governed by the causation of Him who made it. This mind of his recovered its sight and then saw for the first time" (78). He was able to receive the vision of Him who for so long was hidden and invisible (79). Throughout this section, we again have the interplay of divine grace and human action.

In *Virtues*, Philo combined Abraham's exercise of his own reason and divine assistance. He said that Abraham, having formed a proper conception of God, viz. as the Creator of the Universe, the uncreated Being (214), and under the influence of inspiration, left his country, family, and father's house (Gen 12:1-3). He knew that if he stayed there, the influence of Chaldean polytheism would make his mind incapable of arriving at the proper discovery of the true God. If he quitted his native land, he would change his false opinions into true belief.[377] Philo here seems to be combining two things: a belief-changing experience which occurred in Chaldea (213) and divine inspiration leading to his realization that the polytheistic world-view

---

376. Even if one translated the participle by "appeared," the connotation of something encountering him *ab extra* would be present.

377. It looks as if Philo has set Genesis 12:1-3 in Chaldea, rather than Haran, despite Genesis 12:4.

of the Chaldeans would inhibit his complete surrender of false opinions to embrace true ones (214). That advance in the knowledge of God was in mind is confirmed by paragraph 215, which states that at the same time also the divine oracles of God stimulated the desire to attain to a knowledge of the living God by which he was guided. Abraham continued these investigations until he arrived at a more distinct perception of God's existence (not His essence, as Philo emphasized, for this is impossible for humans) and of His providence which governs the world and all things in it.

Thirdly, we look at the Allegorical Writings, beginning with *Migr*. In his comment on the first gift which God had promised Abraham in Genesis 12:1–3 (viz. the Land), Philo stressed that the promise was for the future as indicated by the phrase concerning the land "which I will show you" (43). Hence, there was need of the soul to repose trust in God in expectation of what would be. The soul needed to cling on to such a beneficial hope and consider that, because of God's reliability (βεβαιοτητα), what was not present was already present. Through that approach, it discovered its prize, which is faith, which is the perfect good. For "Abraham believed God" (Gen 15:6; *Migr*. 44).

Having quoted Genesis 12:4 with the reference to Abraham's age when he left Haran and promising to deal later with the symbolic significance of 75, Philo proceeded to remind his reader that at an earlier date Abraham had migrated from Chaldea to Haran (176–77). He then discussed the Chaldean reputation for astronomy and horoscopes and their "theology" of the universe and of Fate (178–79). Just when we would expect a reference to Abraham's abandonment of Chaldean astronomy, to our surprise we read that while Moses partially agreed with the Chaldeans (on the point about the harmony of the universe in all its parts), he disagreed fundamentally on their views about God and about the influence of the stars on human destinies (180–883). Moses also considered it to be his duty to try and change the views of any who held to Chaldean beliefs (184).

There is a treatment of Abraham and Chaldea in *Gig*. 62–64. Philo said that even while still in Chaldea, Abram was a man born of heaven, investigating the sublime nature of heavenly bodies in a truly philosophical manner. "Abram" was interpreted as meaning sublime father which Philo regarded as appropriate for one studying the sublime and heavenly things (62). Philo then leapt over to Genesis 17 and continued that when, however, he became improved, he became a man born of God (63, commenting on Gen.17.1). If God was prepared to call Himself the God of this man, then this man must be a man of God. The change of name to Abraham was an indication of this, for the name meant "the elect father of sound." "Elect" is appropriate because the good man was chosen out of all and purified;

while he was the father of the voice by which we speak. So he was assigned to the one and only God whose minister he became. He made the path of his whole life straight, using the royal road, the road of the only King who governs all things.

In *Congr.* 48–49, Philo commented on the relation of Nachor to his brother Abraham. He did not leave Chaldea and join with Abraham in his migration from the created to the uncreated Being, from the world to the Creator of the world. He did not separate himself from the speculations concerning astronomy, but honored what is created rather than Him who created it.

We are now in a position to consider whether there are different emphases in the portrait of Abraham in the different series of Philo's writings.[378] In *QG*, though both levels of interpretation are present, the allegorical interpretation of the stories and character of Abraham tends to predominate over the literal. As to the latter, God honored him by calling him out of the idolatrous worship of the Chaldeans. The change of name from Abram to Abraham was indicative of the move from a literal study of the heavens to a perception of divine things above. He attained to an unswerving trust in God and was not guilty of doubting God's promise of a son. On the allegorical level, he represents the soul which, though initially in need of making progress (he was at one stage not ready to have children by Virtue and so had to embark on Encyclical studies), ever strove to drive away passions which enslave the soul. He was a symbol of the soul as a sojourner in an alien world. He was eventually granted a vision of the Powers of God.

In the *Exposition of the Law*, specifically the treatise *On Abraham*, Böhm rightly suggests that there is a combination of two levels, which she describes as the concrete historical level of interpretation which leads to the ideal, typical external "biography of salvation" on the one hand, and the inner soul biography of salvation on the other. There is a discernible emphasis on Abraham as the one who found his way to monotheism and the ethical life in harmony with that belief. Here also there is the description of Abraham as the one who attained perfection through instruction and learning.

The emphasis on monotheism and a virtuous life in the picture of Abraham would be aimed at thoughtful Gentiles who were on a spiritual pilgrimage and were at some level of being attracted by the Jewish faith in monotheism and its high ethical standards and so were potential

---

378. Scholars (e.g., Eileen Birnbaum, Martina Böhm, Nancy Calvert-Koyzis, and Maren Niehoff) are not completely agreed on the intended audience of each of the three series of writings, and, consequently, this has repercussions on what each scholar has deemed to be the main emphases in the picture of Abraham.

proselytes.[379] This receives confirmation from the fact that in the closing paragraphs of *On Virtues* Philo specifically said that Abraham was the standard for those who renounced their pagan background and wanted to join the Jewish commonwealth. The change of mind-set and conduct counted for more than any claim to privileges based on descent from certain ancestors. This was confirmed by statements in *Spec.* 1.51–52, 309, which, without specific reference to Abraham, speak of proselytes abandoning their pagan connections and in their genuine love of truth coming over to being servants of God and piety

The many treatises of the *Allegorical Commentary* gives us a not dissimilar picture of how Abraham stood for the soul on its journey from involvement in what was perceptible to the external senses to the attainment of wisdom and virtue. The mind must keep passions under control and not let them control it. The mind within a person was analogous to and linked with the Mind which controls the universe, and to contemplate the mind within was to be put in touch with the Mind which controls the universe. The journey out of Chaldea to Haran was symbolic of the mind's moving away from the astrological study as typified by the Chaldeans, to a contemplation of itself as a reflection of the Mind behind the universe. Abraham's journeying around Canaan indicated the wise soul's quest for peace and solitude. Amid the difficulties of this journey along the royal road to a fuller knowledge of God, the soul can rely on the help of the Logos, God's representative to the cosmos and to the soul. The union with Hagar illustrated the need of the soul first to master the Encyclical Studies before moving on to true (Jewish/Mosaic) philosophy, the teaching of the Law, and so attain to Virtue and the begetting of a child (Isaac) by Virtue (Sarah). For Philo, Abraham stands for the type of soul who through instruction and learning attained to wisdom and virtue, knowledge of the One Who Exists and perfection of character and action. From his treatment of the change of name from Abram to Abraham, it emerged that Philo considered that Abraham had arrived at perfection, though this does not exclude the thought that still further progress was possible and desirable.

All this does not suggest that there are fundamental differences between these three types of writings, but that Philo shapes his material so that there are some aspects which receive more emphasis in one series than

---

379. Böhm, *Abraham*, 391; cf. Calvert-Koyzis, *Monotheism*, 24–29. For a somewhat different perspective, see Dawson, *Allegorical Readers*, 74, 113–26. Dawson thinks that Philo was seeking to help Alexandrian Jews see that the most authentic way to be Greek was to be authentically Jewish and that Philo was translating Greek ideals into Judaism in all of its particularity rather than translating Judaism into a generic, universal philosophy.

in another, and this is probably to be explained by the different audiences which he had in mind when he was writing.

2.14.5 The Faith of Abraham

We have previously had occasion to draw attention to how Philo mentions the faith of Abraham In his handling of this aspect, Genesis 15:6 was clearly important to him. That Abraham believed in God "is a statement brief indeed in words, but of great magnitude and importance when confirmed by action" (*Abr.* 262). We have also seen how Philo did discuss passages which suggested that Abraham did doubt. We now want to raise the question, albeit briefly, on the relation of the undoubtedly intellectual tenor of Abraham's faith (he believed that God existed and that He guided all things by His providence) to what we may call religious experience or a sense of the presence of God. It would go beyond the limits of our study to pursue this in detail. In any case, Noack has investigated what he has called consciousness or awareness of God (*Gottesbewusstsein*) in Philo, and any discussion must be indebted to him. Noack has indicated that this awareness of God is found in different ways in the three different types of writings. Suffice to say that Noack found that in QE Philo suggested that there were times when God gave the wise person a mystical, ecstatic experience; that in the Exposition there is an element of synergism with Abraham's striving after the truth (his repudiation of polytheism and embarking on the quest for the true God) and God through the help of His Spirit assisting the search and bringing it into contact with the creation-related side of God (not the ultimate reality of Him Who Is), and Abraham becoming enhanced in physical beauty, inspired speech, and authority (the philosopher-king or a Jewish form of the "divine man"); and, finally, in the Allegorical Commentary Philo sharply criticized the claim of autonomy for the human reason and emphasized the need to surrender all to God and live from the continuous presence of divine reality,[380] which Noack calls non-ecstatic mysticism.[381]

At least on two occasions Philo described the Spirit of God descending on the patriarch, and as a result he became a prophet (*QG* 3.9; *Virt.* 218).[382]

---

380. Noack, *Gottesbewusstsein*, 202, calls this the irreconcilable antithesis between the egocentric I-consciousness and the theocentric God-consciousness.

381. Noack, *Gottesbewusstsein*, 213

382. The idea of Abraham as a prophet was expressly stated at Genesis 20:7. In *Migr.* 84, Philo commented on Exodus 7:1 that God would make Moses as God to Pharaoh and Aaron as mouth. He stated that later Aaron would "bear the name 'prophet,' when the mind too is inspired [επιθειασας] and entitled 'God.' . . . For it is the prophetic kind, when under the influence of a Divine possession and ecstasy [ενθεω κατοκωχη τε και

At *QG* 3.9, Philo discussed the statement of Genesis 15:12 that at sunset an ecstasy fell upon Abram. Philo took this experience of a trance or ecstasy as an indication that Abram's mind was divinely possessed and received the divine spirit to dwell within it in an experience akin to that of the OT prophets. He maintained:

> A certain divine tranquillity came suddenly upon the virtuous man. For ecstasy, as its very name clearly shows, is nothing else than the departing and going out of the understanding. But the race of prophets is wont to suffer this. For when the mind is divinely possessed and becomes filled with God, it is no longer within itself, for it receives the divine spirit to dwell within it. Nay rather, as he himself has said, it fell upon[383] (Abram), for it does not come upon one gently and softly but makes a sudden attack. (*QG* 3.9)

Philo then referred to the statement that Abram experienced fear.

Clearly Philo here assumes that in this type of special experience, which originated from God and was not in any way self-induced, one's own rational faculties were somehow in abeyance and the divine Spirit was in control, producing a sense of tranquillity, not distracted by anything to do with the sense perceptions.

The other passage is *Virt.* 217 from among the Exposition writings. In context (187–227), Philo was discussing true nobility. This did not reside in the possession of gifted and virtuous ancestors. Good parents may have bad offspring, and vice versa. Abraham was the son of an idolater in Chaldea, but he himself came to realize the existence of the Uncreated Maker of all. This plus divine inspiration (επιθειασας) led him to leave Chaldea and remove himself from its polytheistic environment to enable him to gain a clearer perception not of the essence of God but of His existence and providence (214–15). The two aspects are mentioned together when Philo said "The oracles imparted to him fanned the longing which desired to know the Existent One. Guided by these, he went forth on his search for the One [God] with most unhesitating zeal." The knowledge of God's

---

μανια χρωμενον] that interprets the thoughts of God." This sheds light back on how Philo would understand the idea of Abraham as a prophet. In *Somn.* 2.172, Philo described Isaiah as one of the ancient prophets who under divine inspiration (επιθειασας) uttered the parable of the vineyard (Isa 5:1–7), and the same phrase is used of certain of Moses's utterances (*Mos.* 2.259, 263, 272, 291—the last of these being the story of his own death [Deut 34]).

383. At Moses 2.291, Philo said of Moses, that καταπνευσθεις, he told the story of his death when near the end. The Loeb translates this as fell upon, probably due to the prefix κατα, while Yonge, *Works*, 517, has "inspired," which is also what *LSJ*, 906, offers.

existence and His providence now "has a permanent and firm anchorage in his consciousness."[384]

The aspect of divine help is described in these terms:

> The divine Spirit took possession of him and both endued him with physical beauty and endowed his words with persuasiveness,[385] enabling also his hearers to understand him.

Here not only character—Abraham as a man of virtue—but also even his physical appearance and oratorical powers were heightened. There is inner and external transformation because of the influence of the Spirit of God. The words quoted also mention the effect on those with whom he came into contact,[386] but they do not say what Abraham "felt" as it were, but referred to his being possessed. The assumption seems to be that Abraham was (as we might say) open[387] Godwards: "he craved for kinship with God, and strove by every means to live in familiarity with Him" (218). The result was that the Spirit was able to work divine transformation upon him. This seems to suggest a more permanent relationship between God's Spirit and the human personality than in *QG* 3.9, or, at any rate, something experienced more frequently, since Philo does say at 217 "Whenever, therefore, he was possessed" (οποτε γουν κατασχεθειη), everything in him changed into something better." In *Vit. Mos.* 1.175, Philo mentioned that Moses responded to the understandable panic among the Hebrews at the approach of Pharaoh's army. He encouraged them:

> "Do not lose heart. God's way of defense is not like men's. When God gives help He needs no (military) means. It is characteristic of Him to find a way where there is none. What is impossible for every created being is possible for Him alone and at the right time." He uttered these words while still calm, but after a little while he became possessed and inspired by the spirit who was accustomed to visit him uttered this prophecy and there followed the prediction of the utter destruction of Pharaoh's total

---

384. Noack, *Gottesbewusstsein*, 67.

385. Noack, *Gottesbewusstsein*, 79, points out that rhetorically convincing powers were part of the theory of the philosopher-king which was widespread in the Hellenistic era, a theory going back to Plato. For Cynics-Stoics, the wise man was the true king. In one line of Jewish tradition, "king" was used to interpret "God" in Exodus 7:1 concerning Moses (see Holladay, *Theios Aner in Hellenistic Judaism*, 124–25).

386. There is nothing in the context to suggest that Abraham was predicting the future. The idea could be that he was persuasive in commending monotheism.

387. Philo himself uses this language at *Migr.* 222, when he urged his diavoia to "open the seeing faculty within yourself."

army. The phrase "accustomed to visit him" suggests intermittent inspiration.[388]

To return to *Virt.*, Philo contrasts Abraham's "sovereignty" with that which is gained by "weapons and mighty armies." His sovereignty benefits those around him and he is the noble standard for proselytes. Noack is surely right to see here something of an anti-Roman Imperial sovereignty thrust.[389]

There are passages in the Allegorical Interpretation treatises where Philo envisages a constant need of the mind to orientate itself on God; there can be as it were no let up of this approach. In *Migr.* 9, as part of Philo's interpretation of Genesis 12:1-4, 6, he urges the addressees: "Escape, man, with all your strength and might from the abominable prison house, your body, and from the pleasures and desires which are like its jailors. . . . Depart also from sense perception, your kinsfolk . . . but leave also speech which he [Moses] called father's house, lest you be led astray by the beauty of words and names and be cut off from the real beauty which resides in the things indicated (by these words and names)." The soul needs "the perpetual recollection of God, and the calling down of the help which comes from Him" who is ever ready to help and "draw near for the benefit of those who are worthy to receive His benefits" (56-57).

Both the Exodus (14) and the Passover (25) are interpreted as indicating that the mind (νους) should resolutely and eagerly leave and pass from the pleasures and passions of the body (represented by Egypt).

In *Gig.* 6.1, Philo maintained that the wise man sees God and His powers so long as the pure rays of wisdom shine forth in the soul, but when the light of the intellect is darkened, then passions and vices result. The fact that Abraham bound Isaac (Gen 22:9) was either due to the fact that when he had once tasted divine inspiration, he did not wish to descend to the level of mortal truth,[390] or because he saw that the creature was unstable

---

388. Also in the Exposition series, in Special Laws 4.49, Philo refers to prophetic inspiration: "For no pronouncement of a prophet is ever his own; he is an interpreter prompted by Another in all his utterances, when knowing not what he does is filled with inspiration, as the reason withdraws and surrenders the citadel of the soul to a new visitor and tenant, the Divine Spirit which plays upon the vocal organism and dictates words which clearly express its prophetic message" (in contrast to those who practice divination). As we have seen, prediction is not the only feature of what characterizes "inspiration" from above.

389. Noack. *Gottesbewusstsein*, 103.

390. In the *Allegorical Interpretation* 3.228, Philo had said that it was best to trust in God and not in uncertain reasonings or unsure conjectures, and then immediately quoted Genesis 15:6. A little later, he said that the only true doctrine was to believe in God, whereas to trust in vain reasonings was a mere delusion (229).

and moveable, whereas unwavering steadfastness belongs to the One Who Exists, on whom he is said to have believed (a clear allusion to Gen 15:6) (*Gig.* 6.4; *Immut.* 4). To believe is to recognize and live by the fact that God is unchanging.

A further illustration of this is afforded by *Migr.* 217–19, where Philo mentions how merchants and traders travel vast distances and put up with many discomforts for the sake of profit—how much more ought the soul (ψυχη)/the mind (διανοια) to strive relentlessly in the search for wisdom, earlier described as "the best dwelling place of virtue-loving souls" (28). Abraham was for Philo an example of the wise person who looked within, and, guided by reason, then obeyed the natural Law. The Sinai Law embodied in fact the natural Law, and so, basically, Abraham obeyed what came to be the later written Law. Abraham's rational soul was endowed with the God-given capacity to attend nature's instructions and act upon them.[391] God is, as Watson has put it, the God of the giftedness of the soul.[392]

Still, within *Migr.*, there is a fascinating self-disclosure of Philo about his own experiences, to illustrate God's promise to Isaac "I will be with you" (Gen 26:3; repeated to Jacob at Gen 28:15). He mentioned that on occasions he had had a "writer's block" when writing on some philosophical topic:

> On other occasions, I have approached my work empty and suddenly become full, the ideas falling in a shower from above and being sown invisibly, so that under the influence of Divine possession (υπο κατοχης ενθεου) I have been filled with corybantic frenzy[393] and been unconscious of anything, place, persons present, myself, words spoken, lines written. For I obtained language, ideas, an enjoyment of light, keenest vision, pellucid distinctness of objects, such as might be received through the eyes as a result of clearest shewing. (*Migr.* 35)

In this passage, inspiration comes from above (ανωθεν). It was a gift, unsought, entirely unpremeditated. Philo concentrated on the results of the presence of the Divine upon his ability to express thoughts in writing. This inspiration was intermittent, a high moment in his work as a writer. He also in *Alleg. Leg.* 2.32–33 refers to occasional experiences when wanting

---

391. *Abr.* 57, 60–61, 88, 275; *Migr.* 127–31. See Watson, *Hermeneutics*, 238, who comments that Philo interpreted Sinai in the light of the patriarchs. The Law was embodied in both the universe and in the lives of holy men. Later (244), he says that the unwritten law of nature is the ontological foundation of the written laws.

392. Watson, *Hermeneutics*, 248.

393. Philo uses the same expression about "corybantic frenzy" at *Her.* 69, one of the three passages from Philo's works chosen by Noack to illustrate his theme of the consciousness of God in Philo.

to entertain fitting thoughts he was drenched by a flood of unfitting matters; conversely, when on the point of reflecting on something vile, "I have washed the vile thing away with wholesome thoughts, God having by His grace poured upon my soul a sweet draught in place of the bitter one" (cf. 85). Such experiences are what one might call the occasional moral renewing of the person dedicated to God.[394] The experience was not controlled by Philo, but was due to the grace of God.

In summary, we may say that the whole concept of a journey of the soul and of making progress on that journey is, in general terms, an indication that effort has to be expended,[395] sacrifices made, persistence and steadfastness[396] exercised. Turning back is unthinkable.[397] There may be ecstatic moments on the journey,[398] but one does not live at that level all the time.

When Philo said that God "is not apprehendable even by the mind (τω νω) except only the fact that he is. For it is existence which we apprehend, but apart from that nothing" (*Immut.* 62), he was stating one side of the truth and was safeguarding the concept of the utter transcendence of God, to which he adhered passionately. The other side of the picture is that there is divine help for the journey of the soul in its quest for God. There is the possibility, therefore, of experiencing the presence of God, sometimes in an overwhelming way so that one is taken out of oneself but these are occasional moments.[399]

---

394. In *Fug.* 117, Philo asserts that as long as the most holy Logos is present within the soul (ψυχη), it does not admit any sin whatsoever, but if it has become parted, from our soul, then the way is open for the return of faults. Noack, *Gottesbewusstsein*, 205–6, "non-ecstatic mysticism."

395. See *Somn.* 2.232, where Philo applies the entry of the High Priest into the Holy of Holies to the mind (νους) straining its powers, forgetting everything else, fixing its thoughts on God, making every effort to reach "the inmost shrine" (=Holy of Holies = God's presence).

396. In a comment on Abraham's standing before God mentioned in Genesis 18:22, Philo commented "It is for those who seek intimacy to draw near to each other. To stand fast and acquire an unswerving mind is to be stepping near to the power of God" (*Cher.* 18).

397. See his appeal to his διανοια, to keep going and never to weaken and slacken its resolve to carry on the journey whatever the difficulties (*Migr.* 220, 222).

398. Having interpreted the meaning of Hannah to be "grace," and referring to Eli's assumption that she was drunk, Philo made the comment that "For with those who are God-possessed not only is the soul (ψυχη) accustomed to be stirred and as it were to become frenzied but the body also becomes flushed and reddish-looking, because joy floods and warms it within and extends its quality to the exterior." Not drunk with wine, "they receive copious drafts [Loeb—the loving cup] from perfect virtue."

399. Montes-Peral, *Aleptos Theos*, 164–203, deals with the immanence of God, but in respect of experience of God needs complementing with Noack's study.

2.14.6 The Return to Heaven

Philo believed that the soul, which was of heavenly origin, was imprisoned in the body, was at death liberated, and would return to the divine world whence it came.[400] Abraham and also Isaac and Jacob were thus pilgrims and sojourners while on earth; they were foreigners here and really citizens of heaven. At death, the soul returns to "the metropolis of its native country."[401] This is not the heavenly city/country of Apocalyptic, but the embracing of the concept of the immortality of the soul.[402] According to *Sacr.*, Abraham on his death received immortality and became equal to the angels (5).[403] The same is said of Isaac and Jacob (5–6).

If the major concern of Philo was the spiritual journey of the individual soul to God, then this would seem to have as its corollary that the Covenant was not a major category within Philonic thought,[404] though, of course, Philo regarded himself as a devout Jew and did see Israel as having a special closeness to God as the community of those who see God.[405] In principle, however, what Philo is interested in is open to all.[406]

---

400. *Agri.* 65; *Conf.* 77; *Her.* 82, 88, 274; cf. *Immut.* 150–51 (all in the Allegorical Writings); *Abr.* 258; *QG* 3.11.

401. *QG* 3.11.

402. *QG* 3.11; *Sacr.* 5.

403. For the way Philo's thought in general moved in this direction, see *Sacr.* 34–35.

404. So Hay, *Philo of Alexandria*, 370; Moxnes, *Theology*, 163; Birnbaum, *Judaism*, 132, who comments that Philo's sparse mention of the covenant is surprising. In *QG* 3.40, on Genesis 17:4, Philo described the covenant of God as the incorporeal Word, which is the form and measure of the universe, according to which this world was made. It is put together from the ideas and incorporeal measures and forms in accordance with which this world was made (3.42).

405. Cf. Hays, *Philo*, 370: "God associates with all the wise and virtuous individuals who seek Him."

406. See, e.g., *Prob.* 46, 50, 62–63, 74, and the concluding sentence of the treatise, where Philo referred to the oracle that to live in conformity with nature is the guide to the true life; cf. *Migr.* 185. In *Praem.* 152, Philo praised the proselyte and was critical of Jews who give up their ancestral faith. Moxnes, *Theology*, 131, suggests that Philo was addressing both fellow Jews and Alexandrian Hellenes who showed an interest in the Jewish religion. Birnbaum, *Judaism*, 159, maintains that the relationship between God and biblical Israel is open to anyone who chooses to turn to God and to live virtuously; cf. 178, God's providence is available to everyone, especially those who believe in Him as Creator and Provider. She describes Philo as a potential universalist who was (she borrows a phrase from Jon Levenson) "concerned to extend his particularity indefinitely" (225).

2.14.7 God's Grace

As mentioned earlier, Philo did emphasize the grace of God.[407] Thus, if Abraham was praised for repudiating Chaldean astrology and setting forth to investigate the one true God, the supreme cause and overruling providence of all things, Philo allegorized the statement in Genesis that God led Abraham out of Chaldea, to mean that God led the mind of Abraham from dominance by the organs of the outward senses.[408] The pure mind was inspired by heaven above.[409] Philo categorically stated that it was impossible for anyone "to comprehend by his own unassisted power the true living God unless He Himself displayed and revealed Himself to him."[410] On another occasion, Philo, amid an extensive comment on Genesis 2:7, asserted:

> How could the soul have perceived God if He had not inspired it and touched it according to His power? For the human intellect would not have dared to mount up to such a height as to lay claim to the nature of God, if God Himself had not drawn it up to Himself, as far as it was possible for the mind of man to be drawn up, and if He had not formed it according to those powers which can be comprehended.[411] Indeed, it was a sign of the soul which was imbued with the love of God that it ascribed whatever good and noble theories and feelings it received to God, who was the giver of all benefits.[412] When Abraham fell on his face before God, as mentioned in Genesis 17:3, this was a sign that he recognized the nothingness of himself and of mankind in general, and his utter dependence on the One who created all living things. (*Mut.* 54-56)

---

407. See Zeller, *Charis*; Barclay, *Grace*; *Gift*; Linebaugh, *God*, 52-53.

408. *Leg. All.* 3.41 (interpreting Gen 15:5; cf. a similar interpretation in *Her.* 85; QG 3.1). In *Gig.* 62-63, Philo distinguished between being born of heaven (while still called Abram and studying the things on high) and being born of God when God changed his name to Abraham.

409. *Her.* 184 (Allegorical).

410. *Abr.* 80 (Exposition); cf. QE 22.51; *Praem.* 44, where Jacob is said to have learned of God's existence because God Himself was willing to reveal His existence to His suppliant.

411. *Leg. All.* 1.38.

412. QG 3.4. Barclay, *Grace*, 148, has commented that in Philo "at its moments of deepest and truest reflection, the soul recognizes that what underpins, enables, aids and perfects its own moral struggle is the prevenient grace of God; by the grace of God it is what it is." See the comment on all movements of the soul as gifts of God in Barclay, *Gift*, 221.

More generally, there is God's grace towards sinners. In *The Unchangeableness of God,* Philo commented that were God to judge the human race without mercy and on the standards of strict justice, He would pass on it the sentence of death, since there has never been a human being who, by his own unassisted power, has run the whole course of his life without stumbling. But, in order that the human race might continue, God mixes mercy with justice. He takes into consideration the good actions of even the unworthy and pities them while judging them. Mercy is older than justice in His sight (*Immut.* 75–76).[413]

Side by side with this stress on the grace of God, Philo can also affirm that the righteous are rewarded for their behavior and the wicked will be punished for their wickedness. The causal relationship between lifestyle and true life or spiritual death can be seen, for example, throughout the treatise *On Rewards and Punishments*: "I will now proceed in regular order to mention the rewards which have been proposed for virtuous men, and the punishments threatened to the wicked."[414]

Not infrequently Philo can state that God gives benefits, gifts, or blessings to those who are worthy[415] or who are perfect[416] or who are lovers of wisdom and knowledge.[417] On occasions he can assert that God rejoices to give to those who are αξιοι χαριτος (worthy of His gift/grace/bounty),[418] or that God rejoices to share with those who follow Him and His will, what belongs to Himself (the context is the allegorical interpretation of the birth of Isaac to Abraham, to mean the gift of the bestowal of joy).[419] Because the proselyte has given up so much in order to pass over to a "better colony,"[420] to the clear vision of the truth, and to the worship of the one and truly existing

---

413. Note how justice and punishment are assigned by Philo to one of God's Powers, the ruling Power, in order to dissociate God from anything bad or harmful–see the comments of Barclay, *Gift,* 217–22, on this.

414. *Praem.* 3. See also *Praem.* 87, 113, 119, 126, 152, 162.

415. See *Leg. All.* 1.95; 3.164; *Post.* 139; *Mut.* 26–27; *Somn.* 2.177; *Spec. Leg.* 1.43. At *Mut.* 52, Philo states that "covenants are drawn up for the benefit of those who are worthy of the gift (των δωρεας αξιων), and thus a covenant is a symbol of the grace (χαριτος) which God has set between Himself Who proffers it and man who receives." Barclay, *Gift,* 224, points out that the concept of the worthiness of the recipient serves to safeguard the fairness and rationality of God's blessing, and goes on to say (225–26) that the fact that God exercises discrimination and rewards value mattered to Philo.

416. *Leg. All.* 3.196.

417. *Mut.* 57.

418. *Somn.* 2.177.

419. *Abr.* 204.

420. The metaphor is that of migration to a new settlement or colony.

God, God has laid down through Moses that they should be deemed worthy of every consideration (προνομιας της πασης αξιουσθαι).[421]

Conversely, God rewards those who are bad with appropriate punishment.[422] In one passage, God is likened to an umpire who adjudicates and then bestows prizes on the more excellent class and perdition to the opposite,[423] or, in another passage, personified Justice (Δικη) grants approval to those who are good and punishment to those who are bad.[424]

As we would expect, we meet the concept of reward for virtue in Philo's treatment of Abraham and Sarah.[425] In the *Migration of Abraham*, which dealt with Genesis 12:1-4, 6, Philo commented that God's promise of land was given in the future: "I will show you." From Abraham's departure in response to this, Philo deduced that the soul (Abraham) must have exercised trust in what God had said. Its gratitude was evoked not by what had taken place but by expectation of what was to be. Philo stated that the soul clung to and depended on this hope; it considered without hesitation that things not present were already so, because of the reliability of the One who had made the promise. The soul found faith, the perfect good, as the prize (αθλον). The use of the athletics metaphor probably included a hint at the difficulties which the soul has to cope with in the quest for God and virtue.[426] Then Philo brought in Genesis 15:6, "Abraham believed God." What was said of Abraham in Genesis 15:6 held good equally of his prior action in

---

421. *Virt.* 102-3; cf. *Spec.* 4.178.

422. In addition to passages already referred to in note 414, see *Praem.* 67, and also note 425 below. The reference at *Praem.* 162 is to those who desert their ancestral faith and its holy laws and are led astray into polytheism.

423. *Somn.* 1.151. Here Philo speaks of the wise being assigned "to dwell in the heavenly region of Olympus," while the lot of the bad is in "the depths of Hades." In between these two, there are those who are endeavoring to practice virtue, some of whom succeed, while others slip back (150-52).

424. *Mos.* 2.200.

425. There are several other characters whose outstanding piety and virtue elicits God's gifts: Noah (*Abr.* 34-35, 38-40, 46; *Virt.* 201; *Praem.* 23; *Mos.* 2.58-59); Isaac (*Leg.* 3.87; *Her.* 64; *Abr.* 37); Jacob (*Leg.* 27, 192; *Migr.* 27); the three patriarchs collectively (*Abr.* 50); Moses (*Leg.* 3.14; *Mos.* 1.148, 155, 158; 2.67-69); Phinehas (*Mos.* 2.173, 274). Conversely, there are bad people judged worthy of punishment: Adam (*Virt.* 202); Cain (*Praem.* 69); Ham (Canaan) (*Virt.* 203); the builders of the Tower of Babel (*Conf.* 182); Esau (*Leg. All.* 3.192; *Virt.* 210); those who worshipped the golden calf (*Mos.* 2.162, 171); the one who used the Divine Name irreverently in Leviticus 24.10-16 (*Mos.* 2.193-208); the Sabbath breaker of Numbers 15:32 (*Mos.* 2.227); and the rebels led by Korah in Numbers 16 (*Mos.* 2.53, 85-86, 282-83).

426. So Böhm, *Rezeption*, 272.

Genesis 12 in response to God's promise.[427] The soul's trust in God preceded the fulfilment of what God promised, and is seen as a reward.

Philo interpreted the protection of Sarah while she and Abraham were in Egypt as due to Abraham's obedience in leaving Chaldea at God's command.[428] Abraham's victory in the war against the coalition of kings was due to his faith in God, the champion and defender of the just.[429] As to what happened after the victory, Abraham retained only what had been given him by God and returned the rest of the spoils to the king of Sodom, an indication both that Abraham who was following the will of God, discriminated between the gifts of God and other things, and that God gives perfectly good things to those who are perfect.[430]

In his interpretation of Genesis 17 and God's gift of a covenant to Abraham, Philo stated that there were different kinds of covenant "assuring bounties and gifts to the worthy (παμπολλα χαριτας και δωρεας τοις αξιοις), but the highest form of covenant is (when God says) "I Myself" (αυτος εγω ειμι). God showed Himself, in so far as He who is above all showing can be shown. Philo continued his exposition by saying that whereas God was accustomed to give to some by material and other means, to others He gave Himself alone, making Himself the portion of those who received Him. God considered them worthy of another name (προσρησεως ετερας ηξιωσε). Then Philo mentioned that Abram was re-named Abraham. A key assertion in this exposition is the statement that "God is Himself the beginning and fountain of all His gifts" (η πασων χαριτων αρχη τε και πηγη).[431]

After he had described Abraham's hospitality towards the three strangers/ angels (Gen 18), Philo stated that this hospitality was a byproduct of a greater virtue, namely his piety (θεοσεβεια). The very visit of these three is proof of his virtue, because such holy and divine beings would not have considered stopping and staying if they had seen anything wrong in the souls of those who dwelt there. Philo posed a series of rhetorical questions, all designed to indicate that Abraham's household was like a well-ordered crew obedient to their master. Abraham himself must have been recognized by his visitors as their kinsman and fellow servant of God. These angels, though incorporeal, assumed human form to pay a kindness to the man

---

427. *Migr.* 43–44, which is one sentence in the LCL edition!

428. *Abr.* 90, 98.

429. *Abr.* 232.

430. *Leg. All.* 3.195–97. In *Ebr.* 105, on this same passage from Genesis 14, Philo indicated that Abraham was convinced that everything came from the only wise God who extended his beneficial powers in every direction and who by their agency benefited him.

431. *Mut.* 57–60.

of worth (χαριτι τη προς τον αστειον). "For why was this miracle worked except to enable the wise man to perceive with clearer vision that the Father did not fail to recognize the kind of person he was?"[432]

Philo maintained that God who did not consider it appropriate that He should be perceived by sense-perception, sends forth His Words (τους εαυτου λογους) "to succour the lovers of virtue" and they act as physicians of the soul and heal its infirmities. One of his illustrations of this is the incident mentioned in Genesis 18:33, when the Lord departed from Abraham and Abraham had returned to his "place," which is interpreted by Philo as meaning meeting with the Words or Powers of God.[433]

In response to criticisms of Abraham's willingness to sacrifice his son, Isaac,[434] Philo defended the patriarch's actions vigorously.[435] Among his arguments, he mentioned that previously Abraham had not neglected any of God's commands but offered obedience. At the conclusion of his defense of the literal willingness of Abraham to offer Isaac, Philo maintained that most honest people would be overwhelmed with admiration for his extraordinary piety. Even just one of his arguments was enough to show the greatness and loftiness of his soul. In his allegorical interpretation, Philo suggested that Abraham sacrificed his joy to God as his duty to Him. In preventing him from carrying through the proposed sacrifice, God rewarded his approach by returning the gift (in so far as the recipient's capacity allows).[436]

On the presence of these two strands in Philo, Hays has remarked that Philo's emphasis on grace goes hand in hand with affirming rewards for the righteous and punishments for the wicked.[437] Barclay, whose work has put

---

432. *Abr.* 114-18. In the last quotation from paragraph 118, Colson translates "that the Father did not fail to recognize his wisdom?" (Colson, *Philo Works*, 6:63). The phrase "his wisdom" is an interpretation of τοιουτος ων–probably correct in view of the fact that Abraham is referred to as the wise man.

433. *Somn.* 1.69-71.

434. For a full examination of these, see Section XIIIB below on other Jewish Biblical scholars at Alexandria.

435. Philo began his account at *Abr.* 167 (including the comment that this action surpassed "all other actions which win the favor of God" [πασας οσαι θεοφιλεις υπερβαλλει]) and concluded it at 207.

436. *Abr.* 192, 199, 202, 203. Sandmel, *Philo's Place*, 127, aptly comments that God repaid Abraham's piety by returning the offering which piety intended.

Somn. 1.194 says that offering Isaac was proof of his piety (Cf. *Alleg.* 3.209-210). A comment on the command to Jacob to be pleasing to God and blameless before Him is also worth quoting. Philo said: "The highest prize, that of being well pleasing to God, is set before those who do what is right, and the second prize, not to incur blame, is for those who do not sin" (*Mut.* 48).

437. Hay, *Philo of Alexandria*, 373-79, esp. 378. By contrast, Watson, *Hermeneutics*, 268-69, maintains that Philo shares a tendency with other Jewish interpreters, to

the discussion of Grace on an entirely new footing, notes how Philo stressed the superabundance of divine generosity and the priority of grace, while at the same time generally teaching that God's gifts are congruous with the quality of the recipient, but that this is not debased into a form of payment earned by the good works of the recipient. "If the world is ordained by a system of values instilled by God himself and if the superior values represent God's own nature, it is natural that God should reward what is most like himself with the gifts of his grace. To do otherwise would cut against the values which he himself has instituted in the cosmos."[438] Barclay's point is well illustrated by *Praem.* 126, where Philo says that the bounteous God "glorifies and rewards moral excellence[439] because of its likeness to Himself."

Philo, thus, illustrates the rich diversity present in first-century Judaism. For Philo, the founding father of the nation, while an historical figure, is also an exemplary figure. The journey of his soul out of sense perception to contemplation of the divine through reason and the attainment of virtue, is to be emulated by his descendants, while he was also the prototype of the proselyte searching for spiritual satisfaction. He was to be emulated by the Gentile seeker. God intended Abraham to be the founder of a new race of men.[440]

2.15. Other Jewish Scholars in Alexandria

From Philo's own writings we learn of *other Jewish biblical scholars in Alexandria*, with whose approach and interpretation he disagreed. It has been well known that Philo criticized both those who only interpreted the Scriptures literally and those who have been called "extreme allegorists." For example, as regards the former, he said about the phrase that God "repented" that He had made man in Genesis 6:6, that "some believe that the repentance of the Deity is shown by these words, but they do not rightly so believe, for the Deity is without change" (*QG* 1.93) Or, again, concerning Genesis 8:1, Philo says that some take the πνευμα literally of wind, but Philo maintained that

---

subordinate the divine promise to Abraham's piety: "It is Abraham's faithfulness, obedience, piety, virtue, or intellect that takes center stage."

438. Barclay, *Gift*, 237–38. Cf. Linebaugh, *God*, 55: God acts "in accordance with moral, natural, and rational justice that defines his character and the cosmos he created."

439. Philo used τα καλα, which could also be translated as what is excellent, what is noble, or even virtuous deeds, since in the same paragraph Philo referred to those good men who fulfil the laws by their *deeds*.

440. *Abr.* 46. Cf. the comment in Barclay, *Gift*, 231, that what Abraham learned was foundational for Judaism and exemplary for everyone, since his story encapsulated the twin lessons of truth and virtue.

the correct sense was "the spirit of the Deity" (*QG* 2.28). In *Confusion* 190, he referred to those who interpreted the Tower of Babel story as a reference to the origin of the Greek and barbarian languages. "I would not censure such persons, for perhaps the truth is with them. But I would exhort them not to halt there, but to press on to allegorical interpretations and to recognize that the letter is to the oracle as the shadow is to the substance and that the higher values revealed therein are what really and truly exist" (190). He claimed that Moses had given indications to justify this approach (191).[441] A more critical note is to be found in *Dreams* 1.39, where he referred to "men of narrow citizenship" who interpreted the four wells which Isaac's servants dug in Genesis 26:32 literally, whereas "men of higher thought and feeling" know that the reference was to the four parts of the universe.

On the other hand, *Migr.* 89–93 is an example of his distancing himself from those who, he believed, pushed the allegorical approach too far. He accused them of treating the text "in too easy-going and off-hand manner" (89). They ought to be concerned with both levels of the meaning of the text. He accused them of living in isolation and without consideration for the community of which they were in reality a part. They should not abandon "customs fixed by divinely empowered men greater than those of our time" (90). That the Sabbath, circumcision, the Temple worship, and many other things, have symbolic significance did not mean that they should not be observed literally (92). He concluded "It follows that, exactly as we have to take thought for the body, because it is the abode of the soul, so we must pay heed to the letter of the laws. If we keep and observe these, we shall gain a clearer conception of those things of which these are the symbols" (93).[442]

Building on the work of Hay,[443] Maren Niehoff has greatly expanded our understanding of these exegetes and the situation in Alexandria within which Philo and they worked.[444] Alexandria was a very important center of learning with its famous Museum and Library, and was, in particular,

---

441. Cf. *Det.* 15. Later, towards the end of the treatise (167), in a comment on God's declaration that whoever killed Cain would suffer sevenfold, Philo admitted that he was not sure of the meaning of this. He added "One must suppose that all these things are said figuratively and allegorically; and perhaps what God means to set before us here is something of this sort," and he proceeded to interpret the sevenfold as referring to the seven parts of the irrational soul.

442. In *QG* 3.48, Philo discussed at great length the command to Abraham to circumcise himself and all male members of his household as a sign of God's covenant with him and his descendants (Gen 17:12), without, however, mentioning those who were inclined to minimize the importance of circumcision.

443. Hay, *Philo's References to Other Allegorists*, 41–75; *References to Other Exegetes*, 81–97.

444. For most of this paragraph, see Niehoff, *Jewish Exegesis*, 1–17.

a center of Homeric scholarship. Aristarchus, its fifth librarian (161–131 BC), had exerted considerable influence on Homeric scholarship. He had produced two editions of Homer's work together with two running commentaries. He sought to identify what he considered interpolations in Homer using criteria such as unnecessary repetition and unrealistic and implausible scenes. He used asterisk and obelisk to indicate where he thought additions had been made.[445] Maren Niehoff believes that Jewish exegetes of Philo's generation were familiar with the academic methods used at the Museum by Aristarchus and his many students.[446] Not all agreed with them (e.g., The Letter of Aristeas;[447] and Philo himself),[448] but some embraced them. In other words, they applied literary techniques to the study and interpretation of the Scriptures (LXX).

We are not concerned here with describing all that Philo reveals about how these other Jewish scholars handled various passages from the OT. We shall simply mention that Niehoff has shown, by a detailed examination of the treatment of the Tower of Babel story in Philo, that these other Jewish scholars criticized Philo and his followers for rejecting the notion of myth in the Scriptures, and that they participated in discussions in Alexandria on myth, the unity of humanity, and the possibility of a common language.[449] Our concern is with what emerges about what they said in relation to the passages dealing with Abraham. Philo mentioned in a highly critical way their handling of certain stories about Abraham. We shall consider them in the order in which they appear in Genesis.

Firstly: it is clear that they were critical of Abraham's attempt to pass off Sarah as his sister, as recorded in Genesis 12:10–20. In *QG* 4.60–61, Philo denounced those who were critical of Abraham. "Anyone who says that this (was done) through levity of character . . . is deserving of condemnation." All Philo said in rebuttal was that we should not think that anyone who had attained to perfection would want to remain in sinful transgression. "Let not such a streak of impiety come upon us that we should think unworthy

---

445. Niehoff, *Jewish Exegesis*, 23–24, 26, 29, 49.

446. Niehoff, *Jewish Exegesis*, 3, 14, 186–87. See also Tobin, *Creation*, 156–57.

447. Niehoff, *Jewish Exegesis*, 19, describes his approach as "a conservative reaction to critical scholarship."

448. Niehoff, *Jewish Exegesis*, 187, describes Philo as a relatively conservative figure who applied literary techniques with considerable caution, insisting on the unity and authenticity of the biblical text.

449. In *Gig*. 58, in his discussion of the passage Genesis 6:1–4, and specially on verse 4, Philo said: "Some may think that the Lawgiver is alluding to the myths of the poets about the giants, but indeed myth-making is a thing most alien to him, and his mind is set on following in the steps of truth and nothing but the truth." On this whole issue, see Niehoff, *Jewish Exegesis*, 77–94.

thoughts of the patriarch, father and founder." He then resorted to allegorization—the virtue loving mind [Abraham] by calling virtue [Sarah] "sister" showed thereby that eagerness and zeal for virtue are common to all who are genuine and sincere in their desire for excellence. Then, in a comment on Genesis 20:2 about Abimilech, the king of Gerar, taking Sarah, Philo simply said that he would pass over the opinion of *some who believed that the wise man was a betrayer of the laws of marriage* (61).

In *Abr.* 89, he made an oblique reference to these critical views. He simply said that Abraham's "actions call for anything but contempt. But their greatness is not clear to everyone, but only to those who have tasted virtue and who recognize the greatness of the good things which belong to the soul and therefore are accustomed to deride those which win the admiration of the multitude."

As if to underline the error of their criticism, Philo commented that God rewarded the man of great worth with a great gift (90), implying that Abraham's critics were not in harmony with God's mind.

Secondly, in *QG* 3.3, he posed the question why should God tell Abraham to take a heifer, a she-goat, a ram, together with a turtle dove and a dove (Gen 15:9). He made the comment that he was not unaware that such things gave occasion to idle calumniators to reject the Sacred Writings and to talk nonsense about them. He went on to give an allegorization of the animals and birds. Then, in *QG* 3.8, he discussed "Why does (Scripture) say, 'And Abraham stopped and sat over them?'" (Gen 15:11). Philo said that those who took the passage literally envisaged Abraham sitting and examining the entrails of the slaughtered birds. By contrast, "we disciples of Moses" understand that his intention was not to indicate any form of prognosis, but rather to indicate that the virtuous man restrained wrong-doing and greed and was hostile to quarrels and fights, but loved stability and peace. The virtue of the virtuous man can heal "these civic diseases."

Philo also dealt with this verse in *Her.* 243–48, but did not mention those who took the passage literally as telling the future by the examination of entrails. He said that Moses envisaged the enemies of the soul as birds, while the man of worth (ο αστειος) sat down in their company in order to restrain them. Philo then embarked on a brief discussion of discord and factional disputes in cities and then a longer discussion on the enemies of the soul, during which he commented on those who might be regarded as allies, but who unfortunately engaged in mutual disputes, rather like the wranglings of the Sophists. In such instances, there was need of someone to act as a judge⁴⁵⁰ to throw out what is worthless and preserve what is worth saving (247).

Whom had Philo in mind with those who might be allies? "In so far as their minds are fixed on one end to discover the facts of nature, they may be said to be friends, but in that they do not agree in their solutions of particular problems they may be said to be engaged in civil strife" (246). It looks as if Philo knew of those whose discussions arising out of biblical passages could and did lead to controversy and dissension.[451]

Thirdly, there is the way in which they handled the passage about the change of name from Abram to Abraham in Genesis 17. Philo discussed their views in both *QG* 3.43 and in *Mut.* 60–80. He revealed that they were highly critical of the author of the story and poured scorn on the idea that God had given such a momentous gift by the addition of one letter, alpha, to Αβραμ producing Αβρααμ and the addition of another letter, rho, to Σαρα producing Σαρρα.[452] In *QG* 3.43, Philo referred to the fact that some "who do not belong to the divine chorus ridicule and reproach the one who is blameless in nature, and say reproachfully and chidingly, "Oh what a great gift! The Ruler and Lord of all has graciously given one letter, by which He has increased and made greater the name of the patriarch, so that instead of having two syllables it has three." Oh what great devilishness and impiety (it is) that some presume to bring forward slanders against God." In *Mut.* 60, his criticism runs: "Some of the quarrelsome and captious type of people who wish to attach blame where it is not due . . . and wage war to the death on what is holy . . . but disparage it and hold it up to obloquy" (*Mut.* 60). He then singled out one individual especially for criticism. "Not long ago I heard the scoffing and railing of a godless and impious fellow who dares to speak thus: Vast and extraordinary indeed are the gifts which Moses says come from the hand of the Ruler of all. What a benefit He is supposed to have provided by adding a single letter, an alpha, and again by another addition of rho. . . . And in a sneering way he ran over the list of such cases without a moment's pause" (61). Philo added with some satisfaction that the man committed suicide shortly afterwards in order that[453] "the foul and impure person might not even die a pure death" (62).

---

450. Philo also used the term ο μαιευτικος ομου και δικαστικος ανηρ. Colson translates: "The man-midwife who is also the judge" (Colson, *Philo Works*, 4:409).

451. Winter, *Philo*, 73, discusses this passage, but does not attempt to identify whom Philo envisaged by these potential friends.

452. This shows incidentally that they were operating with the LXX text and not the Hebrew.

453. Philo has an ινα clause here. I think that it is highly probable that Philo did see divine *purpose* here (pace Colson, whose translation in the Loeb volume takes it as a

Philo's response was to say that God had entrusted naming animals to man (Gen 2:19), so one should not think that God Himself altered mere consonants (*Mut.* 62–64). Rather, people should remember that "such changes of names are signs of moral values, the signs small, sensible, obvious, the values great, intelligible, hidden," and he proceeded to explain the etymology of the names Abram and Abraham (65–71). "Stop supposing that the Deity's gift was a change of name, instead of a correction of character (indicated) by symbols" (70). A similar criticism and line of argument is found in *QG* 3.43 (and in 53 in connection with Sarah).

In *QG* 3.43, Philo seems to want to exclude such critics from the Jewish community, since he referred to those "who do not belong to the divine chorus," which Niehoff has translated as "the company of God."[454]

Fourthly: there is their approach to the story of Abraham and the proposed sacrifice of Isaac. After retelling the story of Genesis 22 in his own words, Philo reported, "But quarrelsome critics who misconstrue everything and have a way of valuing censure above praise do not think Abraham's action great or wonderful, as we suppose it to be" (*Abr.* 178). According to Philo, they put forward the following arguments. In the first place, they maintained that Abraham was far from unique in his willingness to offer up a child. Plenty of people, both private individuals and those in authority, had so acted in order to serve their country as a price to redeem it from wars or save it from drought or excessive rainfall. They may have thought that such was an act of piety (ευσεβεια), especially among barbarian nations (179–80). Then, secondly, they pointed out that Moses had forbidden such child sacrifice as an abomination (181).[455] Niehoff believes that in contrasting what Abraham did and what Moses commanded, these Jewish scholars were implying that Abraham presented a primitive era which did not come up to the standards of Moses.[456] Finally, they pointed to India and gymnosophists. When they were afflicted by the diseases of old age, they voluntarily immolated themselves in a funeral pyre, and widows also joined their husbands on their funeral pyre (182). "Why, then, should we praise Abraham, as though the deed which he undertook was unprecedented, when private individuals and kings and whole nations do it when occasion calls?" (183).

result).

454. Niehoff, *Jewish Exegesis*, 154–55.

455. This reference to Moses suggests that these Jewish scholars were not Jews who had assimilated (as Niehoff, *Jewish Exegesis*, 100, correctly observes, pace Sandmel, *Philo's Place*, 128).

456. Niehoff, *Jewish Exegesis*, 102.

When he began his reply, Philo branded their view as "malevolence and bitterness." (184). He argued that where such actions had taken place through pressure or a desire for their own glory, they were not deserving of praise (184–87). He also pointed out that there was no such custom in Babylon and Mesopotamia where Abraham grew up (188). Finally, in view of the fact that the deed was going to take place in an isolated spot far from the public gaze, Abraham was not under any fear of man nor the pressure of public misfortune nor any quest for fame (188–90). He concluded "Let them, therefore, shut up[457] their unbridled evil-speaking mouths, control their envy and hatred of excellence, and not mar the virtues of men who have lived a good life, virtues which they should rather help to glorify by their good report" (191). That Philo was particularly sensitive on this issue is illustrated by the fact that he continued to discuss the issue, even after this apparent conclusion. He stressed both the fact of Abraham's lifelong obedience to God's commands, even when it was costly (192), and the fact that Isaac was the son of his old age, so that Abraham was not giving up one of a numerous family but his only son, and that made his action all the more exceptional (194–96). Philo also pointed out that most fathers would stay away from the sacrifice or avert their gaze, but Abraham actually acted like the presiding priest at a sacrifice (197–98). Philo concluded "Thus, everyone who is not malignant or a lover of evil must be overwhelmed with admiration for his extraordinary piety; and he need not take into consideration at once all the points which I have mentioned, for any single one of them would be enough." Any one of his arguments, he maintained, was enough "to show the greatness and loftiness of (Abraham's) soul" (199).

Fifthly: Philo defended Abraham's approach to the Hittites from whom he wished to purchase land to bury Sarah, as recorded in Genesis 23:1–20. This occurred in the second book of the treatise on Dreams, which is marked by thinly veiled anti-Roman sentiment. Philo offered "his advice to play along with the enemy when you do not have the power to mount successful opposition."[458] He mentioned that type of person who is of an aggressive, treacherous, and malevolent disposition, in whose presence it is best to be guarded in one's language (*Somn.* 2.85–89a), and then came on to the conduct of "wise Abraham" in his negotiations with the Hittites to purchase a piece of land in which to bury Sarah (*Somn.* 2.89b–90). According to Genesis 23:7, Abraham bowed low to the Hittites. Eventually, he purchased a field from one Ephron, which was at Machpelah to the east of Mamre

---

457. Literally "put a door over" (θυρας επιθεντες). Colson renders "set bolt and bar to."

458. Schenck, *Brief Guide*, 115.

(= Hebron) and in which there was a cave, where he buried Sarah. In his interpretation Philo did not bother about the historical details but followed an allegorical explanation.[459] It was not that Abraham was reverencing those who were enemies of reason and who corrupted and spoiled instruction, but because he feared their power and strength and wished to be on his guard not to provoke them. In respect of the cave, Philo interpreted it as standing for virtue, both the weapon of virtue and the most excellent place for wise souls to dwell, the double cave.[460] He could not occupy it if he were engaged in fighting against the enemies of virtue, but only as a champion and servant of reason. By his tactic of gentleness and respectful approach (i.e., that which accorded most closely with reason), Abraham could best further the cause of virtue.

It is true that in *Somn.* 2.89-90 there is no specific reference to someone (τις) or derogatory comment on a different opinion. On the other hand, given that we have encountered criticisms in respect of Abraham's conduct and the trustworthiness of the type represented by him in Genesis in all three types of his work, we can be reasonably confident that the passage from *Somn.* 2.85-90 reflects actual criticism of the patriarch which Philo sought to counter.[461]

There are two other instances where Philo did counter criticism of the patriarch but without the vehemence of three of the instances examined above.[462] The first comes in relation to the story of Genesis 15. When Philo came to discuss Genesis 15:6 and the phrase "Abraham believed God" (*Her.* 90), he claimed that this was an additional reason for praising the patriarch, but immediately went on to say "Yet perhaps, someone (τις) may say, do you consider this worthy of praise?" The next sentence appears to be a

---

459. Cf. the comments in Böhm, *Rezeption*, 260n55.

460. In apposition to the phrase "virtue," Philo places the words "the double cave" (το διπλουν σπηλαιον). Where the Hebrew has the place name Machpelah, the LXX has το σπηλαιον το διπλουν, and it is this phrase that Philo is using. He offered an interpretation of it in *QG* 4.80. There Philo gave both a literal and an allegorical interpretation. He stated without explanation that there were two burial caves under the mountain, one outside and one inside, or two walls, one which enclosed and one which was enclosed. He then gave an allegorical interpretation. A person bears a likeness to a double cave, because the body has a desire for external things, while the mind desires to be guided by reason. The virtuous man makes use of a wall to keep at bay evil passions and to embrace holiness and purity. At *Post.* 62, he offered a different interpretation. The double cave receives pairs of persons noted for their virtue, viz. Abraham and Sarah, Isaac and Rebekah, Leah and Jacob, virtues and those who possess them.

461. This is certainly the view of Böhm, *Rezeption*, 260n55.

462. Perhaps this is the reason why Niehoff does not refer to them.

continuation of the view of the τις of the previous sentence:⁴⁶³ "Who would not pay attention when God speaks and makes promises, even if he were the most unjust and impious of all men?" It looks as if the τις regarded Abraham as a sinner and is suggesting that as such Abraham was bound "to pay attention" (a reference to "believed" of Gen 15:6) when God made such a promise to him.⁴⁶⁴ Philo then began his reply:

> To such a questioner we will answer, "Good sir, do not without due scrutiny rob the Sage of his fitting tribute, or testify that the unworthy possess the most perfect of virtues, faith, or criticize our claim to knowledge on this matter. For if you should be willing to search more deeply and not confine yourself to the mere surface, you will clearly understand that to trust in God alone and join no other with Him is no easy matter." (91–92)

That it is no easy step to take is due to the fact of our involvement with mortality and our inclination to trust in riches, reputation, office, friends, health, strength, and many other things. To distrust the created being and to trust in God alone was the work of a great and heavenly⁴⁶⁵ mind which was no longer being enticed by anything which surrounds us (93). Having said this, Philo then said that given the nature of God, actually an act of faith will be counted as nothing particularly astonishing at the judgment-seat of truth but will be deemed a work which is simply in accord with what is right⁴⁶⁶ (95).⁴⁶⁷

Can we suggest a reason or reasons why the objector had voiced doubts about the quality of Abraham's faith? One reason emerges a little later in the treatise. Proceeding with his commentary on Genesis 15, Philo comes eventually to Genesis 15:7–8 (*Her.* 96), where Abraham responded to God's statement that He had brought Abraham from Ur of the Chaldees in order to give him "this land" as an inheritance (which in Philo's allegorical interpretation is "the inheritance of wisdom which cannot be perceived with

---

463. Yonge, *Works*, 283, recognized this and put this sentence with the preceding one in quotation marks.

464. This interpretation assumes that Abraham is the subject of the "even though" clause, i.e., that Abraham is the sinner, while "pay attention" refers to Abraham's believing God's promise. There are episodes in Genesis 12–25 which reveal Abraham to be a sinner, and these may have been in the minds of those who did not share what probably seemed to them to be Philo's idealised interpretation of the patriarch.

465. Literally, "Olympian." Colson renders "celestial."

466. The translation from "but" onwards paraphrases δικαιοσύνης δ ο αυτο το μονον εργον.

467. Without going into any detail, Moxnes, *Theology*, 134, noted that Philo was meeting an objection in this section.

the external senses but can only be apprehended by the most pure mind," 98). He asked God how he would know that he would inherit "the land." In *Her.* 101, Philo acknowledged that this question seems inconsistent with the belief just ascribed to Abraham when he believed God's promise of innumerable descendants and that this was counted to him for righteousness (Gen 15:5-6). Philo then made the comment "Some one (τις) might say that this is inconsistent with having believed.[468] It is the doubter who feels difficulties whereas what the believer does is not to seek (further confirmation) any longer" (101).

Philo defended Abraham by acknowledging that the difficulties and the fact of faith were both there, but asserted that they applied to different objects. Abraham did believe that he would be the inheritor of wisdom, but he was asking how this should come about (101). God then proceeded to instruct him (102).

What we seem to have here is that the unnamed objector (τις) has spotted an inconsistency in the Scriptural account. As Niehoff has pointed out, Homeric scholars like Aristarchus were concerned with inconsistencies in the work of Homer and were prepared to regard certain passages as interpolations by a later hand. We may surmise that the unnamed objector was using the methods of Homeric scholars in studying the sacred scriptures of Israel, as Niehoff has suggested.[469]

A second passage indicating criticism of Abraham's faith may be found in *Mut.* 175-92, in the section where Philo commented on the promise made by God to Abraham that he would have a son by Sarah, and Abraham's reaction to this, as recorded in Genesis 17:15-19. The Genesis account said that Abraham fell on his face and laughed, and queried the possibility of his and his wife's having a son at their age. Philo began his explanation "Do not think, however, my dear sir, when "he said" is followed by "in his mind" instead of "with his mouth," that the addition has little meaning." Philo then proceeded to argue that Moses showed that the doubt did not last long enough to reach the mouth, but stayed in Abraham's swift moving mind (177-78). Once again, we come across a reference to an unnamed person: "But perhaps someone (τις) might say, why is it that a person, once he has believed, admits of any trace or shadow or change whatsoever arising from unbelief?" (181). Philo dismissed this as unrealistic and, indeed, approaching blasphemy, because it was making out a human being to be like God in

---

468. Colson's translation—"Now perhaps it may be said"—obscures the fact that Philo was not dealing here with a hypothetical issue but rather a real objection.

469. Niehoff, *Jewish Exegesis*, 3, 24, 186-87.

having a faith sound and complete in every way, equal to that of the One Who Exists (182).

This passage again suggests that, on the basis of study of the Scriptures themselves, there was a Jewish scholar (the singular may stand for a group, or the leading representative of a group) who saw flaws in the character of Abraham and was not afraid to enunciate criticism of him

We may also mention a comment which Philo made a little later (188). "But perhaps someone belonging to those of a more courageous outlook might come forward and say that what Abraham said is not the utterance of someone who does not believe but of someone offering a prayer that, if joy, that best of good emotions, were to be born, it should not be born according to any other number than ninety [and a hundred],"[470] in order that the perfect good might come to birth according to perfect numbers (188). Behind this comment there is the fact that Abraham was a hundred and Sara ninety when she conceived and bore Isaac.

Then Philo embarked on a discussion of these numbers. He actually only mentioned examples of the number one hundred as Scriptural illustrations, whereas he said that if we subtract a tenth, the sacred first offering to God, from one hundred, which is 10 x 10, this leaves another perfect number ninety (102). Colson believed that Philo was the one who is putting forward this "more courageous" explanation.[471]

In summary, we may say that it is quite amazing to find that there were some in the Jewish community of Alexandria who could be so critical of the patriarch! Bringing these Jewish scholars "out of the shadows into the light" helps to show that Alexandrine Judaism was by no means monolithic, but marked by diversity and lively discussion.[472] Nor can we assume that Philo was *the* representative of it.[473]

---

470. The manuscripts offer τοις εννενηκονταετεαις ουσι, which would be the age of Sarah according to Genesis 17:17. But Colson, *Philo*, 5:238n1, conjectures τοις εννενηκονταετεαις και εκατοντετεαις ουσι on the grounds that Genesis 17:17 mentioned both numbers (Philo immediately went on to mention "the numbers here named," which would lead one to suppose both 90 and 100 would have been previously mentioned by him). On the other hand, what Philo proceeded to discuss is mainly one hundred, which is the age of Abraham according to Genesis 17:17 (which is probably why Manger proposed to emend to εννενηκονταετεαις, according to Colson's note). The number ninety is the harder reading because Philo goes on to mention the plural "numbers."

471. Colson, *Philo*, 5:137.

472. Among those who recognize this variety are Moxnes, *Theology*, 139–40; Barclay, *Jews*, 103–124; Noack, *Gottesbewusstsein*, 45, 55, 57, 85–87; Böhm, *Rezeption*, 336–37, 367, 419; Niehoff, *Jewish Exegesis*, 4–9, 187.

473. Niehoff, *Jewish Exegesis*, 187.

2.16. The Fourth Book of Maccabees

In *4 Maccabees* we have a writing which, while remaining loyal to Judaism, has made ample use of Greek philosophical concepts (especially the concept of reason) in retelling the heroic struggle of the Maccabean martyrs.[474] The elderly Eleazar was able to conquer emotions and pain by his devout reason. When offered a subterfuge as a way out of his torture, Eleazar retorted "Never may we, the children of Abraham, think so basely that out of cowardice we feign a role unbecoming to us!" (v. 17). At the end of his speech, Eleazar thought of his fellow Jews "Therefore, O children of Abraham, die nobly for your religion!" (v. 22). It was natural for this elderly devout Jew to regard his fellow countrymen and women as descendants of Abraham. They had a special identity which must be preserved, and no compromise was possible to preserve this.

The author composed an eloquent encomium to Eleazar at 7:6-15, and then in verses 16-23 reflected on how those who lived by devout reason could conquer the passions of the flesh, "since they believe that they, like our patriarchs, Abraham and Isaac and Jacob, do not die to God but live to God" (v. 19). A very similar remark occurs at 16:15, "Those who die on account of God live to God just as Abraham and Isaac and Jacob and all the patriarchs."

The seven brothers also despised their suffering, and thus were additional proof to people that "devout reason is sovereign over the emotions" (13:1). The author recorded how they encouraged one another. One recalled the three youths who despised the ordeal of the furnace (13:9), while another reminded them "Remember whence you came, and the father by whose hand Isaac would have submitted to being slain for the sake of religion" (13:12), which is a clear reference to Abraham and Genesis 22. They all encouraged each other with the words "Therefore let us put on the full armor of self-control, which is divine reason. For if we so die, Abraham, Isaac, and Jacob will welcome us, and all the fathers will praise us" (13:16-17). Abraham's obedience to the divine command was held out as an example to

---

474. Townshend, *Fourth Book of Maccabees*, 654, 656-57, dated the work between 63 BC and AD 38, and located it in Egypt, probably Alexandria; Nickelsburg, *Jewish Literature*, 226, suggests a date between AD 20 and 54, possibly around 40, and considers Syrian Antioch as a possible place of composition. With this dating, Anderson, *4 Maccabees*, 534, agrees (he follows E. J. Bickermann's article in the Louis Ginsberg Jubilee Volume). Barclay, *Jews*, 370, 379, 448-49, places the author in Antioch at the end of the first century. See Cummins, *Paul and the Crucified Christ*, 77-79, for an up-to-date discussion on date and provenance (taking account of the work of van Henten, Klauck, and Barclay). He favors ca. AD 90-100 and Syrian Antioch (or possibly a city in Asia Minor) as its place of origin.

emulate, while Abraham, Isaac, and Jacob were envisaged as alive in heaven and would be a kind of reception party for the seven when they died.[475]

After narrating the deaths of the seven brothers, the author praised their mother and included her speeches to them. In his encomium of the mother, the author said that her affection for her children did not cause the mother of these young men to waver. She was of the same mind as Abraham[476] (14:20). He went on later to say "this daughter of Abraham called to mind his unflinching bravery" (15:28). She exhorted them as young men not to fall behind the elderly Eleazar in withstanding the tortures out of loyalty to God and His law (16:17–19). A true son of Abraham would obey the Law, even suffering torture to do so. "For His sake also our father Abraham was zealous to sacrifice his son Isaac, the ancestor of our nation, and when Isaac saw his father's hand wielding a knife and descending upon him, he did not cower" (16:20). Here both Abraham and Isaac were praised: Abraham in his willingness to sacrifice his son and Isaac in his unflinching readiness to be killed. Both are then held up as examples to be imitated. The mother was herself one who imitated Abraham in her willingness to sacrifice her sons as he was in the case of Isaac ("But sympathy for her children did not sway the mother of the young men; she was of the same mind as Abraham," 14:20). Having reported her words to her sons encouraging them to die rather than violate God's commands, the author went on to say that her sons knew that "those who die for the sake of God live to God, as do Abraham and Isaac and Jacob and all the patriarchs" (16:25). So, this is the third time (cf. 7:19; 13:17) that the author had indicated his belief that Abraham and the other founding fathers of the Hebrew nation lived to God in life after death. Finally, in 17:6, the author said of the mother: "Your child bearing was from Abraham," meaning that her sons were true descendants of Abraham.[477]

In the accounts of the sufferings and martyrdom of the seven brothers and of their mother, we meet again the idea of the connection with Abraham. The eldest, described as Αβραμιαιος νεανιας, is reported as not groaning even amidst the most horrendous torture. This adjective, not otherwise attested, is difficult to render into English: probably Abrahamite youth will suffice.[478] All seven were described at 18:23 as οι Αβαμιαιοι παιδες. Their mother is called a "daughter of Abraham" at 18:20 (της Αβααμιτιδος).

---

475. 4 Maccabees espoused immortality of the soul rather than resurrection of the body. See Nickelsburg, *Resurrection*, 139.

476. ομοψυχον as a compound adjective has no separate feminine endings. It agrees with μητερα.

477. As the NRSV translates.

478. With Mühling, *Blickt*, 147. Anderson, "4 Maccabees," 2:55, renders "a true son

At 18:1, the author appealed once more to his fellow Jews: "O descendants of the seed[479] of Abraham, children of Israel, obey this Law and be godly in every way, knowing that godly reason is master of passions and not only of those within but also of those from outside ourselves."

This theme together with Abraham's obedience to God, especially exemplified in his willingness to sacrifice Isaac, are what characterize the use of Abraham in 4 Maccabees.

2.17. The Biblical Antiquities of Pseudo-Philo

Pseudo-Philo's *Biblical Antiquities*[480] belongs to that genre currently given the designation "Rewritten Bible." The work rewrites the biblical story from Adam to the death of Saul.

Before Pseudo-Philo recorded any episode from the life of Abraham, he mentioned that when Abraham's great grandfather, Serug, was born, his mother, Melcha, predicted that from her son there would be born in the fourth generation one who would set his dwelling on high and would be called perfect and blameless. He would be the father of nations, and his covenant would not be broken, and his seed would be multiplied forever (4:11). The phrase "set his dwelling on high" is not easy to interpret.[481] It may be a

---

of Abraham." The NRSV has "worthy of Abraham." No doubt that is what the author thought about the youths, but whether he wished to express that by means of Αβαμιαιος is another matter.

479. The Greek is actually the plural: των Αβραμιαιων σπερματων.

480. Nickelsburg, *Jewish Antiquities*, 268, suggested a date during or after the chaos of the war years, 66-70. He felt that two of Ps. Philo's emphases, viz. the question of Israel's survival in the face of powerful Gentile opposition and the stress on the need for good leaders, would fit in well with that period. Murphy, *Pseudo-Philo*, 6, favors a pre-70 date. (In his article, Murphy is more cautious and states that there is no decisive arguments for before or after the destruction of the temple in AD 70. See Murphy, "Biblical Antiquities," 440.) Harrington, *Pseudo-Philo*, 299, argues for a date before AD 70, indeed around the time of Jesus, because of the lack of any reference to the destruction of the Temple. On the other hand, Vogel, *Heil*, 131, accepts that Ps. Philo presupposes the destruction of Jerusalem. Reinmuth, *Pseudo-Philo und Lukas*, 25, maintains that arguments for a date before or after AD 70 are in neither case conclusive, and Fisk, *Do You Not Remember?*, 34-45, also concludes that we are not able to set a precise date or social setting for the work. Barclay, *Gift*, 266, contents himself with "a date of composition around the first century CE." The work, now only extant in Latin, is thought to have been first composed in Hebrew and translated into Greek, and from Greek into Latin.

481. See the discussion in Murphy, *Pseudo-Philo*, 37-38. Rejecting suggestions that either Mount Moriah or Jerusalem was in mind, he suggests that the phrase either has in mind the vision granted to Abraham and referred to at 18:5 (a suggestion which Fisk, *Do You not Remember?*, 241n161, 253n193, seems to favor), or referred to a post-mortem existence. However, its occurrence as the first of a series of statements glorifying

way of saying that Abraham directed his living in accordance with the living God the creator. The reference to Abraham's perfection and blamelessness is similar to the developing view of Abraham in early Judaism. The remaining phrases come from Genesis 17:4-7.

Pseudo-Philo marked off the family of Abraham from their idolatrous contemporaries.[482] Thus, at 4:16, having said that the inhabitants of the earth fell into worship of the stars, he proceeded to say that Serug and his sons did not act in a similar way (4:17).[483]

As to his treatment of Abraham,[484] the first part of the story of the patriarch in the book of Genesis is radically rewritten. Abraham was actually present at the building of the Tower of Babel.[485] He and eleven others refused to join in the project, because they regarded it as idolatrous, and they affirmed that they believed in one Lord whom alone they worshipped.[486] As a result, they were imprisoned. Subsequently, Abraham was the only one of this group to refuse the chance of escape, such was his absolute trust in God. He confronted death in a fiery furnace, but God protected him and he came out alive (LAB 6), which is reminiscent of the story of the three Hebrew youths in Daniel 3. The exemplary conduct of Abraham is clear. And it was his unswerving faith which led to salvation not only for himself but also for other believers.

The author recorded a declaration of God, in which He indicated that He would choose Abraham and would bring him to Canaan, a land which He had protected during the flood in the time of Noah. There He would establish a covenant with Abraham (7:4). When Abraham got to Canaan, God appeared to him, promised him that he would get "an everlasting seed" from Sarah, and made a covenant with him. Pseudo-Philo then simply said that Abraham knew his wife and she conceived and bore a son (8:3).

The author did not explicitly say that God's choice was based on Abraham's trust in Him in the episode of the furnace of fire just narrated. But,

Abraham seems to tell against a post-mortem existence and might suggest that it has some reference to his earthly life. On the other hand, the view that there is a reference to vision of Genesis 15 seems to shift the initiative for this from God to Abraham.

482. Cf. Josh 24:2, 14-15; Jub 11:6-12:14. This is part of what Fish calls Pseudo-Philo's resculpting of Abraham's image (Fish, *Do You Remember?*, 294).

483. Contrast Jub 11.

484. There is a brief treatment of Abraham in LAB in Sprinkle, *Hermeneutic of Grace*, 57-58.

485. Fish, *Do You Remember?*, 146, calls Pseudo-Philo's Babel story just "a subset of the Abraham narrative."

486. As Calvert-Koyzis, *Monotheism*, 45-46, stresses, the eleven and Abraham see helping in building the tower as tantamount to denying their monotheistic belief: idolatry is the form which rebellion against God takes.

given his resistance to the plans of the people to build a tower and his refusal to accept a way of escape from imprisonment and the fiery furnace (cf. 23:5), it would be natural for the reader to assume that Abraham deserved to receive what God promised him.[487] What Pseudo-Philo has done was to show that Abraham distanced himself completely from human arrogance and sinfulness and was a resolute opponent of idolatry.[488]

Then Pseudo-Philo passed on to Isaac and Jacob and his twelve sons (8:4-14). In the next chapter, the author dealt with the situation of the Israelites as slaves in Egypt and oppressed by the reigning Pharaoh. In particular, the author mentioned Pharaoh's edict that all male Hebrew babies should be killed at birth. Amram, father of the future Moses, disagreed with the elders' view that the Hebrews should abstain from intercourse with their wives, in order to circumvent the Pharaoh's edict. He firmly believed that the universe was more likely to end than that the Israelites would be brought to an end. The time predicted in God's covenant with Abraham (the four hundred years of oppression in a foreign land mentioned in Gen 15:13) would be completed. Amran was persuaded that God would not forget His people forever. His covenant with the fathers was not made in vain (9:3-4).[489] God acknowledged Amran's trust in the covenant which He had made with the fathers (9:7-8).

We might think that it is surprising that Pseudo-Philo passed over so much of Abraham's story as recorded in Genesis. However, as the work unfolds, Abraham "reappears," as it were, later in the book. It is clear that Pseudo-Philo assumed knowledge of the stories of Genesis on the part of his hearers/readers.

In Pseudo-Philo's account of the Golden Calf incident (LAB 12), God, in His conversation with Moses on Sinai, referred to the promise He made to the fathers concerning the land. If Israel had sinned before entering the promised land, how much more would they have sinned if they had actually entered it.[490] He said that He would forsake them but would then turn again

---

487. This is the deed-consequence principle so rooted in Israelite thinking. For the negative side, that God punishes those who transgress the Law, see Reinmuth, *Pseudo-Philo*, 118-23, who points out that the lex talionis principle, i.e., the correspondence between God's recompensing action over against human behavior, is one of the major hermeneutical presuppositions of Pseudo-Philo.

488. As Barclay, *Gift*, 273, puts it, Abraham was well suited to be the foundation of the elect nation.

489. "Amran is like Abraham because he trusts in God, defies the authorities and maintains faith when his compatriots are in despair" (Calvert-Koyzis, *Monotheism*, 48).

490. See Fish, *Do You Not Remember?*, 154-56, for discussion of the syntax involved and a defense of this translation, which is also that of Jacobson and Dietzfelbinger. See also Reinmuth, *Pseudo-Philo*, 53.

and make peace with them, which would mean that they could enter the land and build a place of worship for Him. In contrast to Israel, the other nations meant nothing to Him (12:4). As Fish remarks, God's plan for Israel will not be derailed by the golden calf episode; Israel's sins cannot abrogate the ancient promises (in the Biblical account, there is a very real threat of this in Exodus 32).[491]

Then, in Pseudo-Philo's account of Baalam, he has God speaking to Baalam at night. God pointed out that the people against whom Balak had hired Baalam to prophesy, was the people of whom He had said "Your seed will be like the stars of the heaven" (18:5).[492] God also referred to His demand on Abraham to sacrifice his son Isaac, a demand with which Abraham complied. Because Abraham did not refuse, God gave him back his son (18:4-6). Though in the end Isaac was not sacrificed, God said to Baalam: "Abraham's offering was acceptable before me and on account of his [Isaac's] blood[493] I chose them" (18:5). There was also a reference to God's decision to reveal to Abraham what He intended to do to Sodom (18:5), thus portraying Abraham as a trusted confidante of God (a reference to Genesis 18:17). It would, therefore, be stupid of Balaam to think that he could curse Israel whom God had chosen (18:6).

Moses in his farewell address to the Israelites predicted that they would forsake following God's laws. This would provoke God's anger, but not forever, because He would remember the covenant which He established with their fathers (19:2).

Abraham is mentioned in the speech of Joshua when the latter made a covenant with the people at Shechem (LAB 23). In Joshua's speech (a rewriting of Joshua 24),[494] the initial part is God's review of the history of Israel beginning with a reference to the father of the two brothers, Abraham and Nahor (though Terah is not actually named), as the rock from whom they were hewn,[495] and to their respective wives, Sarah and Melcha, when they

---

491. Fish, *Do You Remember?* 152-62. Fish also draws attention to the fact that the idea of God's replacing the promise to Abraham (Gen 12:2; 15:18; 17:7) and starting a new election-line with Moses (Exod 32:10) was dropped.

492. This prediction took place, according to Pseudo-Philo, when God lifted Abraham above the firmament and showed him the arrangement of the stars (18.5).

493. This seems to be an early reference to the so-called Binding of Isaac, the Aqedah: although Isaac was not actually sacrificed, atoning efficacy was attributed to his willingness to be sacrificed.

494. See Murphy, *Pseudo-Philo*, 107-13, for a full discussion of the differences between Pseudo-Philo and Joshua 24.

495. Here Pseudo-Philo altered the thrust of Deutero-Isaiah, who referred to Abraham as the rock from which Israel was hewn. Fish, *Do You Remember?*, 294-301, comments that Isaiah 51:1-2 has provided Pseudo-Philo with a pool of poetic terms and

all lived beyond the river (Euphrates). Joshua reported God as saying that there, amidst idolatry, Abraham believed in God and was not led astray by that idolatry (23:5). In a reference back to chapters 6–7, God referred to His rescue of Abraham from the flames (i.e., the furnace into which Abraham was flung because he would not agree to the building of the tower of Babel), and how He brought Abraham to Canaan (23:5).

The speech then went on to reproduce some of Genesis 15: there is mention of Abraham's question about an heir since Sarah was childless, and of the vision given to Abraham as he slept.[496] Abraham was shown the "place of fire" for the wicked and "the torches of fire" by which the righteous who have believed in God will be enlightened (23:6). We would expect a phrase to indicate the place where the righteous believers in God dwell after death, but, since "the torches of fire"are said to *enlighten* the righteous believers, a spatial idea seems inappropriate. Murphy suggests that the divine presence is what is meant.[497] God then said that these things would be a witness between Him and Abraham that God would give him offspring from the at present childless Sarah (23:7). Presumably, the meaning is that the vision of the after-world is confirmation that Abraham would have descendants. After likening the dove in the vision to Abraham, the turtledove to the prophets, the ram to the wise (presumably a reference to those who interpret the Law), and the calf to the multitude of peoples, God promised to fulfil all His words (23:7). Then the speech went on to Isaac (23:8). By means of this "flashback," the addressees are reminded of episodes from Abraham's life not reported in chapters 6–8.

The settlement in the land was the result of God's fulfilling His covenant made with the fathers (23:11).

After Kenaz had been appointed leader in place of Joshua, he found out that in the ranks of the Israelites there were numerous men who did not wholeheartedly believe in God. God ordered him to interrogate them to find out exactly what their schemes were (25:1–6). The unfaithful from the tribe of Dan admitted that they had been taught (perhaps a reference to the magical arts)[498] by the Amorites and that these secrets were to be found hidden beneath Abraham's mountain (25:9). This is presumably a reference

familiar Biblical images to enrich his embellishment of Joshua's final speech.

496. There is no mention of God's promise of descendants nor of the comment that Abraham believed God and this was reckoned to him for righteousness, which the apostle Paul made so much of. Two Baruch 4:5 also interpreted the experience of Abraham when Yahweh made a covenant with him in Genesis 15:7–21

497. Murphy, *Pseudo-Philo*, 110.

498. Magical arts associated with idolatry are linked to the Amorites (2 Bar 60:1), as Murphy, *Pseudo-Philo*, 120n12, points out.

to Mount Moriah. It does not, of course, imply that Abraham himself was implicated in idolatrous worship. In order to root out corruption and keep God's people pure, all the unbelieving men from all the tribes were burned (26:5)

Pseudo-Philo also employed the technique of the "flashback" in what he described as Deborah's hymn (LAB 32). She referred to God's choice of the people of Israel, and how He rescued Abraham from the fiery furnace, and gave Abraham a son in his old age. Because the angels and the hosts of heaven envied Abraham,[499] God demanded that Abraham sacrifice his son, a command which Abraham immediately obeyed. Pseudo-Philo inserted a conversation between Isaac and Abraham, in which Isaac acknowledged that he was born for this very purpose and declared that future generations would be instructed about him, and so come to learn that God had counted the human soul to be worthy of being a sacrifice to Him.[500] God intervened to stop the sacrifice and said that His purpose in making the demand on Abraham was to reveal his worth to those who did not know him and to silence those who were constantly speaking derogatory things about him. God Himself would always remember Abraham, and on earth his and Isaac's name would be remembered from one generation to another (32:1–4). The way Pseudo-Philo passed from the patriarchs to the making of the covenant at Sinai at 32:7–8 reinforces the conviction that the Sinai covenant was seen as the climax of the election of the patriarchs and the covenant made with Abraham.[501]

The victory over Sisera was won with the help of the stars which, together with sun and moon, had been ordained by God to be servants for His people (32:9; cf. 32:11). Deborah then summoned the earth, the heavens, the lightnings, and the heavenly angels to go to the fathers in the chambers of their souls with the message "The Most Powerful has not forgotten the least of His promises that He established with us, saying, 'Many wonders will I do for your sons'" (32:13). This is a remarkable indication of the importance of Abraham, Isaac, and Jacob to Pseudo-Philo: the fathers were to

---

499. Cf. the scene in heaven in the book of Job when the Satan impugns the integrity of Job's righteousness and piety.

500. Bassler, *Divine Impartiality*, 41, sees this as a watering down of the promise of divine blessing mediated by Abraham's seed to the Gentile nations into the dissemination of information about the dignified status of the human soul.

501. Vogel, *Heil*, 139, stresses this: "The covenant with the fathers and the Sinai covenant appear here as stations in a course of history subject to the divine predisposition. The Sinai covenant marks the culminating point of the history of Israel's election begun with the covenant with the fathers. The Sinai covenant is not primarily the promulgation of a legal order, but a manifestation of God's faithfulness to His promise."

be informed in their post-mortem abode that God had not forgotten His promises made to them on behalf of their descendants.

Soon afterwards, in a comment probably intended for his contemporaries,[502] the author continued Deborah's hymn: "And from this hour, if Israel falls into distress, it will call upon those witnesses [heaven and earth] along with these servants [sun, moon and stars], and they will form a delegation to the Most High, and He will remember that day [the victory over Sisera] and will send the saving power of His covenant" (32:14). The covenant is the patriarchal and Sinai Covenant melded into one and has soteriological power. God would remember it and send His power to help His people.[503]

There is another brief allusion to Abraham's offering of Isaac in the episode when Jephthah, on his return from defeating the Ammonites, saw his daughter, called Seila, and realized that she would be the victim of his vow to sacrifice the first person whom he met when he got back home. Seila herself accepted her fate and referred to the "binding of Isaac." She said that both the one offered was ready and the one doing the offering was rejoicing. She told her father not to try and annul his vow (40:1-3).

When David went out to meet Goliath, he took seven stones (1 Sam 17:40 has five) and wrote on them the names of five of the fathers (Abraham, Isaac, Jacob, Moses, and Aaron), his own name and that of the Most Powerful (Fortissimus), though we are not told which of these actually killed Goliath (61:5). We see in this expansion of the biblical story the importance of the fathers for Pseudo-Philo. "This symbolic act underlines Israel's very identity. Israel's relationship with its God is its very core . . . it rests on God's covenant with the patriarchs."[504]

If we take into consideration the author's stress throughout the whole of the book, it is not unreasonable to claim that a considerable emphasis falls on God's faithfulness to the covenant which He made with Abraham and the fathers (4:5; 7:4; 8:3; 9:3-4; 11:5; 12:8-10;[505] 13:10; 18:11; 19:2; 23:2,

---

502. So Vogel, *Heil*, 281.

503. Vogel, *Heil*, 283, comments: "When the addressees understand themselves as part of (the people of) the covenant (testamentum), they can derive hope for a saving outcome from their present situation [auf einen heilvollen Verlauf ihrer Gegenwart] from the divine faithfulness to His covenant promises, a faithfulness documented in history."

504. Murphy, *Pseudo-Philo*, 211. Moses was included as the mediator; Aaron for his relation to the cult and priesthood; David himself as God's chosen one.

505. When Moses said to God that He had planted a vine, the planting presumably refers back to the time of Abraham, Isaac, and Jacob. For the importance of this speech of Moses for the author's view of Israel's place in God's cosmic purposes, see Barclay, *Gift*, 275-77.

11, 13; 27:7; 30:7; 32:12–13; 47:3; 49:3).[506] This covenant was irrevocable: God would not go back on it, however Israel behaved and however much she disobeyed His commandments (see 4:11; 7:4; 8:3; 9:3; 10:2; 12:4; 13:10; 15:4; 19:2, 9, 11;[507] 20:4, 11; 23:4; 30:1, 7; 35:2–3). In the end, Israel would be saved. Her election stands.[508] Israel had a role to play in God's purposes which He determined on in eternity before the creation of the world, and He would not go back on that determination (28:4; cf. 12:8–9).[509]

At the same time, Abraham was so described as to provide a fitting model to Pseudo-Philo's contemporaries. In order to come to a complete picture of how Pseudo-Philo regarded Abraham, we need to take account of all the references to him, and not just to what emerges from chapters 6–8. So, what did the author of LAB seek to emphasize about Abraham? For Pseudo-Philo, Abraham was perfect and blameless, prompt to obey God's command. He was a resolute opponent of idolatry and a convinced monotheist. God defended him against his angelic detractors and would never forget Abraham. God favored him with a vision of the world to come, and promised that the covenant made with him would be eternal. He also promised that Abraham would have innumerable descendants and that he would be the father of many nations.

So, the author's addressees should, like Abraham, be faithful to God and avoid assimilation to the Gentiles and their idolatrous ways.[510]

All this could fit in smoothly with a situation after the destruction of Jerusalem and the Temple, and, basically, of the Jewish state. Because of this, there was a crisis for the Jewish people. What had happened to God's promises? Was the covenant abrogated? Were they God's people any longer? Pseudo-Philo's response to such doubts is an unquestioning reassertion of the eternal validity of the covenant made with the fathers and established at Sinai with the people as a whole, and the demand for the people's obedience to God's Law given to them.[511]

---

506. See Murphy, *Pseudo-Philo*, 16, 225, 227–28, 230, 244–46, 263; Fish, *Do You Remember?*, 45–50; Vogel, *Heil*, 131–42; VanLangingham, *Judgment & Justification*, 31; Sprinkle, *Law and Life*, 118–19, 124.

507. At 19:11, God said to Moses that as the rainbow was a sign to Him, so also would be Moses' staff with which he performed the wonders in Egypt. When Israel sinned, God would recall Moses' staff and spare them in His mercy.

508. "LAB offers the most emphatic assertion of God's unfailing mercy to be found in Second Temple Judaism" (Barclay, *Gift*, 267).

509. See Barclay, *Gift*, 275–77, 279.

510. See Calvert-Koyzis, *Monotheism*, 49–50.

511. See Vogel, *Heil*, 132–33.

2.18. The Prayer of Manasseh

The Prayer of Manasseh should be mentioned, though its date is difficult to determine.[512] It is a prayer of repentance attributed to one of the most notorious of Israelite kings, and was prompted by the remark in 2 Chronicles 33:12–13 that Manasseh in his distress humbled himself before God and prayed to Him. God heard his supplication and brought him again to Jerusalem and his kingdom.

The prayer opened with an address to "O Lord God of our fathers, God of Abraham, Isaac, Jacob, and their righteous offspring." This phraseology indicates the importance of the founding fathers for the author. The God of Israel was identified by His relationship to the patriarchs to whom He first revealed Himself and with whom He made a covenant to establish their descendants as His people.

Manasseh prayed "So You, Lord God of the righteous, did not appoint repentance for Abraham, Isaac, and Jacob who were righteous and did not sin against You, but for me, a sinner, whose sins are more in number than the sands of the sea" (vv. 8–9a). He referred to his own idolatry and how he thereby piled sin on sin (v. 10e) and pleaded for God's forgiveness: "For you are the God of those who repent. In me you will manifest your grace; and although I am not worthy, you will save me according to your manifold mercies" (vv. 13f–14).

Was the author thinking of the sinless perfection of the three patriarchs? Though this could hardly be maintained on the basis of the biblical text, it is akin to a growing tendency in post exilic Judaism to enhance the sanctity of Abraham. One suspects special pleading when Garlington argues that what is meant is that Abraham, Isaac, and Jacob remained loyal to God; they did not commit idolatry and apostasy. Because they did not forsake the covenant, they did not in that sense need to repent, whereas Manasseh had apostazied and forsaken Yahweh.[513] Whichever view one adopts, it remains true that in this prayer God's mercy is extended even to such a heinous sinner as Manasseh. Charlesworth aptly comments that "two main ideas permeate the verses: God's infinite mercy and grace and the assurance that

---

512. Charlesworth, *Prayer of Manasseh*, 627, suggests that "it is safe to conclude that it was composed either in the second or first century BC, with the recognition that it also could have been composed during the early part of the first century AD." Werline, *Prayer of Manasseh*, 912, on the other hand, thinks that the date is uncertain: if of Jewish origin, it could be as early as the first century BC, but if of Christian origin, no earlier than the late second century AD.

513. Garlington, *Faith, Obedience, and Perseverance*, 92, 137.

authentic repentance is efficacious," and goes on to list the sinlessness of the patriarchs as another important theme.[514]

In our survey, we now come to writings which may, with varying degrees of confidence, be placed after the destruction of Jerusalem and the Temple and, in some cases, contain a direct response to that catastrophic event.

2.19. The Writings of Josephus

Josephus[515] is a highly significant figure among Jewish writers in the second half of the first century AD.[516] Born and brought up in upper class circles in Jerusalem, he was a participant on the Jewish side in the war against the Romans, but switched sides and supported Vespasian, acknowledging that God had chosen Rome to rule, and, after the conclusion of the war, he settled in Rome on an imperial pension, and began to write.

We begin with a look at references to Abraham in the *Jewish War*, though the major source of information will be his *Jewish Antiquities*. There

---

514. Charlesworth, *Prayer of Manasseh*, 629.

515. See Mason, *Josephus*, 828-32. Josephus-Studies have undergone considerable developments in the last 25 to 30 years, largely due to the work of Steve Mason. Mason has insisted that the work of Josephus be studied first and foremost in relation to its context in Flavian Rome: "He writes artistic narratives, not manuals of factual nuggets that may simply be appropriated as historical facts. . . . Josephus's narratives are themselves, as efforts at communication with real audiences, direct evidence for a new set of historical questions concerning the situation of a Judean living in Flavian Rome." See Mason, *Josephus, Judea, and Christian Origins*, and the volume edited by himself, *Understanding Josephus*. For a balanced critique of this approach and an appeal to put Josephus in the center of attempts to understand the religion of ancient Judaism in the era ca. 300 BC–AD 100, see Klawans, *Josephus*, esp. 5-9, 14-43, 210-222. Klawans, while fully accepting that Josephus was a creative writer and that his literary and ideological interests must be taken into account, successfully argues for the internal consistency and the external confirmability of his statements about the various religious schools in ancient Judaism. McLaren, *Turbulent Times?*, also seeks to hold together Josephus as a writer, while still making use of his writings in the effort of historical reconstruction.

516. Josephus wrote his works in the latter part of the first century AD. He first wrote an account of the Jewish revolt in Aramaic just a few years after the Roman victory. Josephus then rendered this into Greek. This work was then followed by a much more substantial account written in Greek, *The Jewish Antiquities*, together with an appendix, the *Life*. According to the last paragraph of the Antiquities, Josephus published the work in the thirteenth year of the Emperor Domitian's reign, when he was himself 56 years old, i.e., in AD 93-94. Its composition was presumably started after Josephus finished the Greek version of the Jewish War and seems to have been spread over a period of around eighteen years. Subsequently he wrote *Against Apion*, a response to criticisms of Judaism made by a certain Alexandrian scholar, Apion, and a defense of it.

is a brief reference to Abraham as the ancestor of the Jewish nation (4.531), while more significantly there is a reference to Abraham and Sarah in the speech delivered by Josephus from a safe position on the walls of Jerusalem addressing his compatriots within the besieged city and urging them to surrender (5.379–81). Whatever Josephus may or may not have said from the city walls during the siege, the speech as we now have it represents what he considered at the time of writing should have been said, or would be appropriate to the situation (in accordance with the approach to speeches in Greek and Roman historiography). In view of his defection to the side of the Romans, Josephus was not unnaturally regarded by many of his compatriots as a traitor.

Josephus began his speech with an exhortation for the Jews within the city to surrender to the Romans. There would be nothing dishonorable in such a course, as God was on the side of the Romans.[517] The shortage of food would begin to have even more adverse effects as the days went past. All this fell on deaf ears and was greeted with catcalls of derision. Josephus then referred to their history when God had intervened to save them without the use of military means. In particular, he referred to the incident when the Pharaoh Neco with a great army seized Abraham's wife, Sarah. Did Abraham resort to arms? Josephus claimed that Abraham had three hundred and eighteen captains each with an army under them, but Abraham did not use them. Instead, he spread out his hands in prayer towards the temple, relying on "his invisible supporter instead of his own army." The very next day Sarah was returned to Abraham, the Egyptian king fled, adoring the holy site in Jerusalem (which the Jews of today had defiled) and bestowed generous gifts on the Hebrews. Josephus went on to refer to some instances of divine help (e.g., the Exodus, the return of the ark which the "Assyrians" had earlier captured; the raising of the siege by Sennacharib, the king of the Assyrians; Cyrus's deliverance of the captives in Babylon and the granting of permission to return to their homeland); and how internal divisions within the nation had produced the defeat at the hands of Antiochus Epiphanes and later Pompey. Josephus argued that through the sins of the nation God had fled from His sanctuary and now stood on the side of the Romans against whom they were fighting. He appealed to them to surrender and save the country which was on the way to ruin.

517. For this as a major motif of Josephus's *Jewish War*, see, e.g., Mason, *Methods*, 78–79, who puts it sharply with his comment that the Romans were pawns of Judah's God. The *Jewish War* is a story of the rise and fall of nations under divine supervision and God's concern to punish those who violate His Law and Sanctuary. Mason successfully attacks the idea that the *War* was a piece of pro-Flavian propaganda.

The story of the relations of Pharaoh, Sarah, and Abraham has been moulded virtually out of all recognition compared with the account in Genesis 12:10–20.[518] Furthermore, as we shall see below, this account differs from the way the story is presented in the *Jewish Antiquities*. The rhetorical purpose of the speech from the city walls must be taken into consideration.

Later, Josephus wrote the *Jewish Antiquities* to commend his nation, primarily to a non-Jewish, Greek-speaking audience (1.5, 8–9; also at the end of the work at 20.262).[519] He took the story from the Old Testament, beginning from the creation of the world, and then went beyond the Old Testament period up to the start of Nero's reign and the procuratorship in Judea of Gessius Florus. He also dealt with matters concerning the Jewish constitution (as promised at 1.5). He specifically pointed out that the main lesson to be learned from this history was that those who conform to God's will prosper, while those who depart from God's laws end up in irretrievable disaster (1.14, 20).

After some genealogical information about the ancestors of the Hebrews (1.148–53),[520] Josephus began the story of Abraham proper[521] by portraying him as a person of great wisdom, persuasive with his hearers, and not mistaken in his opinions. He began to hold a higher view of virtue than others held. He was also keen to persuade others and to reform the ideas then held about God. Josephus claimed that Abraham was the first to declare that the Creator God was one, and that if any other being contributed to the welfare of human beings, it was by command of this one God.[522] He deduced the oneness of God from the changes to which land and sea were subject, from the course of sun and moon, and from the irregularities of the movements of the heavenly bodies (1.154–56).[523] But, because he sought to

---

518. Mason, *Josephus*, 35–36, maintains that Josephus exercised the freedom to redraw stories to create a truly artistic production.

519. All references are to book 1.

520. We learn that his father, Terah, had Abraham when he was 70, and that Abraham had two brothers, one of whom, Haran, died in Ur of the Chaldees, as a result of which his father decided to migrate to Haran in Mesopotamia. Abraham had married his niece, the daughter of Haran. After Haran's death, because Abraham had no legitimate son, he adopted his nephew, Lot (148–154a).

521. The most thorough treatment of Josephus's portrait of Abraham is that by Feldman, *Josephus's Interpretation*, 223–89.

522. "The significant turning point in Abram's life is his discovery about the deity *apart from and before* he had had any relationship with God" (VanLangingham, *Judgment & Justification*, 34).

523. Feldman, *Interpretation*, 229, 262–63, points out that Abraham here *reversed* the Platonic and Stoic argument for the existence of God from the regularity of the heavenly bodies. Abraham assumed that if these celestial bodies were independent,

convince others of the truth which he had discovered, he was threatened with persecution by the Chaldeans and other people of Mesopotamia, and so he left and migrated to Canaan. This was simply said to be "at the will and with the aid of God." When established in Canaan, he built an altar and offered a sacrifice to God (1.157).

When a famine arose, he decided to go from Canaan to Egypt, not merely to enjoy the plentiful food available there but also to listen to what their priests had to say about the gods (1.161). If their notions of the gods were better than his, then he would follow their views, or else he would convert them to a better way (1.161). The specific mention of the priests as his would-be partners in dialogue underlines the religious dimension of his visit.[524]

Abraham was thus depicted as an open-minded person, eager for the truth, and ready to change his views if honestly convinced, but also prepared to convert others by his arguments.

Because of the Egyptian attitude to women, Abraham persuaded Sarah, who was of great beauty, to agree that both of them would say that he was her brother. Pharaoh desired to have her, but God put a stop to his intentions and sent an illness on him and sedition in his country.[525] Pharaoh's priests told him that he had incurred the wrath of God. Having found out who Sarah was, Pharaoh excused himself to Abraham on the grounds that he had assumed that Sarah was Abraham's sister, not his wife, and that he had intended to marry her (1.162-65).[526] The difference between this account and the attitude of Abraham in the *War* stands out conspicuously.[527]

Pharaoh made a large present of money to Abraham and gave him permission to engage in conversation with the most learned among his subjects, there being different groups at variance with one another in matters of belief. Josephus described these conversations in a way which enhanced Abraham's character and standing. He conferred with each party and, by exposing the inadequacy of their arguments, demonstrated that their views were idle and contained nothing true. So, as a result of these conversations,

---

they would have engineered their own uniform regularity; therefore, since this is not so, they must have been subject to an overruling power.

524. Rightly pointed out by Bird, *Crossing over Land and Sea*, 94.

525. In view of Josephus's clear horror of civil strife (στασις), there could be no greater punishment. See Feldman, *Interpretation*, 140, 178, 390, 563n24, 567, 611.

526. The intention is clearly to remove any blame from Abraham and Sarah.

527. The slant of this story is very different from that of the account in the *War*, to which we earlier referred. Mason, *Josephus*, 110-11, puts it: "It is characteristic of Josephus, in keeping with ancient rhetorical practice, to tell the same story differently on each new occasion."

Abraham's reputation and virtue became more widely known. He was admired as a very wise and sagacious man, with the ability to convince others concerning subjects which he undertook to teach (1.167).[528] Josephus said that he introduced arithmetic and the laws of astronomy to the Egyptians[529] (1.166–68). It would seem that Josephus was not the first to suggest this theory about Abraham,[530] but he took up the idea as part of his aim to counter anti-Jewish propaganda and demonstrate the superiority of Jewish culture.

Josephus touched very briefly on the fact that Abraham and Lot parted company, and said that Abraham took up residence in Hebron, a city seven years older than Tanis in Egypt. Feldman sees this comment about the antiquity of Hebron as a means of helping to underline the antiquity of the Jewish people and their national hero, an aspect important in the eyes of the readers whom he hoped to influence[531] (1.169–70). Later (1.200), in a comment on how Lot received the angels as guests into his house, Josephus said that Lot had learned generosity (χρηστοτης) from Abraham.

Both Franxman and Feldman have pointed out that there is less stress on God's promise of Palestine to Abraham in Josephus[532] (e.g., he omits the use of Gen 13:14–17) because he did not want the land to be a focal point. Feldman attributes this to Josephus's position after the destruction of Jerusalem and as a pensioner of the Romans: he did not wish Romans to think that Jews still harbored a desire for national independence in their homeland.[533] On the other hand, when he came to Genesis 15 Josephus did emphasize the conquest of the Canaanites and possession of their cities (see below).

528. Περι ων αν επιχειρησειε διδασκειν.

529. Την τε αριθμητικην αυτοις χαριζεται και τα περι αστρονομισαν παραδιδωσι. Meyer, *Aspekte*, 125, points out that according to Herodotus, it was the Egyptians who had invented astrology.

530. Josephus had previously referred to Berossus (the fourth-century BC writer of a history of Babylon) as alluding to Abraham (though not by name) as a just and great man, well versed in celestial lore (158). In his *Preparatio Evangelica* 9.17.2–9, Eusebius quotes from Eupolemus who said that Abraham had lived in Heliopolis and had taught the Egyptian priests astrology and other sciences (cf. another fragment, quoted at 9.18.2, where Abraham taught astrology to the Phoenicians, and then later went to Egypt (and did the same there?) [translations of these extracts in Doran, "Pseudo-Eupolemus," *OTP*, 2:880–82]. At Preparatio Evangelica 9.18.1, Eusebius preserved extracts from a summary made of the work of Artapanus (third to second century BC) by Polyhistor in which Artapanus said that Abraham had arrived in Egypt and taught the Egyptian king astrology [translation of this passage in Collins, "Artapanus," *OTP*, 2:897].

531. Feldman, *Interpretation*, 84.

532. Franxman, *Genesis and the "Jewish Antiquities,"* 123; Feldman, *Interpretation*, 154.

533. Feldman, *Josephus's Biblical Paraphrase*, 135–38.

In his account of Abraham's participation in the fight against the five rulers recorded in Genesis 14 (see 1.171-82), Josephus considerably enhanced the military strategy, boldness, and ruthlessness of Abraham. He attained complete success, inflicting heavy losses through his attack during the night and then through the determined pursuit of those who had managed to flee (especially 1.176-78). Josephus also drew the moral lesson that victory does not depend on numbers but on the eagerness and courage of soldiers, for with only 318 men Abraham had won a notable victory over a considerably greater army (1.178). Josephus said that Melchizedek received Abraham and entertained his army hospitably. During the feast, he extolled Abraham and blessed God for having given him victory. "Abraham then offered him the tithe of the spoil, and he accepted the gift" (1.181).[534] Nothing is said about this acting as a precedent for the future.

Josephus blended together the accounts of Genesis 14 and 15 far more closely than the editor of Genesis. He introduced his version of Genesis 15 with the report that God commended Abraham's virtue in refusing to retain the spoils of the war and returning them to the king of Sodom, apart from some remuneration for their efforts to his three allies (1.182-83). God said that he should not lose the *rewards* which he deserved to receive "for such good deeds" (1.183).[535] When Abraham mentioned his childlessness, he received the promise that he would have a son and subsequently numerous descendants. Josephus omitted all mention of Abraham's belief in God's promise and its being counted to him for righteousness. It is also surprising that Josephus did not mention covenant in connection with his account of the event of Genesis 15, though he did mention the ritual of the sacrifice (1.184-85). He mentioned that God predicted that his descendants would find "evil neighbors" in Egypt for 400 years, but then "they would overcome their foes, vanquish the Canaanites in battle, and take possession of their land and cities" (1.185).[536]

Then Josephus gave an abbreviated account of Abraham and Hagar, Hagar's flight into the wilderness and her return, and the birth of Ishmael. He started by mentioning Abraham's distress at Sarah's barrenness (not in Genesis 16) and his plea to God for a son. God reassured him about future

---

534. Koch, *König*, 24, lists this among that stream of Jewish exegesis which sought to devalue Melchizedek because he was a heathen king.

535. The sentence with "rewards" is no doubt inspired by Genesis 15:1, where God introduces *Himself* to Abraham as his protector ("shield") and his great *reward*.

536. This illustrates the comment of Franxman, *Genesis*, 127, on a general tendency of Josephus "to change the divine gift of the Promised Land into a divine prediction of its future conquest, thus seeming to place the right of possession in the force of arms rather than in the divine will manifest in an eternal covenant."

children and commanded Sarah to give Hagar to Abraham. After Hagar had conceived and put on airs as a result, Abraham consigned her to Sarah for chastisement, whereupon Hagar fled. An angel of God met her and commanded her to return. Josephus toned down what was promised for her son, Ishmael, in the future (186-90). After a brief comment on Abraham's age when Ishmael was born, Josephus mentioned that God appeared to Abraham thirteen years later (Gen 17:1). Josephus condensed the conversation between God and Abraham, and, in indirect speech, had God promising him a son by Sarah and ordering that he should be circumcised. Josephus omitted reference to Abraham's disbelief (so Gen 17:17). God said that the son's name should be Isaac, from whom nations and kings would spring, and they would "win possession, by war,[537] of all Canaan from Sidon to Egypt" (1.191-93). There is once again no mention of the covenant, circumcision being designated a means of keeping his posterity unmixed with others (1.192), nor of the change of names (Abram to Abraham and Sara to Sarah).

Genesis 18-19 was rather drastically abbreviated by Josephus. The three visitors (they are from the start angels, according to 1.196) were entertained by Abraham. They enquired after Abraham's wife, and said that they would return the following year[538] and would find her a mother. Josephus reported that Sarah merely smiled at this and declared that such an eventuality was impossible for her and Abraham at their age (1.198). The angels informed Abraham of God's decision to destroy Sodom. There follows only a very brief mention of Abraham's reaction and intercession on behalf of Sodom, though Josephus stressed that Abraham was upset at the thought of the certainty of divine judgment about to fall on the inhabitants. When God responded by asserting that there was not a single good person in Sodom, Abraham held his peace (1.199).

Following the thread of Genesis, Josephus included the episode when Abraham once again passed off Sarah as his sister, this time in the territory of Gera, ruled over by King Abimelech (1.207-212). The reason given by Josephus is that Abraham feared the intemperate lust of Abimelech. God inflicted a painful disease on the king, and then appeared in a dream to him and ordered him not to touch Sarah (1.208). Then Abimelech sent for Abraham, assured him that Sarah was unharmed for God had been watching

---

537. See previous note.

538. This translation assumes an ετος understood with εις το μελλον. At Luke 13:9, εις το μελλον means next year. The phrase has this sense in P. Lond. 1231.4 [dated AD 144] cited in Moulton and Milligen, *Vocabulary*, 396. Thackeray, in the Loeb translation, prefers "one day," while Feldman, *Interpretation*, 210, 251, opts for "some day in the future."

over her, and asked Abraham to win God's favor for him. He offered Abraham the opportunity to stay or leave as he wished, Abraham choosing the former. Abimelech bestowed land and riches on Abraham (1.209-12). In Josephus's account, Abraham comes out much better than in Genesis where Abimelech charged Abraham with deception and protested his own innocence.

Josephus mentioned the birth of Isaac, and reported Sarah's changed attitude towards Ishmael. At first she had treated him as her own son, but after she had given birth to Isaac, she felt that it was not fair that Isaac should be brought up with Ishmael. She feared that Ishmael might do harm to Isaac after the death of Abraham (1.215). She requested that he and his mother be sent away. Abraham at first considered this to be barbarous,[539] but acceded to Sarah's request because God agreed with the plan (1.216-17).

Josephus said that Abraham loved Isaac, who was a child of great virtue, always attentive to his duty to obey his parents, and zealous to worship God (1.222). Abraham had reposed all his happiness[540] on the hope that Isaac would be in good health when he (Abraham) died (1.223).[541] Then God appeared to Abraham and reminded him of "all the favors which He had bestowed upon him,"[542] greatest among them being the happiness en-

---

539. According to 1.191, Abraham was 86 when Ishmael was born. He was 101 when Isaac was born according to 1.213-214. Thus Ishmael, on Josephus's dating, was 15 years old. Hardly the infant child (παις νηπιος) of 1.216! See Franzman, *Genesis*, 154-55.

540. Feldman, *Interpretation*, 270, points out that Aristotle had taught that happiness was the highest of all good things achievable by actions and that Philo had regarded happiness as the ultimate goal of human endeavor (*Cher.* 106). He draws attention to the fact that Josephus, in 222-36, uses forms of the noun ευδαιμονια 4 times and ευδαιμονεω once.

541. Franxman, *Genesis*, 159, aptly comments that there is implicit within Abraham's speech to Isaac the sovereign character of the will of God in the face of which personal feelings are being repressed, but also Abraham's courage and determination.

542. "Favors" is the rendering of the phrase παντα τα οσα ειη παρεσχημενος in the revised and expanded edition of Josephus's *Works* (1999) by W. Whiston. Thackeray in the LCL prefers "benefits." The first meaning of the middle παρεχομαι which LSJ, 1338, gives is "to supply of oneself or from one's own means." Neither here nor at 2.332, where Moses encouraged the Israelites at the Sea of Reeds by stating that God wished in those circumstances to display both his power and his προνοια for them nor at 3.86-88 where, in his speech to the Israelites after descending from Sinai, Moses referred to all that God had done on their behalf, and for Adam, Noah, and Abraham before them, does Josephus actually use the word ευεργεσια, though the idea of "benefactions" is present. Attridge, Spilsbury, and Whitlark have all argued that Josephus has used the concept of Benefactor and benefactions to describe God's relationship towards Israel (see Attridge, *Interpretation of Biblical History*, 79-91, esp. 88; Spilsbury, *God and Israel in Josephus*, 172-91; *Josephus*, 241-60; Whitlark, *Enabling Fidelity to God*, 85-92). Whatever were Josephus's reasons for not using ευεργεσια, it seemed best to respect his usage.

joyed through having a son. He then asked Abraham to sacrifice his son to Him, detailing the place where this was to be done, viz Mount Moriah (1.223–24), a detail not specified in Genesis 22.[543] This was to test the depth of Abraham's religious disposition (θρησκεια), to see whether he preferred what was pleasing to God above the preservation of his son. Where the Genesis account was devoid of any comment on the reaction of Abraham to this command from God, Josephus supplied the lack! Abraham did not think that it was right to disobey God in anything, but that he should serve God in every circumstance of life, since it was by His providence that things happen to those to whom He is gracious (1.225).[544] So, in order that he should not be hindered in obeying God, Abraham concealed his intentions from his wife and his servants (1.225). Josephus then informed the reader that the mountain where Abraham was to sacrifice Isaac was the mountain upon which later King David was to build the temple (1.227). When Isaac asked what they were going to sacrifice, Abraham replied that God was able to provide for men out of what they did not have and to deprive others of what they put too much trust in. God would provide the sacrifice if it was His good pleasure to be present and gracious.

Then Josephus expanded the Biblical account in two ways. First, he attributed to Abraham a moving speech addressed to Isaac concerning his intentions (1.228–31). Abraham recounted how numerous were the prayers he had made to have a son and how solicitous he was for Isaac's well being once he was born and how he longed to leave him as his successor. But since it was by God's will that he had become Isaac's father, it was by God's will that he relinquished him back to the God who gave him. He felt that it was right to return Isaac to Him who had conferred such benefits on him and who had been his benefactor and defender ("I yield you to God, who now claims from us this homage (ταυτης . . . της τιμης) in return for the gracious favor which He has shown me as my supporter and ally," 1.229). Abraham had shown his obedience by his willingness to offer Isaac, and then Josephus reported God's reaction in the following words: "Now that He knew the ardor and depth of his piety, He took pleasure in what He had given him and would never fail to regard with the tenderest care both him and his race; his son should attain to extreme old age and, after a life of felicity, bequeath to a virtuous and lawfully begotten offspring a great dominion" (1.234).[545]

---

543. Genesis does not specify which mountain. It only refers in general terms to the land of Moriah (Gen 22:2) and states that it was three days' journey from where Abraham was living (Gen 22:4).

544. For the importance of divine providence generally in Antiquities, see page 214 and n551.

545. Thus, Abraham had received benefits from God; he now "repaid" God by giving

Abraham thought that God had considered Isaac worthy to leave this life neither by disease nor in warfare nor any other severe way, but with the holy offices of religion. God would receive Isaac's soul and keep it near to Him, and so Isaac would be able to act as a kind of intercessor on behalf of Abraham before God. It would also mean that God would take the place of Isaac as Abraham's "protector and stay" of his old age (1.231).

Secondly, Josephus followed this with the ready compliance of Isaac[546] with his father's proposal. Isaac stated that he would not be worthy of being born if he were not prepared to surrender himself to the will both of God and of his father. It would not have been right to have disobeyed even if only Abraham had willed the sacrifice (1.232). Having said this, Isaac rushed to the altar and the sacrifice would have been accomplished, had not God intervened to stop it.

Josephus then inserted a speech from God which explained God's motives in testing Abraham. He had imposed the test not from any desire for human blood, nor had He made him a father only to rob him of his son in such an impious fashion (μετα τοιαυτης ασεβειας). He indicated that He had asked for the sacrifice to test Abraham's disposition (διανοια)[547] and willingness to obey (1.233). Delighted at Abraham's piety, God promised that He would care for his race and that Isaac should live a happy life and live to a very great age and bequeath a large principality to his descendants, who would expand into nations, whose founding fathers would leave behind an everlasting name, would obtain possession of Canaan by force of arms,[548] and be envied by all (1.233–35).

Thus, Abraham is presented as someone of outstanding virtue, whose faith and trust in God and the action based on these elicited God's continued favor.[549]

Since our concern is with Abraham, we shall only briefly point out that Josephus has greatly expanded the scriptural picture of Isaac, whose piety is enhanced immensely. Either Josephus was acquainted with the incipient Aqedah tradition, or the kind of description which he gave was one of the

---

him τιμη in the form of giving back Isaac, and received further promises for the future. See Whitlack, *Enabling*, 87–92, who calls this "the cooperative dance of reciprocity."

546. We have already mentioned that Josephus had previously commented upon the virtues of the young Isaac in glowing terms (1.222).

547. Loeb translation "soul" is too vague. Feldman, *Interpretation*, 97, reads "his way of thinking."

548. See note 236.

549. Attridge, *Interpretation*, 89. Whitlark, *Enabling*, 98, calls this "grace for the worthy."

influences which led to the development of the Aqedah tradition.[550] As regards Abraham himself, clearly his obedience is underlined. Josephus pulled forward this motif from the divine speech at the conclusion of the episode in Genesis 22:18b, to the divine speech at the beginning of the account with the question whether Abraham preferred what is pleasing to God rather than the preservation of his own son, and the comment that Abraham did not think that it was right to disobey God in anything.

We note a reference to God's providence as that by which all creatures enjoy life. Attridge has shown that the belief in God's providence is one of the leading themes in the Antiquities.[551] God is depicted as having the power to help people even when they do not possess the resources, while conversely He will remove what they have if they have succumbed to trusting too much in them (1.227).

Abraham is shown to be someone who has a firm belief in life after death, and in his address to Isaac we have the idea that Isaac will be able to act as a heavenly intercessor and champion for his ageing father in the presence of God.

Josephus mentioned that after Sarah's death Abraham had many sons by Keturah (1.238-41) and that he provided Rebekah, granddaughter to his brother Nahor, as a wife for Isaac (1.242-55). In the course of this long story, divine guidance is stressed (1.245, 249, 254-55),[552] while there is a reference to Abraham's desire that Isaac should not marry a woman from the Canaanites, but this reference is made in a rather careful and unobtrusive manner (1.253).[553]

The conclusion of Josephus's account of Abraham's life is brief. He stated that Abraham was a man of incomparable virtue and honored by God in a manner corresponding to his zeal ($\sigma\pi o \upsilon \delta \eta$) towards Him (1.256).

Of the five qualities extolled in antiquity-wisdom, courage, temperance, justice, piety-we find that there is mention of wisdom, courage, justice, and piety in Josephus's account of Abraham. Abraham would qualify, therefore, to be placed in the category of great men who have influenced

---

550. Vermes, *Scripture and Tradition in Judaism*, 197, maintains that the Targumic tradition about the binding of Isaac is *implicit* in three works dating from the first century AD: the Antiquities, 4 Maccabees, and Pseudo-Philo's LAB.

551. Attridge, *Interpretation*, 71-107.

552. Though Josephus omits the reference to the angel whom God would send to guide Eliezer, according to Abraham (Gen 24:7)

553. Perhaps because Josephus did not want to give material to fuel the criticism that the Jews disliked the members of other nations. Certainly Feldman, *Interpretation*, 117, believes that to counter this charge was one of the motives behind the writing of the Antiquities.

the course of history, and would assist in one of Josephus's aims which was to counter the criticism that the Jewish nation had not produced men of outstanding qualities or anyone who had contributed useful inventions to civilization.[554]

Summary

Sandmel is rather dismissive of Josephus's concept of Abraham,[555] while Harrisville thinks that Josephus has given us rather a superficial account of Abraham. He has Hellenized the biblical figure and altered the biblical account to suit his purposes.[556] On the other hand, Watson is more positive and thinks that Josephus portrayed the patriarch as a religious reformer and apostle of monotheism both in Chaldea and in Egypt, as well as Abraham's instruction of the Egyptians in Chaldean science.[557] For VanLangingham, Abraham is a role model, an individual whose piety God rewards.[558] Watson has highlighted a motif which occurs at the beginning of Josephus's account of Abraham, while VanLangingham instances a theme which seems to dominate the close of Josephus's account (the willingness to sacrifice Isaac and the closing comments on the patriarch's life).[559] Feldman has given us by far the most complete analysis of Josephus's picture of Abraham. He has worked carefully through the Antiquities,[560] and suggests that Josephus has given us a picture of a national hero who conforms to many of the Graeco-Roman ideals of the great man. Josephus omits material which might cast doubts on the nobility of Abraham and moulds the biblical story to his purposes.[561] Thus, Abraham was of ancient pedigree; embodied the cardinal

---

554. See Feldman, *Interpretation*, xv, 130–31, 232–34, for this as one of Josephus's motives in writing the *Antiquities*. "Abraham emerges as a typical national hero" (288). See also Feldman, *Studies in Josephus's Rewritten Bible*, 546.

555. Sandmel, *Philo's Place*, 75, says, "Josephus does not exhibit any striking, unified, coherent conception of the Patriarch," and points out that there is nothing about Abraham's relation to the Law or Abraham as a source of merit to his descendants or as an example of any kind.

556. Harrisville, *Figure of Abraham*, 62–64.

557. Watson, *Hermeneutics*, 258–59.

558. VanLangingham, *Judgment & Justification*, 34.

559. Neither Watson nor VanLangingham seem to be aware of the work of either Franxman or Feldman, to which we have referred.

560. See particularly Feldman, *Interpretation*, 221–89.

561. Feldman, *Interpretation*, 37–46, discusses the promise of Josephus that he would not modify Scripture (1.17; 20.261) when actually he does add and omit. He believes that Josephus conceived his task not to be just translating from the biblical text, but to be one of interpretation and clarification of scripture. Feldman lists no less than 39 factors which influenced Josephus, concluding with the verdict that the *Antiquities*

ideals of wisdom (including mathematics and astronomy), courage and skill in battle, justice, and piety (conscious of how much he owed to God, he was prepared to surrender back to God what he considered to be God's greatest gift to him, and to put obedience to God above personal happiness); he was kind and humane; persuasive in speech and yet open minded. The final encomium singles out his virtue and his zeal for God's service as a result of which God honored him.[562]

2.20. The Fourth Book of Ezra (or 2 Esdras)

For the author of 4 Ezra,[563] the destruction of Jerusalem and the Temple was an agonizing problem, raising issues about the fairness and justice of God's rule over the world as it concerned Israel in particular ("theodicy"). While different proposals have been put forward to explain the sequence of the thought and Ezra's relationship to the angel interpreter, Uriel, and both to the author's viewpoint,[564] within the last thirty years the case has been persuasively argued for a progression on the part of Ezra from a criticism of God's seeming injustice to a gradual acceptance of the position adopted and propounded by Uriel.[565] Uriel stressed that Ezra was not taking into

---

gives us "a 'more smartened up,' more credible, more interesting, more philosophical, more penetrating psychologically, second edition of the bible, so to speak" (Feldman, *Studies*, 539-70). Any difference between Feldman and Mason in the way they have expressed themselves on Josephus's willingness to shape material to his purposes seems to be one of degree rather than kind.

562. Subsequent to Feldman, though not in such detail, Calvert-Koyzis, *Monotheism*, 68; Mühling, *Blickt*, 306-7, also give positive appraisals of Josephus's picture of Abraham.

563. Box, *IV Ezra*, 542, 552-53, argued for a date ca. AD 100 for the Jewish writing, the "Ezra-Apocalypse," i.e., chapters 3-14, composed in Hebrew, with ca. AD 120 for the final redaction, which was subsequently translated into Greek, from which translations in various languages were made. Nickelsburg, *Jewish Literature*, 287-88, dates to AD 100, thirty years after the fall of Jerusalem, and maintains (294) that it was probably written in Hebrew, translated into Greek, and from Greek into a variety of languages. Metzger, *Fourth Book of Ezra*, 519-20, concurs. Stone, *Fourth Ezra*, 9-10, places it in the latter part of the reign of Domitian; it was originally composed in Hebrew, translated into Greek, and thence into various other languages (1-2). Hogan, *Fourth Book of Ezra*, 624, places it near the end of the first century AD, though also stating that the book may have been completed somewhat later.

564. See Stone, *Fourth Ezra*, 11-21, for a history of interpretation up to 1990.

565. See, e.g., with differing emphases, Stone, *Fourth Ezra*, 24-34; Longenecker, *Eschatology and Covenant*, 40-157; Barclay, *Gift*, 282-97; Najman, *Losing the Temple*, 127-58. See Barclay, *Gift*, 281n4, for criticism of Longenecker. Barclay builds on the work of Stone, but suggests that Stone's use of phrases like "conversion" and "a profound religious experience" may be over dramatic. We shall not embark on a discussion of

consideration the fact that there would be a Last Judgment and another world to come, when the righteous would receive justice, vindication, and blessing, and the wicked would perish. Whereas Ezra was oppressed by the huge number of the unrighteous, Uriel concentrated on the quality of the few righteous who would be saved, and asserted that while God might show mercy in this age, divine justice meant that there could not be mercy at the Last Judgment.[566] Whereas Ezra pleaded for Israel to be spared judgment, Uriel stressed that those to be saved would be the righteous Israelites who had observed and kept God's commandments (cf. 8:45; 9:7).

In chapter three, the seer addressed God in his bewilderment and reviewed the course of history. After Noah, the nations of the human race began to sin once more. "When they sinned, You chose for Yourself one of them, whose name was Abraham; You loved him, and to him alone, secretly, at the dead of night, You showed how the world would end. You made an everlasting covenant with him and promised never to abandon his descendants. You gave him Isaac, and to Isaac You gave Jacob and Esau; of these You chose Jacob for Yourself and rejected Esau; and Jacob grew to be a great nation" (3:13-16). Though not overtly said, the probability is that the author linked the choice of Abraham with his righteousness (cf. 3:11).[567]

We note the stress on God's election of and love for Abraham; on the eternal covenant made with him; the promise never to abandon him (hence the distress at the apparent breach of this promise in the seeming abandonment of Israel evidenced in the destruction of Jerusalem), and on the special revelation given to Abraham of how the world would end—the first evidence of an interpretation of the scene in Genesis 15 when Abraham fell asleep, in terms of a divine revelation about the future. That the author also singled out the revelation of how the world would end from the story of Genesis 15 may be linked with the message of the book which centered very much on the fact that Uriel insisted that the problem raised by Ezra could only be solved by taking into consideration the certainty of a final judgment when the wicked would be condemned and receive their just reward,

---

Stone's use of psychological conceptuality in interpreting the progression through the book: e.g., Stone (32) suggests that Ezra and Uriel in the first three visions/episodes are both the author but are the Janus faces of the author's self, while, on the fourth vision or episode, he describes the author as internalizing his new convictions in Ezra's change of convictions, while externalizing his grief in the figure of the weeping woman. Barclay's exposition seems more convincing.

566. Barclay, *Gift*, 282, 285-87, 290, 293, 298-300.

567. Cf. VanLangingham, *Judgment & Justification*, 36. There seems an implied contrast between those who sinned and Abraham.

while the righteous would be vindicated and they too would receive their just reward.

That Abraham and his immediate descendant(s),[568] Jacob, formed the first stage in the history of God's saving purpose and action again emerges at 6:7–10. In reply to Ezra's question about the interval between the two ages, Uriel said that it would be no larger than between Abraham and Abraham.[569] This last phrase is somewhat puzzling, but the context seems to suggest Abraham and his immediate descendant(s) [here, Jacob].[570] Uriel recalled that Jacob's hand held Esau's heel from the beginning (v. 8). Esau is the end of this age and Jacob the beginning of the age to come (v. 9). Stone agrees with the interpretation which sees Esau as a symbol for the Roman empire. On that assumption, then, the passage suggests that the end of Rome's domination will be followed by the kingdom of Jacob/Israel which will be the beginning of the next age.[571] (Elsewhere, there are passages which suggest that this age is near its end—4:26, 44–50; 5:55; 14:10–11, says that of the ten divisions of time, two and a half still remain.) Ezra was told that the beginning of a person is the hand and the end of a person is the heel, so Ezra was advised not to seek "any interval between the heel and the hand" (6:10b).[572] Myers suggests that history is being seen here *sub specie aeternitatis*: the two ages are coupled together, though they may still be different.[573]

Later, in 7:36–41 (106–111), Abraham figured as the first in a list of those who interceded for the wicked in scripture. At the end of the list, Ezra asked, "If therefore the righteous have prayed for the ungodly now, when corruption has increased and unrighteousness has multiplied, why will it

---

568. Isaac is not in fact mentioned, probably because the author was going to expound Genesis 25.26 and needed to come onto Jacob whose hand grasped the heel of his brother Esau as they emerged from the womb. Stone, *4 Ezra*, 161, calls this an eschatological interpretation of the biblical text based on the idea that it has veiled eschatological meaning.

569. This is the more difficult reading, though Myers, *I & II Esdras*, 190; Metzger, *4 Ezra*, 534, prefer the reading "Isaac."

570. The difficult "between Abraham and Abraham" is best taken as meaning Abraham and his immediate descendant. Stone, *Fourth Ezra*, 160, suggests that "Abraham" means Abraham but also implies his children and draws attention to Hebrews 7:4, 9–10, where the author conceives of Levi as being present in the loins of Abraham when he met Melchizedek.

571. Stone, *Fourth Ezra*, 159–61.

572. Stone, *Fourth Ezra*, 161, suggests that the command not to seek anything between the heel and the hand is an oracular utterance meant to indicate that Ezra should not ask certain questions.

573. Myers, *Esdras*, 202.

not be so then [on the Day of Judgment] as well?"[574] The reply received from Uriel was that the assessment of the Last Judgment would be final and definitive, and would signal the end of the possibility of intercession for sinners. The reference to "the righteous" who interceded for the wicked serves to confirm the assumption that Abraham was chosen by God because like Noah he was righteous in his generation.

Summary

Fourth Ezra clearly regarded God's election of Abraham as the origin of Israel, but, as the work progresses, it becomes crystal clear that the eternal covenant is for those who are righteous within Israel, whereas the unrighteous would receive condemnation and punishment. One might have expected that 4 Ezra would have made more use of the emphasis in so many Second Temple writings of Abraham as the supreme example of obedience in fulfilling the commands of God. In a brief comment, Abraham was said to be the recipient of esoteric revelations, as are Moses (14:5) and Ezra. The choice of Ezra as the character through whom the agonizing questions of his own day were articulated and responded to may have something to do with the paucity of references to Abraham. Ezra was a figure of the period after the return from exile and one associated with the renewal of the Torah as central in the life of Israel (Neh 8–9). What Stone has said is of help in this respect. He has commented that the subject of the worthiness of Ezra is a sustained one throughout the book,[575] and that from chapter 14, the vision of the giving of the Torah, which is deliberately patterned on the story of Moses' call at the burning bush in the wilderness, it is clear that "Ezra was revered as a figure of great status, equal to that of Moses."[576]

---

574. The "when" clause interprets the "now" and indicates that it means the present age.

575. Stone, *Fourth Ezra*, 34; cf. Barclay, *Gift*, 306, where he states that Ezra himself at several points receives revelations as a fitting reward for his devotion to God's Law, and that he serves as a paradigm of the righteous who have "a treasury of works" (7:76-77) and who will reap their reward at the Last Judgment. See also Barclay, *Gift*, 306-8, for Barclay's assessment of the author's discussion of God's mercy and justice and his place in the spectrum of Second Temple handling of this theme.

576. Stone, *Fourth Ezra*, 37, 410-12. In the latter pages, Stone quotes passages from Rabbinic sayings which indicate that Ezra was worthy to receive the Torah in the same measure as Moses.

2.21. The Second Book of Baruch (or The Syriac Apocalypse of Baruch)

Second (or Syrian) Baruch[577] lamented Israel's fate after the calamity of the destruction of Jerusalem in AD 70, and sought an answer to the agonizing questions raised by it. He urged his compatriots to be faithful in adhering to the Law and to hold on to the hope of the future reward of resurrection and immortality after a period of tribulation.

Right at the start of the work, God was reported as indicating to Baruch that He intended to destroy Jerusalem and to scatter the people among the nations (1). When Baruch asked to be relieved of life as he would shrink from beholding such an event, God repeated His intention and then drew a distinction between the earthly city and the heavenly Jerusalem which was destined to be revealed eventually. He had previously revealed this to three people: to Adam, but had taken it away from him when he transgressed God's command; to His servant, Abraham, in the night when the birds and animals had been slaughtered;[578] and to Moses on Mount Sinai. This was part of the author's strategy to direct attention away from the fate of the city and temple in AD 70, and to the transcendent heavenly Jerusalem. Abraham was privileged with such a revelation, an indication of his standing in the author's eyes, along with Moses.

When Baruch gave vent to his frustration at the delay in God's revealing His power and executing justice on the nations and for Israel, he pleaded with God to let His glory appear and to raise from the dead Abraham, Isaac, and Jacob, and all those who were like them, on whose account God had said that He created the world (21:24).

In the final vision given to Baruch and its lengthy explanation, the history of the world from Adam to the arrival of the messiah was divided into alternating periods of light and black waters. Adam's sin inaugurated a period of black waters, which was then followed by a period of bright waters. This was described as "the fount of Abraham, also his generations and advent of his son and of his son's sons, and of those like him" (57:1). As

---

577. Charles, "2 Baruch," 470, 472–74, dates to AD post-90, and argues for a Hebrew original translated into Greek and then into Syriac; Nickelsburg, *Jewish Literature*, 287, dates towards the end of the first century AD, and accepts that the extant Syriac manuscript is a translation from the Greek, which may be a translation of a Semitic original; Klijn, *2 (Syrian Apocalypse of) Baruch*, 616–617, dates to ca. AD 100–120, and suggests a Hebrew original and Palestine as the probable provenance; and Henze, *Second Book of Baruch*, 427, places it not too long after the actual destruction of Jerusalem, in AD 70.

578. LAB 23:6 interpreted this visionary experience differently, as we have already seen.

if to justify this era as one of "bright water," the author pointed out that at that time the unwritten law was named among them, and the works of the commandments were then fulfilled; belief in the coming judgment was then generated; hope of the world that was to be renewed was then built up; and the promise of the life that should come hereafter was implanted (57:2–3). In agreement with this, Abraham and his immediate descendants were described as righteous at 58:1. After them there was a period of "dark water."

Here, then, we observe the idea that in fact the patriarchs observed the law, even though it was not formally given until Sinai. The patriarchs were also credited with eschatological beliefs (coming judgment, renewal of the world, the life to come). We can see that Abraham and the other patriarchs were, by implication, being held up as examples of obedience to the Torah, which was for the author the vital way for Israel to live in the aftermath of the disaster of AD 70.

The closing section of the work is a letter of Baruch to the nine and a half tribes of the Assyrian captivity (2 Bar 78–87).[579] As part of the opening greeting, Baruch asked "Are we not all the twelve tribes bound by one captivity as we also descend from one father?"—a clear reference to the figure of Abraham (78:4). The nine and a half tribes were a literary device meant for Jews of the Diaspora. One of the author's aims was to hold together the people of God in the aftermath of the disaster of the destruction of Jerusalem and the Temple. Baruch asked the addressees to remember the commandments of God, and went on to list features which were characteristic of Jewish identity and which needed, therefore, to be preserved: "Remember Zion and the Law and the holy land and your brothers and the covenant and your fathers and do not forget the festivals and the sabbath" (84:8). The mention of the covenant could be a reference to the Sinai covenant or to the covenant made with Abraham and renewed to Isaac and Jacob. There is no ambiguity about the reference to the fathers which comes after covenant. The "fathers" are "the genealogical foundation for the holding together of the scattered Jewry for which the author strives."[580]

Gwendolen Sayer believes that "the biblical story of Abraham haggling with God over the imminent destruction of Sodom and Gomorrah . . . is the model for Baruch's haggling with God after the destruction of Jerusalem."[581] She notes certain terminological links between Genesis 18 and 2 Baruch; believes that Manasseh is seen as the prototype of "many" unfaithful Jews

---

579. For a defense of the letter as part of the original work, see Murphy, *Structure and Meaning*, 28–29; Whitters, *Epistle of Second Baruch*, 35–65.

580. Vogel, *Heil*, 229.

581. Sayler, *Have the Promises Failed?*, 91–95.

before the destruction of the city (see 41:3; 64-65; 77:3-10); and argues that the worship in Jerusalem was seen by the author as so defiled that Jerusalem was no better than Sodom. While her case is not completely assured, it is a possibility and would be a further indication of the influence of Abraham in the period when 2 Baruch was written.

2.22. The Apocalypse of Abraham

The *Apocalypse of Abraham*, extant now only in Slavonic,[582] dealt with the conversion of Abraham from idolatrous worship to faith in the living God. Abraham was dissatisfied with the gods, which his father and other human beings had made and then worshipped. Various incidents revealed the powerlessness of idols, but Terah would not listen to Abraham's pleas to cease his involvement in the business of manufacturing idols (Apoc. Ab. 1-7). Abraham's dissatisfaction was finally met by a revelation of God to him. God ordered him to leave his home (literally), whereupon it was destroyed with his father as a punishment for his father's idolatry (Apoc. Ab. 8).

In chapters 9-31, the author built on and expanded the account of Genesis 15. God introduced Himself as the One who existed before the world and as its Creator, and commanded Abraham to assemble various birds and animals for sacrifice on a mountain, where Abraham would receive revelations about the created order and things as yet unrevealed (9:6-9). God sent His angel, Jaoel, to be with Abraham always (10:3-6,1 6b), and he guided him on the journey to the mountain (12:1). At the mountain which is revealed to be Horeb (12:3), Azazel, in the shape of one of the unclean birds of prey, sought to dissuade Abraham from sacrificing to God, but he was rebuked by the archangel, Jaoel (13:1-14). Jaoel drew a distinction between Azazel's ungodly, earth-bound followers and Abraham's portion which was in heaven (the righteous). He mentioned that the heavenly garment lost by Azazel through his fall had been set aside for Abraham (13:7-14), and he told Abraham that he should know that God had chosen him (14:2).

Abraham was then taken on a journey to heaven (15:4). The author described the revelations of the heavenly world and human history given to Abraham. He was granted a vision of the heavenly angels and of God's throne (18-20), and then shown what would happen in the future. He was

---

582. Nickelsburg, *Jewish Literature*, 294-99; Rubinkiewicz, *Apocalypse of Abraham*, 681-705, esp. 681-83 (Rubinkiewicz dates the work to after AD 70 and before the middle of the second century). Harlow, *Apocalypse of Abraham*, 296, states that it is generally regarded as an early Jewish composition in response to the destruction of Jerusalem in AD 70.

promised many descendants (20:5, where the language of seed like the stars of the heavens is taken from Gen 15:5). Abraham saw people on the right side of his vision and was told that these represented the ones whom God had prepared to be born of Abraham and to be called His people (22:5).

Abraham asked God why He had allowed Azazel such power to ruin mankind (23:12). When God said that people have committed evil by their own choice, Abraham then queried why God made people who desired evil when He was angered by such behavior (23:14). God showed him the wickedness of mankind (24) and then he was shown the sins of his descendants—even idolatry perpetrated in the Temple[583]—which provoked the anger of God (25). Once again Abraham asked why God had permitted it to be so. In reply God reminded Abraham of how his own father refused to listen to his protests about idols (26:1-7). The temple was destroyed (27:1-3), which provoked an agonized protest from Abraham (27:6). God pointed to the idolatry of the Jews as the reason for the destruction (27:7-8). Their punishment would last for a considerable time (28). Abraham then saw a Gentile who attracted worship (29:3-13),[584] but God would punish the Gentile idolaters with ten plagues (29:14-16), which are explained in 30:1-8, by which time Abraham was back on earth. God would send His Chosen One at the End (31:1), and in the age of justice the righteous from Abraham's seed would live, protected by God, their enemies destroyed, and they would rejoice with God (31:4; cf. 29:17-21).

It would seem that the author of the Apocalypse of Abraham believed that the destruction of Jerusalem in AD 70 had been caused by idolatry[585] and that, therefore, Israelites needed to purge themselves of idolatry if they were to experience restoration (29:17-19).

Significantly, the future of the people of Israel was linked in this Apocalypse with the founding father of the race, Abraham.[586] From an early age,

---

583. See Calvert-Koyzis, *Monotheism*, 80, for a discussion of what the author might have considered idolatrous cultic practices in the temple before its destruction in AD 70.

584. Rubinkiewicz, *Apocalypse of Abraham*, 684, reckons 29:3-13 to be a Christian interpolation, referring to the coming of Jesus and his treatment at the hands of Jews and Gentiles; cf. Nickelsburg, *Jewish Literature*, 297. According to Calvert-Koyzis, *Monotheism*, 82, Hall argued that the vision (29:3-7) is original, and it is the interpretation (29:8-13) which is a Christian interpolation (see Hall, "Christian Interpolation," 107-111). If that is correct, the man in the original version was in league with Azazel, attracted worship to himself from both Gentiles and some Jews, and was presumably an evil figure of the time before the end.

585. Nickelsburg, *Jewish Literature*, 298.

586. See Poirier, *On a Wing and a Prayer*, 96-97. Nickelsburg, *Jewish Literature*, 297-98; Sayer, *Promises*, 138, broadly agree that this Apocalypse was grappling with

Abraham was one who rejected idolatry and sought the one true Creator God. He was called beloved of God and friend of God (9:6; 10:5; 16:3; 19:3; 28:2). God revealed to him the future, and he was assured that the people had a place in God's purposes for the future. But it would be the righteous from Abraham's descendants who would receive God's mercy and blessing. What would characterize them? They would refuse to countenance idolatry. In other words, they would follow the example of their progenitor, Abraham.

2.23. The Testament of Abraham

Although *The Testament of Abraham* is difficult to date and has a complicated pre-history,[587] it offers an interesting picture of Abraham rather different in some respects from the picture obtained so far.

The work opened with the report that Abraham at nine hundred and ninety years old had reached the "measure of his life." This life had been marked by quietness, gentleness, righteousness, generous hospitality to all and sundry, and piety (1:1-2). God sent Michael to inform him of his impending death so that he could put his affairs in order, because God had greatly blessed him (1:4). Michael addressed Abraham "Hail, honored father, righteous soul elect of God, true friend of the Heavenly One" (2:3).[588]

The story revolved round the fact that constantly Abraham refused to accept that he was about to die (7:12). He consented when Michael returned a second time with the message, on condition that he was allowed a journey through the universe to see the inhabited earth (9:6), a request which God granted (9:8). During this trip, Abraham saw the sinful behavior of people

---

the fact that the destruction of Jerusalem had called in question the efficacy of God's covenant with Abraham, and the survival of Israel was perceived to be at stake.

587. This is extant in two recensions, A (the longer form) and B (the shorter version). There may have been ultimately a common ancestor, but then different intermediate Vorlage. Scholarly opinion seems to favor recension A as preserving the contents and order of the original composition. Nickelsburg, *Jewish Literature*, 253, believes that the work probably originated in Egypt at a time that cannot be precisely determined. Sanders, *Testament of Abraham*, 874-75, maintains a date for the original of ca. AD 100, plus or minus 25 years, and argues for Egypt as the provenance of both the original story and the Recension A manuscript. Allison Jr., *Testament of Abraham*, 300, thinks that if the work originated in Egypt, then it probably originated before the revolt of AD 115-117, since this left Egyptian Jews decimated.

588. Michael continued throughout the book to address Abraham in the most glowing terms, e.g., righteous Abraham (2:6; 15:9); all-pious Abraham (13:2); and God's friend (15:9). At 4:6, Michael said to God that he had not seen on earth a man like Abraham who was merciful, hospitable, righteous, truthful, God-fearing, and who refrained from every evil deed. God told Michael that Abraham had not sinned (10:3) and told Death that Abraham was his true friend (16:5).

and invoked punishment on the sinners whom he saw (10:1–11). So severe was his judgment that God ordered Michael to bring him to heaven to see the process of judgment there and to learn mercy, or else all humanity would be destroyed (10:12–15). This Abraham did (11–14). In the end he asked for forgiveness because he had been so severe in his judgment (14:10–15).

On his return to earth (15:1–2), he still refused to come to terms with the fact that his life was due to draw to a close (15:10), but then God sent Death to him in a beautiful and attractive form (16:7–16). Finally, Death took his soul by subterfuge (20:8–9). Abraham's body was buried, and the angels escorted his soul to heaven (20:8–12).[589]

Alongside the fulsome tributes to Abraham's sheer goodness, there is another strand. There is Abraham's stubborn refusal to admit that his death was near,[590] and the fact that Abraham admitted that he was a sinner and a completely worthless servant of God (9:3), and, later, having realized how severe had been his judgments, admitted to Michael that he had sinned before God and requested Michael to join with him in seeking God's forgiveness, to which God responded with "Abraham, Abraham, I have heeded your voice and your supplication, and I forgive you (your) sin" (14:10–14). The Testament of Abraham must be one of the few Jewish writings in which negative features are part of the portrait of Abraham.

The message is that "even to [the pious, all-holy, righteous, hospitable Abraham] there came the common and inexorable bitter cup of death and the unforeseen end of life" (1:3). Nickelsburg comments: "Through this parody the author transforms the exceptional patriarch into a character who stands in solidarity with the rest of humanity and with whom his readers can empathize."[591]

Sanders, however, offers a different line of interpretation, seeing the judgment scene as central. He notes the lack of any stress on specific Jewishness. There is no mention of converting to Judaism. Everyone is judged by the same standards. If good deeds outweigh bad ones, the soul will enter life;

---

589. The present ending is clearly a Christian addition because of the Trinitarian formula: "Let us too, my beloved brethren, imitate the hospitality of the patriarch Abraham and let us attain to his virtuous behavior, so that we may be worthy of eternal life, glorifying the Father and the Son and the Holy Spirit, to whom be the glory and the power forever. Amen" (20:15).

590. Mühling, *Blickt*, 325, sees this as serving to increase the entertainment value of the writing, while Nickelsburg, *Jewish Literature*, 251, had earlier spoken of the author's use of "parody."

591. Nickelsburg, *Jewish Literature*, 251.

if not, it is sentenced to punishment. The means of atonement are repentance and premature death.[592]

There is no reason why a writer might not wish to get across more than one message, and we need not make an either-or choice in this matter.

2.24. The Pirke Aboth (The Sayings of the Fathers)

The *Pirke Aboth* (*Sayings of the Fathers*)[593] was incorporated into the Mishnah which was a codification of Jewish laws made around AD 200. The material is, of course, much older than the date of the publication of the Mishnah. While the sayings in chapters 1–4 are attributed to particular teachers, that is not the case in chapter 5[594] which contains a reference to Abraham.

Chapter 5 opens with: "By ten sayings the world was created. And why does the scripture teach this? Could not the world have been created by one saying? But it was in order to exact penalty from the wicked who destroy the world that was created by ten sayings, and to give good reward to the righteous who establish the world that was created by ten sayings" (5.1). The ten sayings are the divine utterances in Genesis 1. The passage continued by saying that the ten generations from Adam to Noah provoked God and He brought the flood upon them. The ten generations from Noah to Abraham also provoked God "until Abraham our father came and received the reward of them all" (5.3). The meaning appears to be that God put up with the sinners until Abraham, who by his righteousness made up for the sins of his ancestors and received the reward which the previous generations should in fact have received.[595] Then come "Ten trials Abraham our father was tried with, and he bore them all, to make known how great was the love of Abraham our father" (i.e., for God) (5.40).[596]

Later in the chapter, it is said:

---

592. Sanders, *Testament*, 876–78. Sanders sees the work as a witness to a universalistic and generalized Judaism: "Judaism is depicted here as a religion of commonplace moral values, which nevertheless insists both on the strictness of God's judgment and on his mercy and compassion" (876–77).

593. Herford, *Pirke Aboth*, 686–714. There is a modern translation in Young, *Meet the Rabbis*, 121–44.

594. Chapter 5 is dominated by groups of related things based on numbers: ten, seven, four, and three.

595. Herford, *Pirke Aboth*, 707.

596. Young, *Rabbis*, 136, translates: "This is to make known how great was His love for our father Abraham." For Jubilees as the origin of the concept of the ten trials of Abraham, see 81n56.

Every one who has three things is one of the disciples of Abraham our father. And every one who has three other things is one of the disciples of Balaam[597] the wicked. If he has a good eye and a lowly soul and a humble spirit, he is of the disciples of Abraham our father. If he has an evil eye and a boastful soul and a haughty spirit, he is of the disciples of Balaam the wicked. What is the difference between the disciples of Abraham our father and the disciples of Balaam the wicked? The disciples of Balaam the wicked inherit Gehenna and go down to the pit of destruction, as it is said, "But You, O God, will bring them down to the pit of destruction. Men of blood and deceit shall not live out half their days; but I will trust in You." But the disciples of Abraham our father inherit the Garden of Eden and inherit the world to come;[598] as it is said: "That I may cause them that love me to inherit substance, and that I may fill their treasuries." (5.22)[599]

The phrase "disciples of Abraham"[600] indicates that Abraham was regarded as worthy of imitation. All loyal Jews should look to the ancestor of the race and live as he did. The writer constantly referred to Abraham as "our father," which probably contains an allusion to the covenant which God made with him and which was the commencement of their story.[601]

2.25. Summary

This run through post-biblical Jewish literature reveals a fairly consistent picture of Abraham. We could say that five major themes seem to emerge. Firstly, in some writings Abraham is set forth as one who *turned away from the idolatry characteristic of his milieu* in Ur of the Chaldees and Haran, and sought to come to a knowledge of the one true Creator God. He can be portrayed as an example of faith. He thus became the first proselyte in history.

597. Herford, *Pirke Aboth*, 709, considered that the reference to Balaam might be alluding to Jesus.
598. Charles, *APOT*, 2:709, himself added a note to Herford's comments, to the effect that with "Garden of Eden" and "world to come" the text had been conflated and that one or other of these phrases should be excised.
599. The two quotations are from Ps 55:23; Prov 8:21, respectively.
600. The Jews/Pharisees in the Fourth Gospel refer to themselves as "disciples of Moses" (John 9:28) as well as "the seed of Abraham" (John 8:33). The two phrases are not, of course, antithetical, but rather complementary.
601. There is a reference to Abraham at 6:11, a passage about the five possessions of the Holy One with quotations to support each item, but this is regarded by Herford, *Pirke Aboth*, 713, as a later addition since the quotation is not really an apposite support for the inclusion of Abraham.

Secondly, he is portrayed as *righteous, obedient, and faithful to God*. It is also occasionally said that he even kept the Law, so in touch with God's will was he. Where there is talk about his being tested by God, it is affirmed that in all such tests of his faith and obedience, Abraham proved himself absolutely faithful and loyal.

Thirdly, *as a result of his righteousness, he was rewarded by God*. God made a covenant with him and gave him promises concerning descendants and land.

In the fourth place, he is held up as *someone worthy of emulation* by Jews undergoing the test of their fidelity to God and His covenant.

Fifthly, future generations are depicted as appealing to this covenant which God made with Abraham, and renewed with Isaac and Jacob, in order to remind God to keep His promises and so preserve Israel from destruction.

Among some writings which probably emanated from the Diaspora, Abraham is set forth as a scholar-philosopher, an inventor, and a bringer of culture. In this idea we can see both the pride of Jewish writers and also an apologetic defense of Judaism over against their environment.

Occasionally, motifs like his becoming the father of many nations, his being a prophet, a healer, and a warrior-statesman are mentioned, but these do not become such developed themes which would compel one to describe them as characteristic of Second Temple Judaism.

This picture runs the risk of being a synthesis, of presenting a schematic view for the whole of Judaism, whereas scholars recognize that Judaism was by no means a monolithic entity; indeed, not a few scholars are prepared to speak of Judaisms[602] Another possible approach might be to use Josephus's four sub-groups within Judaism plus apocalptic Judaism and Hellenistic Judaism and look at representatives of each (e.g., Sirach for the Sadducees; Psalms of Solomons for the Pharisees; perhaps the spirit of the Maccabean marrtyrs to illustrate the ethos of the later Zealots; Jubilees and the Qumran writings for the Essenes; 4 Ezra and 2 Baruch for Apocalyptic Judaism; Wisdom of Solomon, Philo and those criticized by Philo, and Josephus for Hellenistic Judaism) and see what characterizes their picture of Abraham and what, if any, distinctive features emerge. Therefore, alongside this summary, we propose with some hesitations to use Josephus's description of four groupings in contemporary Judaism and supplement it with two other categories, and see if a picture of Abraham characteristic of the group emerges.

---

602. Though see Haacker, *Verdienste und Grenzen*, 5, who thinks that the pendulum has swung too far in speaking of Judaisms.

Of groups mentioned by Josephus we start with the Sadducees. If we accept Maier's description of Sirach as "the spiritual forefather" of the Sadducees, we could with some caution use Sirach as a representative of the best in Sadduceeism.[603] Sirach represented Abraham as faithfully and obediently carrying out the law; he introduced circumcision; he was promised many descendants and land and that he would be both a father of nations and a blessing to the nations. The covenant God made with him was of considerable benefit to his descendants.

The Prayer of Manasseh thought of Abraham as obedient. It combined a confession of sin with a fervent plea for forgiveness due to God's grace. We can only speculate what the original Sitz im Leben of this prayer was. Could it have been used to express contrition and repentance in worship, whether by an individual or corporately? If we accept that it was used in the worship of the Temple, then it would be used by the priests who were responsible for the liturgy of the Temple, viz the "higher clergy" who seem to belong to the Saducean party.

Here is perhaps the place to mention what the material about John the Baptist in the Synoptic Gospels can contribute to our theme. According to Matthew's Gospel, John the Baptist asked the Sadducees and Pharisees who had come out to (? inspect) his baptism, "Who warned you to flee from the wrath to come?" He himself denounced reliance on descent from Abraham: "Don't say among yourselves, "We have Abraham as our father," for I tell you that God is able to raise up children for Abraham from these stones" (Luke 3:7).[604] Clearly the author of Matthew's Gospel felt that confidence in descent from Abraham characterized the Sadducees as well as the Pharisees.

The second group mentioned by Josephus was the Pharisees. Some scholars are hesitant about the view that the Psalms of Solomon originated from within Pharisaic circles, but they seem closest to the Pharisees. These Psalms certainly see the covenant with Abraham as of immense importance

---

603. This suggestion is strengthened if we accept the thesis frequently asserted by Mack that the hymn in praise of the fathers was a mythic etiology of Second Temple Judaism, centered on the covenants which undergird the priesthood and seen as a theocratic community which was the flowering of all God's works in creation and history (Mack, *Wisdom*, 6, 54–56, 60, 64–65, 73, 77, 86, 105, 153, 179). Note also the comment by Blenkinsopp, *Interpretation and Tendency to Sectarianism*, 14: "Ben Sira... a devout scribe, might be considered a typical representative of the theocratic point of view." Similarly, Klawans, *Josephus*, 26–27, 177, 240n123, takes Sirach as a representative of the Saducean viewpoint.

604. Luke 3:8 has John the Baptist addressing *the crowds* who had streamed out to the Jordan to hear John's preaching and to be baptised. Probably Matthew has edited the Q original, which is better preserved by Luke with "crowds." Cf. Matt 16:1 for another instance of where Matthew conjoins "Pharisees and Sadducees" (Mark 8:11 has "Pharisees"; Luke 11:14–16, probably Q, has "crowds").

for Israel's self-understanding and her future. God chose the descendants of Abraham, and made a covenant with the fathers. He has loved the descendants of Abraham and has put His name on them. This relationship is one which will last forever. This is broadly in agreement with the way the fourth evangelist represents the Jews/Pharisees, especially in John 8:31–59.

No documents survive from the third group mentioned by Josephus, viz. the Zealots. However, the zeal which inspired the Maccabean fighters to resist the inroads of Hellenism and to strive for freedom from the rule of Antiochus IV Epiphanes gives us something of an insight into the mind set of those who were determined to resist Roman rule in the first century AD.[605] In seeking to inspire his sons, the dying Mattathias appealed to the example of "the fathers." He pointed to Abraham's faithfulness when tested (1 Macc 2:52). So too, at the present time, his sons were to be courageous and strong in keeping the Law (2:64). "Pay back the Gentiles in full and obey the commands of the Law" (2:68). Likewise, the militant spirit of Judith[606] and the way in which she rallied the flagging spirits of the menfolk in Bethulia; and the defiance of the seven brothers together with the way their mother urged her sons on to keep loyal to the God of their ancestors and to His laws can help us to enter into the spirit of those who were prepared to fight to the last drop of their blood against those whom they deemed to be blasphemous idolaters occupying God's holy land.[607]

The fourth of Josephus's parties in Judaism was the Essenes. We shall proceed on the assumption that this movement existed prior to the Qumran group which was a radical wing of the movement and which broke away from the parent body. The Qumran library exhibits works which reflect a particular ideology and other writings which are akin to but not as radically orientated as the works in this first category. This points to the fact that even after their break away, the members of the Qumran community kept the works which they had previously read and been helped by. The book of Jubilees belonged to the earlier history of the Essenes. It spoke of the ten trials or testings which God imposed on Abraham and stressed that he was found faithful in them all. The author emphasized Abraham's obedience to the Law and stressed the command to circumcise himself and his household. It also showed Abraham observing the festivals even before the Sinai laws were

---

605. We are not, of course, suggesting that either this or the other examples to be mentioned were actual Zealots, but that their "zeal" was akin to, and helps us to understand, the mindset of the later Zealots.

606. Compare the spirit of Esther in the canonical scriptures.

607. The resistance of the aged Eleazar and the seven brothers and their mother was of course a passive resistance. But the *spirit* is not dissimilar to that which animated the Zealots.

promulgated. It defended a solar based calendar. While it mentioned Abraham's inventive proclivity, it was his obedience to God's command and laws that dominated the portrait. He was promised descendants and the Land. Any friendship with Gentiles or inter-marriage with them was branded as disobedience to God.

It is possible that an early version of the Testaments of the Twelve Patriarchs existed. If it did, we may surmise that such references to Abraham as might have occurred were references to the way in which Israel benefitted from what God promised Abraham, Isaac, and Jacob. That the patriarchs would enjoy the life of the age to come was also a feature of the Testaments. The Apocalypse of Weeks probably belonged to the Essene heritage of Qumran. It stressed the righteousness of Abraham, which stood out in comparison with the sinfulness of humans before and after him.

Of the literature emanating from the Qumran community after its separation from the parent body, the Damascus Document stressed Abraham's obedience and how he observed the commands of God (his observance of the command to circumcise and to sacrifice Isaac were mentioned). The covenant made with him had ongoing validity, and the members of Qumran were the beneficiaries of it at the present time. The Genesis Apocryphon underlined Abraham's obedience and also mentioned his ability to heal.

In addition to Josephus's four groups in Palestine, we will mention Hellenistic Jewish writers, some of whom we can locate in Alexandria. The author of the Wisdom of Solomon stressed Abraham's obedience and the soteriological value of the covenant which God made with him for his descendants. Abraham occupied a considerable place in the numerous works of Philo of Alexandria, and it is not easy to summarize briefly what he said. Although Abraham was an historical figure, he was especially a paradigm of the journey of the soul, which Philo extracted from the Genesis material through the allegorical mode of interpretation. Thus, Abraham's various journeys became illustrations of the journey of the soul, which should seek to liberate itself from the prison house of the body and flee from the pleasures and the appetites of the outward senses. The move from Chaldea was the move from "astrology" to a deeper view of God; that from Haran was the soul seeking to leave behind the outward senses and contemplating the mind, which was a fragment of the divine, a copy of the Logos which holds the universe together; the wandering around Canaan was the soul seeking solitude. Because of his view of the mind, Philo can say that Abraham kept the natural law of which the written Law of Sinai was a copy. Although Philo can speak of the grace of God drawing the soul to Himself, the primary impression is that faith has a very intellectual character and becomes the crown, rather than the starting point, of the journey. Faith is passing through the created order to the attainment of belief in the one true Creator who sustains all things by His providence. Abraham's willingness to sacrifice his only son, Isaac, and his fortitude when Sarah died, were examples of reason conquering passions. Genesis 15:6 was quoted several times by Philo. He seems to take the faith of this verse as an advance on the trust which led Abraham to leave Ur of the Chaldees and as true of all Abraham's life. Faith in the one true Creator became something of a reward for the quest of the soul.

Philo's own writings reveal other Jewish biblical scholars who were prepared to use the literary critical methods of Homeric scholars, both those earlier and those contemporary with them, in their study of the LXX. They were not afraid to voice their criticism of Abraham's conduct as shown in the book of Genesis. They stand out against the prevailing trend in Judaism as a whole to celebrate the obedience and goodness of Abraham.

The Testament of Abraham mentioned Abraham's incomparable goodness and his obedience to God, and yet at the same time it acknowledged that Abraham was a sinner in need of God's forgiveness. For example, the story depicted Abraham as refusing to accept the fact that he was about to die, even when this was conveyed to him from God. It is noteworthy to come across a negative component in the presentation of Abraham in a Jewish writing, as opposed to learning of criticisms via a third party.

In 4 Maccabees, which may have originated in Syrian Antioch, Abraham was praised as one obedient to God's commands and, therefore, as an example to be emulated. As he was willing to sacrifice his only son, so any Jew should be willing to sacrifice their life in loyalty to God. Like Abraham, such will be raised to enjoy immortality.

Josephus himself, although born and brought up in Israel, spent his years as a writer in Rome and wrote with an eye on a non-Jewish audience, seeking to defend the Jewish faith to this audience. Josephus depicted Abraham as rejecting idolatry and turning to the one, true God, in fact the first monotheist in history. He was a man eager for the truth and of great wisdom, introducing arithmetic and astrology to the Egyptians. He was a very virtuous person who obeyed God faithfully. Josephus made a great deal of his willingness to offer up Isaac to God, which elicited favors from God. Abraham believed in life after death.

Finally, we mention writings which probably originated in Israel after the destruction of the Temple. Fourth Ezra mentioned that God chose Abraham and made an everlasting covenant with him, which had soteriological value for those descendants of Abraham who would keep the Law. God also revealed to him how the world would end. In addition, Abraham was mentioned as the first intercessor before God in scripture.

The author of 2 Baruch described Abraham's dissatisfaction with idolatry and underlined Abraham as a man who obeyed God and kept His commands (the unwritten law) even before the Law was given on Mount Sinai. The Apocalypse of Abraham recorded how Abraham was dissatisfied with the idolatry of his native Ur and how God revealed to him the future. He was promised innumerable descendants, but many would prove to be wicked and it would only be the righteous among his seed who enjoy the life of the age to come.

Hopefully, this way of Summarizing the findings helps to indicate the variety as well as the agreement among Jews in the Second Temple period about the founding father, Abraham. On the whole, it has shown that the five aspects mentioned above were shared by most Jews of this period.

Bibliography

Abegg, Martin G. "4QMMT, Paul, and 'Works of the Law.'" In *The Bible at Qumran: Text, Shape, and Interpretation*, edited by Peter W. Flint, 203-16. SDSSRL. Grand Rapids: Eerdmans, 2001.
Adler, William. "Demetrius the Chronographer." In *The Eerdmans Dictionary of Early Judaism*, edited by John J. Collins and Daniel C. Harlow, 530. Grand Rapids: Eerdmans, 2010.
Alexandre, Manuel. *Rhetorical Argumentation in Philo of Alexandria*. BJS 322. SPM 2. 1999. Reprint, Atlanta: SBL, 2007.
Allen, Leslie C. *Ezekiel 1-19*. WBC 28. Dallas: Word, 1994.
———. *Ezekiel 20-48*. WBC 29. Dallas: Word, 1990.
Allison, Dale C., Jr. "Testament of Abraham." In *The Eerdmans Dictionary of Early Judaism*, edited by John J. Collins and Daniel C. Harlow, 298-300. Grand Rapids: Eerdmans, 2010.
Alt, Albrecht. *Essays on Old Testament History and Religion*. Oxford: Blackwell, 1966.
Anderson, Hugh. "3 Maccabees (First Century BC)." In vol. 2 of *The Old Testament Pseudepigrapha*, edited by James H. Charlesworth, 509-29. New York: Doubleday, 1985.
———. "4 Maccabees." In vol. 2 of *The Old Testament Pseudepigrapha*, edited by James H. Charlesworth, 531-64. New York: Doubleday, 1985.
Arenhoeval, Diego. *Die Theokratie nach dem 1. und 2. Makkabäerbuch*. WS 3. Mainz: Matthias-Grünewald, 1967.
Assefa, Daniel. "Book of Dreams (1 Enoch 83-90)." In *The Eerdmans Dictionary of Early Judaism*, edited by John J. Collins and Daniel C. Harlow, 552. Grand Rapids: Eerdmans, 2010.
Atkinson, Kenneth. "Enduring the Lord's Discipline: Soteriology in Early Judaism." In *This World and the World to Come: Soteriology in Early Judaism*, edited by Daniel M. Gurtner, 145-63. LSTS 74. London: T. & T. Clark, 2011.

———. "The Psalms of Solomon." In *The Eerdmans Dictionary of Early Judaism*, edited by John J. Collins and Daniel C. Harlow, 1238-40. Grand Rapids: Eerdmans, 2010.

Attridge, Harold W. *The Interpretation of Biblical History in the Antiquitates Judaicae of Flavius Josephus*. HDR 7. Missoula, MT: Scholars for HTR, 1976.

———. "Philo the Epic Poet (Third to Second Century BC)." In vol. 2 of *The Old Testament Pseudepigrapha*, edited by James H. Charlesworth, 781-84. New York: Doubleday, 1985.

Avemarie, Friedrich. "Erwählung und Vergeltung. Zur optionalen Struktur rabbinischer Soteriologie." *NTS* 45 (1999) 108-26.

———. *Tora und Leben: Untersuchungen zur Heilsbedeutung der Tora in der frühen rabbinischen Literatur*. TSAJ 55. Mohr: Tübingen, 1996.

Avemarie, Friedrich, and Hermann Lichtenberger, eds. *Bund und Tora. Zur theologischen Begriffsgeschichte in alttestamentlicher, frühjudischer und urchristlicher Tradition*. WUNT 92. Mohr: Tübingen, 1996.

Bächli, Otto. *Israel und die Völker: Eine Studie zum Deuteronium*. ATANT 41. Zürich: Zwingli, 1962.

Baltzer, Klaus. *The Covenant Formulary in Old Testament, Jewish, and Early Christian Writings*. Philadelphia: Fortress, 1971.

Barclay, John M. G. "'By the Grace of God I Am What I Am': Grace and Agency in Paul and Philo." In *Divine and Human Agency in Paul and His Cultural Environment*, edited by John M. G. Barclay and Simon J. Gathecole, 140-57. London: T. & T. Clark, 2006.

———. "'I Will Have Mercy on Whom I Have Mercy': The Golden Calf and Divine Mercy in Romans 9-11 and Second Temple Judaism." *Early Christianity* 1 (2010) 82-106.

———. *Jews in the Mediteranean Diaspora from Alexander to Trajan (323 BCE-117 CE)*. Berkeley: University of California Press, 2004.

———. "Unnerving Grace: Approaching Romans 9-11 from the Wisdom of Solomon." In *Between Gospel and Election: Explorations in the Interpretation of Romans 9-11*, edited by Florian Wilk and J. Ross Wagner, 91-109. WUNT 257. Tübingen: Mohr Siebeck, 2010.

———. "Who Was Considered an Apostate in the Jewish Diaspora?" In *Tolerance and Intolerance in Early Judaism and Christianity*, edited by Graham N. Stanton and Guy Stroumsa, 80-96. Cambridge: Cambridge University Press, 1996.

Baumgart, Norbert C. *Die Umkehr des Schopfergottes: Zu Komposition und religionsgeschichtlichem Hintergrund von Gen 5-9*. HBS 22. Freiburg: Herder, 1999.

Behm, Johannes. "διατίθημι διαθήκη." *TDNT* 2:104-134.

Berthelot, Katell. "Hecateus of Abdera." In *The Eerdmans Dictionary of Early Judaism*, edited by John J. Collins and Daniel C. Harlow, 718-19. Grand Rapids: Eerdmans, 2010.

Bird, Michael F. *Crossing over Land and Sea: Jewish Missionary Activity in the Second Temple Period*. Peabody, MA: Hendrickson, 2010.

———. "Waiting for Salvation: The Story of Salvation in Judith." In *This World and the World to Come: Soteriology in Early Judaism*, edited by Daniel M. Gurtner, 15-30. LSTS 74. London: T. & T. Clark, 2011.

Birnbaum, Ellen. *The Place of Judaism in Philo's Thought: Israel, Jews, and Proselytes*. BJS 290. SPM 2. Atlanta: Scholars, 2007.

Blanton, Thomas R., IV. *Constructing a New Covenant: Discursive Strategies in the Damascus Document and Second Corinthians*. WUNT 2.233. Tübingen: Mohr Siebeck, 2007.

Blaschke, Andreas. *Beschneidung: Zeugnisse der Bibel und verwandter Texte*. TANZ 28. Basel: Francke, 1998.

Blenkinsopp, Joseph. "Abraham as Paradigm in the Priestly History in Genesis." *JBL* 128 (2009) 225–41.

———. "Interpretation and Tendency to Sectarianism: An Aspect of Second Temple Judaism." In *Aspects of Judaism in the Graeco-Roman Period*, edited by E. P. Sanders, et al., 1–25. Vol. 2 of *Jewish and Christian Self-Definition*. London: SCM, 1981.

Bloch, Renée. "Midrash." In *Approaches to Judaism: Theory and Practice*, edited by William S. Green, 29–50. BJS 1. Missoula, MT: Scholars, 1978.

Boccaccini, Gabriele. *Beyond the Essene Hypothese: The Parting of the Ways between Qumran and Enochic Judaism*. Grand Rapids: Eerdmans, 1998.

Bockmuehl, Marcus. *Revelation and Mystery in Ancient Judaism and Pauline Christianity*. 1990. Reprint, Grand Rapids: Eerdmans, 1997.

Böhm, Martina. "Abraham und die Erzväter bei Philo. Überlegungen zur Exegese und Hermeneutik im frühen Judentum." In *Philo und das Neue Testament: Wechselseitige Wahrnehmungen*, edited by Roland Deines and Karl-Wilhelm Niebuhr, 377–95. WUNT 172. Tübingen: Mohr Siebeck, 2004.

———. *Rezeption und Funktion der Vätererzählungen bei Philo von Alexandria: Zum Zusammenhang von Kontext, Hermeneutik und Exegese im frühen Judentum*. BZNW 128. Berlin: de Gruyter, 2005.

Borgen, Peder. *Bread from Heaven: An Exegetical Study of the Concept of Manna in the Gospel of John and the Writings of Philo*. SNT 10. Leiden: Brill, 1965.

———. *Early Christianity and Hellenistic Judaism*. Edinburgh: T. & T. Clark, 1996.

———. "Judaism in Egypt." In *Early Christianity and Hellenistic Judaism*, by Peder Borgen, 71–102. Edinburgh: T. & T. Clark, 1996.

———. *Philo of Alexandria: An Exegete for His Time*. SNT 86. Leiden: Brill, 1997.

———. "Some Hebrew and Pagan Features in Philo's and Paul's Interpretation of Hagar and Ishmael." In *The New Testament and Hellenistic Judaism*, edited by Peder Borgen and Søren Giversen, 151–64. Aarhus: Aarhus University Press, 1995.

Borgen, Peder, P. Kåre Fuglseth, and R. Skarsteneds, eds. *The Philo Index: A Complete Greek Word Index to the Writings of Philo of Alexandria*. Grand Rapids: Eerdmans, 2000.

Bowley, James E. "Artapanus." In *The Eerdmans Dictionary of Early Judaism*, edited by John J. Collins and Daniel C. Harlow, 386. Grand Rapids: Eerdmans, 2010.

———. "Cleodemus Malchus." In *The Eerdmans Dictionary of Early Judaism*, edited by John J. Collins and Daniel C. Harlow, 476–77. Grand Rapids: Eerdmans, 2010.

Box, George H. "IV Ezra." In *Pseudepigrapha*, edited by Robert H. Charles, 542–624. Vol. 2 of *The Apocrypha and Pseudepigrapha of the Old Testament in English*. Oxford: Clarendon, 1913.

Braulik, Georg. *Deuteronium, 1:1–16:17*. ECB AT 15. Würzburg: Echter, 1986.

———. *Deuteronium 2, 16:18–34:12*. ECB AT 28. Würzburg: Echter, 1992.

———. *Die deuteronomischen Gesetze und der Dekalog: Studien zum Aufbau von Deuteronomium 12–26*. SBS 145. Stuttgart: KBW, 1991.

———. "Die Freude des Festes: Das Kultverstandnes des Deuteronium—die älteste biblische Festtheorie." In *Studien zur Theologie des Deuteroniums*, by Georg Braulik, 161–218. SBAAT 2. Stuttgart: KBW, 1988.

———. *Die Mittel deuteronomischer Rhetorik.* AB 68. Rome: Pontifical Biblical Institute, 1978.

———. "Gesetze als Evangelium. Rechtfertigung und Begnadigung nach der deuteroniumischen Tora." In *Studien zur Theologie des Deuteronomiums*, by Georg Braulik, 123–60. SBAAT 2. Stuttgart: KBW, 1988.

———. "The Sequence of the Laws in Deuteronomy 12–26 and in the Decalogue." In *A Song of Power and the Power of Song: Essays on the Book of Deuteronomy*, edited by Duane L. Christensen, 313–35. SBTS 3. Winona Lake, IN: Eisenbrauns, 1993.

———. *Studien zu den Methoden der Deuteronomiumsexegese.* SBA 42. Stuttgart: KBW, 2006.

Brewer, David I. *Techniques and Assumptions in Jewish Exegesis before 70 CE.* TSAJ 30. Tübingen: Mohr, 1992.

Brueggemann, Walter. *A Commentary on Jeremiah: Exile and Homecoming.* Grand Rapids: Eerdmans, 1998.

———. *Genesis: Interpretation.* Atlanta: John Knox, 1982.

———. *Old Testament Theology: Essays on Structure, Theme, and Text.* Minneapolis: Fortress, 1992.

———. *Theology of the Old Testament: Testimony, Dispute, Advocacy.* Minneapolis: Fortress, 1997.

Brueggemann, Walter, and Hans W. Wolff. *The Vitality of Old Testament Traditions.* 2nd ed. Atlanta: John Knox, 1982.

Bruin, Tom de. *The Great Controversy: The Individual's Struggle between Good and Evil in the Testaments of the Twelve Patriarchs and in their Jewish and Christian Contexts.* NTOA/SUNT 106. Göttingen: Vandenhoeck & Ruprecht, 2015.

Callaway, Mary. *Sing, O Barren One: A Study of Comparative Midrash.* SBLDS 91. Atlanta: Scholars, 1986.

Calvert, Nancy. *Philo's Use of Traditions about Abraham.* SBL 1994 Seminar Papers. Atlanta: SBL, 1994.

Charles, Robert H. "2 Baruch, or the Syriac Apocalypse of Baruch." In *Pseudepigrapha*, edited by Robert H. Charles, 470–526. Vol. 2 of *The Apocrypha and Pseudepigrapha of the Old Testament in English.* Oxford: Clarendon, 1913.

———, ed. *The Apocrypha and Pseudepigrapha of the Old Testament in English.* 2 vols. Oxford: Clarendon, 1913.

———, ed. *Testaments of the XII Patriarchs.* London: A & C Black, 1908.

Charlesworth, James H., ed. *The Old Testament Pseudepigrapha.* 2 vols. New York: Doubleday, 1983, 1985.

———. "Prayer of Manasseh." In vol. 2 of *The Old Testament Pseudepigrapha*, edited by James H. Charlesworth, 625–37. New York: Doubleday, 1985.

Chesnutt, Randall D. "The Wisdom of Solomon." In *The Eerdmans Dictionary of Early Judaism*, edited by John J. Collins and Daniel C. Harlow, 1242–44. Grand Rapids: Eerdmans, 2010.

Childs, Brevard S. *Exodus: A Commentary.* OTL. London: SCM, 1974.

Christensen, Duane L. *Deuteronomy 1–21:9.* WBC 6A. 2nd ed. Michigan: Zondervan, 2001.

———. *Deuteronomy 21:10–34:12.* WBC 6B. Michigan: Zondervan, 1997.

———. "Form and Structure in Deuteronomy 1-11." In *Deuteronomium: Enstehung, Gestalt und Botschaft*, edited by Norbert Lohfink, 135-44. Leuven: Leueven University Press, 1985.

———, ed. *A Song of Power and the Power of Song: Essays on the Book of Deuteronomy*. SBTS 3. Winona Lake, IN: Eisenbrauns, 1993.

Christiansen, Ellen J. *The Covenant in Judaism and Paul: A Study of Ritual Boundaries as Identity Markers*. AGAJU 27. Leiden: Brill, 1995.

Christiansen, Irmgard. *Die Technik der allegorischen Auslegungswissenschaft bei Philon von Alexandrien*. BGBH 7. Tübingen: Mohr, 1969.

Clements, Ronald E. "A Review of Rolf Rendtorff, *Das überlieferungsgeschichtliche Problem des Pentateuch*. BZAW 147. Berlin: de Gruyter, 1977." *JSOT* 3 (1977) 46-56.

———. *Deuteronomy*. OTG. Sheffield: JSOT, 1980.

———. *God's Chosen People: A Theological Interpretation of the Book of Deuteronomy*. London: SCM, 1968.

———. *Jeremiah: Interpretation*. Atlanta: John Knox, 1988.

———. *Old Testament Prophecy: From Oracles to Canon*. Louisville: Westminster John Knox, 1996.

Coats, George W. "The Yahwist as Theologian? A Critical Reflection." *JSOT* 3 (1977) 28-32.

Collins, John J. *Jewish Wisdom in the Hellenistic Age*. OTL. Louisville: Westminster John Knox, 1997.

———. "Philo the Epic Poet." In *The Eerdmans Dictionary of Early Judaism*, edited by John J. Collins and Daniel C. Harlow, 1080. Grand Rapids: Eerdmans, 2010.

———. "Pseudo-Hecateus." In *The Eerdmans Dictionary of Early Judaism*, edited by John J. Collins and Daniel C. Harlow, 718. Grand Rapids: Eerdmans, 2010

Collins, John J., and Daniel C. Harlow, eds. *The Eerdmans Dictionary of Early Judaism*. Grand Rapids: Eerdmans, 2010.

Collins, John J., and Gregory E. Sterling, eds. *Hellenism in the Land of Israel*. CJAS 13. Notre Dame, IN: University of Notre Dame Press, 2001.

Colson, F. H., et al., eds. *Philo I-IX: Suplements I-II*. Cambridge, MA: Harvard University Press, 1929-62.

Cox, Ronald R. "Travelling the Royal Road: The Soteriology of Philo of Alexandria." In *This World and the World to Come: Soteriology in Early Judaism*, edited by Daniel M. Gurtner, 167-80. LSTS 74. London: T. & T. Clark, 2011.

Cross, Frank M. "Exile and Apocalyptic." *Canaanite Myth and Hebrew Epic: Essays in the History of the Religion of Israel*, 291-325. Cambridge, MA: Harvard University Press, 1973.

Crüsemann, Frank. "Die Eigenstandigkeit der Urgeschichte: Ein Beitrag zur Diskussion um den 'Jahwisten.'" In *Die Botschaft und die Boten: Festschrift für Hans Walter Wolff zum 70. Geburtstag*, edited by Jörg Jeremias und Lothar Perlitt, 11-29. Neukirchen-Vluyn: Neukirchener, 1981.

———. *The Torah: Theology and Social History of Old Testament Law*. Edinburgh: T. & T. Clark, 1996.

Davies, William D. *The Gospel and the Land: Early Christianity and Jewish Territorial Doctrine*. Berkeley: University of California Press, 1974.

———. *Jewish and Pauline Studies*. London: SPCK, 1984.

———. "Law in First-Century Judaism." In *Jewish and Pauline Studies*, by William D. Davies, 3–26. London: SPCK, 1984.

———. "Reflections on Tradition: The 'Abot Revisited.'" In *Jewish and Pauline Studies*, by William D. Davies, 27–48. London: SPCK, 1984.

———. *The Territorial Dimension of Judaism*. Berkeley: University of California, 1982.

Dawson, David. *Allegorical Readers and Cultural Revision in Ancient Alexandria*. Berkeley: University of California Press, 1992.

Deines, Roland, and Karl-Wilhelm Niebuhr, eds. *Philo und das Neue Testament: Wechselseitige Wahrnehmungen. Internationales Symposium zum Corpus Judaeo-Hellenisticum 1.-4. Mai 2003, Eisenach/Jena*. WUNT 172. Tübingen: Mohr Siebeck, 2004.

Delling, Gerhard. "τελος κτλ." *TDNT* 8:49–57.

Denvers, William G. *What Did the Biblical Writers Know & When Did They Know It? What Archaeology Can Tell Us about the Reality of Ancient Israel*. Grand Rapids: Eerdmans, 2001.

Diepold, Peter. *Israels Land*. BWANT 5.15. Stuttgart: Kohlhammer, 1972.

Dillon, John. *The Middle Platonists 80 BC to AD 220*. Rev. ed. London: Duckworth, 1996.

Doran, Robert. "Cleodemus Malchus (Prior to the First Century)." In vol. 2 of *The Old Testament Pseudepigrapha*, edited by James H. Charlesworth, 883–87. New York: Doubleday, 1985.

———. "Eupolemus." In *The Eerdmans Dictionary of Early Judaism*, edited by John J. Collins and Daniel C. Harlow, 611–12. Grand Rapids: Eerdmans, 2010.

———. "Pseudo-Eupolemus." In *The Eerdmans Dictionary of Early Judaism*, edited by John J. Collins and Daniel C. Harlow, 612–13. Grand Rapids: Eerdmans, 2010.

———. "Pseudo-Eupolemus." In vol. 2 of *The Old Testament Pseudepigrapha*, edited by James H. Charlesworth, 873–82. New York: Doubleday, 1985.

———. "Pseudo-Heccateus (Second Century BC–First Century AD)." In vol. 2 of *The Old Testament Pseudepigrapha*, edited by James H. Charlesworth, 905–918. New York: Doubleday, 1985.

Ego, Beate. "Abraham als Urbild der Toratreue Israels. Traditionsgeschichtliche Überlegungen zu einem Aspekt des biblischen Abrahamsbildes." In *Bund und Tora, zur theologischen Begriffsgeschichte in alttestamentlicher, frühjüdischer und urchristlicher Tradition*, edited by Friedrich Avemarie and Hermann Lichtenberger, 25–40. WUNT 92. Tübingen: Mohr, 1996.

Eichrodt, Walter. *Ezekiel*. OTL. London: SCM, 1970.

———. *Theology of the Old Testament*. Vol. 1. OTL. London: SCM, 1961.

Elliott, Mark W. *The Survivors of Israel: A Reconsideration of the Theology of Pre-Christian Judaism*. Grand Rapids: Eerdmans, 2000.

Endres, John C. *Biblical Interpretation in the Book of Jubilees*. CBQMS 18. Washington, DC: Catholic Biblical Association of America, 1989.

Eshel, Esther. "Genesis Apocryphon." In *The Eerdmans Dictionary of Early Judaism*, edited by John J. Collins and Daniel C. Harlow, 664–67. Grand Rapids: Eerdmans, 2010.

Evans, Craig A. "Abraham in the Dead Sea Scrolls: A Man of Faith and Failure." In *The Bible at Qumran: Text, Shape, and Interpretation*, edited by Peter W. Flint, 149–58. Grand Rapids: Eerdmans, 2001.

———, ed. *The Interpretation of Scripture in Early Judaism and Christianity: Studies in Language and Tradition*. JSPPS 33. 2000. Reprint, London: T. & T. Clark, 2004.

Fallon, F. "Eupolemus (Prior to First Century BC)." In vol. 2 of *The Old Testament Pseudepigrapha*, edited by James H. Charlesworth, 861–72. New York: Doubleday, 1985.

Feldman, Louis H. "Hellenizations in Josephus's Jewish Antiquities: The Portrait of Abraham." In *Josephus, Judaism, and Christianity*, edited by Louis H. Feldman and Gohei Hataeds, 133–53. Detroit: Wayne State University Press, 1987.

———, and Gohei Hataeds (eds.). *Josephus, Judaism, and Christianity*. Detroit: Wayne State University Press, 1987.

———. "Josephus's Biblical Paraphrase as a Commentary on Contemporary Issues." In *The Interpretation of Scripture in Early Judaism and Christianity: Studies in Language and Tradition*, edited by Craig A. Evans, 124–201. JSPPS 33. 2000. Reprint, London: T. & T. Clark, 2004.

———. *Josephus's Interpretation of the Bible*. HCS 27. Berkeley: University of California Press, 1998.

———. *Studies in Josephus's Rewritten Bible*. SJSJ 58. Atlanta: SBL, 1998.

Fish, Bruce N. *Do You Not Remember? Scripture, Story, and Exegesis in the Rewritten Bible of Pseudo-Philo*. JSPSS 37. Sheffield: SAP, 2001.

———. "One Good Story Deserves Another: The Hermeneutics of Invoking Secondary Biblical Episodes in the Narratives of Pseudo-Philo and the Testaments of the Twelve Patriarchs." In *The Interpretation of Scripture in Early Judaism and Christianity: Studies in Language and Tradition*, edited by Craig A. Evans, 217–38. JSPSS 33. 2000. Reprint, London: T. & T. Clark, 2004.

Flury-Schölch, André. *Abrahams Segen und die Völker: Synchrone und diachrone Untersuchungen zu Gen 12:1-3 unter besonderer Berüchsichtigung der intertextuellen Beziehungen zu Gen 18:22; 26:28; Sir 44; Jer 4; und Ps 72*. FzB 115. Wurzburg: Echter, 2007.

Fox, Michael V. "Greek Version of Esther." In *The Eerdmans Dictionary of Early Judaism*, edited by John J. Collins and Daniel C. Harlow, 604–5. Grand Rapids: Eerdmans, 2010.

Franxman, Thomas W. *Genesis and the "Jewish Antiquities" of Flavius Josephus*. BO 35. Rome: Pontifical Biblical Institute, 1979.

Fretheim, Terrence E. *Abraham: Trials of Family and Faith*. Columbia, SC: University of South Carolina Press, 2007.

Früchtel, Ursula. *Die kosmologischen Vorstellungen bei Philo von Alexandrien: Ein Beitrag zur Geschichte der Genesisexegese*. ALGHJ 2. Leiden: Brill, 1968.

Füglister, Notker. "Psalm 105 und die Väterverheitzung." In *Die Väter Israels: Beiträge zur Theologie der Patriarchenüberlieferungen im Alten Testament*, edited by Manfred Görg, 41–59. Stuttgart: KBW, 1989.

Garnet, Paul. "Qumran Light on Pauline Soteriology." In *Pauline Studies: Essays Presented to F. F. Bruce*, edited by Donald A. Hagner and Murray J. Harris, 19–31. Exeter: Paternoster, 1980.

———. *Salvation and Atonement in the Qumran Scrolls*. WUNT 2.3. Tübingen: Mohr, 1977.

Gerstenberger, Eerhard S. *Psalms*. 2 vols. FOTL 14–15. Grand Rapids: Eerdmans, 1988, 2001.

Gilbert, Maurice. *La critique des dieux dans le Livre dela Sagesse (Sg. 13–15)*. AB53. Rome: Pontifical Biblical Institute, 1973.

Goldstein, Jonathan A. *First Maccabees*. AB 41. New York: Doubleday, 1976.

Görg, Manfred, ed. *Die Väter Israels: Beiträge zur Theologie der Patriarchenüberlieferungen im Alten Testament*. Stuttgart: KBW, 1989.

Grabbe, Lester L. *Etymology in Early Jewish Interpretation: The Hebrew Names in Philo*. BJS 115. Atlanta: Scholars, 1988.

Gray, John. *I & II Kings*. OTL. London: SCM, 1964.

Gross, Heinrich. "Zu theologischen Bedeutung von hālak (gehen) in den Abraham-Geschichten (Gen 12–25)." In *Die Väter Israels: Beiträge zur Theologie der Patriarchenüberlieferungen im Alten Testament*, edited by Manfred Görg, 73–82. Stuttgart: KBW, 1989.

Gross, Walter. "Erneuerter oder Neuen Bund? Wortlaut und Aussageintention in Jer 31:31–34." In *Bund und Tora*, edited by Friedrich Avemarie und Hermann Lichtenberger, 41–66. WUNT 92. Tübingen: Mohr, 1996.

Gruen, Erich S. "Jewish Perspectives on Greek Culture." In *Hellenism in the Land of Israel*, edited by John J. Collins and Gregory E. Sterling, 62–93. CJAS 13. Notre Dame, IN: University of Notre Dame Press, 2001.

Gurtner, Daniel M. "On the Other Side of Disaster: Soteriology in 2 Baruch." In *This World and the World to Come: Soteriology in Early Judaism*, edited by Daniel M. Gurtner, 114–26. LSTS 74. London: T. & T. Clark, 2011.

———, ed. *This World and the World to Come: Soteriology in Early Judaism*. LSTS 74. London: T. & T. Clark, 2011.

Haag, E. "Die Abrahamtradition in Gen 15." In *Die Väter Israels: Beiträge zur Theologie der Patriarchenüberlieferungen im Alten Testament. Festschrift für Josef Scharbert zum 70. Geburtstag*, edited by Manfred Görg, 83–106. Stuttgart: KBW, 1989.

Hall, Robert G. "The 'Christian Interpolation' in the Apocalypse of Abraham." *JBL* 107 (1988) 107–11.

Halpern-Amaru, Betsy. "The Book of Judith." In *The Eerdmans Dictionary of Early Judaism*, edited by John J. Collins and Daniel C. Harlow, 855–57. Grand Rapids: Eerdmans, 2010.

———. *Rewriting the Bible: Land and Covenant in Postbiblical Jewish Literature*. Valley Forge, PA: Trinity, 1994.

Hansen, G. Walter. *Abraham in Galatians: Epistolary and Rhetorical Contexts*. JSNTSS 29. Sheffield: SAP, 1989.

Hanson, J. "Demetrius the Chronographer (Third Century BC)." In vol. 1 of *The Old Testament Pseudepigrapha*, edited by James H. Charlesworth, 843–54. New York: Doubleday, 1985.

Hanson, Paul D. *The Dawn of Apocalyptic: The Historical and Sociological Roots of Jewish Apocalyptic Eschatology*. Philadelphia: Fortress, 1975.

Harlow, Daniel C. "Apocalypse of Abraham." In *The Eerdmans Dictionary of Early Judaism*, edited by John J. Collins and Daniel C. Harlow, 295–98. Grand Rapids: Eerdmans, 2010.

Harrington, Daniel J. "Pseudo-Philo." In vol. 2 of *The Old Testament Pseudepigrapha*, edited by James H. Charlesworth, 297–377. New York: Doubleday, 1985.

———. "'Saved by Wisdom' (Wis 9:18): Soteriology in the Wisdom of Solomon." In *This World and The World to Come: Soteriology in Early Judaism*, edited by Daniel M. Gurtner, 181–90. London: T. & T. Clark, 2011.

Haspecker, Josef. *Gottesfurcht bei Jesus Sirach: Ihre religiöse Struktur und ihre literarische und doktrinäre Bedeutung*. AB 30. Rome: Papal Biblical Institute, 1967.

Hatch, Edwin, and Henry A. Redpath. *A Concordance to the Septuagint*. 2 vols. 1897. Reprint, Graz: Akademische Druck-u.-Verlagsanstalt, 1954.

Hay, David M., ed. *Both Literal and Allegorical: Studies in Philo of Alexandria's Questions and Answers on Genesis and Exodus*. BJS 232. Atlanta: Scholars, 1991

———. "Philo of Alexandria." In *The Complexities of Second Temple Judaism*, edited by Donald A. Carson, et al., 357–79. Vol. 1 of *Justification and Variegated Nomism*. Tübingen: Mohr Siebeck, 2001.

———. "Philo's References to Other Allegorists." *SPh* 6 (1980) 41–75.

———. "References to Other Exegetes." In *Both Literal and Allegorical: Studies in Philo of Alexandria's Questions and Answers on Genesis and Exodus*, edited by David M. Hay, 81–97. BJS 232. Atlanta: Scholars, 1991.

Hayes, Christine E. *Gentiles Impurities and Jewish Identities: Intermarriage and Conversion from the Bible to the Talmud*. Oxford: Oxford University Press, 2002.

Hayes, John H., and Stuart A. Irvine. *Isaiah, the Eighth-Century Prophet: His Times and His Preaching*. Nashville: Abingdon, 1987.

Heard, R. Christopher. *Dynamics of Diselection: Ambiguity in Genesis 12–36 and Ethnic Boundaries in Post-Exilic Judaism*. SBLSS 39. Atlanta: SBL, 2001.

Heilgenthal, Roman H. *Werke als Zeichen: Untersuchungen zur Bedeutung der menschlichen Taten im Frühjudentum, Neuen Testament und Frühchristentum*. WUNT 2.9. Tübingen: Mohr, 1983.

Hempel, Charlotte. "The Damascus Document." In *The Eerdmans Dictionary of Early Judaism*, edited by John J. Collins and Daniel C. Harlow, 510–12. Grand Rapids: Eerdmans, 2010.

Hengel, Martin. *Judaism and Hellenism: Studies in their Encounter in Palestine during the Early Hellenistic Period*. 2 vols. London: SCM, 1974.

Henton Davies, Gwynne. *Exodus*. TBC. London: SCM, 1967.

———. "Genesis." In vol. 1 of *The Broadman Bible Commentary*, edited by Clifton J. Allen, 101–304. Nashville, TN: Broadman, 1969.

Henze, Matthias. "Second Book of Baruch." In *The Eerdmans Dictionary of Early Judaism*, edited by John J. Collins and Daniel C. Harlowads, 426–28. Grand Rapids: Eerdmans, 2010.

Herford, R. T. "Pirke Aboth (Sayings of the Fathers)." In *Pseudepigrapha*, edited by Robert H. Charles, 686–714. Vol. 2 of *The Apocrypha and Pseudepigrapha of the Old Testament in English*. Oxford: Clarendon, 1913.

Hertzberg, Hans W. *I & II Samuel*. 2nd rev. ed. OTL. London: SCM, 1960.

Hess, Richard S., et al., eds. *He Swore an Oath: Biblical Themes from Genesis 12–50*. 2nd ed. Carlisle: Paternoster, 1994.

Himmelfarb, Martha. *A Kingdom of Priests: Ancestry and Merit in Ancient Judaism*. JCC. Philadelphia: University of Pennsylvia Press, 2006.

Hogan, Karina M. "Fourth Book of Ezra." In *The Eerdmans Dictionary of Early Judaism*, edited by John J. Collins and Daniel C. Harlow, 623–25. Grand Rapids: Eerdmans, 2010.

Holladay, Carl H. *Theios Aner in Hellenistic Judaism: A Critique of the Use of This Category in New Testament Christology*. SBLDS 40. Missouola, MT: Scholars, 1977.

Hollander, Harm W. *Joseph as an Ethical Model in the Testaments of the Twelve Patriarchs*. SVTP 6. Leiden: Brill, 1981.

Hossfeld, Frank-Lothar, and Erich Zenger. *Die Psalmen 1: Psalm 1–50*. NEB. Wurzburg: Echter, 1993.
———. *Psalms 2: A Commentary on Psalms 51–100*. Hermeneia. Minneapolis: Fortress, 2005.
Hübner, Hans. *Die Weisheit Salomons*. ATD Apokryphen Band 4. Göttingen: Vandenhoeck & Ruprecht, 1999.
Jacobs, Naomi S. "The Book of Tobit." In *The Eerdmans Dictionary of Early Judaism*, edited by John J. Collins and Daniel C. Harlow, 1214–15. Grand Rapids: Eerdmans, 2010.
Japhet, Sara. *The Ideology of the Book of Chronicles and its Place in Biblical Thought*. 2nd rev. ed. BEATAJ 9. Frankfurt am Main: Lang, 1997.
Jenks, Alan W. *The Elohist and North Israelite Traditions*. SBLMS 22. Missoula, MT: Scholars, 1977.
Jeremias, Jorg, and Lothar Perlitt, eds. *Die Botschaft und die Boten: Festschrift für Hans Walter Wolff zum 70. Geburtstag*. Neukirchen-Vluyn: Neukirchener, 1981.
Johnson, Aubrey R. *The Cultic Prophet in Ancient Israel*. Cardiff: University of Wales Press, 1962.
———. *Sacral Kingship in Ancient Israel*. 2nd ed. Cardiff: University of Wales Press, 1967.
———. *The Vitality of the Individual in the Thought of Ancient Israel*. 2nd ed. Cardiff: University of Wales Press, 1964.
Johnson, Sara R. "The Third Book of Maccabees." In *The Eerdmans Dictionary of Early Judaism*, edited by John J. Collins and Daniel C. Harlow, 907–9. Grand Rapids: Eerdmans, 2010.
Johnstone, William. *1 & 2 Chronicles*. 2 vols. JSOTSS 253–54. Sheffield: Sheffield Aacademic, 1997.
Kaiser, Otto. *Isaiah 13–39*. London: SCM, 1974.
Kamesar, Aryeh, ed. *The Cambridge Companion to Philo*. Cambridge: Cambridge University Press, 2009.
Kaminsky, J. S. *Yet I loved Jacob: Reclaiming the Biblical Concept of Election*. 2007. Reprint, Eugene, OR: Wipf & Stock, 2016.
Kampen, John, and Moshe J. Bernstein, eds. *Reading 4 QMMT: New Perspectives on Qumran Law and History*. SBLSS 2. Atlanta: Scholars, 1996.
Kasher, A. *Jews, Idumaeans, and Ancient Arabs*. TSAJ 18. Tübingen: Mohr, 1988.
Kee, Howard C. "The Testaments of the Twelve Patriarchs (Second Century BC)." In vol. 1 of *The Old Testament Pseudepigrapha*, edited by James H. Charlesworth, 775–828. London: Darton Longman & Todd, 1983.
Kilian, Rudolf. "Nachtrag und Neuorienteriung: Anmerkungen zum Jahwisten in den Abrahamserzählung." In *Die Väter Israels: Beiträge zur Theologie der Patriarchenüberlieferungen im Alten Testament*, edited by Manfred Görg, 155–67. Stuttgart: KBW, 1989.
Kittel, Gerhard, and Gerhard Friedrich, eds. *Theological Dictionary of the New Testament*. Translated by Geoffrey W. Bromiley. 10 vols. Grand Rapids: Eerdmans, 1964–1976.
Klawans, Jonathan. *Impurity and Sin in Ancient Judaism*. Oxford: Oxford University Press, 2000.
———. *Josephus and the Theologies of Ancient Judaism*. Oxford: Oxford University Press, 2012.

———. *Purity, Sacrifice, and the Temple Symbolism and Supersessionism in the Study of Ancient Judaism*. Oxford: Oxford University Press, 2006.

Klijn, A. F. J. "2 (Syriac Apocalypse of) Baruch." In vol. 1 of *The Old Testament Pseudepigrapha*, edited by James H. Charlesworth, 615–79. New York: Doubleday, 1985.

Knibb, Michael A. "Exile in the Damascus Document." *JSOT* 25 (1983) 99–117.

———. "Similitudes of Enoch (1 Enoch 37–71)." In *The Eerdmans Dictionary of Early Judaism*, edited by John J. Collins and Daniel C. Harlow, 585–87. Grand Rapids: Eerdmans, 2010.

Knoppers, Gary N., and J. Gordon McColnville, eds. *Reconsidering Israel and Judah: Recent Studies on the Deuteronomistic History*. SBTS 8. Winona Lake, IN: Eisenbrauns, 2000.

Koch, Klaus. "Der König als Sohn Gottes in Ägypten und Israel." In *"Mein Sohn bist du" (Ps 2:7): Studien zu den Königspsalmen*, edited by Eckart Otto und Erich Zengler, 1–32. SBS 192. Stuttgart: KBW, 2002.

Konradt, Matthias. "Die aus Glauben, diese sind Kinder Abrahams' (Gal 3:7): Erwägungen zum galatischen Konflikt im Licht frühjüdischer Abrahamtraditionen." In *Text, Ethik, Judentum und Christentum, Gesellschaft: Ekkehard W. Stegemann zum 60. Geburtstag*, edited by Gabrielle Gelardini, 25–48. Vol. 1 of *Kontext der Schrift*. Stuttgart: Kohlhammer, 2005.

Kreuzer, Siegfried. "'Der den Gottlosen rechtfertigt' (Röm 4:5): Die frühjüdische Einordnung Gen 15 als Hintergrund für das Abrahambild und die Rechtfertigungslehre des Paulus." *TB* 33 (2002) 208–219.

Kugler, Robert A. *The Testaments of the Twelve Patriarchs*. GAP. Sheffield: SAP, 2001.

———. "The Testaments of the Twelve Patriarchs." In *The Eerdmans Dictionary of Early Judaism*, edited by John J. Collins and Daniel C. Harlow, 1296. Grand Rapids: Eerdmans, 2010.

Kuhn, Karl G. "προσηλυτος." *TDNT* 6:727–44.

Kurzewitz, Christian. *Weisheit und Tod: Die Ätiologie des Todes in der Sapientia Solomonis*. TANZ 50. Tübingen: Franke, 2010.

Leslie, Elmer A. *Jeremiah: Chronologically Arranged, Translated, and Interpreted*. New York: Abingdon, 1954.

———. *The Psalms: Translated and Interpreted in the Light of Hebrew Life and Worship*. New York: Abingdon, 1959.

Levenson, Jon D. *The Death and Resurrection of the Beloved Son: The Transformation of Child Sacrifice in Judaism and Christianity*. New Haven: Yale University Press, 1993.

Levison, John R. *Portraits of Adam in Early Judaism: From Sirach to 2 Baruch*. JSPSS 1. Sheffield: JSOT, 1988.

Liddell, H. G., and R. Scott. *A Greek-English Lexicon*. Rev. by H. S. Jones. Oxford: Clarendon, 1968.

Limbeck, Meinrad. *Die Ordnung des Heils: Untersuchungen zum Gesetzesverständnis des Frühjudentums*. KBANT. Düsseldorf: Patmos, 1971.

Linebaugh, Jonathan A. *God, Grace, and Righteousness in Wisdom of Solomon and Paul's Letter to the Romans: Texts in Conversation*. SNT 152. Leiden: Brill, 2013.

Lohfink, Norbert, ed. *Das Deuteronomium: Entstehung, Gestalt und Botschaft*. BETL 68. Leuven: Leuven University Press, 1985.

———. *Die Väter Israels im Deuteronomium: Mit einer Stellungnahme von Thomas Römer*. OBO 111. Freiburg: Universitätsverlag Freiburg, 1991.

———. "Dtn 12:1 und Gen 15:18: Das dem Samen Abrahams geschenkte Land als der Geltungsbereich der deuteronomischen Gesetze." In *Die Väter Israels: Beiträge zur Theologie der Patriarchenüberlieferungen im Alten Testament*, edited by Manfred Görg, 183–210. Stuttgart: KBW, 1989.

———. *Höre, Israel! Auslegung von Texten aus dem Buch Deuteronium*. WB. Düsseldorf: Patmos, 1965.

———. "Kerygmata des Deuteronomischen Geschichtswerks." In *Die Botschaft und die Boten: Festschrift für Hans Walter Wolff zum 70. Geburtstag*, edited by Jörg Jeremias und Lothar Perlitt, 87–100. Neukirchen-Vluyn: Neukirchener, 1981.

———. "The Small Credo of Deuteronomy 26:5–9." In *Theology of the Pentateuch: Themes of the Priestly Narrative and Deuteronomy*, by Norbert Lohfink, 265–89. Minneapolis: Fortress, 1994.

———. *Theology of the Pentateuch: Themes of the Priestly Narrative and Deuteronomy*. Minneapolis: Fortress, 1994.

Longenecker, Bruce W. *Eschatology and the Covenant: A Comparison of 4 Ezra and Romans 1–11*. JSNTSS 57. Sheffield: JSOT, 1991.

Lorenzen, Stefanie. *Das paulinische Eikon-Konzept. Semantische Analysen zur Sapientia Solomonis, zu Philo und den Paulusbriefen*. WUNT 2.250. Tübingen: Mohr Siebeck, 2008.

Machiela, Daniel A. *The Dead Sea Genesis Apocryphon: A New Text and Translation with Introduction and Special Treatment of Columns 13–17*. STDJ 79. Leiden: Brill, 2009.

Mack, Burton L. *Logos und Sophia: Untersuchungen zur Weisheitstheologie im hellenistischen Judentum*. SUNT 10. Göttingen: Vandenhoeck & Ruprecht, 1973.

———. *Wisdom and the Hebrew Epic: Ben Sira's Hymn in Praise of the Fathers*. CSHJ. Chicago: University of Chicago Press, 1985.

Maier, Gerhard. *Mensch und freier Wille: Nach den jüdischen Religionsparteien zwischen Ben Sira und Paulus*. WUNT 12. Tübingen: Mohr, 1971.

Marböck, Johann. *Weisheit im Wandel: Untersuchungen zur Weisheitstheologie bei Ben Sira*. BBB 37. Bonn: Peter Hanstein, 1971.

Martin-Achard, Robert. *A Light to the Nations*. Edinburgh: Oliver and Boyd, 1962.

Martinez, Florentino G. "4QMMT in a Qumran Context." In *Reading 4QMMT: New Perspectives on Qumran Law and History*, edited by John Kampen and Moshe J. Bernstein, 15–27. SBLSS 2. Atlanta: Scholars, 1996.

Mason, Rex A. *The Books of Haggai, Zechariah, and Malachi*. CBC. Cambridge: Cambridge University Press, 1977.

———. *Micah Nahum Obadiah*. OTG. Sheffield: JSOT, 1991.

Mason, Steve. "Josephus." In *The Eerdmans Dictionary of Early Judaism*, edited by John J. Collins and Daniel C. Harlow, 828–32. Grand Rapids: Eerdmans, 2010.

———. *Josephus and the New Testament*. 2nd ed. Grand Rapids: Baker Academic, 2013.

———. *Josephus, Judea, and Christian Origins: Methods and Categories*. Peabody, MA: Hendrickson, 2009.

———, ed. *Understanding Josephus: Seven Perspectives*. JSPSS 32. Sheffield: SAP, 1998.

Maston, Jason. *Divine and Human Agency in Second Temple Judaism and Paul: A Comparative Study*. WUNT 2.297. Tübingen: Mohr Siebeck, 2010.

Mays, James L. *Micah*. OTL. London: SCM, 1976.

McConville, J. Gordon. *Deuteronomy*. AOTC 5. Downers Grove, IL: IVP Academic, 2002.

———. *Grace in the End: A Study in Deuteronomic Theology*. SOTBT. Carlisle: Paternoster, 1993.

McConville, J. Gordon, and J. Gary Millar. *Time and Place in Deuteronomy*. JSOTSS 179. Sheffield: SAP, 1994.

McGlynn, Moyna. *Divine Judgment and Divine Benevolence in the Book of Wisdom*. WUNT 2.139. Tübingen: Mohr Siebeck, 2001.

McLaren, James S. *Turbulent Times? Josephus and Scholarship on Judaea in the First Century CE*. JSPSS 29. Sheffield: SAP, 1998.

Metzger, Bruce M. "The Fourth Book of Ezra." In vol. 1 of *The Old Testament Pseudepigrapha*, edited by James H. Charlesworth, 517–59. London: Darton, Longman & Todd, 1983.

Meyer, Gunter. "Aspekte des Abrahamsbildes in der hellenistisch-jüdischen Literatur." *Ev. Th.* 32 (1972) 118–27.

Middendorp, Th. *Die Stellung Jesu ben Siras zwischen Judentum und Hellenismus*. Leiden: Brill, 1973.

Mihaly, E. "A Rabbinic Defense of the Election of Israel: An Analysis of Sifre Deuteronomy 32:9, Pisqa 312." *HUCA* 36 (1969) 103–63.

Millar, J. Gary. *Now Choose Life: Theology and Ethics in Deuteronomy*. NSBT 6. Leicester: Apollos, 1998.

Millar, J. Gary, and J. Gordon McConville. *Time and Place in Deuteronomy*. JSOTSS 179. Sheffield: SAP, 1994.

Montes-Peral, Luis A. *AKATALEPTOS THEOS: Der unfassbare Gott*. ALGHJ 16. Leiden: Brill, 1987.

Moo, Jonathan A. *Creation, Nature, and Hope in 4 Ezra*. FRLANT 237. Göttingen: Vandenhoeck & Ruprecht, 2011.

———. "The Few Who Obtain Mercy: Soteriology in 4 Ezra." In *This World and the World to Come: Soteriology in Early Judaism*, edited by Daniel M. Gurtner, 98–113. LSTS 74. London: T. & T. Clark, 2011.

Moore, Carey A. *Judith*. AB 40. New York: Doubleday, 1985.

———. *Tobit*. AB 40A. New York: Doubleday, 1996.

Mowinckel, Sigismund. *The Psalms in Israel's Worship*. Vol. 1. Oxford: Blackwell, 1962.

Mühling, Anke. *"Blickt auf Abraham, euren Vater": Abraham als Identifikationsfigur des Judentums in der Zeit des Exils und des Zweiten Tempels*. FRLANT 236. Göttingen: Vandenhoeck & Ruprecht, 2011.

Müller, Paul G. *ΧΡΙΣΤΟΣ ΑΡΧΗΓΟΣ: Der religionsgeschichtliche und theologische Hintergrund einer neutestamentlichen Christusprädikation*. EH 23.28. Bern: Herbert Lang, 1973.

Murphy, Frederick J. "Biblical Antiquities (Pseudo-Philo)." In *The Eerdmans Dictionary of Early Judaism*, edited by John J. Collins and Daniel C. Harlow, 440–42. Grand Rapids: Eerdmans, 2010.

———. *Pseudo-Philo: Rewriting the Bible*. New York: Oxford University Press, 1993.

———. *The Structure and Meaning of Second Baruch*. SBLDS 78. Atlanta: Scholars, 1985.

Myers, Jacob M. *I & II Esdras*. AB 42. New York: Doubleday, 1974.

Najman, Hindy. *Losing the Temple and Recovering the Future: An Analysis of 4 Ezra* Cambridge: Cambridge University Press, 2014.

———. *Seconding Sinai: The Development of Mosaic Discourse in Second Temple Judaism*. SJSJ 77. 2003. Reprint, Atlanta: SBL, 2009.
Neef, Heinz-Dieter. "Aspekt alttestamentlicher Bundestheologie." In *Bund und Tora*, edited by Friedrich Avemarie and Hermann Lichtenberger, 1–23. WUNT 92. Tübingen: Mohr, 1996.
Nelson, Richard D. *Joshua*. OTL. Louisville: Westminster John Knox, 1997.
Nicholson, Ernest W. *Deuteronomy and Tradition*. Oxford: Blackwell, 1967.
———. *Preaching to the Exiles: A Study of the Prose Tradition in the Book of Jeremiah*. Oxford: Blackwell, 1970.
Nickelsburg, George W. E. *1 Enoch 1: A Commentary on the Book of Enoch, Chapters 1–36, 81–108*. Hermeneia. Minneapolis: Fortress, 2001.
———. "Abraham the Convert: A Jewish Tradition and Its Use by the Apostle Paul." In *Biblical Figures Outside the Bible*, edited by Michael E. Stone and Theodore A. Bergren, 151–75. Harrisburg, PA: Trinity, 1998.
———. *Jewish Literature Between the Bible and the Mishnah: A Historical and Literary Introduction*. London: SCM, 1981.
———. *Resurrection, Immortality, and Eternal Life in Intertestamental Judaism and Early Christianity*. HTS 56. Expanded ed. Harvard: Harvard University Press, 2006.
Nickelsburg, George W. E., and James C. VanderKam. *1 Enoch 2: A Commentary on the Book of Enoch, Chapters 37–82*. Hermeneia. Minneapolis: Fortress, 2012.
Niehoff, Maren. *Jewish Exegesis and Homeric Scholarship in Alexandria*. Cambridge: Cambridge University Press, 2011.
———. *Philo on Jewish Identity and Culture*. TSAJ 86. Tübingen: Mohr Siebeck, 2001.
———. "Philo's Views on Paganism." In *Tolerance and Intolerance in Early Judaism and Christianity*, edited by Graham N. Stanton and Guy G. Stroumsa, 135–58. Cambridge: Cambridge University Press, 1998.
Nissen, Andreas. *Gott und der Nächste im antiken Judentum: Untersuchungen zum Doppelgebot der Liebe*. WUNT 15. Tübingen: Mohr, 1974.
Noth, Martin. *Exodus*. OTL. London: SCM, 1962.
Novenson, Matthew V. *Christ among the Messiahs: Christ Language in Paul and Messiah Language in Ancient Judaism*. Oxford: Oxford University Press, 2012.
Oeming, Manfred. "Is Genesis 15:6b ein Beleg für die Anrechnung des Glaubens zur Gerechtigkeit?" *ZAW* 95 (1983) 182–97.
———. "Der Glaube Abrahams: Zur Rezeptionsgeschichte von Gen 15:6 in der Zeit des zweiten Tempels." *ZAW* 110 (1998) 16–33.
Otto, Eckart, and Erich Zengler, eds. *"Mein Sohn bist du" (Ps 2:7): Studien zu den Königspsalmen*. SBS 192. Stuttgart: KBW, 2002.
Pascher, Joseph. *Η ΒΑΣΙΛΙΚΗ ΟΔΟΣ: Der Königsweg zu Wiedergeburt und Vergottung bei Philon von Alexandreia*. SGKA 17.3–4. 1931. Reprint, New York: Johnson Reprint, 1968.
Patrick, Dale. *Old Testament Law*. London: SCM, 1986.
Pearce, Sara J. K. *The Land of the Body*. WUNT 208. Tübingen: Mohr Siebeck, 2007.
Petersen, David L. *Zechariah 9–14 & Malachi*. OTL. London: SCM, 1995.
Poirier, John C. "On a Wing and a Prayer: The Soteriology of the Apocalypse of Abraham." In *This World and the World to Come: Soteriology in Early Judaism*, edited by Daniel Gurtner, 87–97. LSTS 74. London: T. & T. Clark, 2011.

Rahlfs, Alfred, and Robert Hanhart, eds. *Septuaginta*. Stuttgart: Deutsche Bibelgesellschaft, 2006.

Rajak, Tessa. *Josephus: The Historian and His Society*. 2nd ed. London: Duckworth, 2002.

Rappaport, Uriel. "First Book of Maccabees." In *The Eerdmans Dictionary of Early Judaism*, edited by John J. Collins and Daniel C. Harlow, 903–5. Grand Rapids: Eerdmans, 2010.

Redditt, Paul L. *Haggai, Zechariah, Malachi*. NCB. London: Marshall Pickering, 1995.

Reinmuth, Eckart. *Pseudo-Philo und Lukas: Studien zur Liber Antiquitatum Biblicarum und seiner Bedeutung für die Interpretation des lukanischen Doppelwerks*. WUNT 74. Tübingen: Mohr, 1994.

Rendtorff, Rolf. "Die Erwählung Israels als Thema der deuteronomischenTheologie." In *Die Botschaft und die Boten: Festschrift für Hans Walter Wolff zum 70. Geburtstag*, edited by Jörg Jeremias and Lothar Perlitt, 75–86. Neukirchen-Vluyn: Neukirchener, 1981.

———. "Pentateuchal Studies on the Move." *JSOT* 3 (1977) 43–45.

———. "The 'Yahwist' as Theologian? The Dilemma of Pentateuchal Criticism." *JSOT* 3 (1977) 2–9.

Robertson, R. G. "Ezekiel the Tradegian (Second Century BC)." In vol. 1 of *The Old Testament Pseudepigrapha*, edited by James H. Charlesworth, 803–19. New York: Doubleday, 1985.

Römer, Thomas. "Deuteronomy in Search of Origins." In *Reconsidering Israel and Judah: Recent Studies on the Deuteronomistic History*, edited by Gary N. Knoppers and J. Gordon McColnville, 112–38. SBTS 8. Winona Lake, IN: Eisenbrauns, 2000.

———. *Israels Väter: Untersuchungen zur Väterthematik im Deuteronium und in der deuteronomischen Tradition*. OBO 99. Freiburg: Freiburg Universitätverlag, 1990.

Roo, Jacqueline C. R. de. *"Works of the Law" at Qumran and in Paul*. NTM 13. Sheffield: Sheffield Phoenix, 2007.

Rost, Leonard. *Judaism Outside the Hebrew Canon*. New York: Abingdon, 1976.

Rowland, Christopher C. *The Open Heaven: A Study of Apocalyptic in Judaism and Early Christianity*. London: SPCK, 1982.

Rowley, Harold H. *The Missionary Message of the Old Testament*. London: Carey, 1944.

———. *The Relevance of Apocalyptic: A Study of Jewish and Christian Apocalypses from Daniel to Revelation*. New and rev. ed. London: Lutterworth, 1963.

Royse, James R. "The Works of Philo." In *The Cambridge Companion to Philo*, edited by Adam Kamesar, 32–64. Cambridge: Cambridge University Press, 2009.

Rubinkiewicz, R. "Apocalypse of Abraham." In vol. 1 of *The Old Testament Pseudepigrapha*, edited by James H. Charlesworth, 681–705. New York: Doubleday, 1985.

Runia, David T. *Exegesis and Philosophy: Studies on Philo of Alexandria*. Hampshire, UK: Variorum, 1990.

———. "God and Man in Philo of Alexandria." *JTS* 39 (1988) 48–75.

———. *On the Creation of the Cosmos according to Moses: Introduction, Translation, and Commentary*. PACS 1. 2001. Reprint, Atlanta: SBL, 2005.

———. *Philo of Alexandria and the Timaeus of Plato*. PA 44. 2nd ed. Leiden: Brill, 1986.

———. "Secondary Texts in Philo's Quaestiones." In *Both Literal and Allegorical*, edited by David M. Hay, 47–79. BJS 232. Atlanta: Scholars, 1991.

Sanders, Edward P. *Paul and Palestinian Judaism: A Comparison of Patterns of Religion.* London: SCM, 1977.
———. "Testament of Abraham." In vol. 1 of *The Old Testament Pseudepigrapha*, edited by James H. Charlesworth, 871–902. New York: Doubleday, 1985.
Sandmel, Samuel. *Philo's Place in Judaism: A Study of Conceptions of Abraham in Jewish Literature.* Cincinnati: Hebrew Union College Press, 1956.
Sauer, Georg. *Jesus Sirach/Ben Sira.* ATD Apokryphen Band 1. Göttingen: Vandenhoeck & Ruprecht, 2000.
Sayler, Gwendolyn B. *Have the Promises Failed? A Literary Analysis of 2 Baruch.* SBLDS 72. Chico, CA: Scholars, 1984.
Schenck, Kenneth. *A Brief Guide to Philo.* Louisville: Westminster John Knox, 2005.
Schiffman, Lawrence. "The Place of 4QMMT in the Corpus of Qumran Manuscripts." In *Reading 4QMMT: New Perspectives on Qumran Law and History*, edited by John Kampen and Moshe J. Bernstein, 81–98. SBLSS 2. Atlanta: Scholars, 1996.
Schlier, Heinrich. "ανατελλω ανατολη." *TDNT* 1:351–53.
———. *Der Brief an die Galater.* KEKNT. 5th ed. Göttingen: Vandenhoeck & Ruprecht, 1971.
Schliesser, Benjamin. *Abraham's Faith in Romans 4: Paul's Concept of Faith in the Light of the History of Reception of Genesis 15:6.* WUNT 2.224. Tübingen: Mohr Siebeck, 2007.
Schmid, Hans H. *Der sogenannte Jahwist: Beobachtungen und Fragen zur Pentateuchforschung.* Zürich: TVZ, 1976.
———. "In Search of New Approaches in Pentateuchal Research." *JSOT* 3 (1977) 33–42.
Schnabel, Eckhart J. *Law and Wisdom from Ben Sira to Paul.* WUNT 2.16. 1985. Reprint, Eugene, OR: Wipf & Stock, 2011.
Schramm, Brooks. *The Opponents of Third Isaiah: Reconstructing the Cultic History of the Restoration.* JSOTSS 193. Sheffield: SAP, 1995.
Schreiner, Josef. "Segen für die Völker in der Verheissung an die Väter." *BZ* 6 (1962) 1–31.
Schrenk, Gottlob. "πατηρ κτλ." *TDNT* 5:945–1022.
Schwartz, Daniel R. "MMT, Josephus, and the Pharisees." In *Reading 4QMMT: New Perspectives on Qumran Law and History*, edited by John Kampen and Moshe J. Bernstein, 67–80. SBLSS 2. Atlanta: Scholars,
Schwarz, Eberhard. *Identität durch Abgrenzung: Abgrenzungsprozesse in Israel im 2. Vorchristlichen Jahrhundert und ihre traditonsgeschichtlichen Voraussetzungen. Zugleich ein Beitrag zur Erforschung des Jubiläenbuches.* EHS 23.162. Frankfurt am Main: Lang, 1982.
Segal, Michael. "The Book of Jubilees." In *The Eerdmans Dictionary of Early Judaism*, edited by John J. Collins and Daniel C. Harlow, 843–46. Grand Rapids: Eerdmans, 2010.
———. *The Book of Jubilees: Rewritten Bible, Redaction, Ideology, and Theology.* SJSJ 117. 2007. Reprint, Atlanta: SBL, 2012.
Seifrid, Mark A. "Righteousness Language in the Hebrew Scriptures and Early Judaism." In *The Complexities of Second Temple Judaism*, edited by Donald A. Carson, et al., 415–42. Vol. 1 of *Justification and Variegated Nomism*. Grand Rapids: Baker Academic, 2001.

Sellin, Gerhard. "Gotteserkenntnis und Gotteserfahrung bei Philo von Alexandrien." In *Monotheismus und Christologie: Zur Gottesfrage im hellenistischen Judentum und im Urchristentum*, edited by Hans-Josef Klauck, 17–40. Freiburg: Herder, 1992.

Skehan, Patrick W., and Alexander A. di Lella. *The Wisdom of Ben Sira*. AB 39. New York: Doubleday, 1987.

Spilsbury, Paul. "God and Israel in Josephus—A Patron-Client Relationship." In *Understanding Josephus: Seven Perspectives*, edited by Steve Mason, 172–91. JSPSS 32. Sheffield: SAP, 1998.

———. "Josephus." In *The Complexities of Second Temple Judaism*, edited by Donald A. Carson, et al., 241–60. Vol. 1 of *Justification and Variegated Nomism*. Grand Rapids: Baker Academic, 2001.

Sprinkle, Preston M. "The Hermeneutic of Grace: The Soteriology of Pseudo-Philo's Biblical Antiquities." In *This World and the World to Come: Soteriology in Early Judaism*, edited by Daniel Gurtner, 50–67. LSTS 74. London: T. & T. Clark, 2011.

———. *Law and Life: The Interpretation of Leviticus 18:5 in Early Judaism and in Paul*. WUNT 2.241. Tübingen: Mohr Siebeck, 2008

Stanton, Graham, and Guy G. Stroumsa, eds. *Tolerance and Intolerance in Early Judaism and Christianity*. Cambridge: Cambridge University Press, 1996.

Steck, Odil H., et al. *Das Buch Baruch: Der Brief des Jeremia. Zu Ester und Daniel*. ATD Apokryphen Band 5. Göttingen: Vandenhoech & Ruprecht, 1998.

Sterling, Gregory E. "Philo." In *The Eerdmans Dictionary of Early Judaism*, edited by John J. Collins and Daniel C. Harlow, 1063–70. Grand Rapids: Eerdmans, 2010.

———. "Philo's *Quaestiones*: Prolegomena or Afterthought?" In *Both Literal and Allegorical: Studies in Philo of Alexandria's Questions and Answers on Genesis and Exodus*, edited by David M. Hay, 99–123. BJS 232. Atlanta: Scholars, 1991.

Stokes, Ryan E. "The Book of the Watchers (1 Enoch 1–36)." In *The Eermans Dictionary of Early Judaism*, edited by John J. Collins and Daniel C. Harlow, 1332–34. Grand Rapids: Eerdmans, 2010.

Stone, Michael E. *Fourth Ezra*. Hermeneia. Minneapolis: Fortress, 1990.

Stuckenbruck, Loren T. "Epistle of Enoch (1 Enoch 91–108)." In *The Eerdmans Dictionary of Early Judaism*, edited by John J. Collins and Daniel C. Harlow, 583–85. Grand Rapids: Eerdmans, 2010.

Syren, Roger. *Forsaken Firstborn: A Study of a Recurrent Motif in the Patriarchal Narratives*. JSOTSS 133. LHB/OT Studies 133. Sheffield: JSOT, 1993.

Terian, Abraham. "The Priority of the Quaestiones among Philo's Exegetical Commentaries." In *Both Literal and Allegorical: Studies in Philo of Alexandria's Questions and Answers on Genesis and Exodus*, edited by David M. Hay, 29–46. BJS 232. Atlanta: Scholars, 1991.

Ternibi, Cristina. "Philo's Thought within the Context of Middle Judaism." In *The Cambridge Companion to Philo*, edited by Adam Kamesar, 95–123. Cambridge: Cambridge University Press, 2009.

Thackeray, H. St. J. *Josephus: Jewish Antiquities Books 1–111*. LCL. 1930. Reprint, Cambridge, MA: Harvard University Press, 1998.

Thiessen, Matthew. *Contesting Conversion: Genealogy, Circumcision & Identity in Ancient Judaism and Christianity*. Oxford: Oxford University Press, 2011.

Thompson, Thomas L. *The Historicity of the Patriarchal Narratives*. BZAW 133. Berlin: de Gruyter, 1974.

Thomson, Peter J. "Transformation of Post-70 Judaism: Scholarly Reconstructions and Their Implications for Our Perception of Matthew, Didache, and James." In *Matthew, James, and Didache: Three Related Documents in Their Jewish and Christian Settings*, edited by Huub van de Sandt and Jürgen K. Zangenberg, 91–121. Symposium 45. Atlanta: SBL, 2008.

Tobin, Thomas H. *The Creation of Man: Philo and the History of Interpretation*. CBQMS 14. Washington DC: Catholic Biblical Association of America, 1983.

———. *Paul's Rhetoric in Context: The Argument of Romans*. Peabody, MA: Hendrickson, 2004.

Townsend, R. B. "The Fourth Book of Maccabees." In *Pseudepigrapha*, edited by Robert H. Charles, 653–85. Vol. 2 of *The Apocrypha and Pseudepigrapha of the Old Testament in English*. Oxford: Clarendon, 1913.

Van der Horst, Pieter W. "Ezekiel the Tragedian." In *The Eerdmans Dictionary of Early Judaism*, edited by John J. Collins and Daniel C. Harlow, 620. Grand Rapids: Eerdmans, 2010.

Van Landigham, Chris. *Judgment & Justification in Early Judaism and the Apostle Paul*. Peabody, MA: Hendrickson, 2006.

Van Ruiten, Jacques T. A. G. M. *Abraham in the Book of Jubilees: The Rewriting of Genesis 11:26–25:10 in the Book of Jubilees 11:14–23:8*. SJSJ 161. Leiden: Brill, 2012.

Van Seters, John. *Abraham in History and Tradition*. New Haven: Yale University Press, 1975.

———. "The Yahwist as Theologian? A Response." *JSOT* 3 (1977) 15–20.

VanderKam, James C. *The Book of Jubilees 1–2*. Leuven: Peeters, 1989.

———. "Greek at Qumran." In *Hellenism in the Land of Israel*, edited by John J. Collins and Gregory E. Sterling, 175–81. CJAS 13. Notre Dame, IN: University of Notre Dame Press, 2001.

Vermes, Geza. *The Complete Dead Sea Scrolls in English*. Penguin Classics. Rev. ed. London: Penguin, 2004.

———. *Scripture and Tradition in Judaism: Haggadic Studies*. SPB 4. 2nd ed. Leiden: Brill, 1983.

Vogel, Manuel. *Das Heil des Bundes: Bundestheologie im Frühjudentum und im frühen Christentum*. TANZ 18. Tübingen: Francke, 1996.

Von Rad, Gerhard. "Das Gottesvolk im Deuteronium." In *Gesammelte Studien zum Alten Testament*, 9–108. Vol. 2. Altes Testament 48. 1929. Reprint, München: Chr. Kaiser, 1973.

———. "The Form-Critical Problem of the Hextateuch." In *The Problem of the Hextateuch and Other Essays*, by Gerhard von Rad, 1–78. Edinburgh: Oliver & Boyd, 1966.

———. *Genesis: A Commentary*. London: SCM, 1961.

———. *The Theology of Israel's Historical Traditions*. Vol. 1 of *Old Testament Theology*. Edinburgh: Oliver & Boyd, 1962.

Vriezen, Theodosius C. *An Outline of Old Testament Theology*. Oxford: Blackwell, 1958.

Wagner, N. E. "A Response to Professor Rolf Rendtorff." *JSOT* 3 (1977) 20–27.

Wehnert, Jürgen. *Die Reinheit des "christlichen Gottesvolkes" aus Juden und Heiden: Studien zum historischen und theologischen Hintergrund des sogenannten Aposteldekrets*. FRLANT 173. Göttingen: Vandenhoeck & Ruprecht, 1997.

Weimar, Peter. "Genesis 15: Ein reaktionskritischer Versuch." In *Die Väter Israels: Beiträge zur Theologie der Patriarchenüberlieferungen im Alten Testament*.

Festschrift für Josef Scharbert zum 70. Geburtstag, edited by Manfred Görg, 361-411. Stuttgart: KBW, 1989.

———. "Sinai und Schöpfung: Komposition und Theologie der priesterschriftlichen Sinaigeschichte." *RB* 95 (1988) 337-85.

Weinfeld, Moshe. *Deuteronomy and the Deuteronomic School*. 1972. Reprint, Winona Lake, IN: Eisenbrauns, 1992.

———. "The Emergence of the Deuteronomic Movement: The Historical Antecedents." In *Deuteronomium: Enstehung, Gestalt und Botschaft*, edited by Norbert Lohfink, 76-98. Leuven: Leuven University Press, 1985.

Weiser, Artur. *The Psalms*. OTL. London: SCM, 1962.

Weiss, Konrad. "Φερω κτλ." *TDNT* 9:56-59.

Welch, Adam C. *The Code of Deuteronomy: A New Theory of Its Origin*. London: James Clark, 1924.

———. *Deuteronomy: The Framework of the Code*. Oxford: Oxford University Press, 1932.

———. *Jeremiah: His Time and His Work*. Oxford: Blackwell, 1955.

Wenham, Gordon J. "Review of H. H. Schmid, *Der sogenannte Jahwist: Beobachtungen und Fragen zur Pentateuchforschung*. Zürich: TVZ, 1976." *JSOT* 3 (1977) 57-60.

Werline, Rodney A. "Prayer of Manasseh." In *The Eerdmans Dictionary of Early Judaism*, edited by John J. Collins and Daniel C. Harlow, 912-13. Grand Rapids: Eerdmans, 2010.

Werrett, Ian. "Salvation through Emulation: Facets of Jubilean Soteriology at Qumran." In *This World and the World to Come: Soteriology in Early Judaism*, edited by Daniel M. Gurtner, 211-28. LSTS 74. London: T. & T. Clark Internatiional, 2011.

Westermann, Claus. *Genesis 12-36: A Commentary*. CC. Minneapolis: Augsburg, 1985.

———. *The Promise to the Fathers: Studies on the Patriarchal Traditions*. Philadelphia: Fortress, 1980.

Whiston, William. *The New Complete Works of Josephus*. Introduction and Commentary by Paul L. Meier. New and expanded ed. Grand Rapids: Kregel, 1999.

White Crawford, Sidnie. *Rewriting Scripture in Second Temple Times*. SDSSRL. Grand Rapids: Eerdmans, 2008.

Whitters, Mark F. *The Epistle of Second Baruch: A Study in Form and Message*. JSPSS 42. Sheffield: SAP, 2003.

Whybray, R. Norman. "Response to Professor Rendtorff." *JSOT* 3 (1977) 11-14.

Wildberger, Hans. *Isaiah 1-12*. CC. Minneapolis: Fortress, 1991.

———. *Isaiah 13-27*. CC. Minneapolis: Fortress, 1997.

———. *Isaiah 28-39*. CC. Minneapolis: Fortress, 2002.

Williamson, Paul R. *Abraham, Israel, and the Nations: The Patriarchal Promise and Its Covenantal Development in Genesis*. JSOTSS 315. Sheffield: SAP, 2000.

Williamson, Ronald. *Philo and the Epistle to the Hebrews*. ALGHJ 4. Leiden: Brill, 1979.

Wilson, Ian. *Out of the Midst of the Fire: Divine Presence in Deuteronomy*. SBLDS 151. Atlanta: Scholars, 1995.

Wilson, R. R. "The OT Genealogies in Recent Research." *JBL* 94 (1975) 168-89.

Wilson, Walter T. *Philo of Alexandria: On Virtues*. PACS. Atlanta: SBL, 2011.

Winninge, Mikael. *Sinners and the Righteous: A Comparative Study of the Psalms of Solomon and Paul's Letters*. CB. NT Series 26. Stockholm: Almquist & Wiksell International, 1995.

Winston, David. *The Wisdom of Solomon*. AB 43. New York: Doubleday, 1979.

Winston, David, and John Dillon. *Two Treatises of Philo of Alexandria: A Commentary on De Gigantibus and Quod Deus Sit Immutabilis*. BJS 25. Chico, CA: Scholars, 1983.

Winter, Bruce W. *Philo and Paul among the Sophists: Alexandrian and Corinthian Responses to a Julio-Claudian Movement*. 2nd ed. Grand Rapids: Eerdmans, 2002.

Wisdom, Jeffrey R. *Blessing for the Nations and the Curse of the Law: Paul's Citation of Genesis and Deuteronomy in Gal 3:8–10*. WUNT 2. 133. Tübingen: Mohr Siebeck, 2001.

Witte, Markus. *Die biblische Urgeschichte. Redaktions- und theologiegeschichtliche Beobachtungen zu Gen 1:11–11:26*. BZAW 265. Berlin: de Gruyter, 1998.

Wolff, Hans W. "The Elohistic Fragments in the Pentateuch." In *The Vitality of the Old Testament Traditions*, edited by Walter Brueggemann, 67–82. 2nd ed. Atlanta: John Knox, 1982.

———. "The Kerygma of the Yahwist." In *The Vitality of the Old Testament Traditions*, edited by Walter Brueggemann, 41–66. 2nd ed. Atlanta: John Knox, 1982.

Worthington, Jonathan D. *Creation in Paul and Philo: The Beginning and the Before*. WUNT 2.317. Tübingen: Mohr Siebeck, 2011.

Wright, N. T. *Pauline Perspectives: Essays on Paul, 1978–2013*. London: SPCK, 2013.

Yeung, Maureen W. *Faith in Jesus and Paul: A Comparison with Special Reference to "Faith That Can Remove Mountains" and "Your Faith Has Healed/Saved You."* WUNT 2.147. Tübingen: Mohr Siebeck, 2002.

Yinger, K. L. *Paul, Judaism, and Judgment according to Deeds*. SNTSMS 105. Cambridge: Cambridge University Press, 1999.

Yonge, C. D. *The Works of Philo*. New updated ed. Peabody, MA: Hendrickson, 1993.

Young, Brad H. *Meet the Rabbis: Rabbinic Thought and the Teachings of Jesus*. Peabody, MA: Hendrickson, 2007.

Zeller, Dieter. *Charis bei Philon und Paulus*. SBS 142. Stuttgart: KBW, 1990

Zenger, Erich. "Der Gott Abrahams und die Völker. Beobachtungen zu Psalm 47." In *Die Väter Israels: Beiträge zur Theologie der Patriarchenüberlieferungen im Alten Testament*, edited by Manfred Görg, 413–30. Stuttgart: KBW, 1989.

Zimmerli, Walter. *Old Testament Theology in Outline*. Edinburgh: T. & T. Clark, 1978.

Index of Ancient Documents

Biblical Literature

Genesis

1:28	5
5:21–24	102
6:18	29
9:9–17	29
11:9	5
11:10–29	3
11:10–32	3
11:29	74
11:30	8, 75
12–17	14
12:1–5	4, 7–8, 76
12:3	5, 11, 15, 20, 25
12:4	8
12:7	8, 10, 23, 30
12:12–20	6, 16
12:15	6
12:17	6
13	8
13:1	6
13:14–17	10
13:14–18	6
13:15	23, 30
13:15–16	8
14:	7–8
14:18–20	7
15:	8
15:1–5	10
15:1–6	7, 9
15:2	8, 29
15:2–3	8
15:4	8
15:5	8, 23, 26
15:6	8, 9, 21
15:7	9, 10, 30
15:9–11	10
15:9–21	10
15:13–16	10
15:18–19	10
15:18–21	10
16:7–12	11
16:12	11
16:15	11
17:1	12
17:2	12, 29
17:3	12
17:3–8	12
17:4	12
17:5–6	25
17:6	12, 29
17:7	12, 13
17:8	12, 23
17:9–14	12, 13
17:12	12, 17
17:12–13	13
17: 15–16	12
17:15–17	13
17:16	13
17:17–19	12

Genesis (continued)

17:18	13
17:19	18
17:19–21	12
17:21	12
17:23	13
17:23–27	12
17:27	13
18:1–15	15
18:14	29
18:17–18	16
18:18	5, 15, 29
18:19	15, 21
18:32	16
18:33	15
19:29	16
20:1–18	16
20:2	16
20:7	11, 16, 21, 72
20:12	17, 18
20:14–16	17
21:4	12
21:12–13	17
21:14–20	17
21:12–20	17
21:22–34	17
22:1–18	18–20, 23, 29
22:14–18	20
22:18	5
23	20
24:2–9	21
24:12	21
24:21	21
24:24	4
24:27	21
24:42–44	21
24:48	21
24:56	21
24:60	20
25	21
25:7	103
25:8–10	21
25:10–34	22
25:12–18	21
25:18	11
25:19–21	21
26:1	22
26:1–11	16
26:2–4	22
26:3	22
26:4	5, 30
26:5	22
26:12	22
26:24	22
27:41–45	24
27:46—28:9	24
28:2–4	25
28:4	22
28:11–15	24–25
28:13	22, 30
28:19	24–25
31:42	22
21:53	22
32:9	22
35:1	25
35:7	25
35:9	25
35:11	26
35:11–12	22, 25
48:4	25
48:16	30
49:30–31	25
50:13	25
50:24	22, 25

Exodus

1:1–5	26
1:12	26
1:20	26
2:24	26
3:1—4:17	28
3:6	30
3:6–8	26
3:8	28
3:10	26
3:12	28
3:14	27
3:14–17	27
3:15	27
3:16–17	27
3:17	28
4:5	28
4:12	28
4:15	28

INDEX OF ANCIENT DOCUMENTS

6:2–4	29	4:41–44	33
6:2–8	28, 29	4:44—28:68	33, 34
6:8	29	5:3	34
6:9–13	28	5:16 3	4
25–31	30	6:10	37
26:30	29	6:11	35
32–34	30	6:18	35
32:1–14	30	6:23	35
33:1–3	30	7:8	36
33:19	28	7:9	38
		8:1	36
		8:3	34

Leviticus

		8:16	34
		9:5	36
7:18	9	9:27	36
13:17	9	10:11	36
13:23	9	10:15	36–38
13:28	9	10:22	34
13:37	9	11:19	36
13:41	9	12–26	32, 33
18:21	19, 80	12:1	33, 36
20:3	80	12:1–7	33
21:9	80	12:1—28:68	34
21:15	80	13:17	36
25:38	10	17:16–17	32
26:13–45	31	18:10	19
26:42	31	19:8	36
26:45	31	24:5	34
		26:3	36
		26:7	36

Numbers

		27:3	36
		28:11	36
11:12	31	29–30	33, 34
12:8	15	29:1	33
16:41–50	117	29:1—30:20	34
18:27	9	29:9	37, 38
32:5–11	31	29:10–15	33
		29:13	36, 37
		29:25–26	36

Deuteronomy

		30:5	34
		30:9	38
1:1–5	33	30:20	36
1:1—4:40	33, 34	31	34, 37
1:8	35, 37	31–33	34
1:10	35	31:16	35
1:35–36	35	31:26	32
4:1	35	32–33	37
4:31	35	32:6	34
4:37	37		

Deuteronomy *(continued)*

32:17	34
34	34, 37
34:4	37

Joshua

1:5	40
1:6	40
2:9	41
2:24	41
3:10	41
5:2–9	40
5:4–7	40
5:6	40
10:42	41
21:43	40
21:45	41
22:28–29	41
23:4–5	41
23:12–13	41
23:15–16	41
24	61
24:2	39, 196
24:2–3	55
24:2–13	40
24:3	40
24:13	41
24:14–28	40

Judges

2:12	42
2:17	42
2:19	42
2:20	42
2:22	42
3:1–3	42
3:4	42

Ruth

4:18–22	12

1 Samuel

12:6–12	43
12:15	43

2 Samuel

7:12	43

1 Kings

18:36	43, 61

2 Kings

13:22–23	62
13:23	43
22	32
23	33

1 Chronicles

2:14	12
28:9	59
29:10	58
29:18	58, 61

2 Chronicles

15:2	59
20:7	58, 64
30:6	59, 61
30:9	59
33:12–13	203

Ezra

9:6–8	59
9:16–21	60
10	18

INDEX OF ANCIENT DOCUMENTS

Psalms

47:1–5	53
47:6–8	53
47:9	53, 55
72:2	57
72:5–7	57
57:8	57, 70
72:9–11	57
72:8–14	57
72:17	57
72:20–56	58
105:5	55
105:6	55, 61
105:7	55
105:8–10	56
105:10–12	55
105:12–41	56
105:24	55
105:42	56, 58
105:44–45	56
105:45	56
132:11	9

Isaiah

1–39	47
2:7–9	32
19:24–25	64
29:17–24	47
29:22	47–48
41:8	45, 58, 64
42:1–7	15
45:23	9
49:3–6	15
51:2–3	46
54:1	46
55:6–7	59
63:7—64:11	46
63:15	47
63:15–17	46
63:16	46, 47
63:17	47
63:18	46
64:10–11	46

Jeremiah

2:5	50
2:7	51
3:15–16	50
3:16	49
3:17	50
3:18	49, 51
3:19	51
3:22	49
3:23–25	49
3:24–25	50
4:1	50
4:1–2	49
4:2	49, 64
10:16	51
11:5	51
12:7–9	51
12:14	51
14:20	50
14:20–21	49
16:18	51
17:4	51
29:13–14	59
31–34	49
33	49
33:14–26	62
33:23–26	48
33:24	62
33:25–26	62
33:26	48, 62
34:18–20	10
39:10	51

Ezekiel

11:15–16	22
33:10	46
33:21–22	51
33:23–24	51
33:23–29	51, 63
33:24	22
33:25–26	52, 63
33:29	51

Amos

3:7	11

Micah

4:1–4	64
5:10	32
7:8–20	52, 57

Zechariah

8:20–23	64

Extra Biblical Jewish Literature

Additions to Daniel (Prayer of Azariah)

3.13	87
3.16–17	87
3.19–22	87

Additions to Esther

13.9–17	88
14.1–19	88

The Apocalypse of Abraham

1–7	222
8	222
9–31	222
9.6	224
9.6–9	222
10.3–6	222
10.5	224
10.16	222
12.1	222
12.3	222
13.1–14	222
14.2	222
15.4	222
16.3	224
18–20	222
19.3	224
20.5	221
22.5	221
23.12	221
23.14	221
24–25	221
26.1–7	221
27.6–8	221
28.2	224
29.3–19	221
31.1	221
31.4	221

2 Baruch

1	220
21.24	220
57.1	220
57.2–3	221
58.1	221
78–87	221
78.4	221
84.8	221

Dead Sea Scrolls

Damascus Document

1.3–12	90
2.14	89
3.1–3	90
3.13–14	90
4.9–10	90
5.20—6.2	90
8.14–18	90
12.11	90
14.4–5	91
16.6	91

War Scroll (1QM)

13.7–8	90
14.8–9	90

Genesis Apocryphon

2–5	91
6–17	91
19–22	91
19.14–17	92
19.25	92
20.10–15	92
21.8–14	93
22.1–26	93

4Q 174

1–4	91

4Q 214b

2–6	95

4Q225II

1.4	94
1.8–14	94
11.4–11	94

4Q 252

1	94
2	94
8	94

4Q 393

	94

4Q 464

3.8–9	95

4Q542

	96

1 Enoch

1–36	100
37–71	100
72–80	100
81–82	100
83–90	100–101
89.10–12	101
91	100
91.11–12	101
92–105	100
93.5	101
93.8–10	101
106–7	100

4 Ezra

3.11	217
3.13–16	218
4.26	218
4.44–50	218
5.55	218
6.7–10	218
7.36–41	218
7.76–77	219
8.45	217
9.7	217
14.5	219
14.10–11	218

Josephus

Jewish War

4.531	205
5.379–81	205

Jewish Antiquities

1.5	206
1.8–9	206
1.14	206
1.17	216
1.20	206
1.148–53	206
1.154–56	206
1.157	207
1.161	207
1.162–65	207
1.166–70	208
1.171–82	209
1.182–85	209
1.186–93	210
1.191	211
1.196	210
1.198–99	210

INDEX OF ANCIENT DOCUMENTS

Jewish Antiquities (continued)

1.200	208
1.207–12	210
1.209–12	211
1.213–14	211
1.215–17	211
1.222	213
1.223	211
1.223–25	212
1.227	214
1.227–31	212
1.231–35	213
1.234	213
1.238–56	214
20.261	216

The Book of Jubilees

1.29—2.1	77
2.17–33	83
2.18–20	74
6.1–10	74
6.18–19	74
6.32–37	84
7.38	86
8.10–21	74
9.14–15	74
10.14	74, 86
10.29–34	74
11.14	74
11.16	76
11.16–24	74
12.9	74
12.17	75
12.19–20	76
12.24–26	76
12.27	77, 86
13.4	78
13.9	78
13.25–27	78
14.4–7	78
14.10	79
14.20	74
14.20–24	79
15.6–17	79
15.19	79
15.21	79
15.25–32	79, 82
15.27	80
15.28	80
15.30–34	80
16.1–4	80
16.10–14	80
16.16–18	80
16.17–18	83
16.19–31	80
16.26	83
17.15–18	81
18.1	81
18.8	82
18.11–12	81
18.15–16	81
19.3	82
19.8–9	82
19.11	82
19.15	82
19.16–29	82
20–22	82
20.1–11	83
21.3–5	83
21.21–25	83
22.10–13	83
22.15	83
22.16–19	83
22.20–22	83
22.24	83
23.10	84
25.1–10	82
26.24	85
30.11–19	84
31.26	85
32.1–2	85
32.16–21	85
32.23–26	85
41.1	82
45.13–15	86
45.16	84

Judith

1–7	108
5.6–10	109
8.26–27	109

INDEX OF ANCIENT DOCUMENTS

1 Maccabees

1.23–28	97
1.45–48	97
2.26	97
2.49–68	97
2.50–51	97
2.52	97, 230
2.61–62	97
2.64	97, 230
2.68	230
4.10–11	98
8.17–18	105
12.5–19	98
12.23	98

3 Maccabees

1.1–5	99
6.1–15	99
6.15–29	99
6.30–41	100

4 Maccabees

7.6–15	193
7.16–23	193
7.19	193–94
13.1	193
13.9	193
13.12	193
13.16–17	193
13.17	194
14.20	194
15.28	194
16.15	193
16.17–19	194
16.20	194
16.25	194
17.6	194
18.1	195
18.20	194
18.23	194

Pirke Aboth

1–4	226
5	226
5.1	226
5.3	226
5.22	227
5.40	226
6.11	227

Philo

De Opifico Mundi

139	118
143–44	118
146	118
155	131

Legum Allegoriae

1.35	135
1.38	177
1.95	178
2.32–33	174
2.54	140
2.58–59	140
2.85	174
3.1	146
3.14	179
3.27	179
3.41	177
3.87	179
3.140–44	156
3.159–60	156
3.161	118
3.164	178
3.192	178, 179
3.195–97	180
3.196	178
3.203	131
3.203–7	133
3.209–10	181
3.217	152
3.218	125, 129
3.228–29	150, 173
3.243–44	149
3.244	129, 155
3.244–45	148

de Cherubim

5	129
7	157
7–8	139, 150
9	129
18	175
18–19	159
31	146
45	138

De Sacrifiies Abelis et Caini

5	141, 176
5–6	175
5–7	156
34–35	176
78	130
91–96	133

Quod Deterius Potiori insidiari soleat

15	183
59	129
89–90	143
90	118
159	141, 145
164–65	153
167	183

de Posteritate Caini

14–18	161
17–21	147
27–28	159, 161
38	139
62	189
101–2	143
139	178
167–69	161

de Gigantibus

6	173
6–8	173
12–16	118
49	161
53–55	141
58	184
60	118
62–63	177

62–64	118–19, 167
63	167
64	142

Quod Deus sit Immutabilis

1	150
3	150
4	150, 173
45	130, 178
45–46	118
55	161
60–64	153
62	161, 175
75–76	178
143–44	143
150–51	176
159–60	143
161–62	142
162	143

de Agricultura

41	138
65	147, 176
159–61	154
160–61	157

de Plantatione

14	118
18	118
20–23	130

de Ebrietate

82	127, 130
94	144
100	147
105	180

de Sobrietate

8–9	139
55–57	160

de Confusione Linguarum

30–31	160, 161
77	176
77–79	147

INDEX OF ANCIENT DOCUMENTS

148	130	139–40	155
182	179	146	142–43
190–91	183	148–50	140
		148–75	138

de Migratione Abrahami

		150	155
2	117, 126, 138, 143,	151	140
3	139	151–53	153
7–8	142	152	153
9	140, 173	157	144
12	139	159–63	140
13	138–40	169	144
14	140	170	153
17	141	171–81	146
20–21	140	173–75	153
23	140	176	144
27	141, 179	176–84	167
28	174	177	143
30	141	177–79	144
35	171	178–81	164
38	141	181–82	144
38–40	127, 130	184	144
43	150, 155, 167	185	142
43–44	144, 151, 180	185–87	144
44	137, 167	187	142
56	153	205	140
56–57	73	205–6	139–40
58	142	217–19	146, 174
60	142	220	175
66–68	139	222	142, 172, 175
67–68	140	244	174
70–85	153	263	140
84	170	272	138

Quis Rerum Divinarum Heres Sit

86–105	153		
89–98	183		
92	137	8–9	154, 157
106–8	153	30	156, 158
118–27	138	64	179
122	138	69	174
126	138	82	176
126	148	82–83	147
127	143	85	118, 177
127–29	154	88	147, 176
127–31	174	90	189
127–47	138	91–96	190
128	138	96–97	144
130	131	98	146, 191
132–34	161	100–101	152
137–38	142	101–2	191

Quis Rerum Divinarum Heres Sit (continued)

184	177
243–48	185
246–47	186
254	136
274	176

De Congressu Eruditionis Gratia

1	148
2–6	129
5	148
9	148, 173
11	148
14	173
14–18	148
19	148
22	149
24	148
25	173
35	149
46	162
48	138
48–49	168
56–57	173
57–58	162
60–61	162
63	129, 148
67	149
71	149
72	148
74–76	149
77	149
78–79	148
79	149
81–84	155
92	138
109	138, 162
119	138
121	148
121–22	155, 162
123	163
125	163
132	159–60
132–33	160
144	149
154	149
155–56	155
156	149
173	162
180	129, 148, 155

De Fuga et Inventione

46	142
117	175
157	157
213	156

De Mutatione Nominum

3–6	157
15	157
15–17	127
16–17	146
19	127
24	156–57
26–27	178
27–29	157
48	181
51–54	158
52	178
52–53	139
54–56	177
57	178
57–60	180
58–60	158
60–80	186
62–64	187
65–71	187
66–67	158
69–70	158
70	159
78	129
84–85	158
87	158
102	192
128	138
151–53	138
154	125
166	152
166–67	125, 157
175–78	152
175–85	152
175–92	191
176–78	152

INDEX OF ANCIENT DOCUMENTS

182	192	38–40	179
186	152	46	179, 182
188	192	48–59	125
201	157	50	179
204	157	52–54	126
209	157	54	125–26
216–17	157	56–58	126
223	118	57	126, 174
253–63	148	60–207	126
270	155, 159	60–61	174
		60–62	126

De Somniis 1 and 2

		66–72	127
1.34	118	68	165
1.52	164	68–70	146
1.52–54	165	69–70	164
1.58	165	70	165
1.59–60	156	71	165
1.60	142, 154	72–73	147
1.62–64	154	72–75	128
1.65–70	154	75–76	147
1.68–71	181	77–82	128
1.70	154	78–80	165
1.71	154	79	146, 164
1.135–40	118	80	177
1.146	118	84	128, 144, 151
1.150–52	179	88	128
1.151	147	88–99	129
1.166–68	147	89	185
1.194	156, 181	90–98	180
2.85–90	188–89	95	164
2.172	170	99	129
2.177	178	99–103	155
2.225–29	161	101–3	129
2.226–28	160	107–32	129
2.228	160	111–13	125, 130
2.230	160	114–18	181
2.232	175	116	130
2.234–37	156	118	130
2.243–44	138	119	130
2.253	162	121–22	130
		125	130
		138–41	130

de Abrahamo

		145	130
5–6	125	147–66	130
7–14	145	160	164
7–47	125	167	181
34–35	179	167–207	176
37	179	178–83	187

267

de Abrahamo (continued)

184–99	188
185	145
188	145
188–92	131
189–94	145
192	181
193–94	145
194–96	131
195	145
199	131, 181
201–7	131
202–3	181
204	178
206	129
208–16	131
216	145
219	131
222	145
223–44	131
258	176
262	151, 170
270	132
272–73	133
275	133
276	125

de Decalogo

38	131
134	118

de Specialibus Legibus 1–4

1.1–11	137
1.43	178
1.44	142
1.51–52	136, 169
1.81	118
1.146	118
1.309	136, 169
3.207	118
4.18	125
4.49	172
4.123	118, 125
4.168	143

de Virtutibus

88	136
102–3	179
187–227	171
189–91	134
201	179
202	179
203	179
210	179
211–19	137
212–13	135, 164
212–19	125, 134
213	166
214	134, 166
214–15	167, 171
214–16	135
215–16	134
216	131
217	134, 136, 171
218	131, 170, 172
218–19	134
218–20	136
220–22	136

de Praemiis et Poenis

3	178
23	179
24–51	125
27	131, 135
27–30	137
44	126, 135, 177.
49	137
58	137
67	179
69	179
87	178
113	178
119	178
126	178, 182
152	176, 178
162	178–79
163	118

de Vita Mosis 1 and 2

1.7	125
1.71–76	125
1.76	126

1.148	179
1.155	179
1.175	172
2.53	282
2.58–59	179
2.67–69	179
2.85–86	179
2.162	179
2.171	179
2.173	179
2.193–208	179
2.200	179
2.227	179
2.259	171
2.263	171
2.272	171
2.274	179
2.282–83	179
2.291	171

Quaestiones et Solutiones in Genesesum

1.93	182
2.28	182
3.1	120–21, 164–65, 177
3.2	121, 151–52
3.3	185
3.4	177
3.8	120–21, 185
3.9	170–72
3.10	121–22
3.11	120, 122, 176
3.13	120, 122
3.15–16	120
3.16	121
3.18	120
3.20	122, 129
3.21	121
3.22–24	120
3.25	122
3.27	122
3.28–31	122
3.32	123
3.35	122
3.36	120
3.39–42	123
3.40	176
3.42	124, 176
3.43	120, 123, 151, 186–87
3.44	123, 133
3.45	122
3.46–47	137
3.48	183
3.52–53	120
3.53	123, 187
3.54	122
3.54–59	124
3.56	152
3.62	124
4.2	121
4.8	121, 124
4.17	124
4.20	121
4.28	121
4.29	121
4.60–61	184
4.61	185
4.73	121
4.80	189
4.84	132
4.137	120

Quaestiones et Solutiones in Exodum

2.45	177
4.8	129
4.11	129

Quod Omnis Probus Liber Sit

46	176
50	176
62–63	176
74	176

Pseudo-Philo: Liber Antiquitatum Biblicarum

4.11	195
4.16–17	196
6	196
7.4	196
8.3	196
8.4–14	197
9.3–4	197

Pseudo-Philo: Liber Antiquitatum Biblicarum (continued)

9.7–8	197
12	197
12.4	198
12.8–9	202
12.12	202
18.4–6	198
18.5	195
19.2	198
19.11	202
23	198
23.5–8	199
23.6	220
23.11	199
25.1–6	199
25.9	199
28.4	202
32	200
32.1–4	200
32.7–9	200
32.11	200
32.13	200
32.14	201
40.1–3	201
61.5	201

Prayer of Manasseh

8–9	203
10	203
13–14	203

Psalms of Solomon

9.9–10	108
18.3–4	108

Testament of Abraham

1.1— 2.4	224
1.3	225
2.3	224
2.6	224
4.6	224
7.12	224
9.3	225
9.6	224
9.8	224
10.1–11	225
10.3	224
10.12–15	225
13.2	224
14.10–14	225
14.10–15	225
15.1–2	225
15.9	224
15.10	225
16.5	224
16.7–16	225
20.8–12	225

Testament of the Twelve Patriarchs

T. Asher

7.7	113

T. Benjamin

1.1	114
10.2–6	114

T. Dan

7.1–2	113

T. Joseph

6.7	113

T. Judah

17.5–6	112
24.4, 5	112
25.1	112

T. Levi

2.6–10	111
5.1	111
5.3	111
6.3–7	111

6.9	111	\u00a0	

Wisdom of ben Sirach

6.9	111	42.15–25	68
8.15	111	42.15–43	33, 68
15.1–4	112	43.33	68
18.6	112	44.1–15	68
18.14	112	44.1—50.21	68
19.5	112	44.2	68–70
		44.19–21	68–70
T. Naphtali		44.21	68
		44.23	70
1.10	113		

Wisdom of Solomon

Tobit

1.3–18	71	1.1—6.11	115
2.2–4	71	6.12—9.18	115
3.1–10	72	10	115
3.16–17	71	10.5	116
4.1–12	71–72	10.15	116
4.6–18	71	11.1–14	115
4.7	72, 73	12.3–6	116
4.8–9	73	12.21	117
4.17–22	86	12.22	116
		18.6	117
		18.22	117

Index of Modern Scholars

Adler, William, 103
Alexandrzze, Manuel
Allen, Leslie C., 22, 51
Allison, Dale C., 224
Anderson, Hugh, 99, 193-94
Arenhoeval, Diego, 98
Assefa, Daniel, 101
Atkinson, Kenneth, 107-8
Attridge, Harold W., 104, 211, 213-14
Aune, David E., 136

Bächli, Otto
Baltzer, Klaus, 114
Barclay, John M.G., 114-15, 117-18, 137, 177-78, 182, 193, 195, 201-2, 216-17, 219
Bassler, Jouette M., 200
Bauer, Walter, 18, 116
Bertholet, Kafell, 104
Bird, Michael F., 108, 207
Birmbaum, Ellen, 119, 126, 134, 136-38, 162, 176
Blanton, Thomas R., 89-90
Blaschke, Andreas, 13, 40
Blenkinsopp, Joseph., 14, 59, 229
Bloch, Renée, 48
Boccaccini, Gabriele., 73, 77, 86
Böhm, Martina., 117, 119-20, 122, 126-27, 129, 131-32, 134, 136-37, 139, 146, 148-49, 152, 156-58, 160, 162, 168, 179, 189, 192
Borgen, Peder., 117, 148-49
Bowley, James E., 103, 106

Box, George H., 216
Braulik, Georg, 32, 38
Brueggemann, Walter, 25, 26, 28, 49
Bright, John, 50
Bruin, Tom de, 111

Callaway, Mary, 46
Calvert, Nancy, 146
Calvert-Koyzis, Nancy, 76, 117, 168, 196-97, 202, 216, 223
Charles, Robert H., 73, 110, 112, 220, 227
Charlesworth, James H., 103, 203-4
Cheshnutt, Randall D., 115
Childs, Brevard S., 26-29
Christensen, Ellen J., 11, 91
Christiansen, Irmgard, 118
Clements, Ronald E., 3, 32-33, 45, 47-48, 51
Coates, George W., 3
Cohn, Leopold, 120
Collins, John J., 103-5, 208
Colson, F.H., 129, 134, 136, 139, 155, 181, 186, 188, 191-92
Cox, Ronald R., 143
Cross, Frank M., 14
Cummins, Stephen A., 193

Dawson, David, 169
Denvers, William G., 22
Diepold, Peter, 48, 50-51
Di Lella, Alexander A., 67-70
Dobler, Axel von, 10.,
Doran, Robert, 104-6, 208

Dunn, James G., M, 112

Easton, Susan, 9
Ego, Beate, 4, 19, 39
Eichrodt, Walter, 22, 28, 57, 63
Endres, John C., 82-86
Eshel Esther, 91
Evans, Craig A., 76, 92

Fallon, F., 106
Fieldman, Louis H., 206-8, 210-11, 213-16
Fish, Bruce N., 195-98, 202
Flüchter, Sascha, 9
Flury-Shölch, André, 4-5, 15, 20, 22-23, 38, 50, 57
Fox, Michael V., 87
Franxman, Thomas W., 208-9, 211
Fretheim, Terence E., 4, 11, 30
Früchtel, Ursula, 119, 121, 138-39, 143, 149, 160
Füglister, Notker, 56

Garlington, Don, 203
Gaston, Lloyd, 9
Gerstenberger, Erhard S., 53
Goldstein, Jonathan A., 96, 98
Grabbe, Lester, 123, 128, 140
Gray, John, 43, 62, 107
Gross, Walter, 49
Gruen, Erich S., 98, 105-7
Grindham, Sigurd, 76

Haag, E., 3
Haacker, Klaus, 228
Hall, Robert G., 223
Halpern-Amarnu, Betsy, 5, 28, 74, 76, 78-81, 108
Hansen, G., Walter, 20, 69
Hanson, J., 103
Hanson, Paul D., 46-47
Harlow, Daniel C., 222
Harrisville, Roy A., 215
Harrington, Daniel J., 114, 195
Haspecker, Josef, 70
Hay, David M., 119-20, 176, 181, 183
Hayes, Christine E., 80, 82-83
Hayes, John H

Heard, R., Christopher, 7, 11, 16-18
Henton Davies, Gwynne, 4, 7, 10, 25-26, 29, 152
Henze, Matthias, 220
Herford, R.T., 226-27
Hofius, Otto, 112
Hogan, Karina M., 216
Holladay, Carl H., 172
Hollander, Harm W., 111
Hossfeld, Frank-Lothar, 57
Hübner, Hans, 114-16

Isaacs, Marie E., 136

Jacobs, Naomi S., 71
Jenks, Alan W., 3
Jeremias, Joachim, 69
Johnson, Aubrey R., 17, 53, 57
Johnson, Sara R., 99
Johnstone, William, 58
Jonge, Marius de, 111

Kaiser, Otto, 47, 64
Kaminsky, J.S., 7, 14
Kasher, A., 102
Kee, Howard C., 110, 112-13
Klawans, Jonathan, 204, 229
Klijn, A.F.J., 220
Knibb, Michael A., 89, 100
Koch, Klaus, 93, 209
Konradt, Matthias, 14, 85, 132, 134
Kottsieper, Ingo, 86-88
Kraus, Hans Joachim, 54
Kugler, Robert A., 110-11
Kuhn, Karl G., 136

Lee, Chee-Chiew, 49
Lella, Alexander A., di, 67-70
Leslie, Elmer A., 50, 54, 56-57
Levenson, Jon D., 19, 23, 176
Levison, John R., 20
Liddell, Henry George, 132, 155, 171
Linebaugh, Jonathan A., 115-16, 177, 182
Lohfink, Norbert, 32-34, 40
Longenecker, Bruce W., 216

Machiela, Daniel A., 92

INDEX OF MODERN SCHOLARS 275

Mack, Burton L., 68, 143, 229
Maier, Gerhard, 107
Marböck, Johann, 68, 70
Martin-Achard, Robert, , 54
Mason, Rex A., 52
Mason, Steve, 204–7
Maston, Jason, 69
Mays, James L., 32–34, 52
McConville, J., Gordon, 32
McGlynn, Moyna, 114, 116
McLaren, James S., 204
Metzger, Bruce M., 216, 218
Meyer, Gunter, 75, 98, 103, 107, 128, 208
Middendorp, Th, 70
Mihaly, E., 86
Millar, J., Gary, 32
Milligan, George, 210
Montes-Peral, Luis A., 175
Moo, Jonathan A
Moore, Carey A., 72, 76, 108–10
Mowinckel, Sigismund, 53, 55, 57
Mühling, Anke, 11, 13, 16–17, 19, 45, 47, 59–60, 71, 73, 75–78, 85, 87, 89, 95, 104–5, 109–10, 127, 134, 194, 216, 225
Müller, Paul G., 143
Murphy, Frederick J., 195, 198–99, 201–2, 221
Myers, Jacob M., 218
Moxnes, Halvor, 133, 148, 151–52, 176, 190, 192
Moulton, James H., 210

Najman, Hindy, 217
Neeef, Heinz-Dieter, 11, 13
Nelson, Richard D., 40–41
Nicholson, Ernest W., 32–33, 48
Nickelsburg, George W.E., 67, 71, 73, 86–87, 89, 91, 96, 100–1, 107–8, 110, 193, 113–14, 194–95, 216, 220, 222–25
Niebuhr, Karl-Wilhelm, 76
Niehoff, Maren, 104, 117, 119–20, 130, 183–84, 187, 189, 191–92
Noack, Christian, 119, 134–36, 170–75, 192
Noth, Martin, 28, 58, 152

Oeming, Manfred, 9–11, 59–60, 81, 94

Pascher, Joseph, 143
Patrick, Dale, 32
Pearce, Sara J.K., 152
Poirier, John C., 223

Rahlfs, Alfred, 70–72, 87
Rappaport, Uriel, 96.,
Reinmuth, Eckart 195, 197
Rendtorff, Rolf, 3
Robertson, R.G., 104
Römer, Thomas, 34
Rost, Leonard, 110
Rowland, Christopher C., 100
Rowley, Harold H., 54
Royse, James R., 120
Rubinkiewicz, R., 222–23
Runia, David T., 120

Sanders, Edward P., 70, 224, 226
Sandmel, Samuel, 76, 117, 122, 158, 181, 187, 215
Sauer, Georg, 67–70
Sayler, Gwendolyn B., 221, 223
Schenck, Kenneth, 188
Schnabel, Eckhard J., 69
Schliesser, Benjamin, 9–10, 59–60, 69, 78
Schmid, Hans H., 1
Schramm, Brooks, 46
Schwartz, Eberhard, 73, 84
Segal, Michael, 73, 80
Skehan, Patrick W., 76–70
Spilsbury, Paul, 211
Sprinkle, Preston M., 82, 196, 202
Sterling, Gregory E., 117, 120
Stokes, Ryan E., 100
Stone, Michael E., 216–19
Stuckenbruck, Loren T., 100
Syrén, Roger, 11, 13–14, 18

Terian, Abraham, 120
Thackeray, H.St.J., 211
Thiessen, Matthew, 101–2
Thompson, Thomas L., 22
Tobin, Thomas H., 137

Townsend, R.B., 193

Van der Horst, Peter W., 104
Van Landigham, Chris, 69, 76, 202, 206, 215, 217
Van Ruiiten, Jacques T.A.G.M., 73–74, 77, 92, 95
Van Seters, John, 3, 22
VanderKam, James C., 73, 76, 78, 96, 100–1, 112, 202
Vermes, Geza, 89, 91, 94–96, 214
Vogel, Manuel, 13, 29, 70, 86, 90–91, 94, 117, 195, 200–2, 221
Von Dobler, Axel, 10
Von Rad, Gerhard, 4, 6–7, 9–11, 14, 23, 25, 32–33, 63, 102
Vriezen, Theodosius C., 28

Wagner, N.E., 3
Walter, N., 104
Watson, Francis, 115, 117, 133, 174, 181, 215
Weimar, Peter, 3, 8–10, 29
Weinfeld, Moshe, 32–33
Weiser, Artur, 54, 57
Welch, Adam C., 33, 50, 58
Wenham, Gordon J., 3
Werline, Rodney A., 203

Werrett, Ian, 75, 82, 85
Westermann, Claus, 4–10, 15, 19–24, 45, 47, 62, 77
Whiston, William, 211
White Crawford, Sidnie, 86, 91–93, 95
Whittiers, Mark F., 221
Whitlark, Jason A., 211–13
Whybray, R., Norman, 3
Wildberger, Hans, 48
Williamson, H.G.M., 59, 151, 155
Wilson, Ian, 33
Wilson, Walter T., 134, 136
Winnige, Mikael, 107
Winston, David, , 114–16, 161
Winter, Bruce W., 149, 154, 186
Wintermute, O.S., 73
Wisdom, Jeffrey R., 50, 83
Wolff, Hans W., 7, 52, 54
Wright, N., Thomas, 67, 107–8

Yeung, Maureen W., 23, 59, 69, 133
Yinger, K.L., 107
Yonge, C.D., 134, 171, 190
Young, Brad H., 226

Zeller, Dieter, 118, 158, 177
Zenger, Erich, 53–55
Zimmerli, Walter, 27–28